Eva Zeisel

On Design

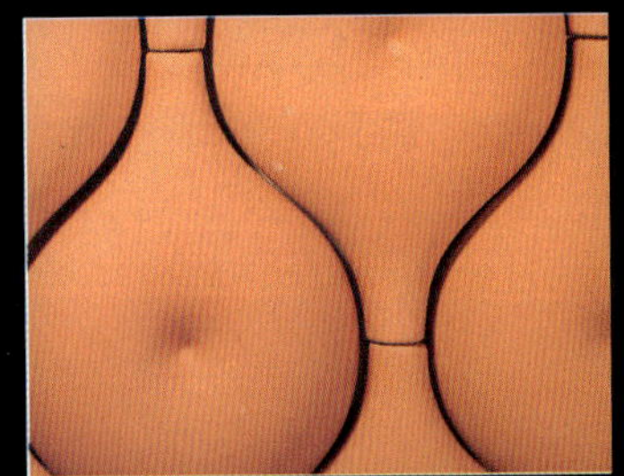

Eva Zeisel

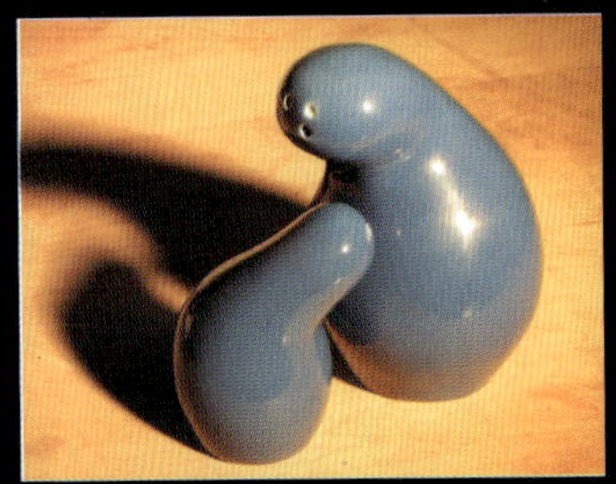

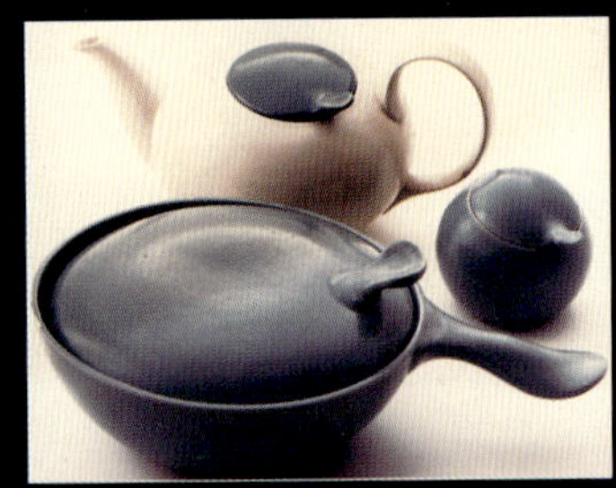

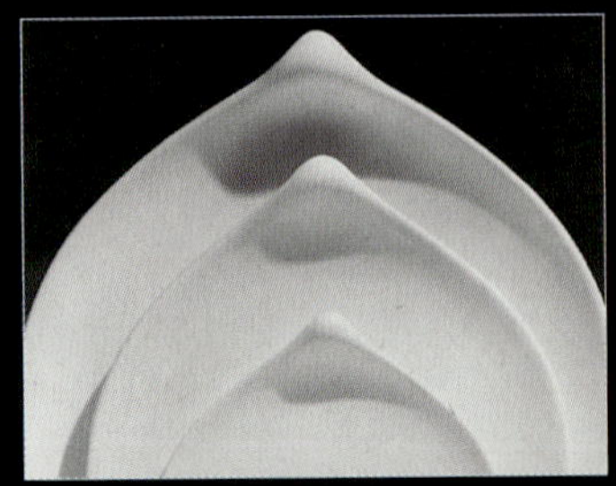

On Design

THE MAGIC LANGUAGE OF THINGS

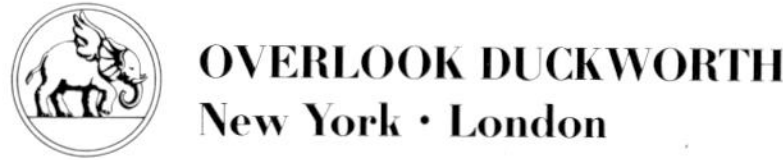
OVERLOOK DUCKWORTH
New York • London

This edition first published in paperback in 2011 by
Overlook Duckworth, Peter Mayer Publishers, Inc.

NEW YORK:
Overlook
141 Wooster Street
New York, NY 10012
www.overlookpress.com
For bulk and special sales, please contact sales@overlookny.com

LONDON:
Duckworth
90-93 Cowcross Street
London EC1M 6BF
www.ducknet.co.uk
info@duckworth-publishers.co.uk

Cataloging-in-Publication Data is available from the Library of Congress
A catalogue record for this book is available from the British Library

Cover design by Yellowstone Ltd.
Layout and type formatting by Bernard Schleifer
Printed in China
ISBN 978-1-59020-689-8 US
ISBN 978-0-7156-4211-5 UK
10 9 8 7 6 5 4 3 2 1

To Jean Richards and Brent C. Brolin
with deep gratitude for their help with this book

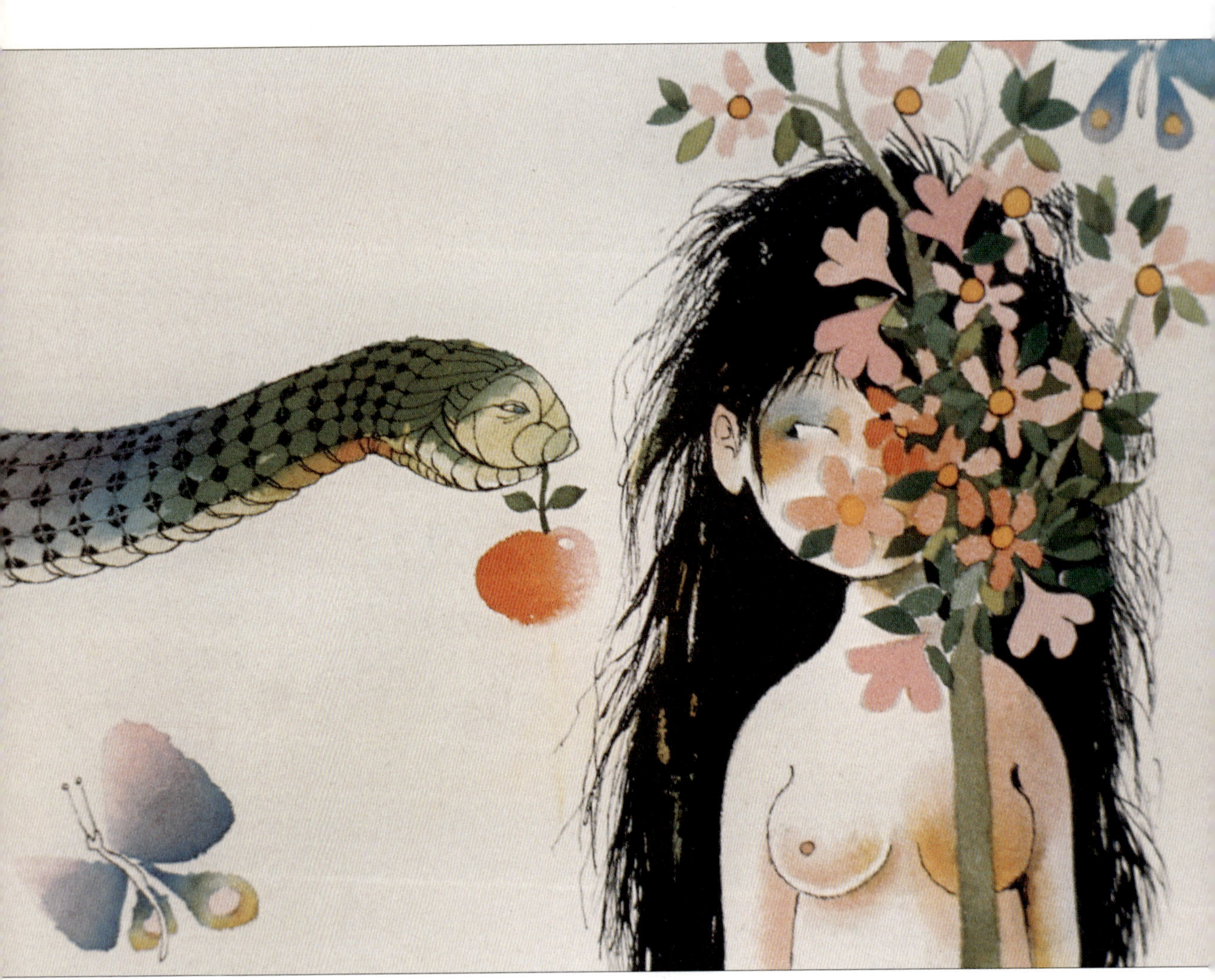

Before Eve found how good the apple tasted,

she saw how lovely it looked.

Fig. 1. Watercolor by Irene Haas.

Contents

Eva Zeisel
On Design

Introduction: The Magic Language of Design

This picture book is meant to teach a language that will speak to those for whom we—designers—make things. This language is not meant for monologues, nor for self-expression, but to speak to others. It is not intended to proclaim eternal values, to make designs innovative, or to champion the cause of artistic individualism. Nor does it proclaim any new, or follow any old, moral precepts or principles of "good design."

When you begin your work, nothing exists. When it is finished it looks as if it just happened, spontaneously, effortlessly, convincingly. It looks as though it had been there all along.

To create things to be used, to be loved, to be with, to give as a gift, to fit into a normal day, to match a festive mood, to be proud of, is to create the culture of life that surrounds us. This is a personal activity, a thoughtful activity of imagining and visualizing and making critical decisions. Neither the "juggling" of basic forms, nor fortuitous artistic accidents, nor the insertion of the computer as intermediary, can replace the personal dialogue between maker and thing, which leads to a design that communicates to others.

When you have put the first line on paper, or begun forming the model, you have created the partner for your dialogue. You will continue a conversation with the object you are making until this at-first-imagined thing has become real and convincing. You might ask it, for instance, if I add a sixteenth of an inch here or take it away there, is it relevant? Does it weaken a line? Does it deepen a shadow or soften the form to fill in a space, or scoop it out?

Your image will come to life through this dialogue, and in the development of that conversation the object will be articulated into what you intended: it will become stately or flabby, solid or light, cute or imposing, old-fashioned, funny, miniature, monumental, harmonious, irritating or convey a sense of suspense or of serenity. In short, it will say what you want it to say to those for whom you have made it. This will be true whether it is an eyeglass frame, a motorcycle, a harp, a chair, a teapot, or a building.

What your design looks like is almost entirely up to you. Designers communicate feelings to the viewer through line and form. The object may look light and airy, as though its massive weight had yielded to the gentle breeze, or it can look solid, as though the object would never consider such a challenge to the force of gravity. It can look firm and compact, or as though it is about to lift off and take flight.

These qualities can exist in any medium and at any scale, as we will see. Therefore the possibility for an emotional relationship between the object and the viewer can exist for architects, goldsmiths, weavers, potters, tinsmiths, stained-glass makers, car designers, and the makers of every other designed object.

Whether we make things or they just happen, whether we grow them or form them, things speak to us. They tell us where we are—waking up in our beds or flying above the clouds in an airplane. They talk to us through their shapes, contours, color, weight, temperature, surface, sound, and most clearly, their associations. For instance, the weight, temperature, and sound of a plastic plate might disappoint us. Objects might look graceful or scrawny. They might be stately, or plump and fat. They might be cold and hard, soft and warm, or they might seem bigger or smaller than they actually are. They might seem tremendous and monumental, or miniature and tiny. Their sounds call us to church, or announce the approaching trolley car. We might enjoy the sound of a well-strung tennis racket meeting the ball, or the festive clinking of glasses. They cheer us or shock us by their color. We might follow their movements like clouds across the sky. They might hold us in suspense. They might fill us with tenderness and smiles, or irritate us by their incongruous forms. They fit in or clash with our surroundings. They speak in many national dialects. They speak of faraway places and things of old, of modern life and cultures long dead. They inspire. They soothe and bathe a home with grace, and provide intangible pleasures and joy. This is the magic of the language of design.

Essay: The Roots of 20th Century Design

Throughout the ages, the things around us spoke to us in a magical idiom.

However, the magic language was lost in the twentieth century. In 1901, the German architect Hermann Muthesius described the style for which the last century will be known. He wrote:

> The new art movement broke out with such violence, power, and sound-force that . . . one can only call it an explosion.

This new movement declared a "catastrophic break" with the past. New "truths" were sharply set against old "truths." What began as an emotional response became codified and rationalized during the next two decades in the "New Movement," later known as the Modern Movement. Its optimistic social message and invigorating missionary élan notwithstanding, modernism's negative urge, its violent break with the past, was conveyed in moralistic statements that had no relevance to design. The attempt not to repeat what had come before frustrated creative pleasure, which depends upon a positive impulse. The modern movement restricted itself to a limited vocabulary of lines and forms. It introduced rules and principles that would dictate what distinguished good design from bad. These new rules aimed at silencing communication between the maker of things and his public. Things lost their magic.

Applied Art: The Division of the Technical Form from the Art Form

At the outset of the nineteenth century, division of labor had become the leading idea for improving the efficiency of industrial production. London's Great Exhibition of 1851 (the Crystal Palace Exhibition) was the first programmatic manifestation of industrial production. Prince Albert, who had taken part in its organization, announced, "The great division of labor may be called the moving power of civilization."

Yet the jury of the exhibition remarked on the "defects of English work on account of separation of artists from workmen." According to the catalog of the exhibition, "the decadence in English design was more pronounced than anywhere else on the European continent, because the division of labor in France and Italy had not proceeded as far, where the designer was still taking part in the construction and design of the whole product." (Although art nouveau tried to remedy this situation, it created designs outside of mainstream production and had a relatively short lifespan.)

The division of labor disrupted the unity of the designer's creative process. It divided his profession into that of the designer of the technical form, the form produced by the machine for use, and the designer of the art form, the artist, whose work was to be applied to the technical form to cover its nakedness. Similarly, architect and critic Gottfried Semper wrote of a division between the "technical form" as anti-aesthetic and the "art form" as aesthetic. The division of these two functions of the designer resulted in *applied art*, or art to be applied to the surface of the useful technical form. The catalog of the 1851 exhibition speaks of "design as applied to a branch of industry...."

Some of the world's greatest museums are called museums of applied art, such as the *Österreichisches Museum für Angewandte Kunst* in Vienna, and the Russian Museum of Prekladnoy Art, literally meaning art "added to." Despite such official recognition, the factory designer received little respect from his employer. In Gottfried Semper's 1878 book, *Style in the Technical and Tectonic Arts*, he describes the sorry lot of the "designer for industry":

> Business aims to make the arts subservient to it . . . but it has achieved this in the most unfortunate way because of the necessity of the division of labor for such large-scale enterprise. Business divides, for instance, the "ornamental" from the "formal-technical" in a purely mechanical manner. This reveals the lack of understanding and lack of sensitivity for the real relationships among the various functions through which the artist realizes his work. A large number of artists, many of them gifted, are working in steady employment for the French and English industries, in a kind of dual subservience. Their employer thinks of them, on the one hand, as burdensome taste-makers and form-beautifiers, whom he does not consider his equals, seldom paying them well, while on the other hand, he expects them to guarantee the sales of the products they design, as everything depends on this in the end...
>
> The preparation of the clay body requires someone to knead the clay, and a foreman must be put in charge of overseeing the firing of the kiln. The only difference is that, while the manufacturer gives free rein to these workmen

> because he is aware of the inadequacy of his technical knowledge, like every donkey, however, he believes that he knows something about art. If the artist's contribution does not suit the tastes of the manufacturer, it is criticized, misrepresented and destroyed . . .

With the modern movement came a change in aesthetics. The technical form, which earlier had been considered in need of beautification, came to be thought of as beautiful in itself. The catalogue of the Dresden Exhibition of 1906 states: "The elements of the technical form, insofar as they demonstrate the beauty of the solid materials, the suitability to a purpose, represent the highest artistic forms."

Geometry—A Reaction to Nineteenth Century Comfort and Sentimentalism

Another aspect of the magic language of design also changed at the end of the nineteenth century.

The nineteenth-century designer working in the style of nostalgic sentimentalism was described as "invisible but always present." He made the bourgeois home so comforting and comfortable that its occupant felt that the things surrounding him were his intimate friends, there to bring him solace. The heavy drapes and soft armchairs were meant to comfort body and soul. A "comforter" comforted the sleeper. This was a most personal and communicative style, as described in a nineteenth-century French magazine:

> [The clock] will sing the poem which transfigures the short hours. The pleasure of the eye adds itself to the anxiety of the hour and alleviates its pathos. In the same way, the mute grace of the mirror will so enhance the beauty of the coquette who gazes into it with alarm that her exact age will seem to benefit through the charming sympathy of the artist.

This late nineteenth-century style also evoked faraway countries and times. To quote the prominent English designer, illustrator, and teacher of this period, Walter Crane:

> We can get decorations "in any style" nowadays to order. We can be ancient Egyptian, or Greek, or Roman, or Pompeian, or Byzantine, or Celtic, or Italian, or German, Gothic or Renaissance, whichever we please, Louis Quatorze or Louis Seize—worse luck, but none of them seems to please for long....

The designers of the twentieth century, however, were repulsed by the emotionalism implied by the curvaceous lines of the nineteenth century. The modern movement was born of an emotional reaction to nineteenth-century sentiment and its comfortable, lively curves. In 1925 Le Corbusier wrote:

> Our parents wanted that a radiant atmosphere should glorify our gloomy life; but we want the objects to be our mute slaves rather than soulful friends. We want instruments. We exact from them punctuality, accuracy, and unobtrusive presence.

Architect Peter Behrens once wrote of a professor who exclaims, "Hurrah, hurrah for the straight line," upon looking at a geometric chair.

The Viennese architect Adolf Loos praised the exactitude of the compass' sweep "against the uncertainty of the accident of dreams of humanity…."

With great suddenness, geometric forms replaced natural and historical ones. The Austrian architect Otto Wagner changed the lively historical ornaments decorating the facades of his buildings to rectangles. The Viennese architect Josef Hoffmann was nicknamed "Hoffmann of little squares." During the first two decades of the twentieth century, geometry became fashionable in highbrow as well as lowbrow designs. (By the 1920s, the limited style of art nouveau, the individualistic style of lively forms, had also died down.) If the modernists wanted to stop the intensely emotional individual expressions they had inherited, they made the right choice to reduce its formal language to rectilinear geometry. In 1927, Dutch designer Gerrit Rietveld, one of the leaders of the De Stijl movement of that time wrote:

> They [the modernists] consider the straight line and the right angle as truly universal, while the acute angle is arbitrary, and therefore individual.

One of the most powerful means of silencing communication used by the modern movement was the exclusion of the compound curve (the S-curve) along with the acute angle from its form language, since they might invite emotional associations.

At the beginning of the twentieth century, the modern movement adopted a curve that prevented all communication: the stress curve. Although it grants élan and movement to the modern form language, it avoids all communicative or sentimental expressions. The stress curve does not invite emotional associations as it can only be described as a rational rather than an emotional line.

In 1964, Arthur Drexler, the director of the Architecture and Design Department of the Museum of Modern Art, summed up the modern form language in these words:

> It employs simple geometric shapes, clearly independent of each other, of smoothness and precision of finish and polish, [characterized by] a religious avoidance of any applied ornament with its connotation of a personal idiosyncrasy and consisting of surprisingly few shapes. The introduction of angles and compound curves are usually considered gratuitous and sometimes extravagant…. The more closely an object approximates a single geometric figure, the more perfect the design.

Throughout the twentieth century, the modern movement fought the emotionalism and communicative lines of the nineteenth century: the magic language of design was muted.

Structure

While the solid technical form, a product of the division of labor, was hidden under its ornamental cover, another technical form appeared in the public eye during the nineteenth century with increasing frequency: the sweeping lines of metal bridges and the transparent metal structures of buildings. The sweep of their arches, their light, lacy grandeur, could not but fascinate. The fascination with these forms culminated in the monument to these shapes, a symbol of progress, the Eiffel Tower (1889). It soared a thousand feet above an exhibition filled with fake splendor. These metal structures did not meet the nineteenth-century definition of beauty. Yet the early modern reformers embraced them as part of their vocabulary of modern design. Around 1900, Muthesius spoke of the "truth" of construction and Wagner advocated the energetic assertion of construction. Frank Lloyd Wright called modern iron and steel construction the triumphs of engineering. In 1913, the Belgian architect Henry van de Velde wrote:

> We found ourselves in the presence of surprising creations, denuded of all ornaments in the shocking nakedness of a rational, logical construction.... We found ourselves face to face with things which showed us their real face. For the first time we were in the presence of organic technical elements and without all that could induce us to misunderstand their function.... What might have worried us . . . is that as soon someone signaled this new architecture, the discussion immediately became heated.

He asked:

> Whether these structural forms, the Bridge over the Firth of Forth, the Great Hall of Machines at the Exhibition of 1889, or the Eiffel Tower, which came in time to rekindle the discussion, were beautiful or not? Will these metallic constructions sustain a new style?

This question was answered by Le Corbusier, who wrote: "In 1889 the Eiffel Tower was the aggressive expression of 'le Calcul,' in 1900 the aesthetes wanted to destroy her, in 1925...she appears pure like a crystal."

The form language of the modern movement integrated the elements of structure. The Germans called the designer the "constructor" (der Konstruktor). The French, in the late 1920s, spoke of the German Bauhaus as "la maison des constructeurs." A design magazine was called *Structure*. In mid-century, Ludwig Mies van der Rohe declared that it took him "years to make clear, honest construction, to find an answer to the question of 'truth.'" Structure was not only an essential building element, but also an architectural ornament. This was also true in the design of wood and metal furniture, jewelry, etc. One hundred years after the controversy surrounding the Eiffel Tower's incongruous intrusion upon the Beaux Arts architectural landscape of Paris, I. M. Pei's Louvre pyramid renews this discussion. From the design of chairs to the exuberant designs of airports, structure remains part of our modern design vocabulary. In my feeling, structure as a style often inhibits personal communication between the designers and their public.

Simplicity

"Strict simplicity" also muted the magic language of things. Simplicity is not a natural phenomenon: the shells of the sea, the leaves of the forest, the clouds of the sky, the wings of the butterfly, the palace of the spider — none would pass the test of modern simplicity.

In the early twentieth century, simplicity, as with geometry, was an emotional reaction to the richness of curves and shapes and the wealth of bulges and crevices of the nineteenth century. Peter Behrens, whose students included Le Corbusier as well as Walter Gropius and Mies van der Rohe, declared that "Simplicity is riches." He preached the elimination of all natural and historic shapes. Frank Lloyd Wright stated, "Simplicity is a sign of maturity." This flight into simplicity soon was rationalized in a program called Neue Sachlichkeit ("New Objectivity"), which explained the need for simple forms in social terms. Early in the century, German unions proposed simple furniture designs for working class interiors. Even as late as 1961, the art critic Sir Herbert Read wrote that

> [I]f the urgent problem is the transformation of a million slum dwellings into cities of order ... man ... will find the question of ornament and decoration singularly futile and academic, a waste of time and money.

As recently as the 1970s, the slogan of the Philadelphia Museum of Art's exhibition *Design Since 1945*—"Reduce! Reduce! Reduce!"—reflects that century's continued desire to break away from the nineteenth century's richness of form and expression of emotion. And in 1988, the title of an exhibition at the Cooper-Hewitt Museum in New York City (now the National Design Museum) was called "The Triumph of Simplicity."

When simplicity becomes a requirement of design, it can inhibit the designer's natural and playful inclinations, and the things he designs can become less communicative, even mute.

Individuality

In the nineteenth century, a new hero had been born, the engineer—the great organizer, the rationalizer of industry who made the new age function and grow. The catalog of the Crystal Palace Exhibition described the role of such a genius as the directing mind for "over thousands [of workers] who combined to realize his will, and who within the short span of seven months completed a structure as vast and as novel as the [huge] structure of this Temple of Peace."

At the end of the nineteenth century, Gustav Eiffel spoke of that thousand-foot tower in personal terms, saying "I" built this tower and "I" inscribed the names of the savants on it. The modern movement rejected the way in which such an obviously collective effort could be expropriated by its designer as *his* own individual achievement. It felt that design should be a collective effort. The modern movement expressed its irritation with any overpowering individuality and removed it by eliminating the speaker of the magic language.

Early in the twentieth century, Otto Wagner described how "the city dweller preferred to disappear among the masses as 'numbers.'" In the 1920s, Gropius, on behalf of the Bauhaus, declared:

> Together we endeavored to develop [something] above an individual, a teachable form language meant to convey an objective knowledge of visual facts. It was the aim of the Bauhaus to save the artist from arbitrariness and separateness in order to have him become an ingredient of the real spirit of the time, far from the cult of the "I" . . . People, like machine parts, were interchangeable…all men have the same needs at the same hour each day of their lives

In 1931, I wrote:

> [The modern movement] wants to change one's taste and is remarkable for rejecting and reducing. It prefers geometric shapes and noble materials, and rejects anything that goes beyond the basic form as an *individual note*. But as such a strong formal limitation is not justified either from the point of view of the soul nor from an objective point of view, this form direction can only be considered as mere aestheticism far removed from real life.

The magic language of design was to be replaced by the collective expression of the time. This aspect of modern design most severely suppressed the designer's natural generosity in conveying his feelings to his audience.

Functionalism

In the first years of the twentieth century, Wagner and Semper formulated a tenet of the modern movement: they declared that only what is useful can be beautiful. Thus, the idea of beauty of utility replaced the earlier, beaux arts definition of beauty, that only what is not useful can be beautiful. With this new aesthetic declaration, diametrically opposed to the previous idea of beauty, came a new focus for design: the *useful object*. This new aesthetic became the basis for a style called "functionalism"—a style in which objects were made to look functional. The leaders of the modern movement did not think of functionalism as a style. In fact, Le Corbusier declared that the styles were dead. They thought of functionalism as a new truth. The functional look was widely accepted by the mid-twentieth century.

Streamlining

In the late 1920s and early 1930s, industrial design burst onto the public scene, and some designers became celebrities. Streamlining, a popular symbol of the speed that characterized modern life (locomotives, cars, airplanes, etc.), became the hallmark of such designers as Norman Bel Geddes, Henry Dreyfuss, Raymond Loewy, Walter Dorwin Teague, and others.

By the end of the 1930s, the first professional school of industrial design had opened in Pittsburgh and later moved to Brooklyn as the industrial design department of Pratt Institute. It was headed by Alexander Kostellow and Rowena Reed. It was here that I taught for thirteen years. A photograph from an early cover of a Pratt Institute catalogue showed a hand holding a chisel, portraying industrial design as a technical profession and clearly illustrating the loss of the magic language.

Evolution and Progress

Our deep-seated belief that what comes later is better than what came before has led us to overvalue novelty. The wealth of new technical inventions created the idea of endless progress: an advance toward a richer, better future. This attitude has led the Industrial Designers Society of America to call its magazine *Innovation*.

As long ago as 1815 Rachel Varnhagen, a woman from Frankfurt, wrote to her brother:

> The whole earth has now been traveled and is known: compass, telescope, human rights, who knows what else has been discovered... whatever happens anywhere is known anywhere else in a fortnight...I see all of existence as a progression, as an intense gain in perception, I truly think that earthly life is not a strict repetition, but a forward-stepping change. I am expecting the Great and the New, miracles of Invention, of discovery, of revelation. Oh Evolution! I am sure it is coming....

In 1823, a German traveling in England wrote a letter to the German architect Friedrich Schinkel, extolling the progress of the industrial revolution:

> The wonders of the new time, my friend, are here, the machine and the buildings for it called factories—in the distance they make a wonderful sight, particularly at night when thousands of windows are resplendent with gaslight. And in addition, there is a forest of still higher steam machine chimneys, which stand upright like needles.

And, Nicholas Nickleby, Charles Dickens's character, exclaims, "Behold the peaceful industries of our island, her rivers covered with steamboats, her roads with locomotives, her skies with balloons of a power and a magnitude unknown in history, the boundless conquest achieved by British perseverance and labor...." In the 1840s, the Hungarian poet Sandor Petöfi predicted that the invention of the locomotive would inspire brotherhood between nations.

In 1859, one year after Charles Darwin's *Origin of Species*, Herbert Spencer captured the optimism of the age and its trust in virtually automatic progress in his *First Principles of Evolution*. He predicted the endless benefits which technology was to bring to every field, easing the burdens of life, freeing time for leisure travel and art (which he called "play").

The word "forward" began to be widely used. The earliest Socialist newspaper, for example, was called "*Vorwärts*" in Germany and "*Avanti*" in Italy. The idea of continuous progress was accepted in general parlance: the magazine of the Smithsonian Institute mentions the "progress of science" in the context of the Eiffel Tower. Otto Wagner, a forerunner of the modern design movement, named both Darwin and Spencer as his guiding spirits. Further on in the early twentieth century, Adolf Loos declared that "no one can stop the evolution of humanity," and that evolution brought about the elimination of ornament. Our minds are so influenced by the evolutionary calendar that we do not allow ourselves to accept the validity of our present aesthetic yearnings, to admit to our preference for ornament and the compound curve, for instance. If one expresses an interest in ornament, the response is usually that one is going "*back* to ornament." This, of course, frustrates our uninhibited creative process and deprives the magic language of its color.

Our belief in evolution leads us to the assumption that what comes later will be better than what came before. We use the term "'avant-garde design,'' meaning design marching forward, with modern design in the lead. We speak of progressive architecture, progressive education, of the Progressive political party, the avant-garde music movement, implying that everything is moving forward, that the new is better than what came before. Today, designing mostly means to make something new, an attitude that has a negative impact on the work of the designer.

Inherent in creativity is a happy, positive attitude. It is a discovery, an exploration. However, in creating something that does not exist already, the designer focuses on how not to design something. This negative approach frustrates the urge to speak freely through lines, through the softness or hardness of the material, through colors—the physical urge to make something to touch. Any negative conditioning in the path of creativity is a hindrance.

Our inherent belief in evolution has led to our appreciation of novelty. While "variety" is an aesthetic term and attracts attention, "novelty" is a commercial term and attracts buyers. The main focus of much of today's design effort is innovation; the communicative aspect of design has been lost.

Due to our fascination with the forms of technical inventions on the one hand, and the limiting vocabulary of the modern movement on the other, our designs have moved from the realm of feeling into that of reasoning. In 1925, in his critique of the Paris exhibition of the decorative arts, Angel Zarraga, a Spanish painter, wrote:

> Our sensitivities have been profoundly modified by the impact of...the new possibilities of reinforced concrete, naval architecture, the forms of airplanes... [These] new conditions and inventions, plus the famous "all is but cylinders, cones, and spheres," have given us a taste for the solid form ... From this point, to imagine that our reason is in command was just one step. We took that step....

However, beauty is not appreciated through reason—it is enjoyed through feelings. There is no objective beauty; it goes directly to the heart—a glowing rainbow over a field of ripe wheat needs no explanation. The program of the modern movement made it impossible to express feelings. Following its principles, the designs of the last century have lost emotional appeal. The design process has become sensible instead of sensitive.

Our Goal:
The Playful Search for Beauty

From time immemorial, man has tried his hand at making pretty things.

According to the late Cyril Smith, professor of metallurgy at the Massachusetts Institute of Technology, "Man's capacity for aesthetic enjoyment may have been his most practical characteristic, for nearly all the industrially useful properties of matter and ways of shaping materials had their origins in the playful search for beauty. Beauty is at the root of man's discovery of the world around him, and makes him want to live." Since designers are the authors of our physical culture, the things they create should make our lives pleasurable, comfortable, and elegant.

Today, at the beginning of the twenty first century, we are starting to shed the moralistic theories and restrictive tenets of the modern movement. Rather than trying to create a better world through "good design," we should use our newly found freedom to search for delightful lines and forms.

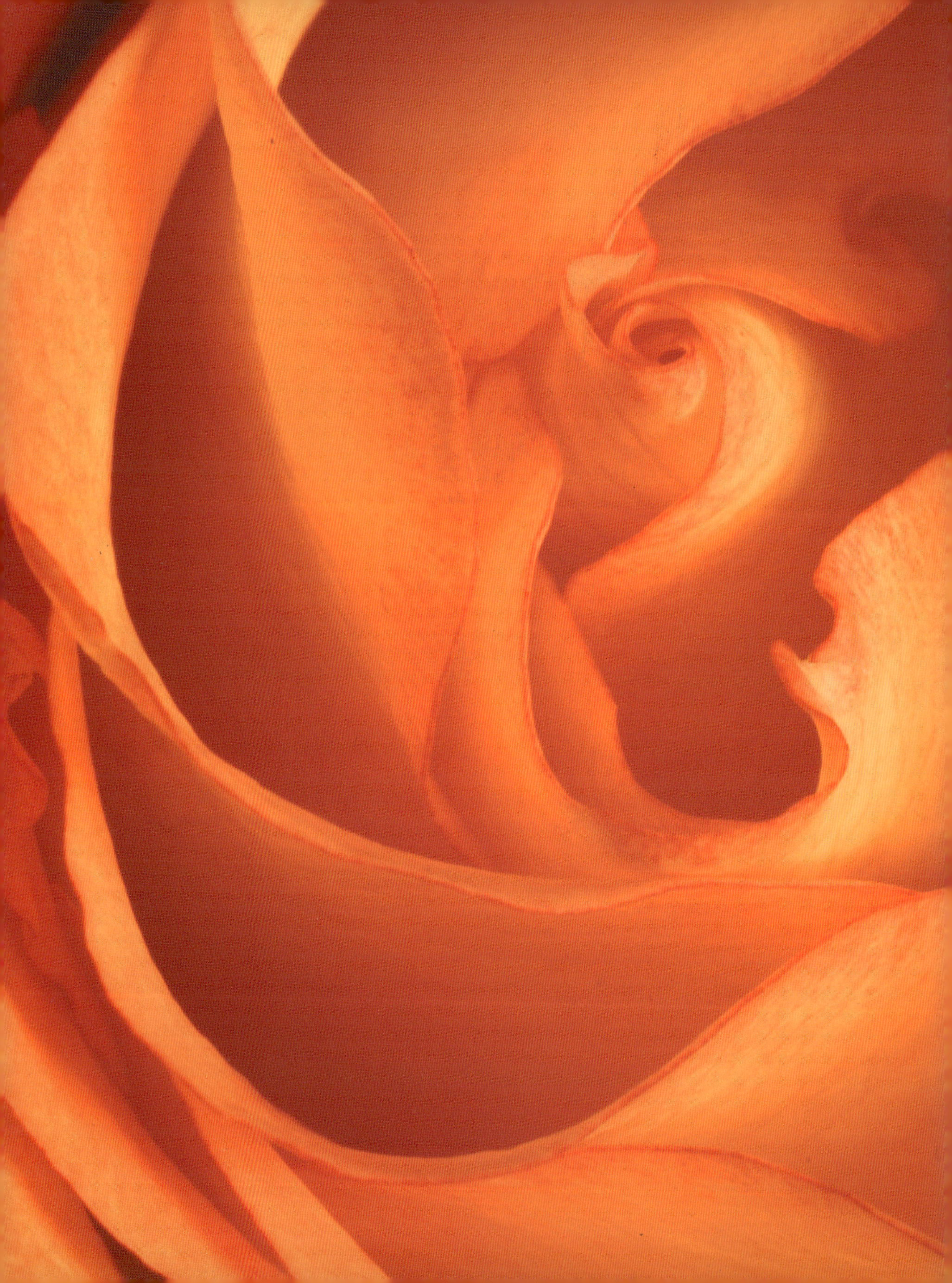

To See: Affinitive Seeing

Before we can make things that are pleasant to see, we must find pleasure in seeing the things that are offered to our sight. We take note of the flamboyant, extraordinary sights, but we must also seek out the innumerable irrelevant shapes and lines on which our glance can alight and invest them with meaning, as patterns or forms we can enjoy. We must learn to see . . . and to enjoy.

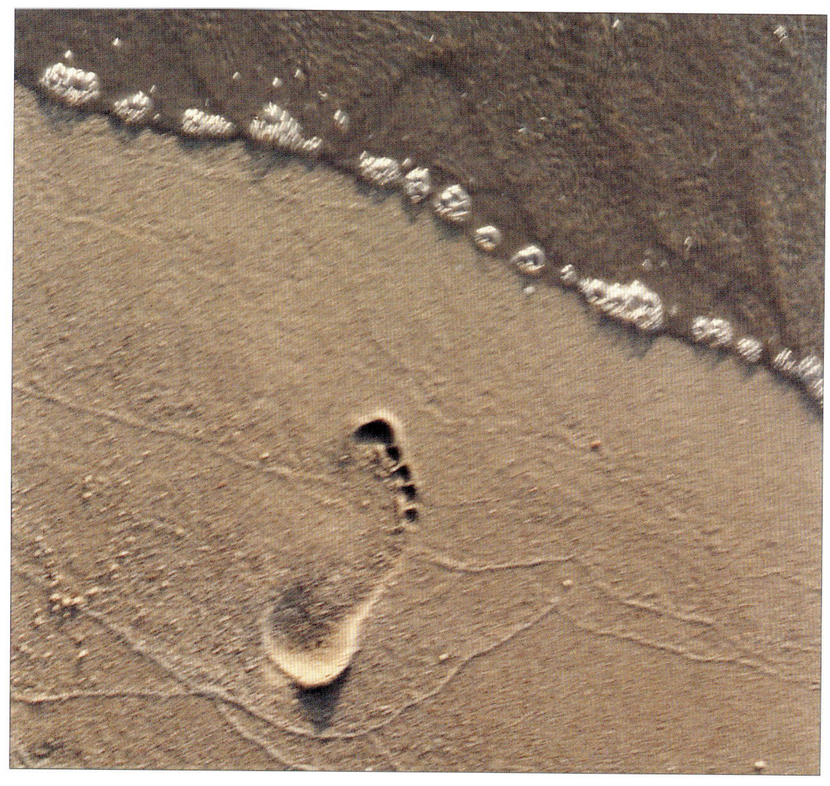

Fig. 2: Rose.

Fig. 3: Footprint.

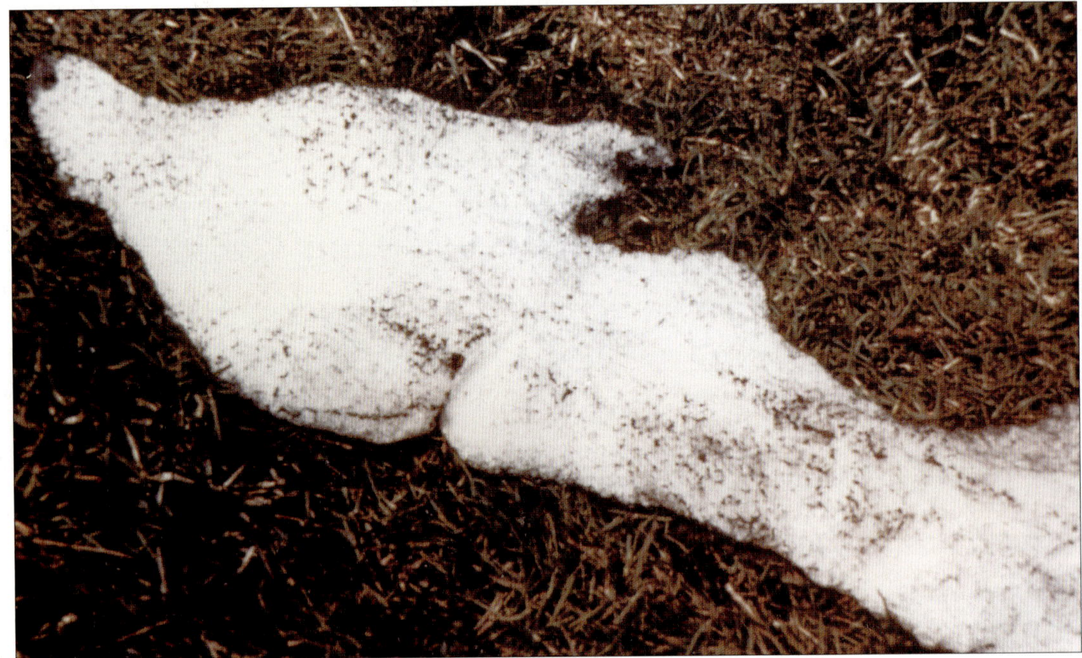

Fig. 4: Patch of snow.

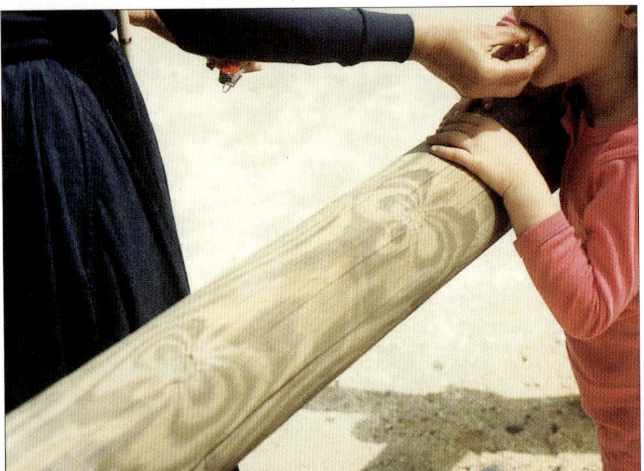

Fig. 5: Wooden railing.

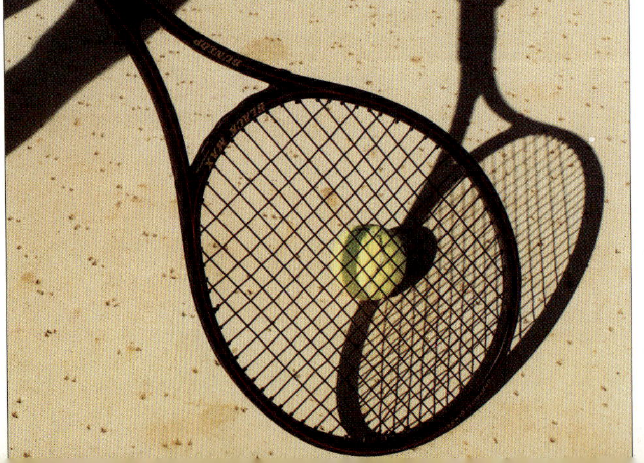

Fig. 6: Tennis racquet.

Fig. 7: Ivy leaves.

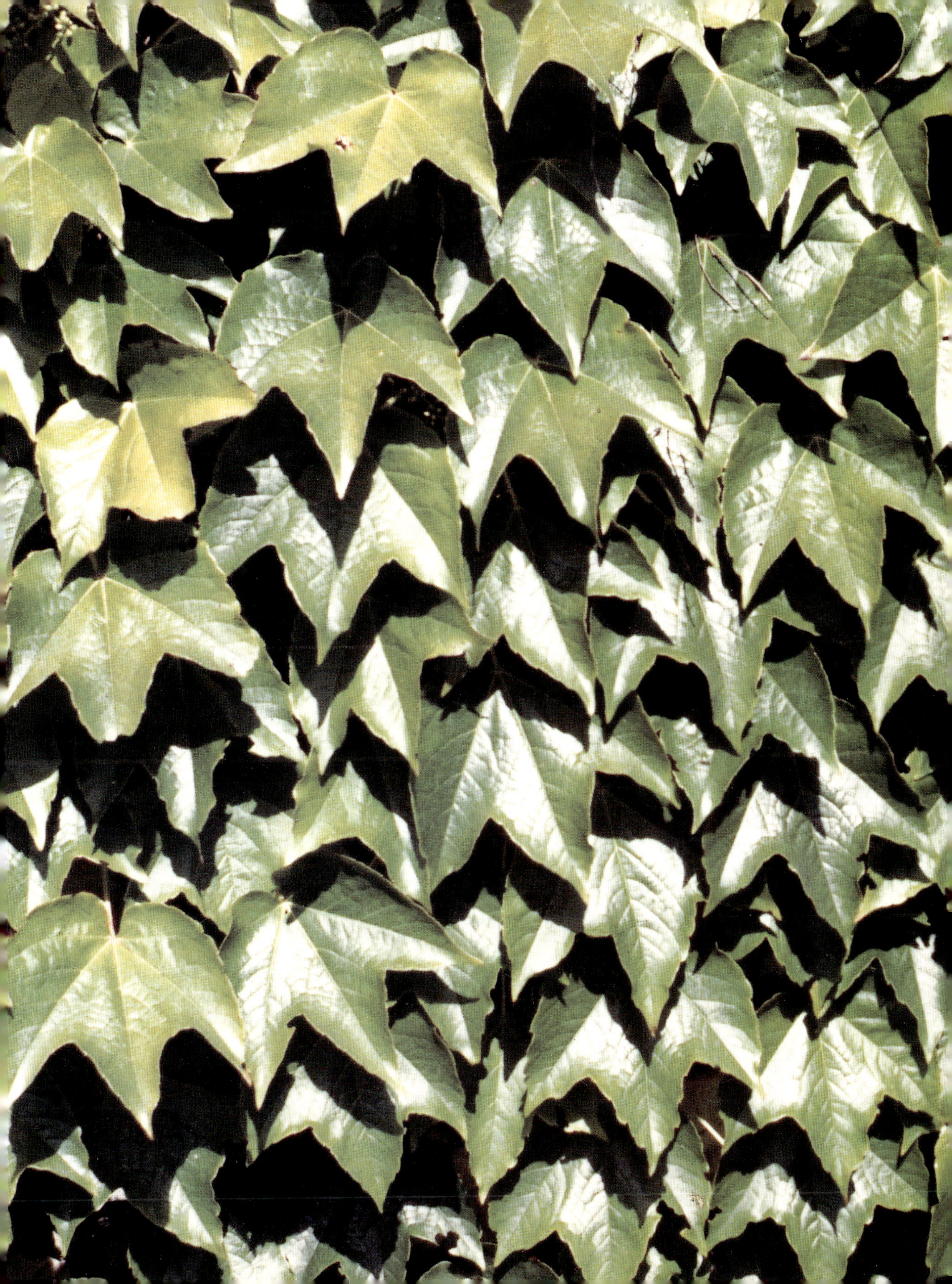

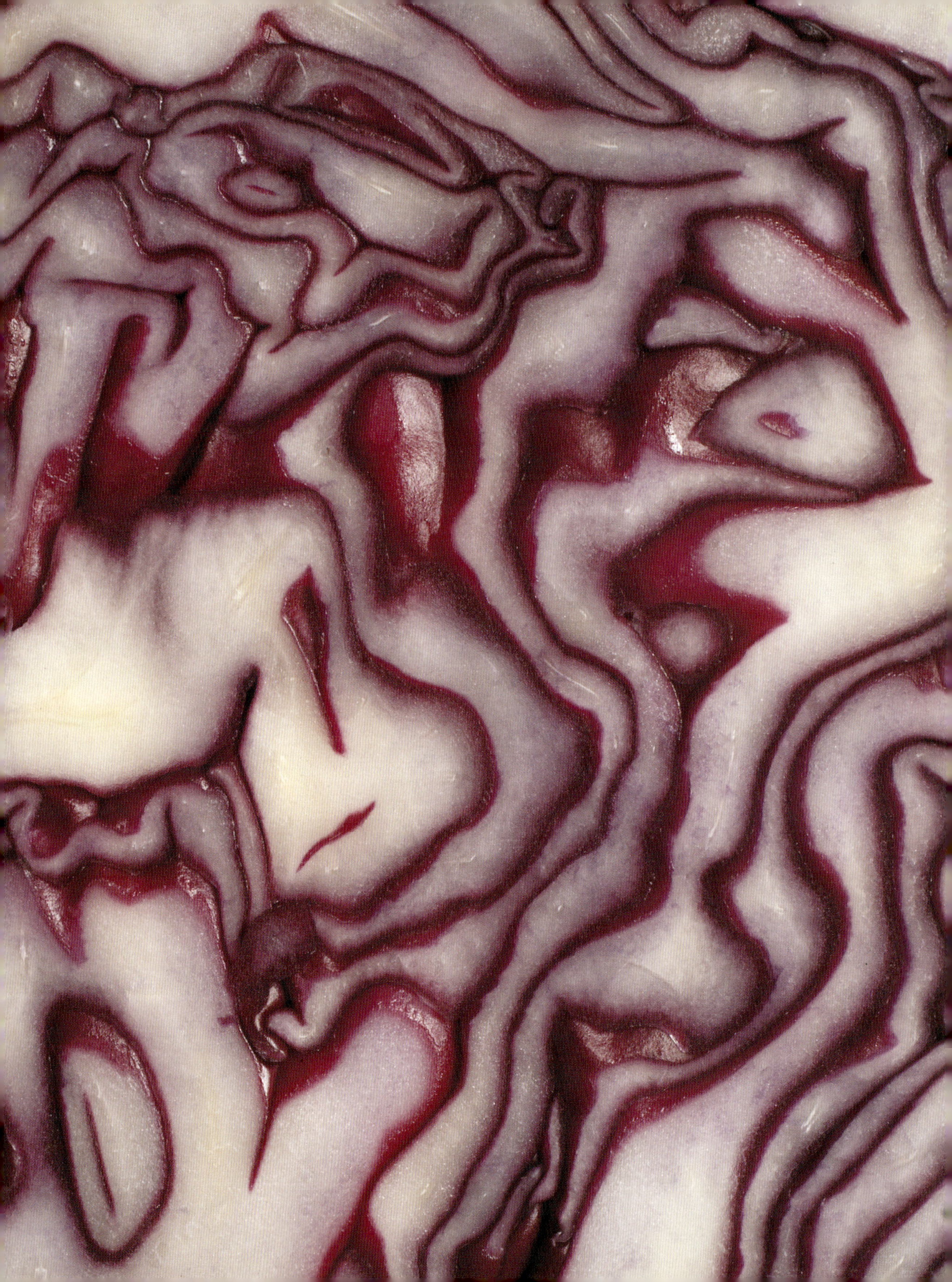

As we see, we project our style preferences—our moods—and those preferences become a filter, through which we select those things that correspond to the lines and shapes of our preferred style—whatever it happens to be at any given time. In one mood, or stylistic period, we may see cabbages that are comparable to an Art Nouveau hair comb, while in another—when we are in the mood for geometric designs—we delight in a nature composed of technical forms.

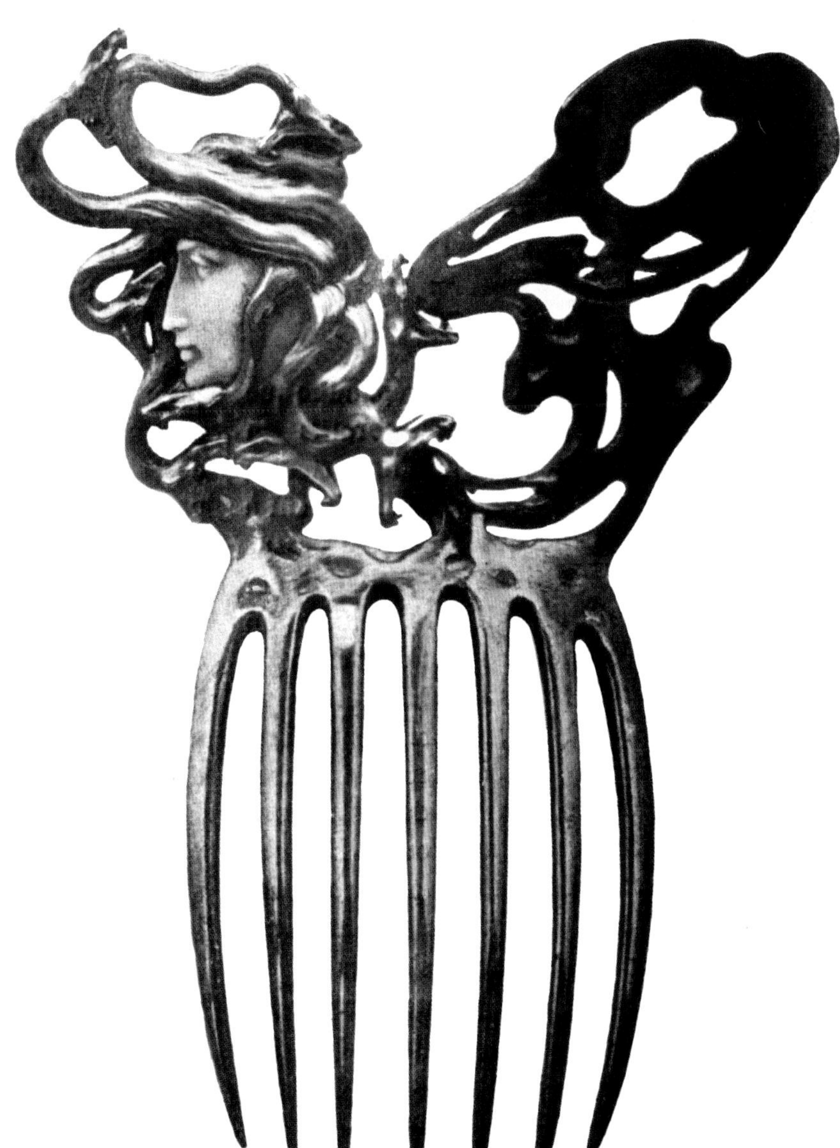

ig. 8. Cross-section f a cabbage.

Fig. 9: Art Nouveau hair comb.

Images also convey meanings and tell stories of faraway lands, of lonely roads, or funerals of forgotten people. In Japan, people often meditate and reflect as they gaze upon stones in open courtyards.

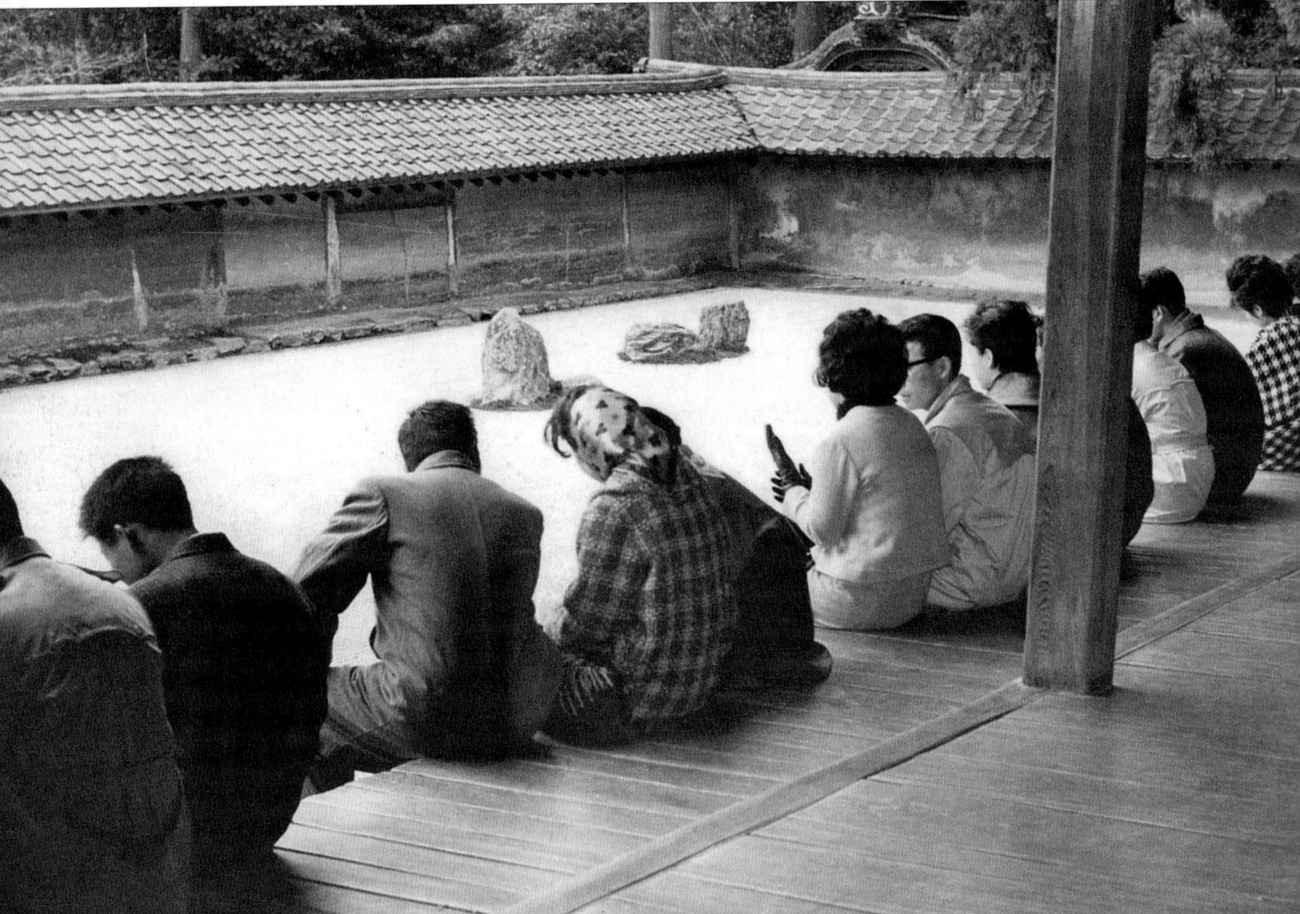

Fig. 10: Japanese sand garden.

Fig. 11: Tre

Our glances will naturally alight on something and pass over where there is nothing. This is one of the most relevant aspects of design.

Coming into Manhattan, I come upon the lovely sight of many brightly-lit ornamental spires spotting the skyline at a distance from one another. If these jewel-like mirages appeared side by side, with no space in between them, their impact would be far less powerful. Without "nothing" surrounding them, they would tend to blur together—they would present a "forest" instead of individual "trees." The greater the visual importance of empty spaces surrounding something, the more important and valuable that something appears.

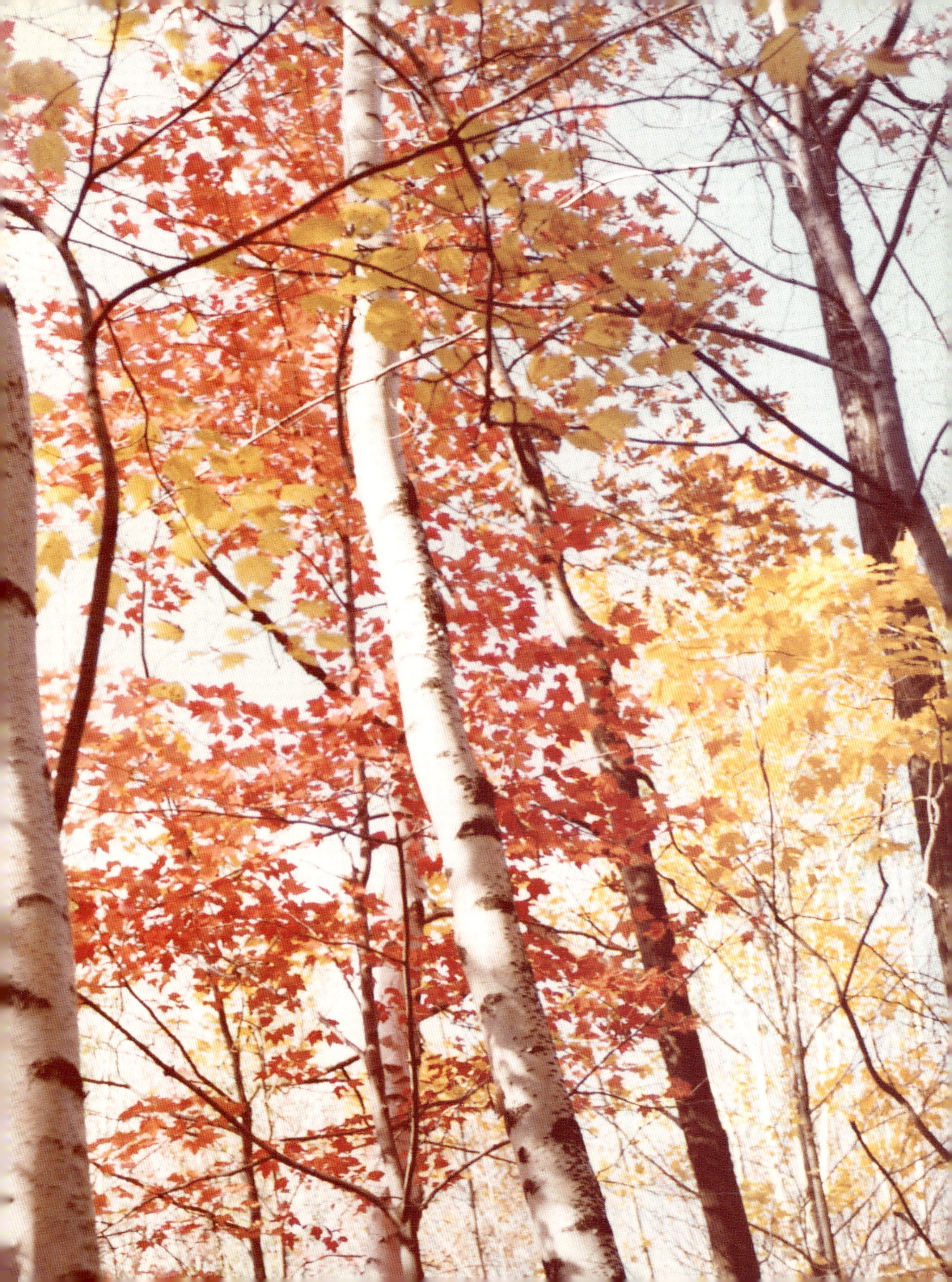

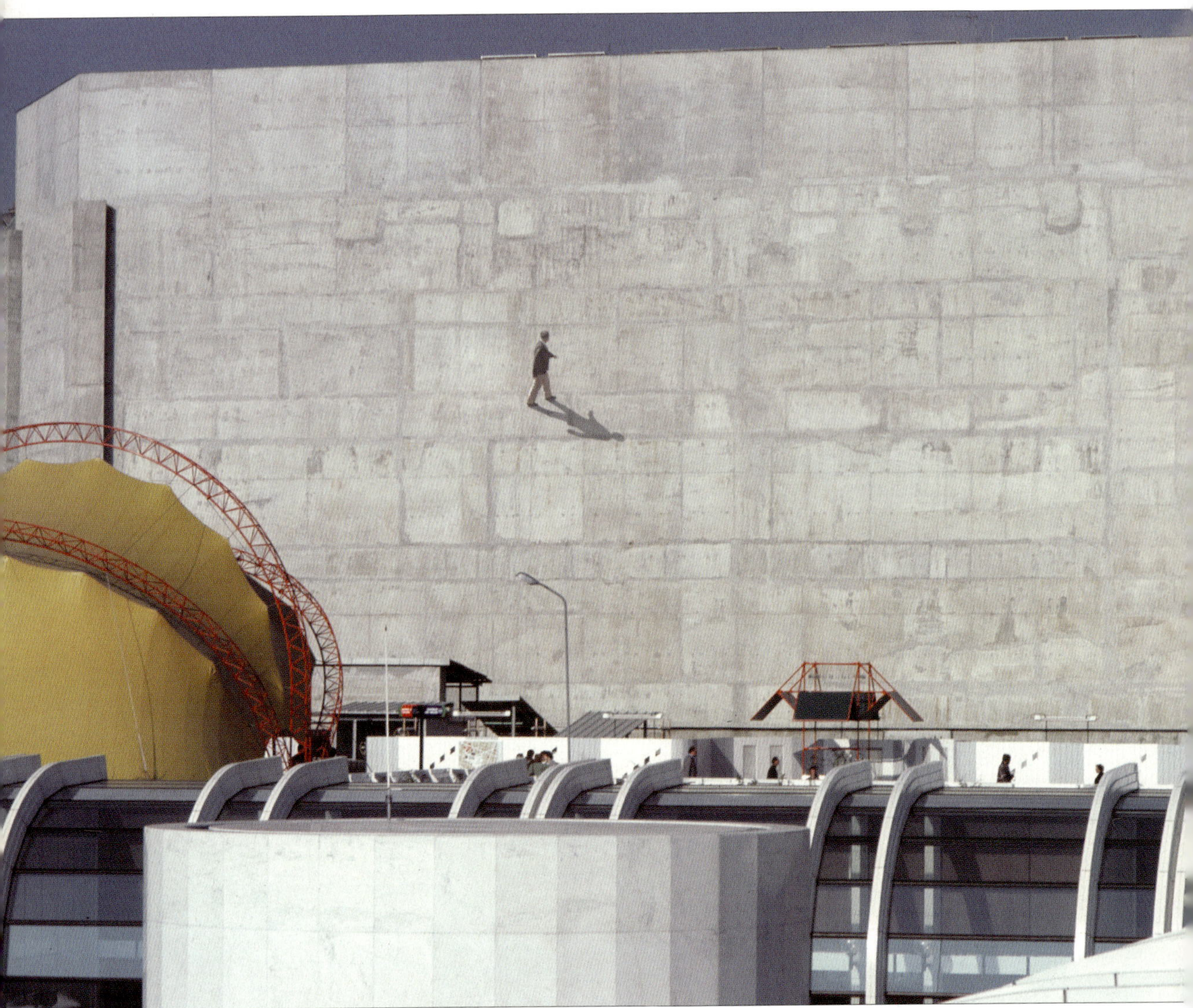

Fig. 12: Figure of man in mural on a wall at Les Halles, Paris.

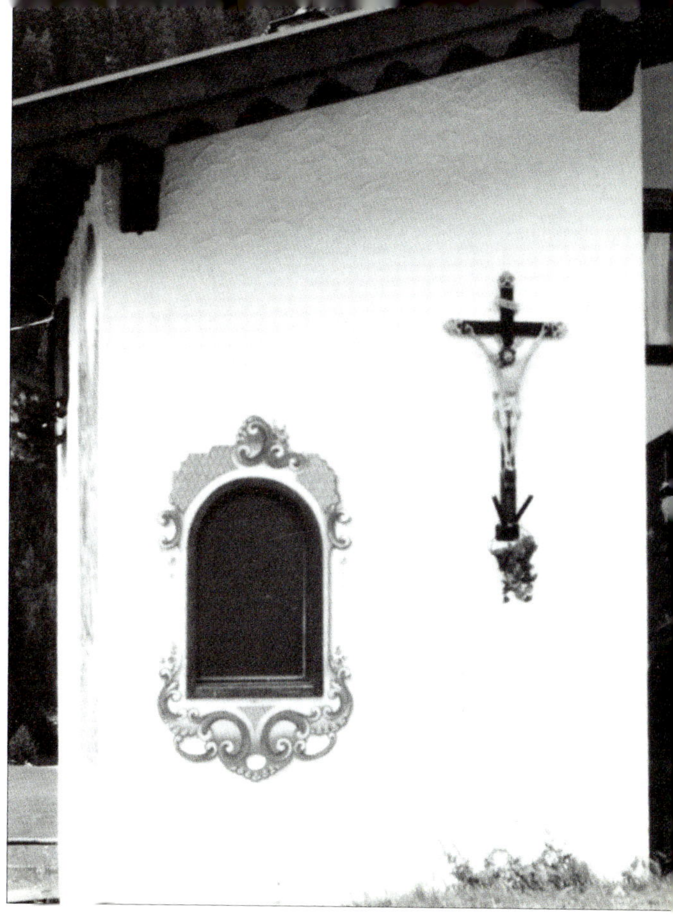

Fig. 13: Wall painting, Bavaria.

Fig. 14: Painted door in Greece.

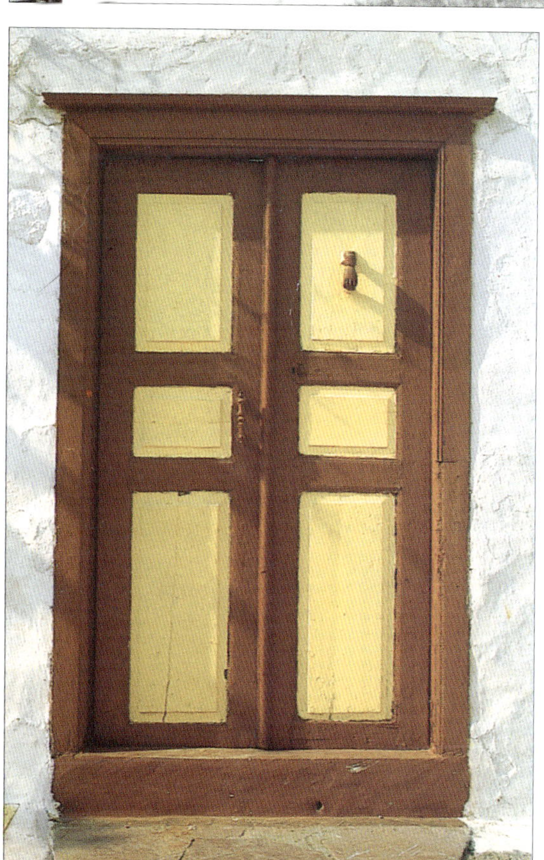

Variety—Not Originality

"Variety is that element of beauty that attracts attention," according to Roger Fry, English art critic and painter. Self expression, the search for novelty—also called "innovative design"—the demonstration of one's personality, the search for originality, trying to create something that's different, are all motivations *which do not lead to variety.* They are all negative impulses, urging you *not* to do something, causing the designer to hold back, rather than to give. All negative attitudes inhibit the process of creation; they stop the joy of aesthetic play.

The restrictive injunctions inherited from the modern movement are examples of such negative motivations—and they are still subconsciously adhered to by the postmodern generation. So, too, is the notion of "good design," for it implies that there is "bad design" (which, however, might please people who are not designers).

Only a positive attitude of generosity, a friendly dialogue with our work from the beginning to the end of its development, will produce pleasant variety.

Fig. 15: Fence.

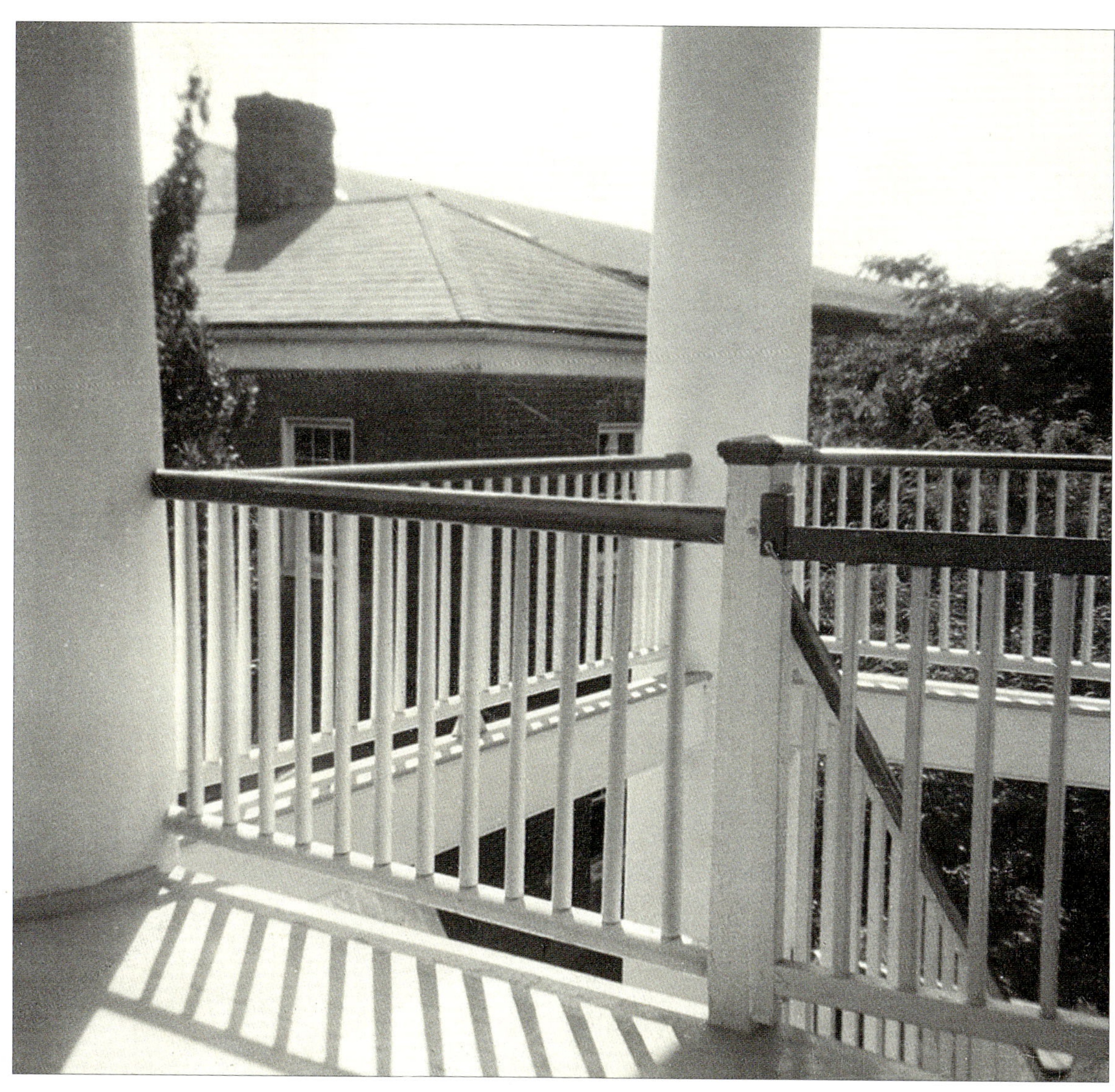

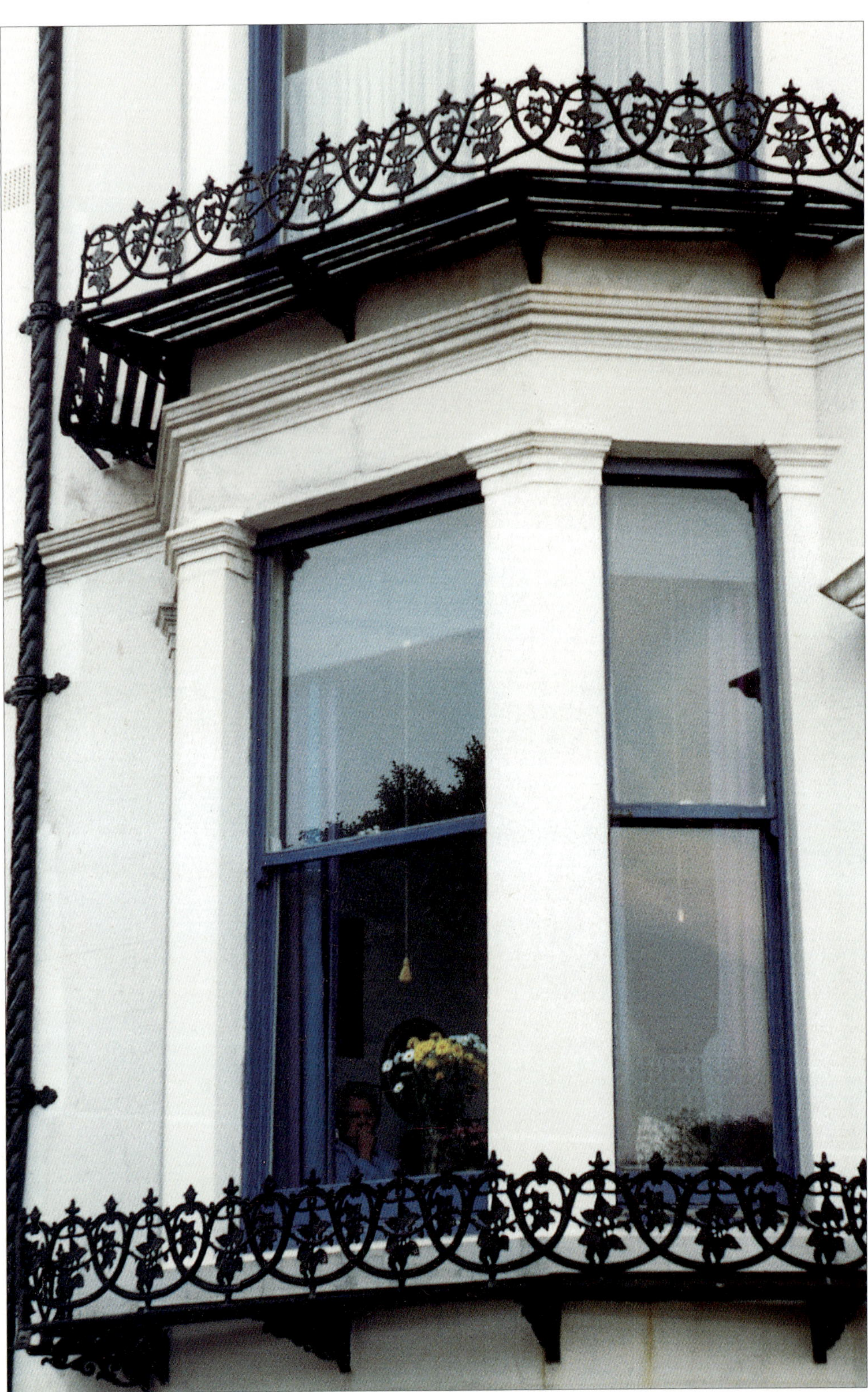

Fig. 16: Decorative grille.

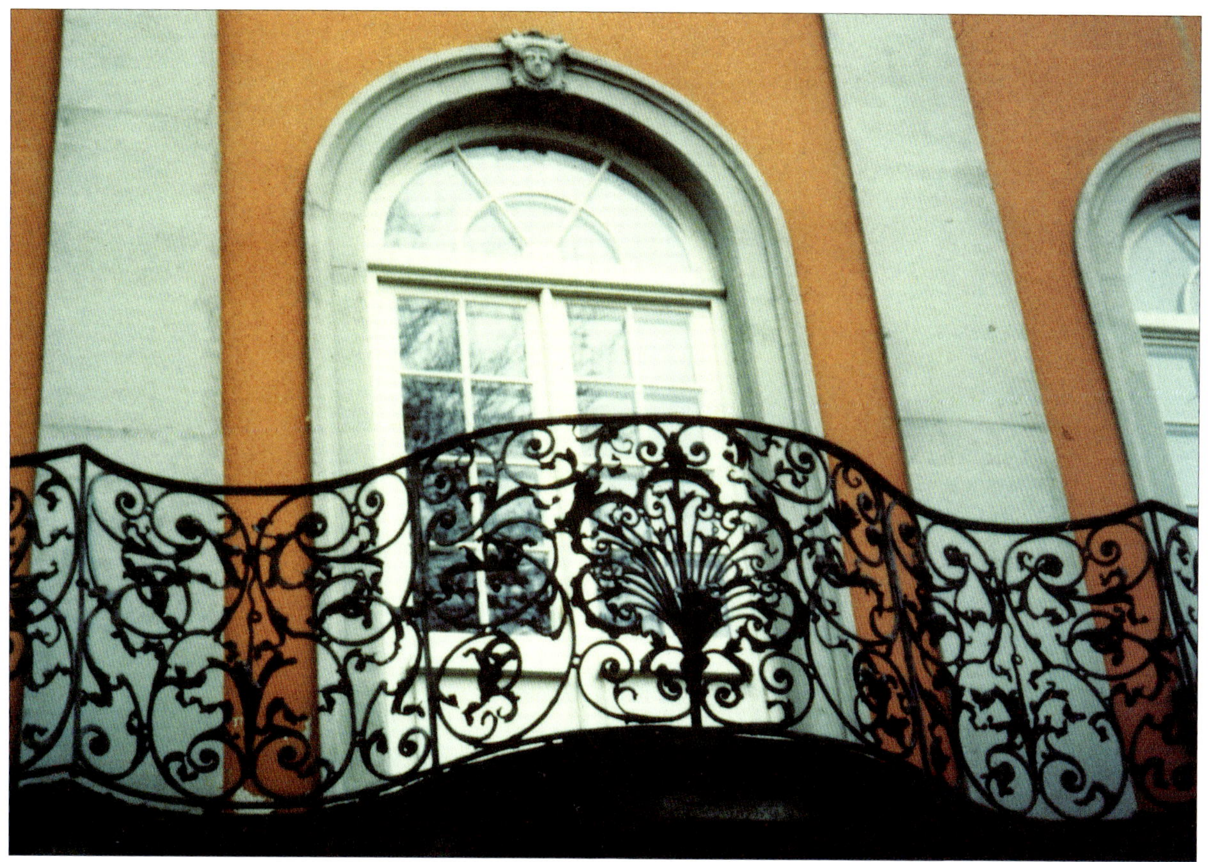

Fig. 17: Decorative grille.

Fig. 18: Grille.

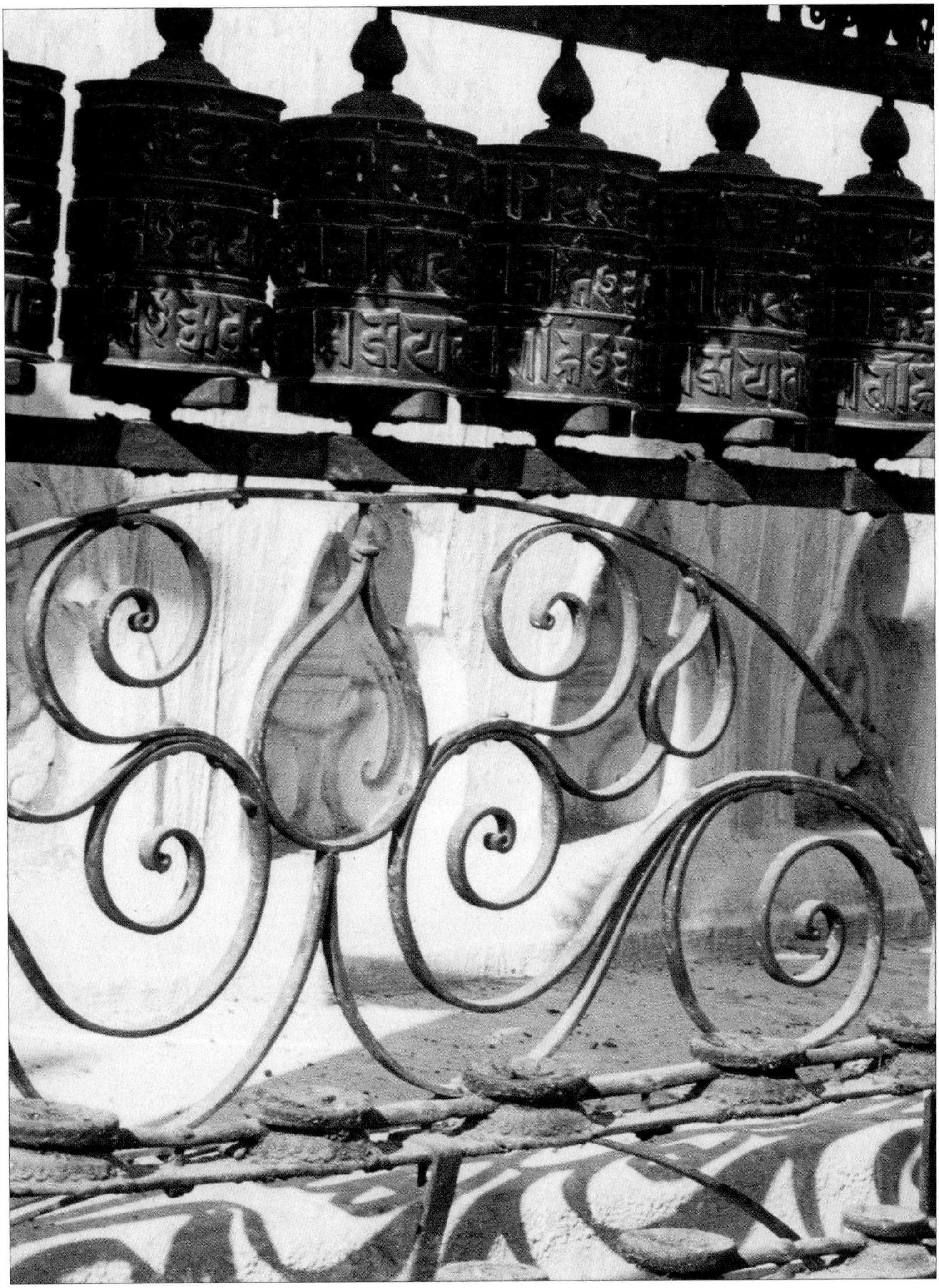

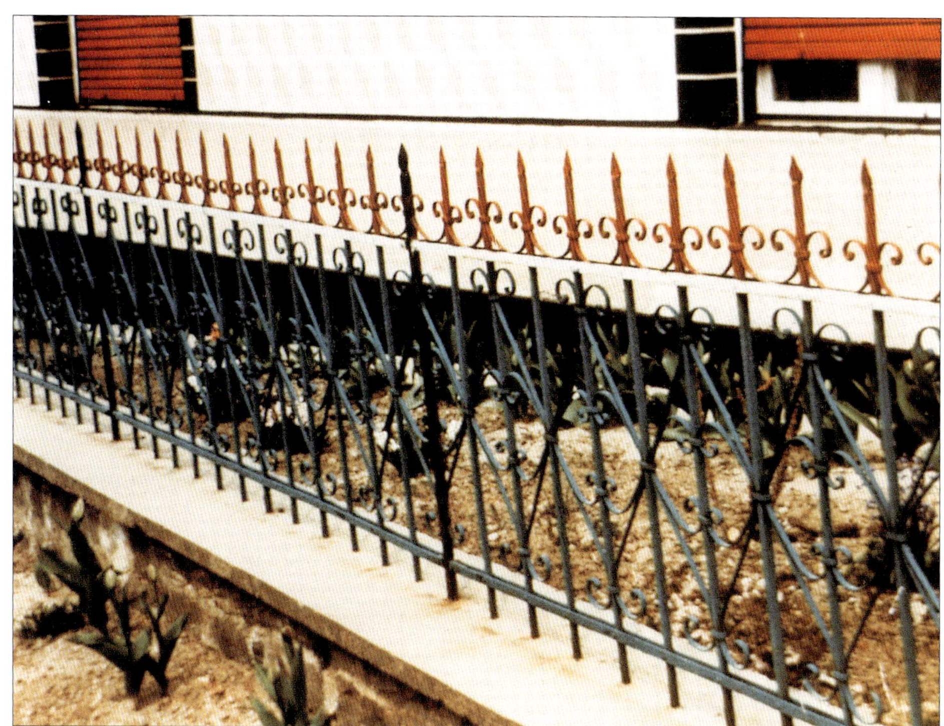

Fig. 19: Fence.

Fig. 20 Fence.

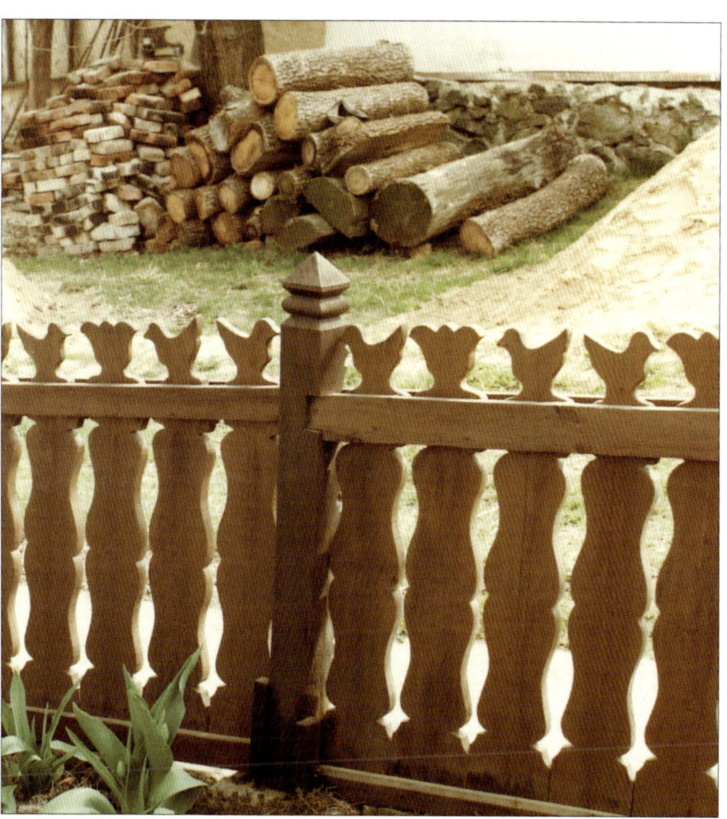

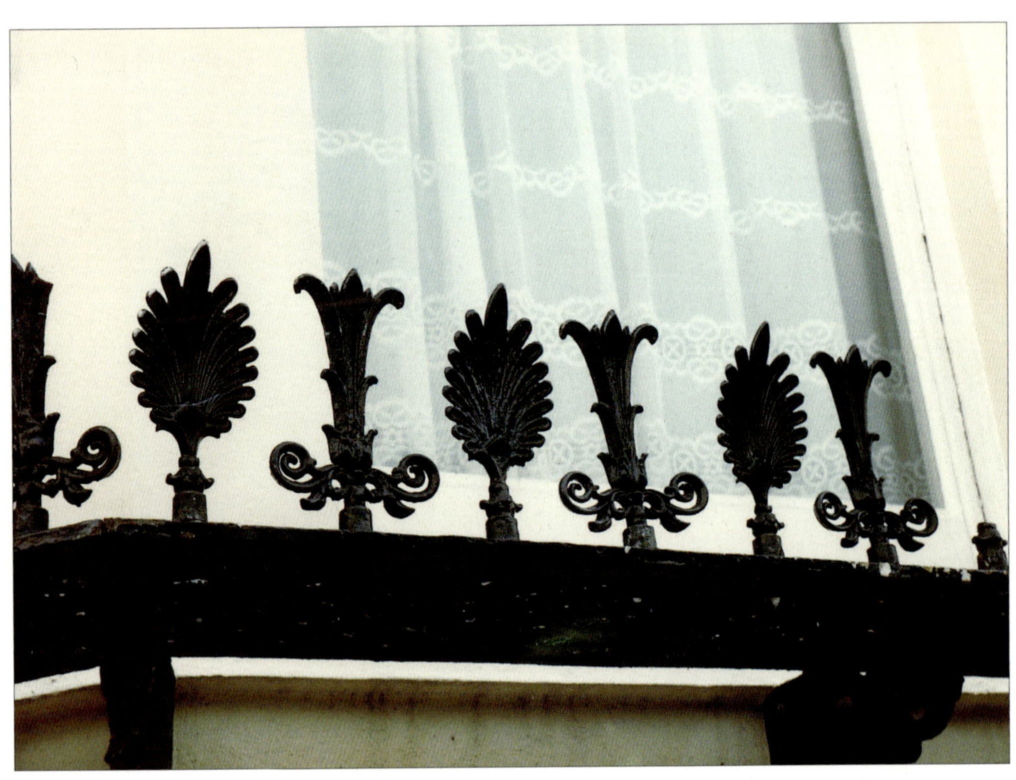

21: Cresting.

22: Fence.

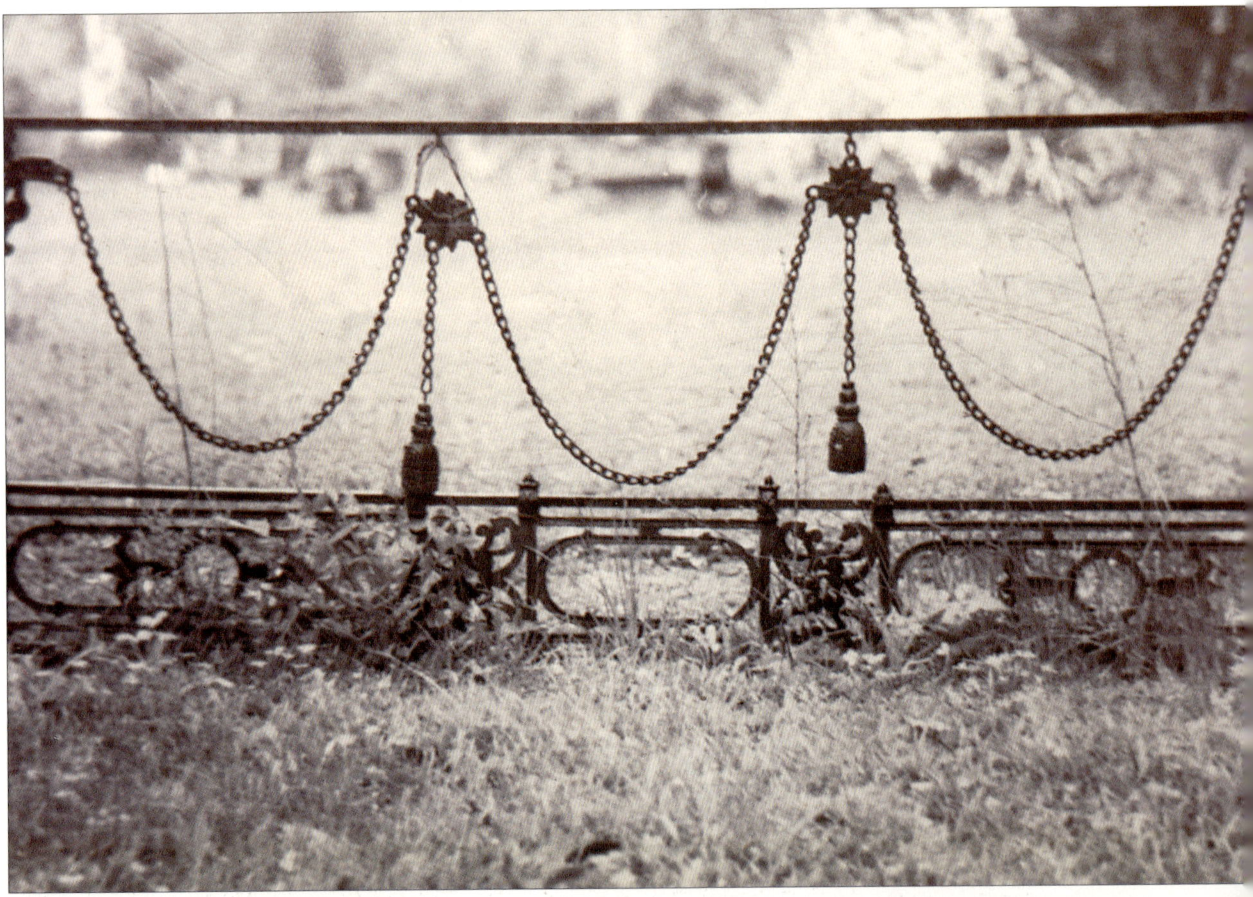

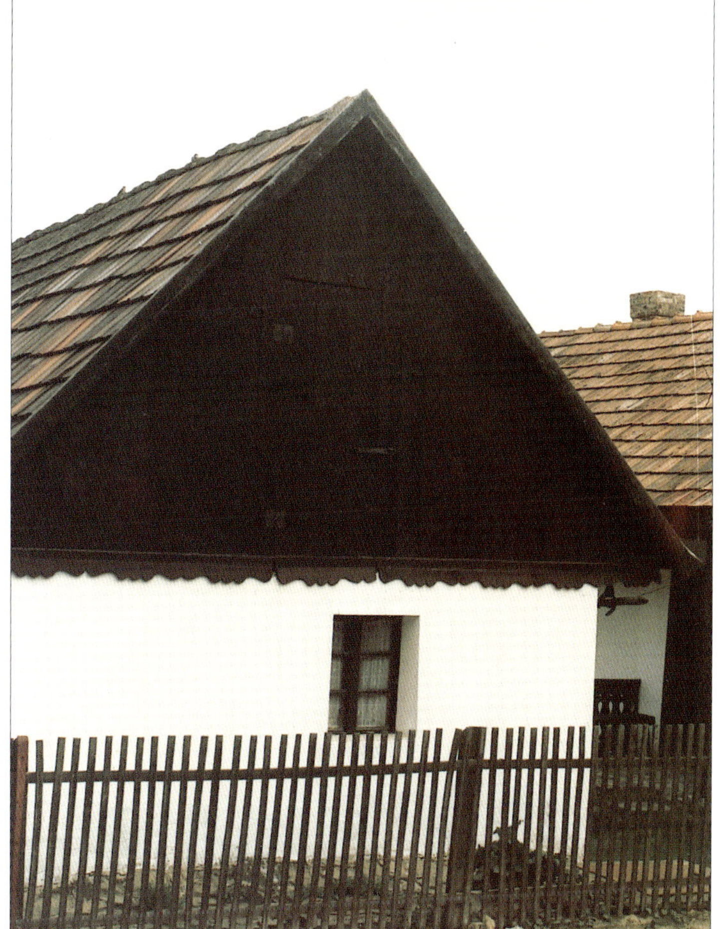

23: Fence.

24: Fence.

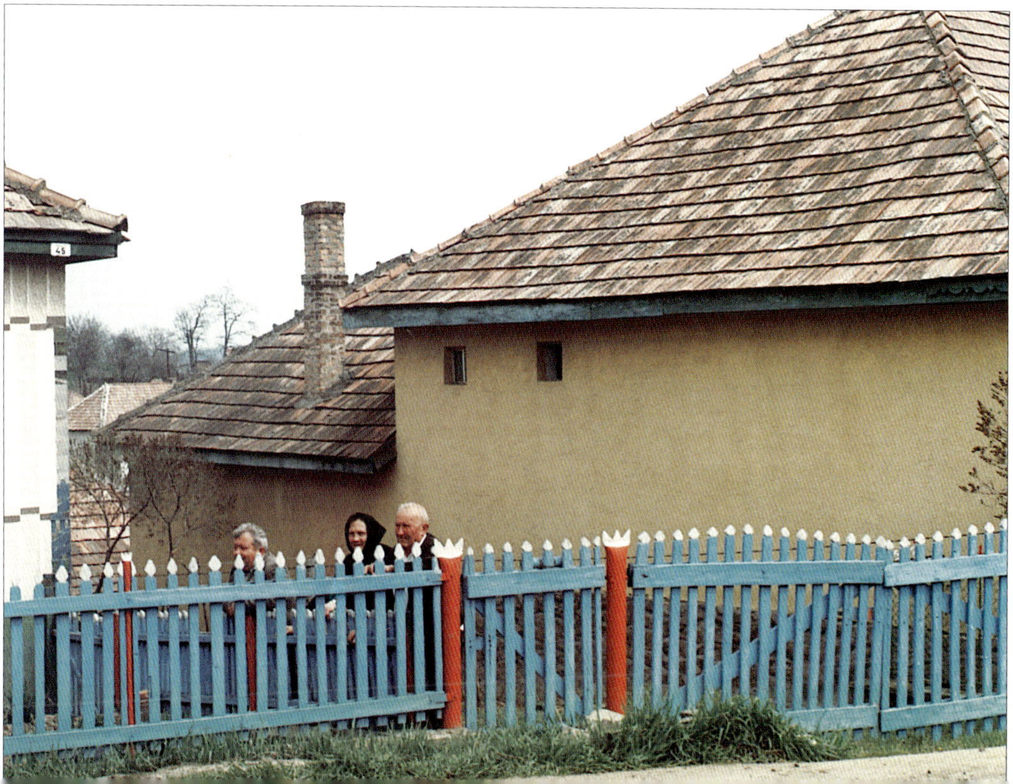

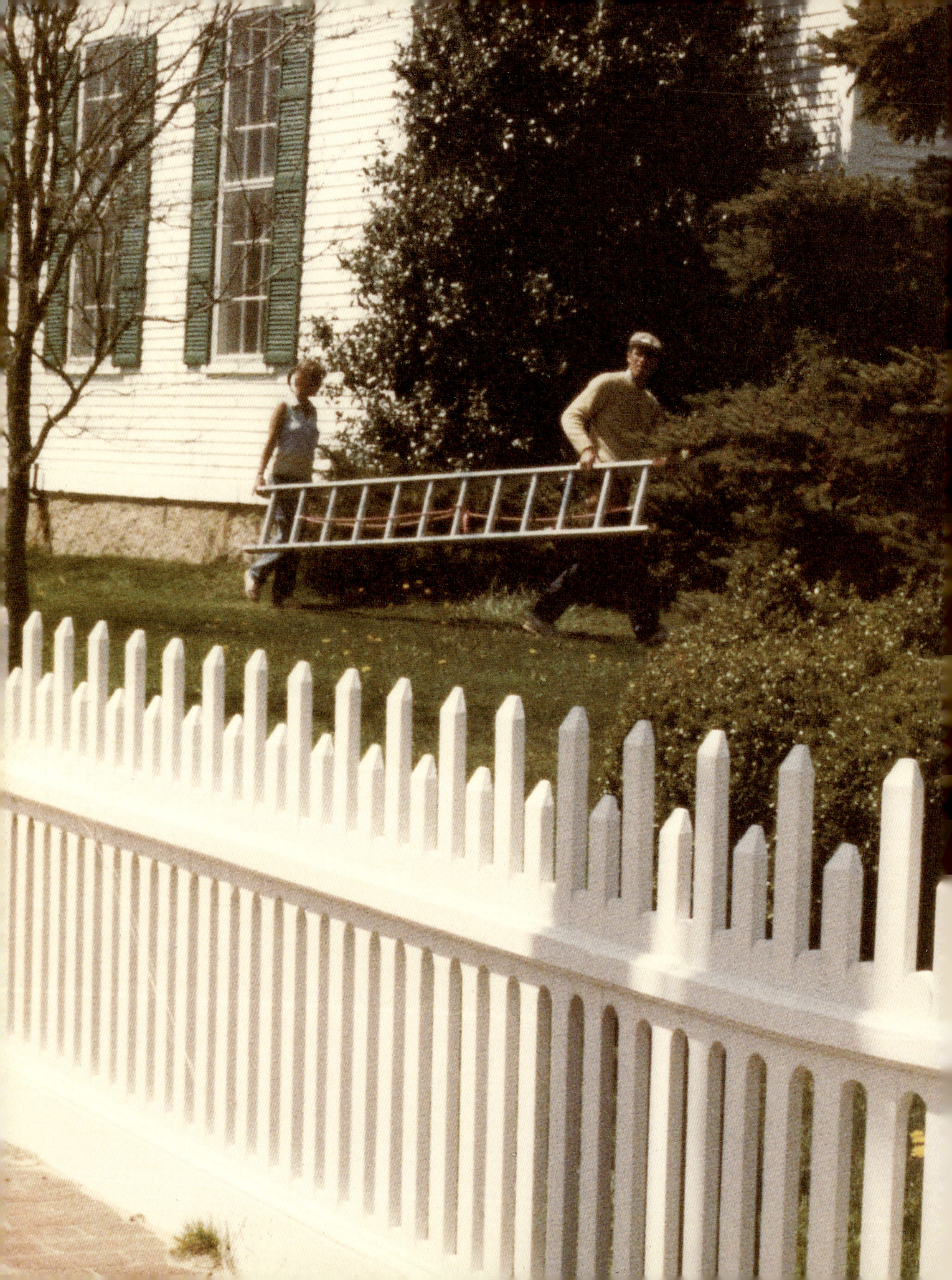

Fig. 25: Fence.

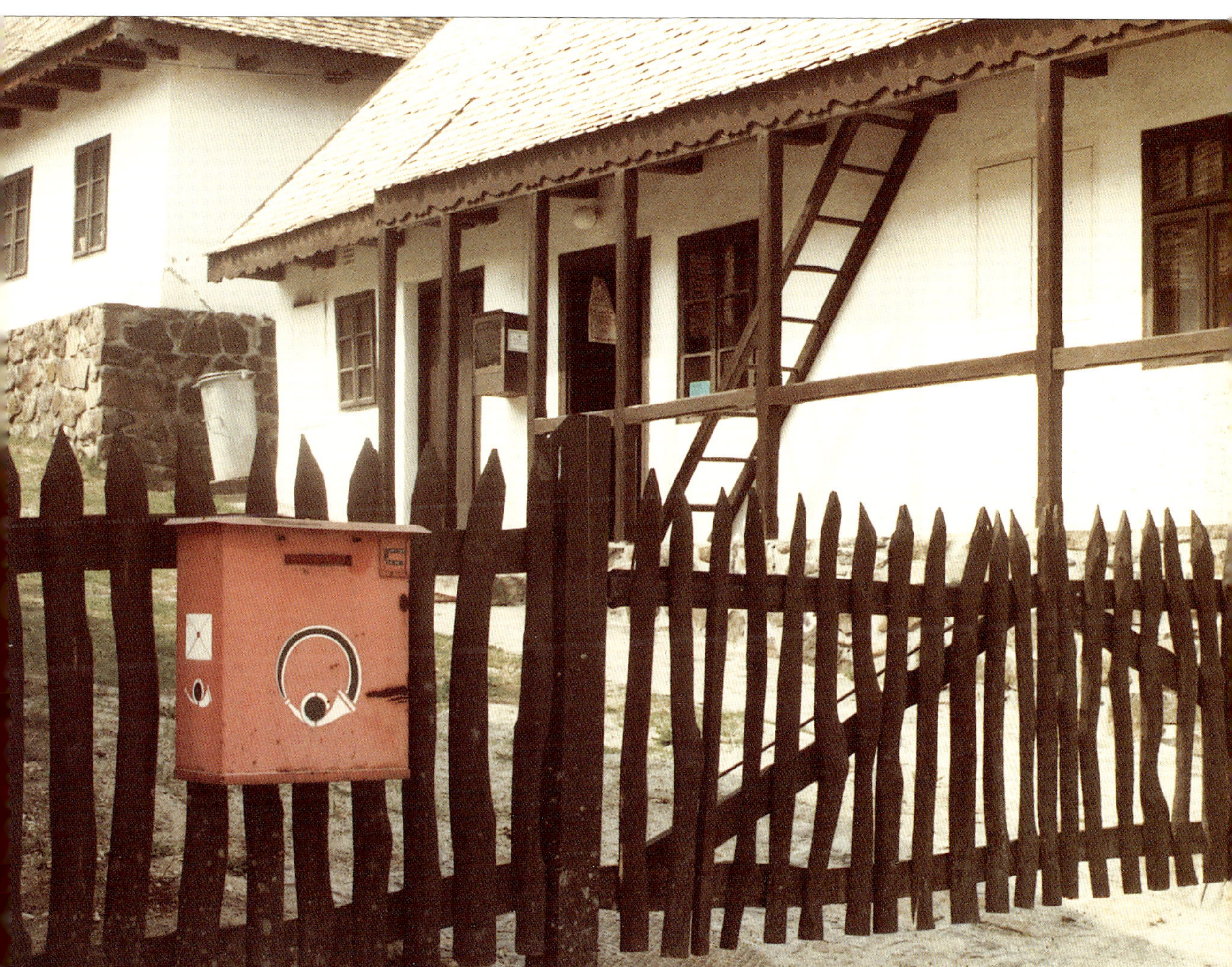

Fig. 26: Fence.

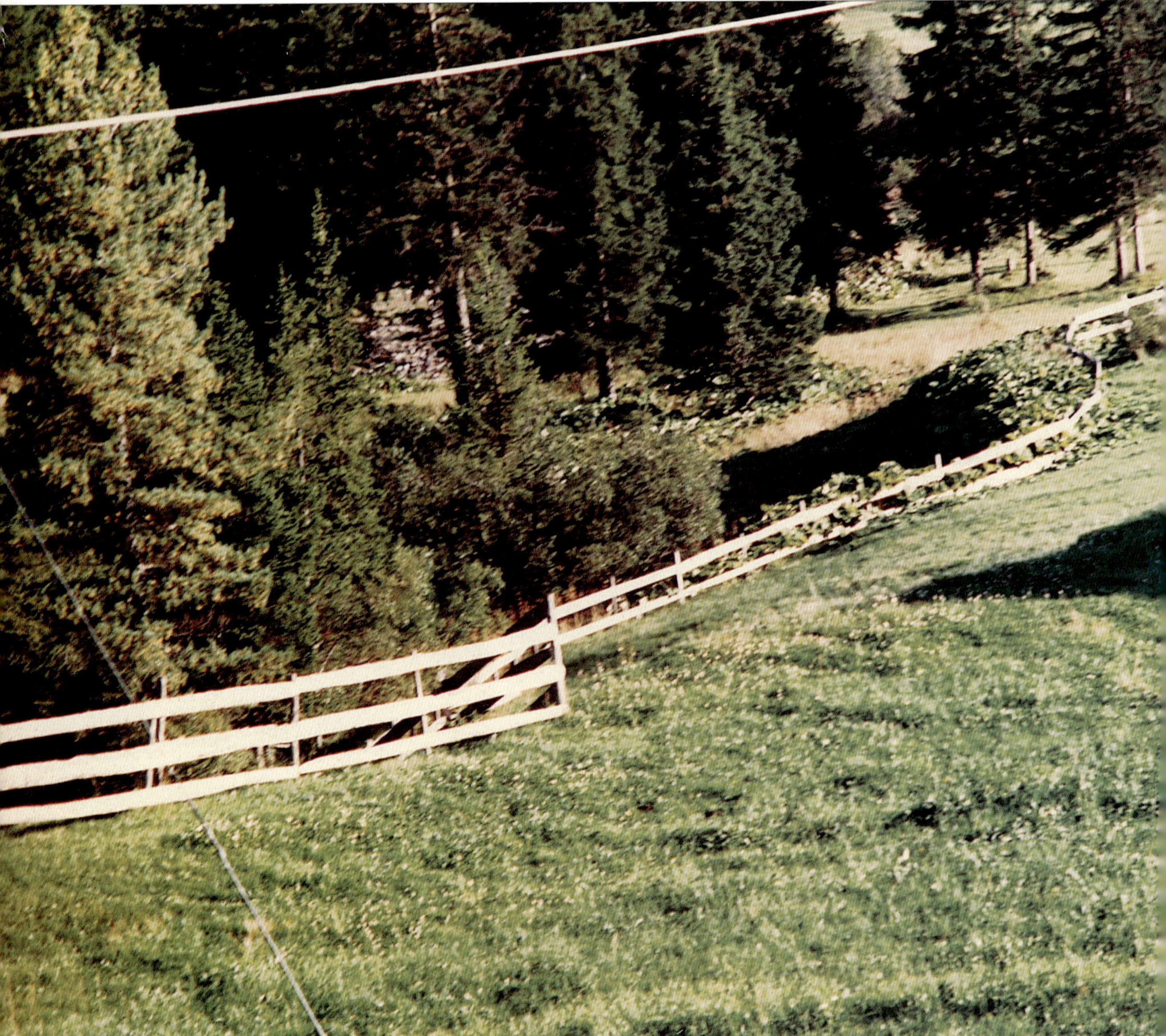

Fig. 27: Fence.

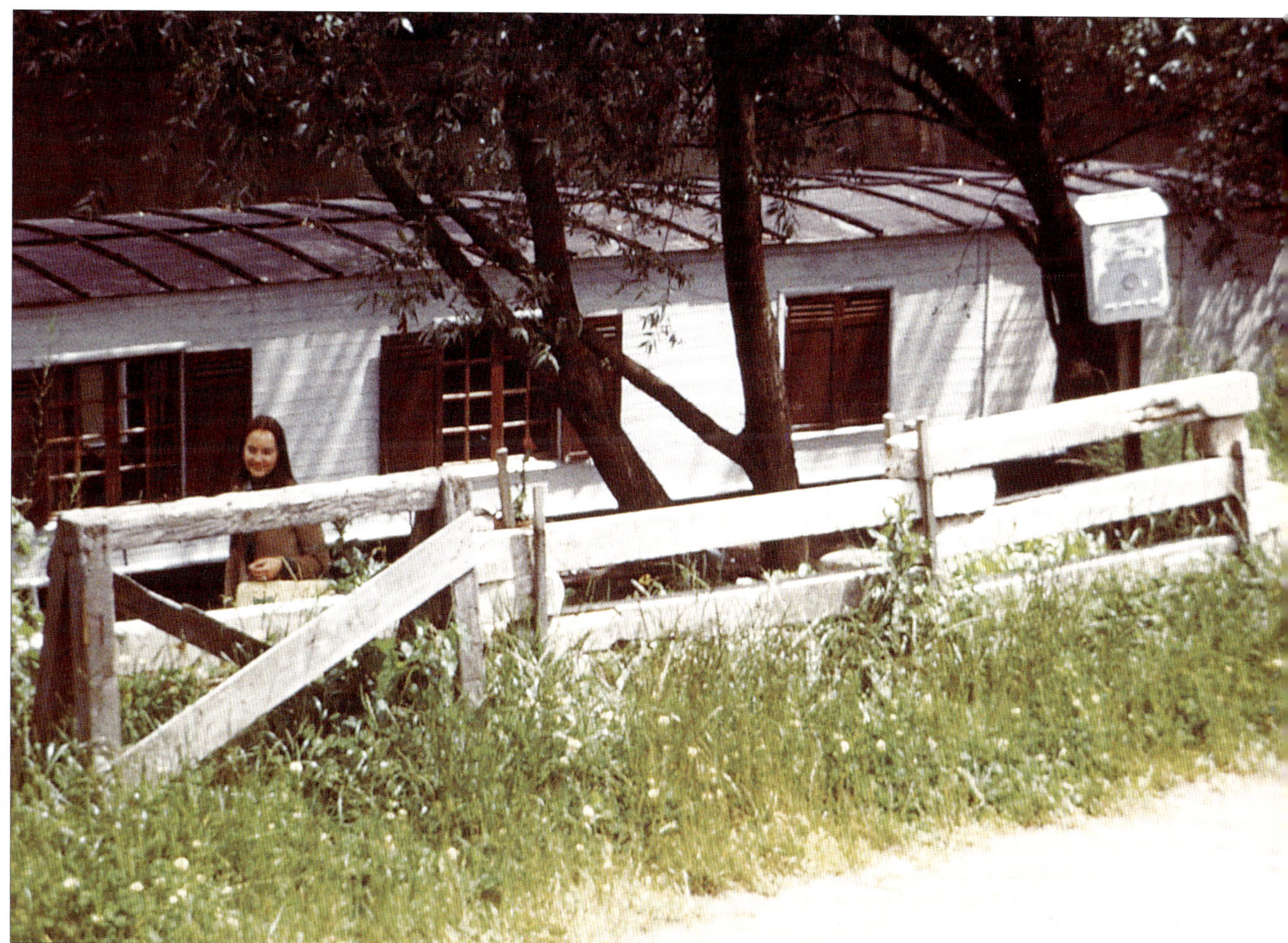

Fig. 28: Fence.

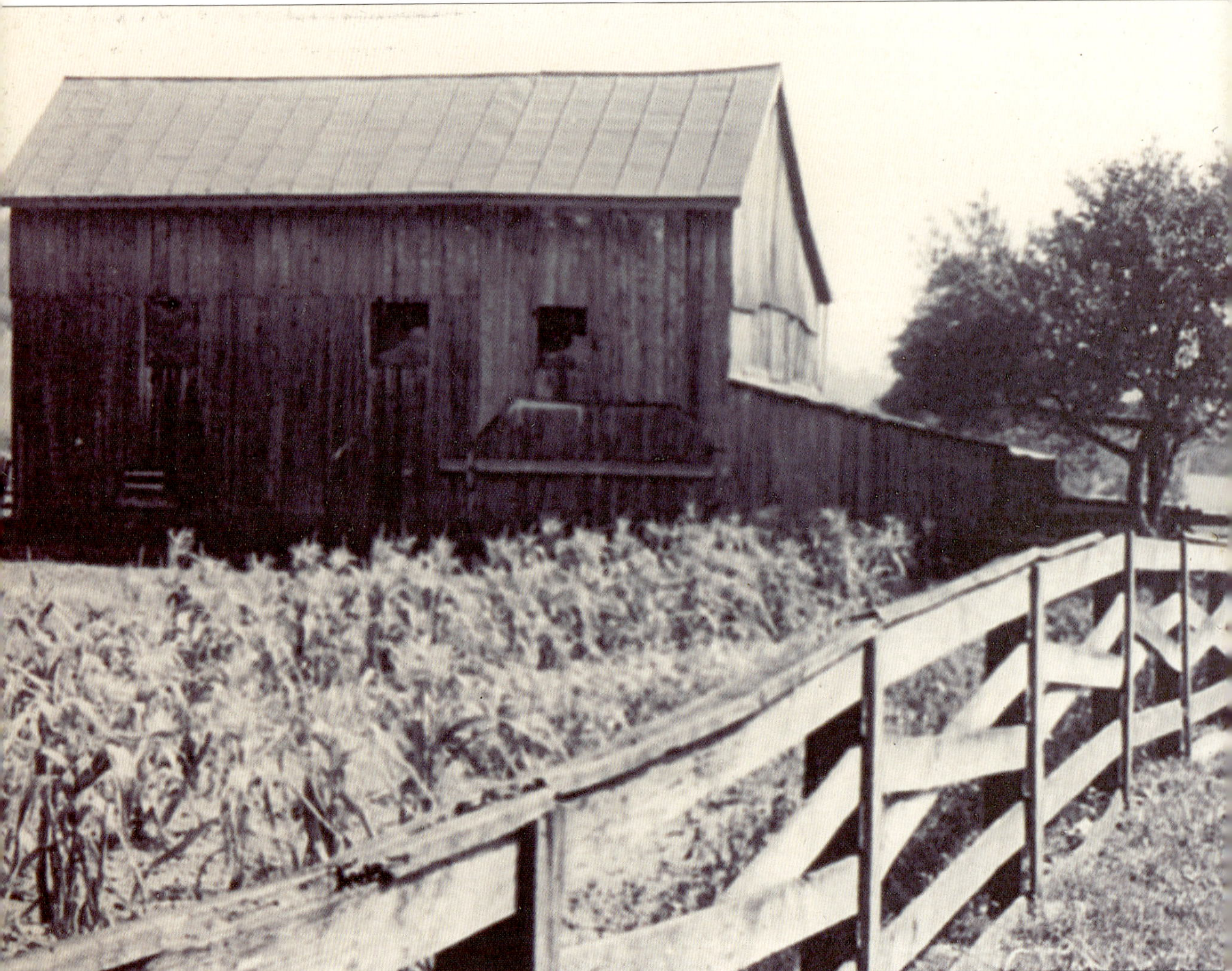

Fig. 29: Fence.

Fig. 30: Fe

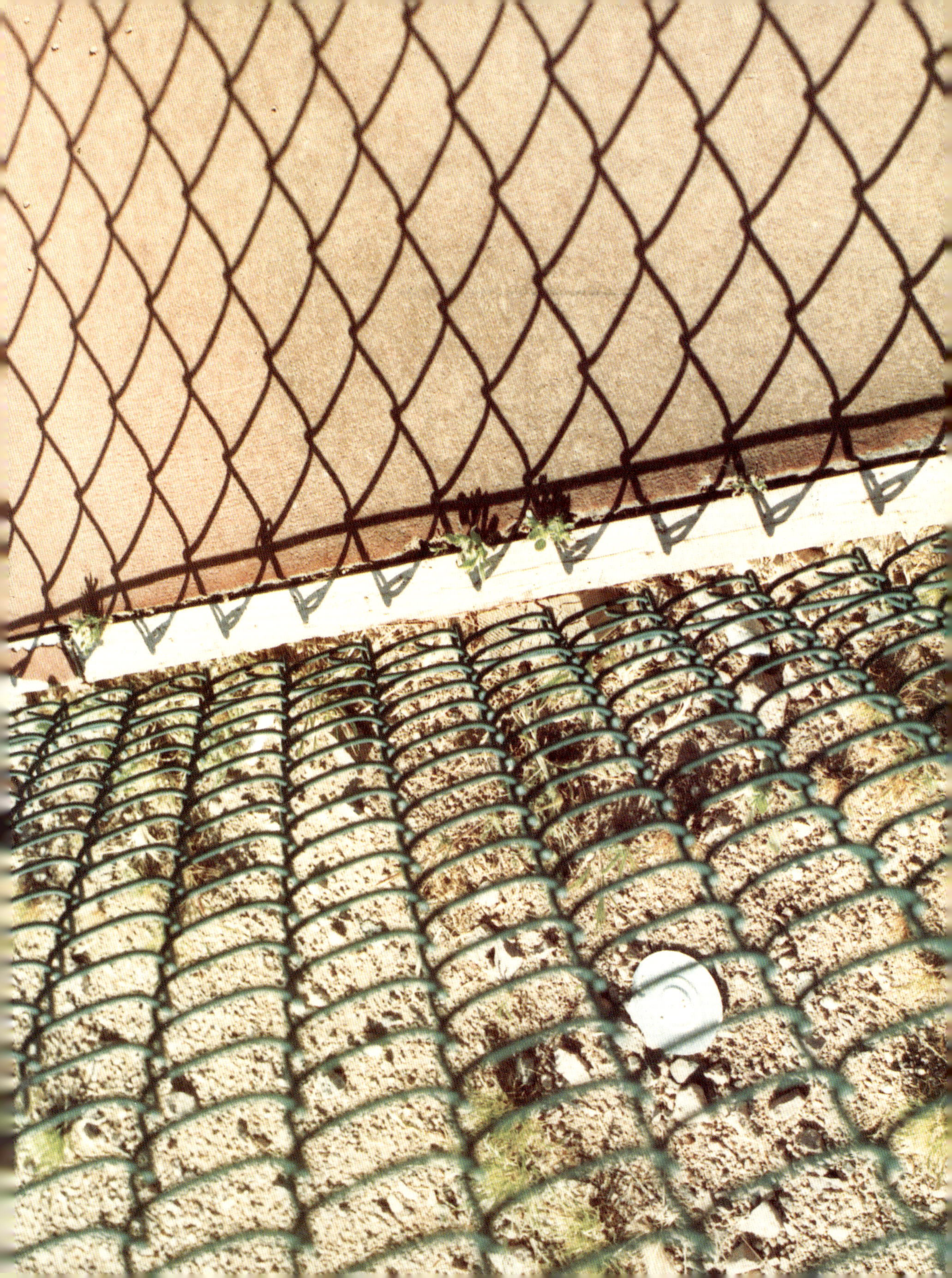

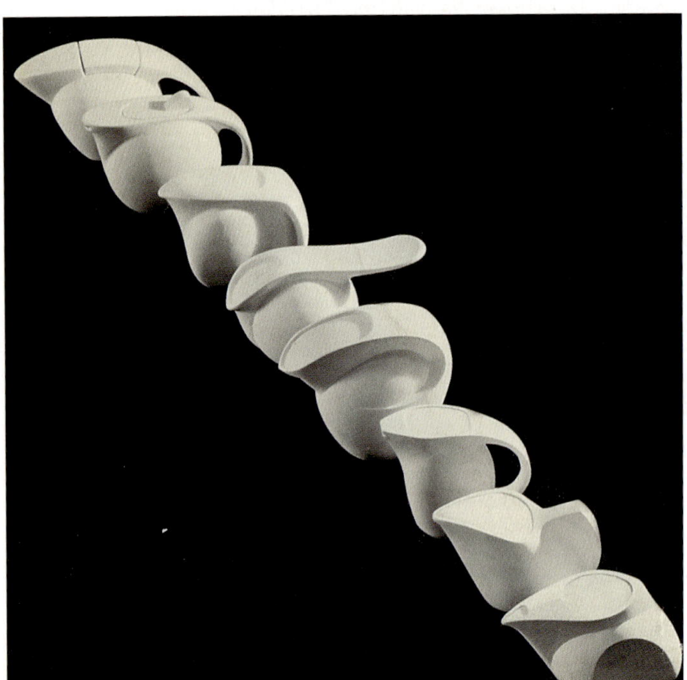

Fig. 31: Streamlined pitchers, student work, Pratt Institute, 1940s.

Facing p

Fig. 32: Hungarian

Fig. 33: Detail of Romanesque church.

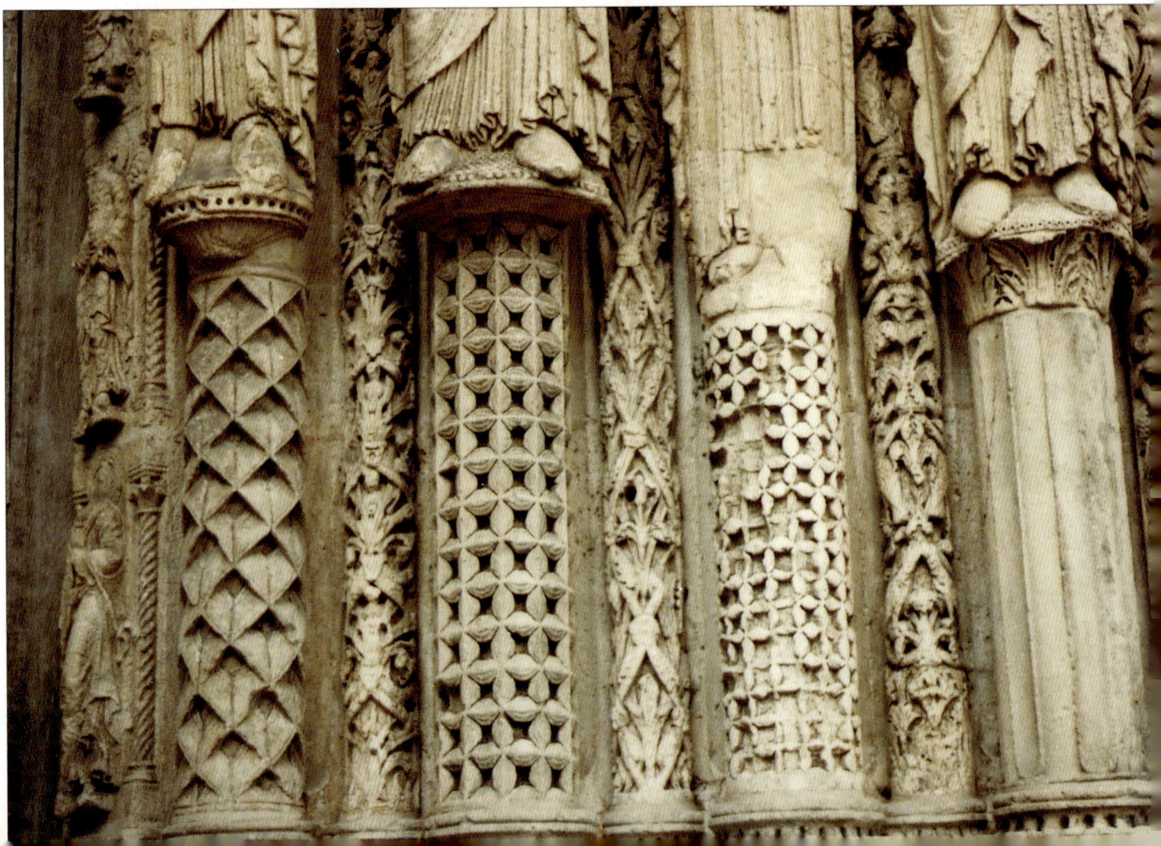

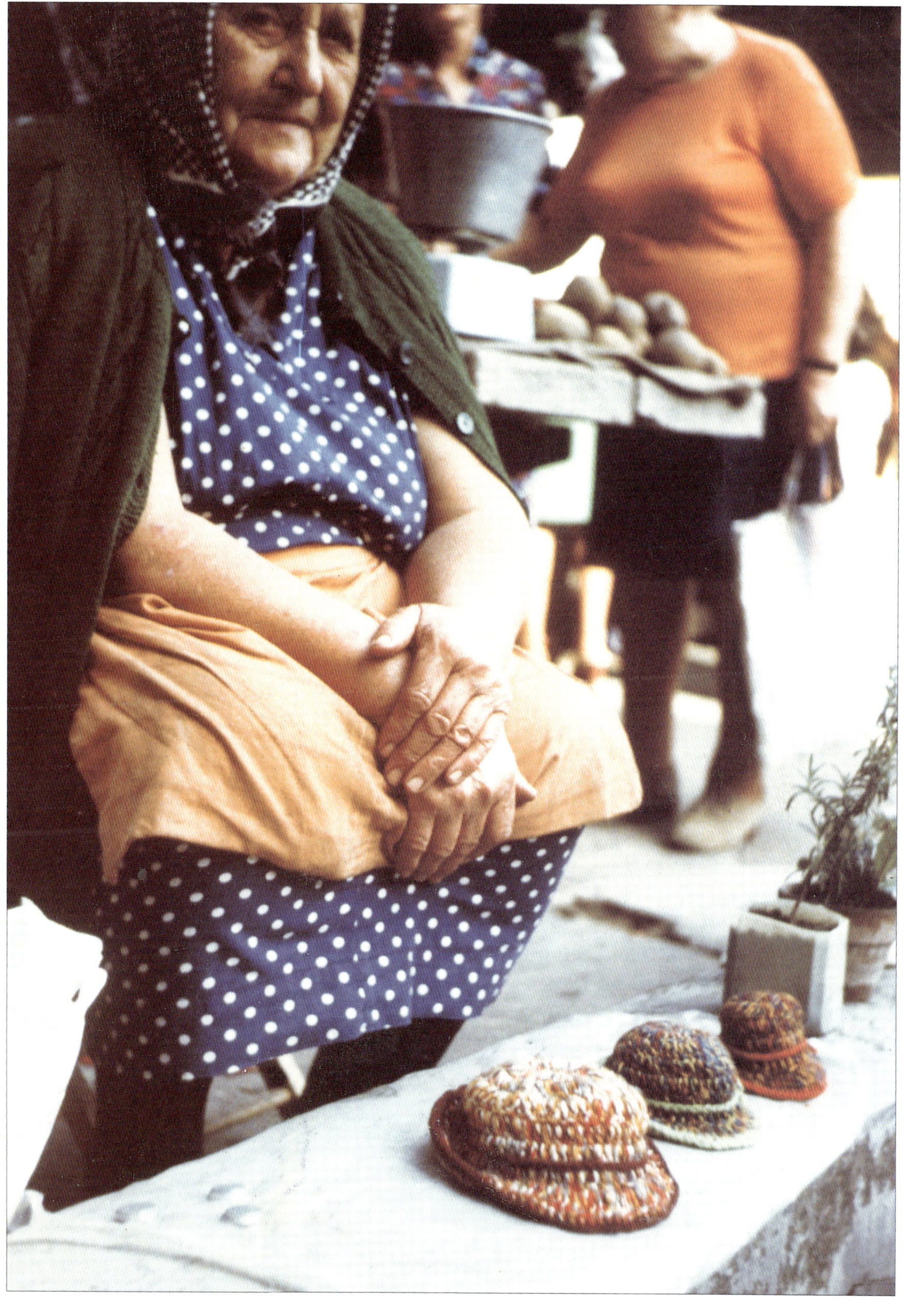

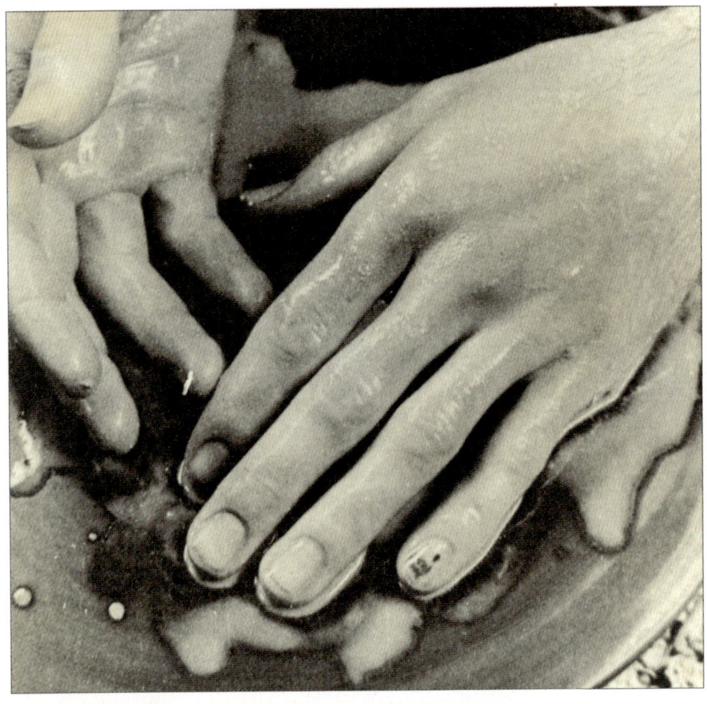

Fig. 34: Hands in clay.

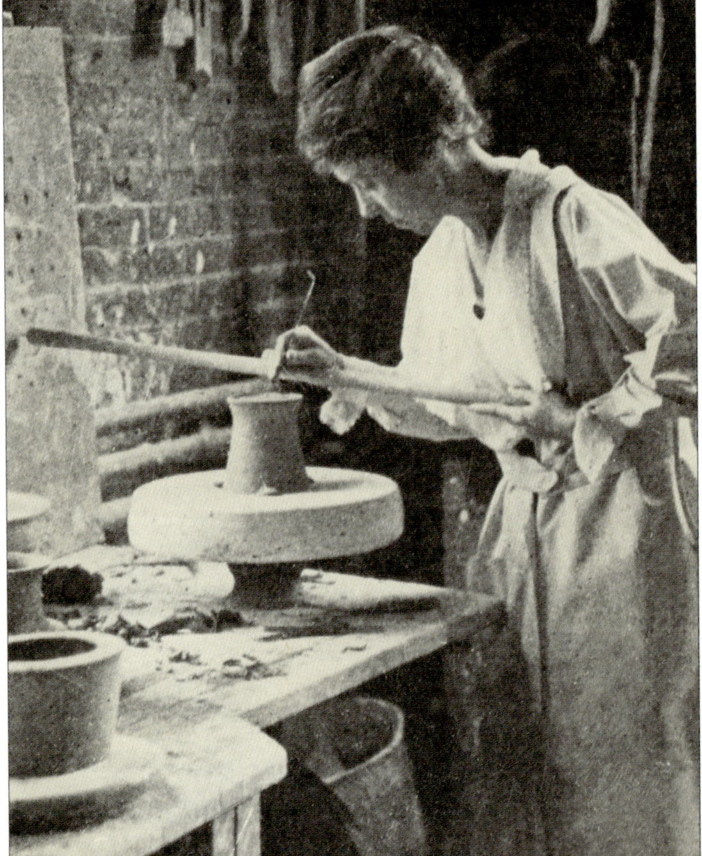

Fig. 35: Potter at turntable.

Spontaneity

It has become fashionable for some artists to present the public with objects that appear uncontrolled, that look as though they had been created by accident. In pottery, the attractive, "spontaneous" quality of these objects is often produced by interactions of fire and chemicals that are only vaguely under the control of the maker. The technique might be called "loosely controlled accident."

Interest in the process of creation had its origin in the mid-nineteenth century with English art critic and social theorist John Ruskin's pronouncement that art is pleasure in work. But when designers luxuriate in the process rather than paying attention to mastering their craft, it can lead to uncontrolled, inarticulate forms.

The delight in making, the pleasure in the act of creating, is a part of every art. This pleasure, this enjoyment of the process, is most noticeable in those arts in which the maker is most directly connected with the end product. Thus, for the potter, the process involves the intimate pleasure of squeezing and caressing the soft, cool clay.

The next step, the control and articulation of line and surface, does not provide the same degree of sensuous, indulgent, physical pleasure. It calls, instead, for a disciplined articulation in the vital dialogue between the maker and the object. It is a process of give and take, of the clear formulation and control of the sweep of the line, the modulation of shade, the disposition of mass. It is the step that brings the object from the sphere of purely sensuous pleasure, provided by direct contact with the material, into a spiritual sphere.

In other media, of course, there are other reasons for the seemingly uncontrolled chaos, for example, the apparently haphazard heap of lumber in the exhibition of modern art at Minneapolis's Walker Art Center, or, to go back a few decades, the quasi-spontaneous drip paintings of Jackson Pollock. Although these are not decorative arts, the attitude they represent has influenced the decorative arts of today.

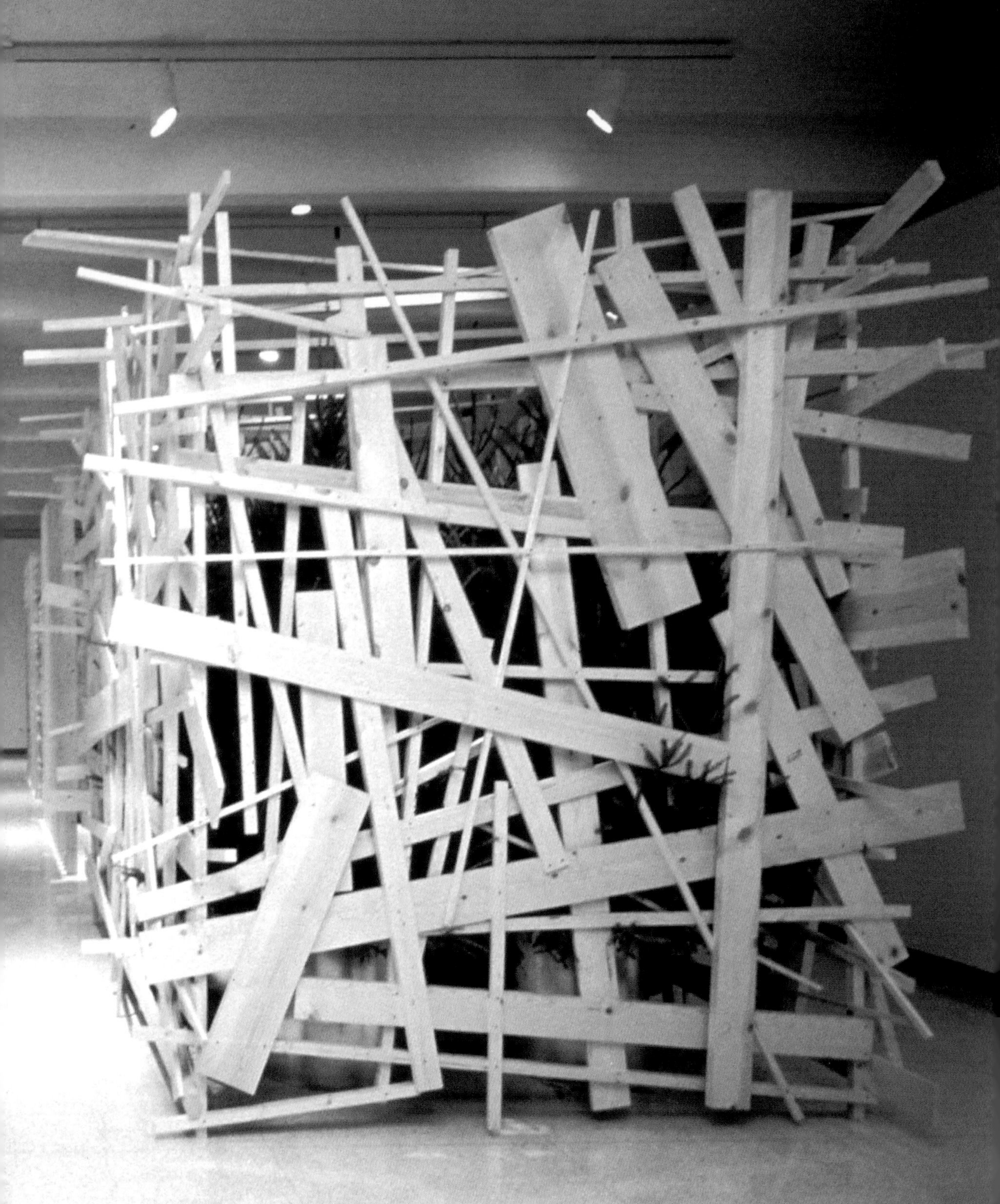

Fig. 36: Installation view of #4. Architecture Tomorrow: Franklin D. Israel, Walker Art Center 1988–89, Minneapolis, Minnesota.

To the sensitive public, however, the difference between spontaneity and helplessness is often indistinguishable. Convincing, exultant spontaneity, which conveys the unhampered freshness of the maker's attitude, is a rare commodity. Spontaneity may come directly from the heart of a child, or from the prehistoric cave dwellers about whom we know so little. But the appearance of spontaneity generally comes only after years of diligent apprenticeship—as in traditional cultures—or, for a modern designer, after long years of practical experience.

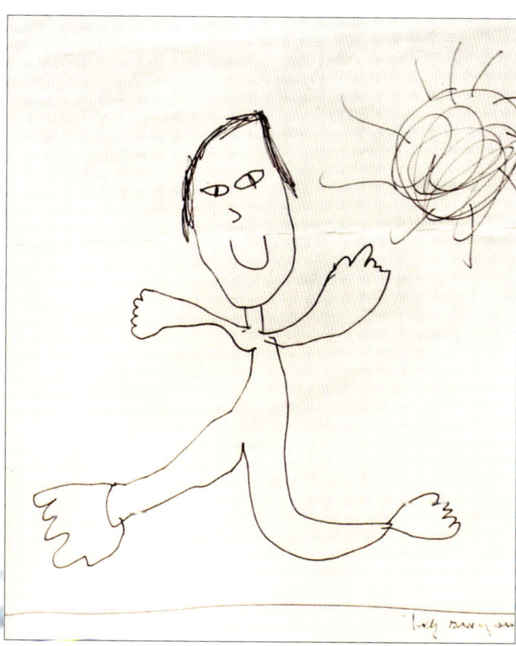

Fig. 37: Child's drawing.

Fig. 38: Cave painting.

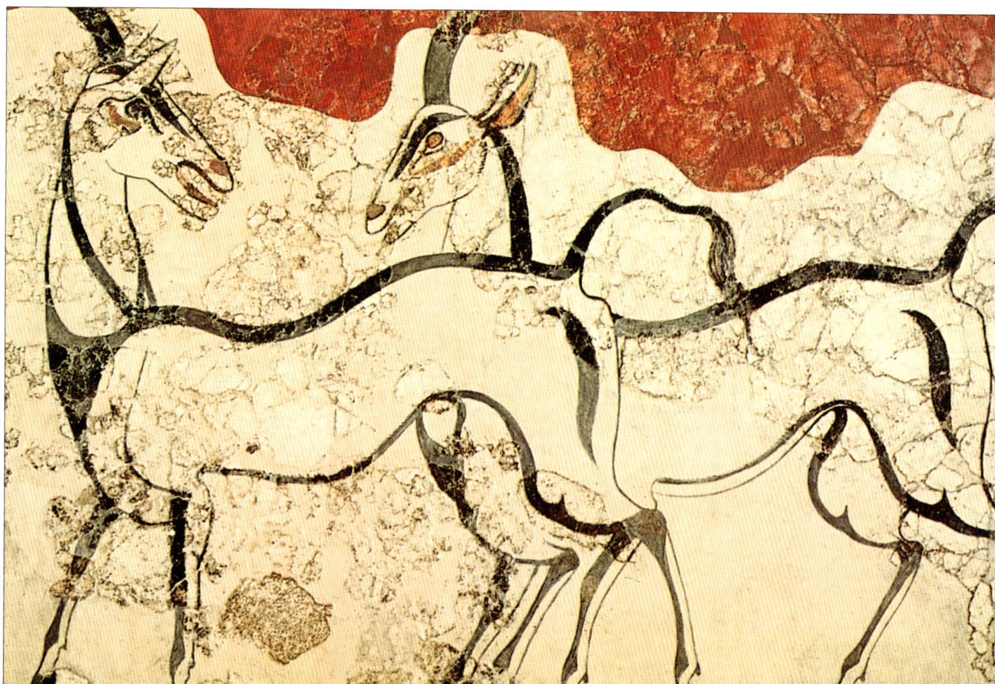

When we admire and quasi-participate in the act of sweeping the paintbrush over a pot or a canvas, we also admire the assurance with which the artist, with so few lines, so few strokes, can so perfectly describe a hand or create the illusion of a silk brocade. If we try to understand our enchantment with the spontaneity of Rembrandt, Velazquez or Goya, we will learn that the reason lies with their perfect draftsmanship, their sureness of line, their complete control of the materials and subject matter of their art. When spontaneity is used as a cover-up for any deficiency, such as a lack of articulation that comes from lack of craftsmanship, the result is disturbing rather than pleasurable to behold.

Spontaneity, as a style, has seized the fashion fancy of the decorative and pure arts almost from the beginning of modern movements in the arts. The Impressionists dissolved shape into light, and Rodin displayed his genius in the impressions of his fingers in the clay, forever preserving his fingerprints in bronze. Demonstrations of spontaneity, proclaiming the practitioner's freedom from academic constraints grew in large part from the exuberance produced by the dawn of a new style. But the present fashion for spontaneity originates from negative reasons. It is most readily observed in pottery. Few of the artist/craftsmen who practice the arts nowadays approach their chosen discipline through years of apprenticeship, which was the case in previous centuries, and is still the case in traditional societies. The adoption in the West of the Japanese controlled-accident style of pottery known as Raku, for example, amounts in most cases to the imitation of a technique without an understanding of the cultural roots that produced it. Western "Raku" products are often the result of lack of precision and demonstrate the artistic inarticulateness of the maker rather than a calculated artistic purpose.

Spontaneity is, of course, a most engaging aspect of communication. It gives us a feeling of immediacy, of participating in the act of creating the work. By contrast, one may feel excluded when looking at something that is precisely formed and well finished. If we speak of spontaneity not as a style but as an approach to work, we realize that most designers first express their ideas in loose, spontaneous sketches or models. But very soon, a more controlled development begins, a dialogue between ourselves and the preliminary documentation of our idea. Then there are two: the thing and ourselves. We start to articulate the thing by asking it how it will respond if we do this to it, or we do that to it. At each response, we decide whether what we did to this thing is relevant or irrelevant. Does it disturb us or make us happier to look at it or to touch it?

At this point we may lose the freshness of spontaneity, that cheerful element of design which brings the viewer into a more intimate contact with the maker of the work than is possible when confronting the well-controlled disciplined work of a classical artist.

Line

Walter Crane, the nineteenth century graphic artist and writer who was director of the Royal College of Art in London, wrote the most beautiful words about the meaning of line. "The first necessity of a design," he says, "is definition." Therefore,

> Line is all important, line determinative, line emphatic, line delicate, line expressive, line controlling and uniting. In all degrees of intensity the designer possesses a means of considerable force and sympathetic power...
>
> The association of restfulness with horizontal lines . . . the suggestion of fixity and solidity by the use of horizontal with verticals, the stern and logical character given to a design in which angular forms are used, the expression of movement by the wave of the meandering line. The line actually described by human action, the lines of energy and resistance by the sharp irregular zigzag, the lines of grace and rhythmic speediness, by gently flowing and recurring curves. The lines of vigor, of structural force, of life itself, in the radiating group, or the upward spiral of aspiration.
>
> Line is, indeed, a language, a more sensitive and vigorous speech of many dialects, which can adapt itself to all purposes.

Fig. 39: Zig-zag chair. Gerrit Rietveld (1934).

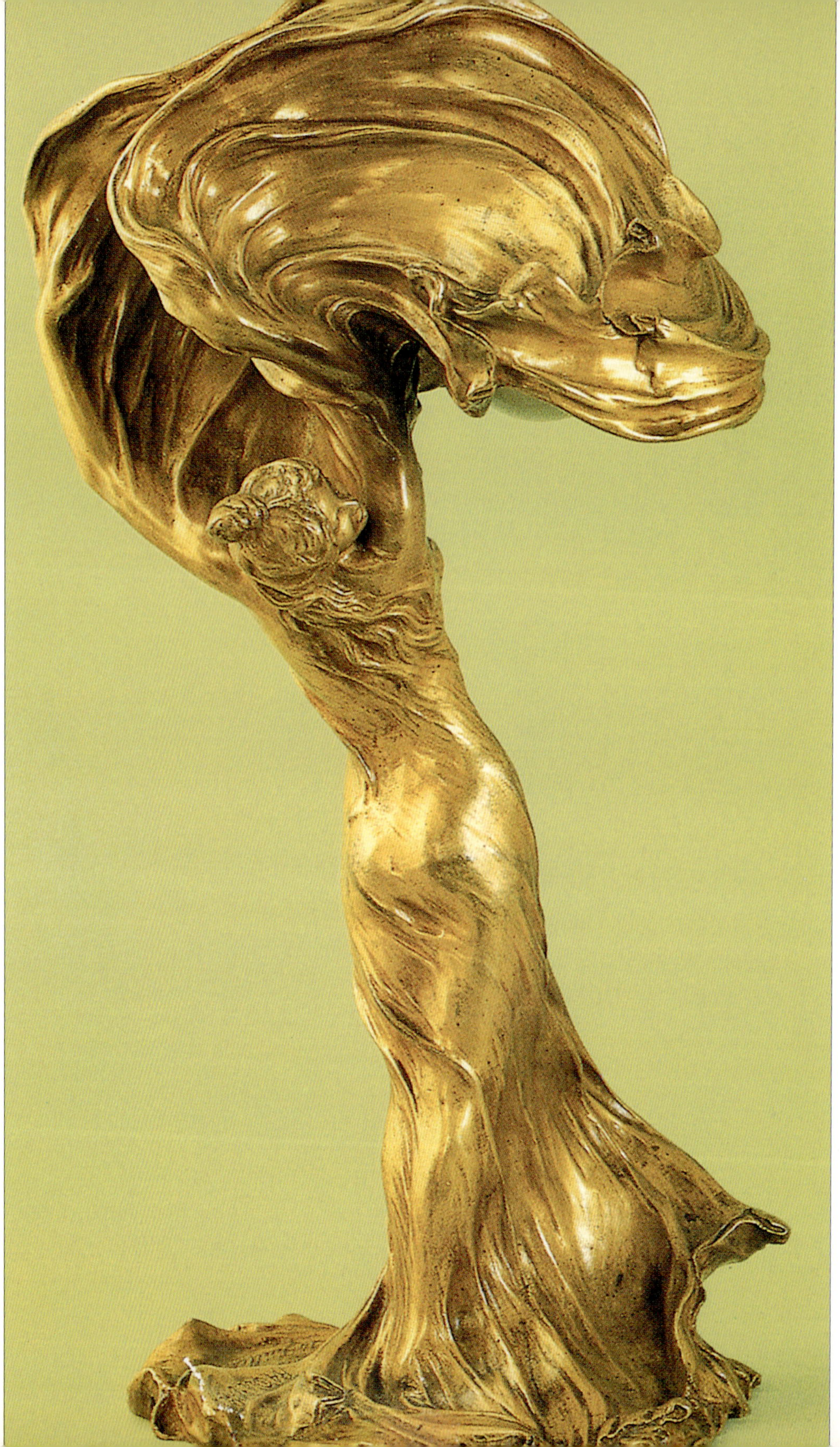

Irrespective of style and time, and whenever they intrude upon our sight, lines convey the same meaning, based upon our associations with nature.

Fig. 41: Drawing by Walter Crane.

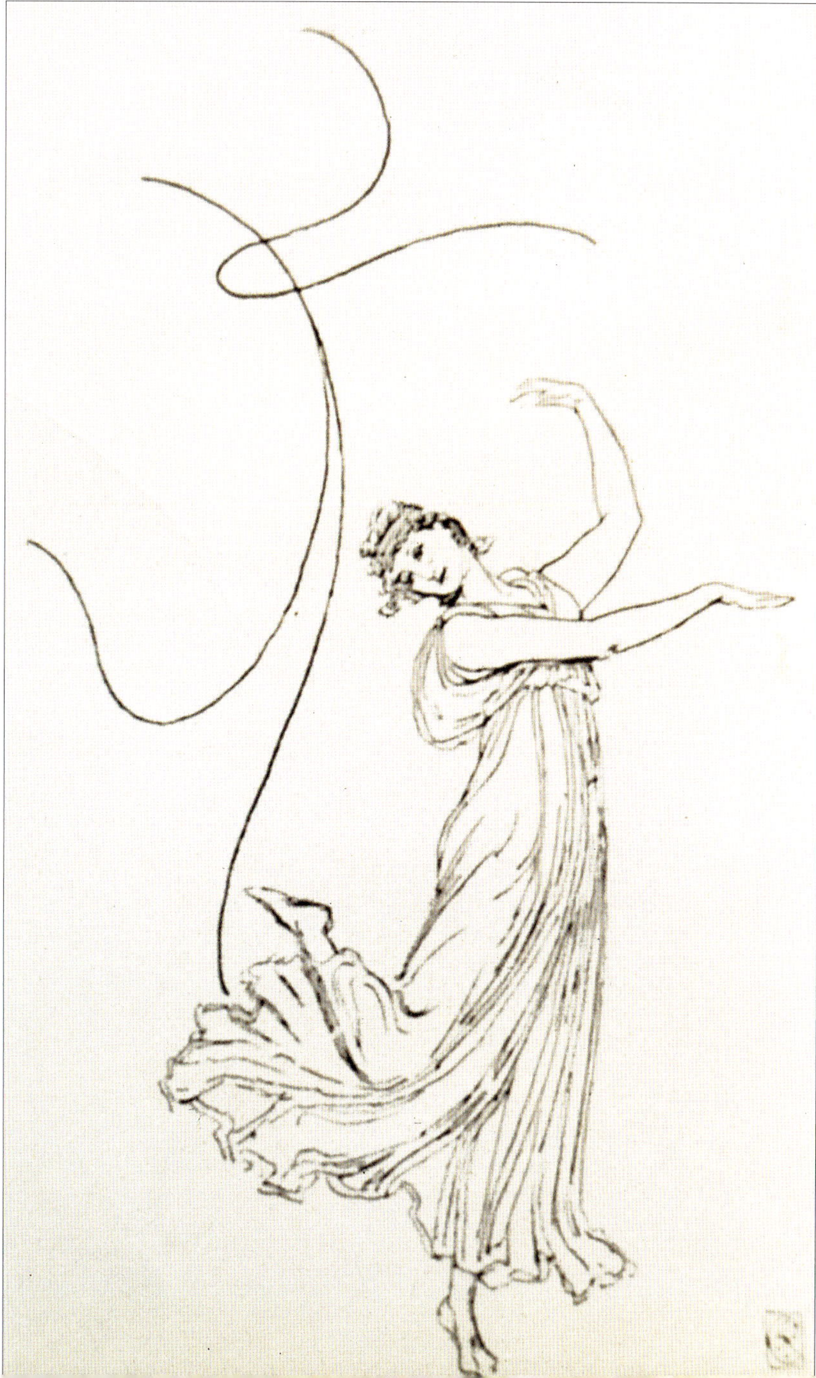

Fig. 40: Sculpture by Raoul Larche, Paris, 1900, Macklowe Gallery, New York.

Small variations of line can change the character of a thing. Of the three cones on these two pages, one looks sunken in a bit (fig. 42), another nearly geometric (fig. 44), and the third puffed up, filled with air. Although the designer must respect such small deviations in line, we should not overvalue the lines we first sketch when developing our ideas. We should play with them to articulate what we want to say, clearly and beautifully.

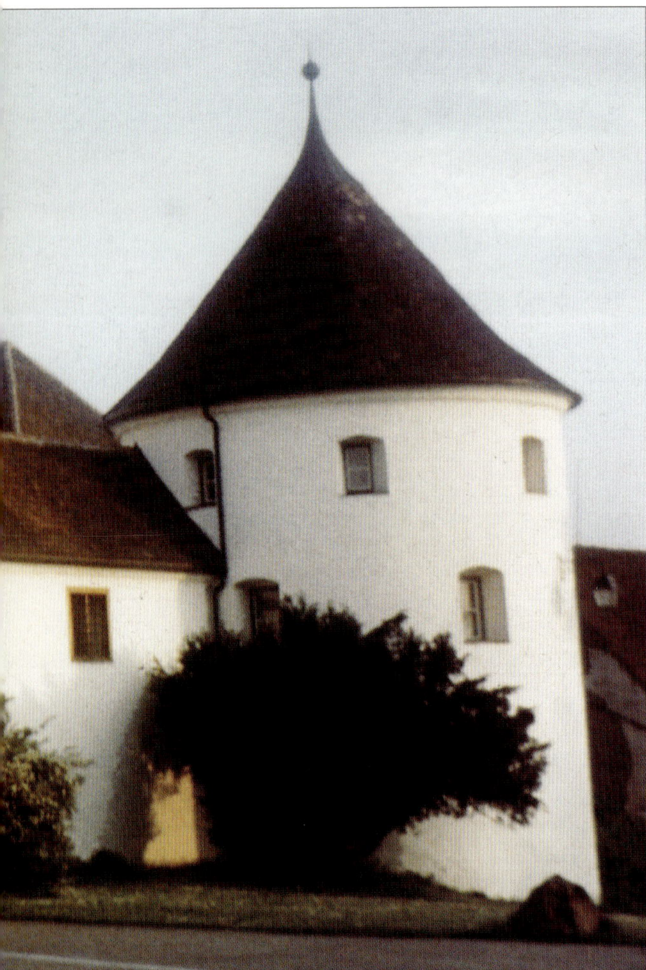

Fig. 42: Conical roof, southern France.

Fig. 44: Conical roof, New York City.

Fig. 43: Conical structure, student work.

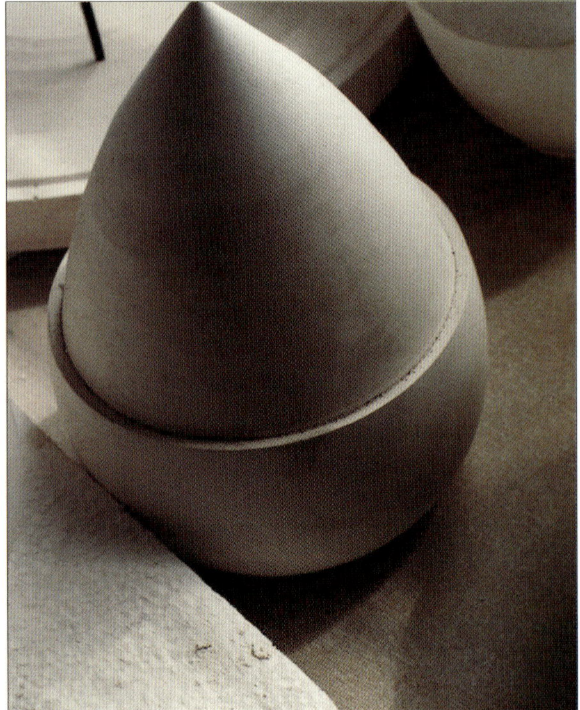

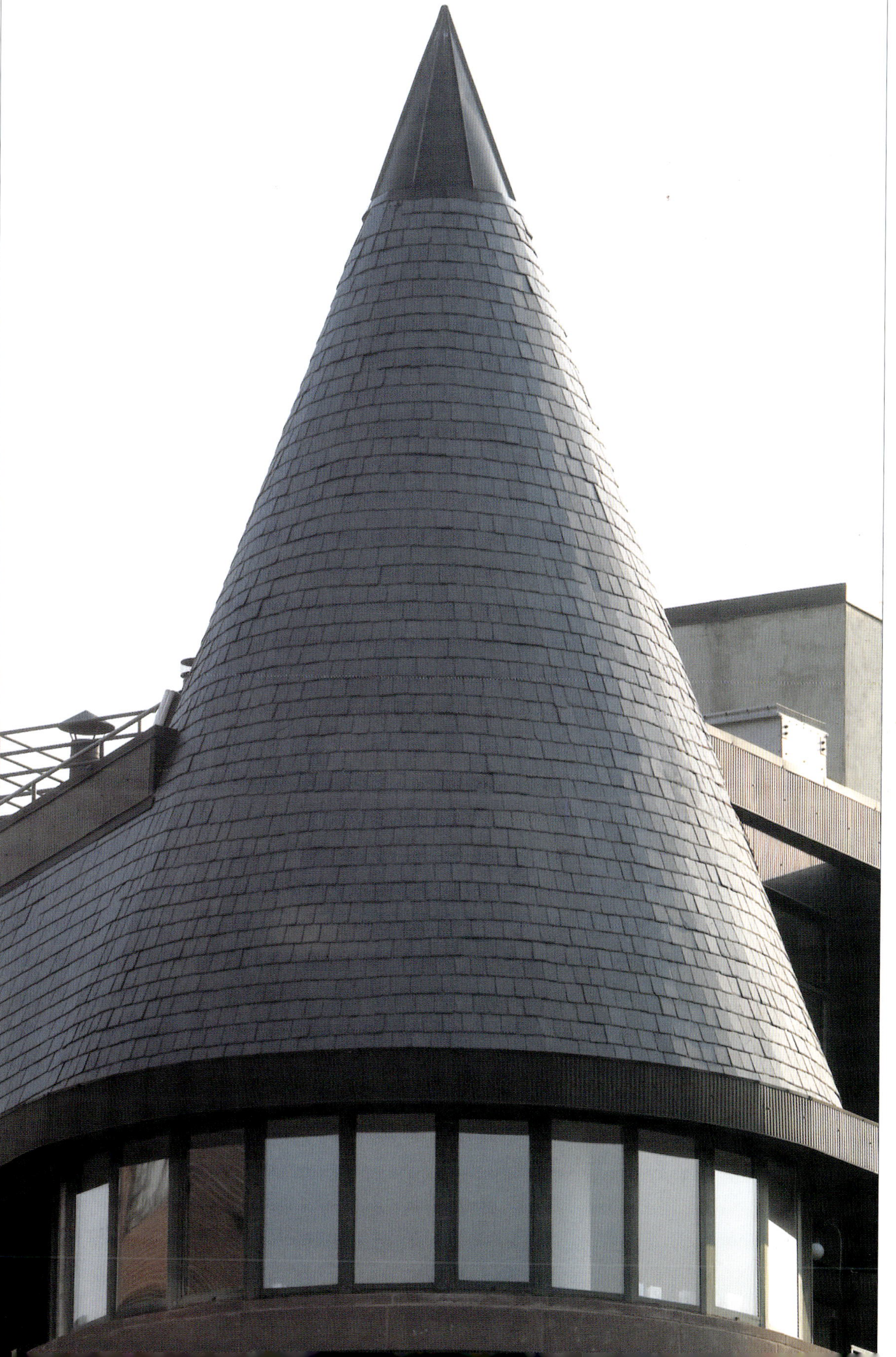

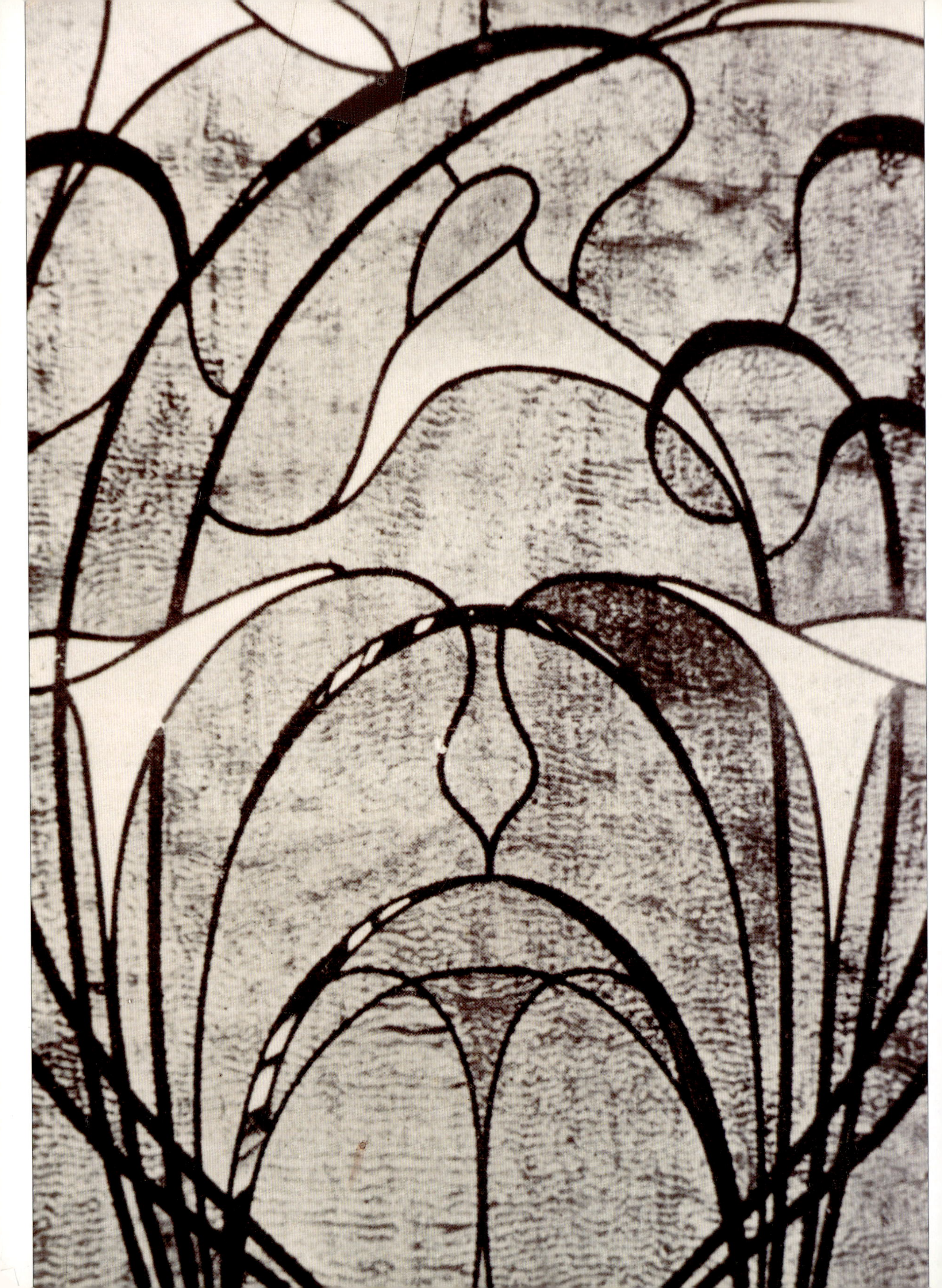

From lines we can read the style. The sinewy lines of Art Nouveau sometimes break at unexpected places. Should we unearth a cup handle of those years, we could read its style from its curves.

Fig. 45: Art Nouveau stained glass.

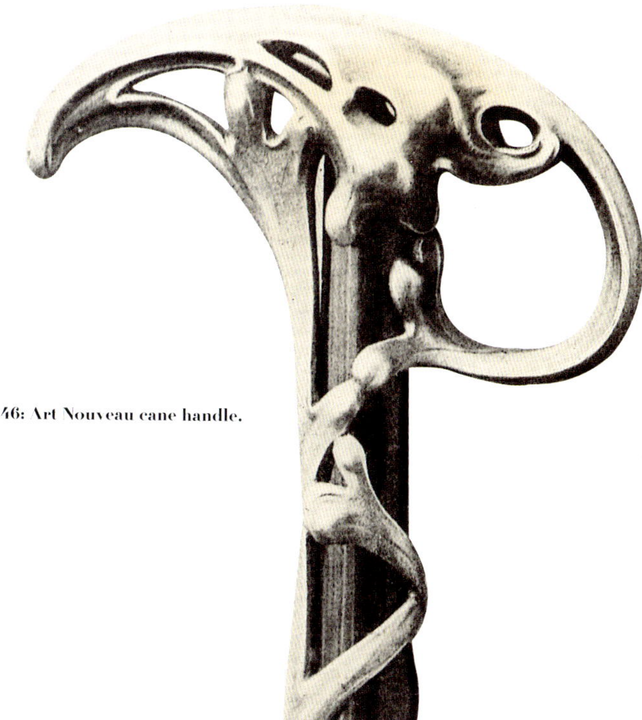

Fig. 46: Art Nouveau cane handle.

Fig. 47: Art Nouveau gravy boat.

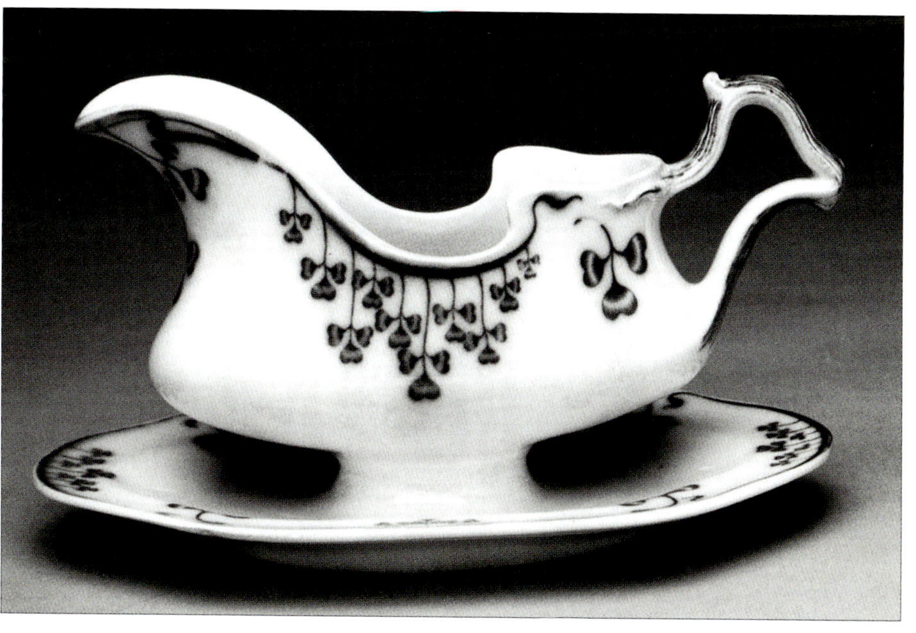

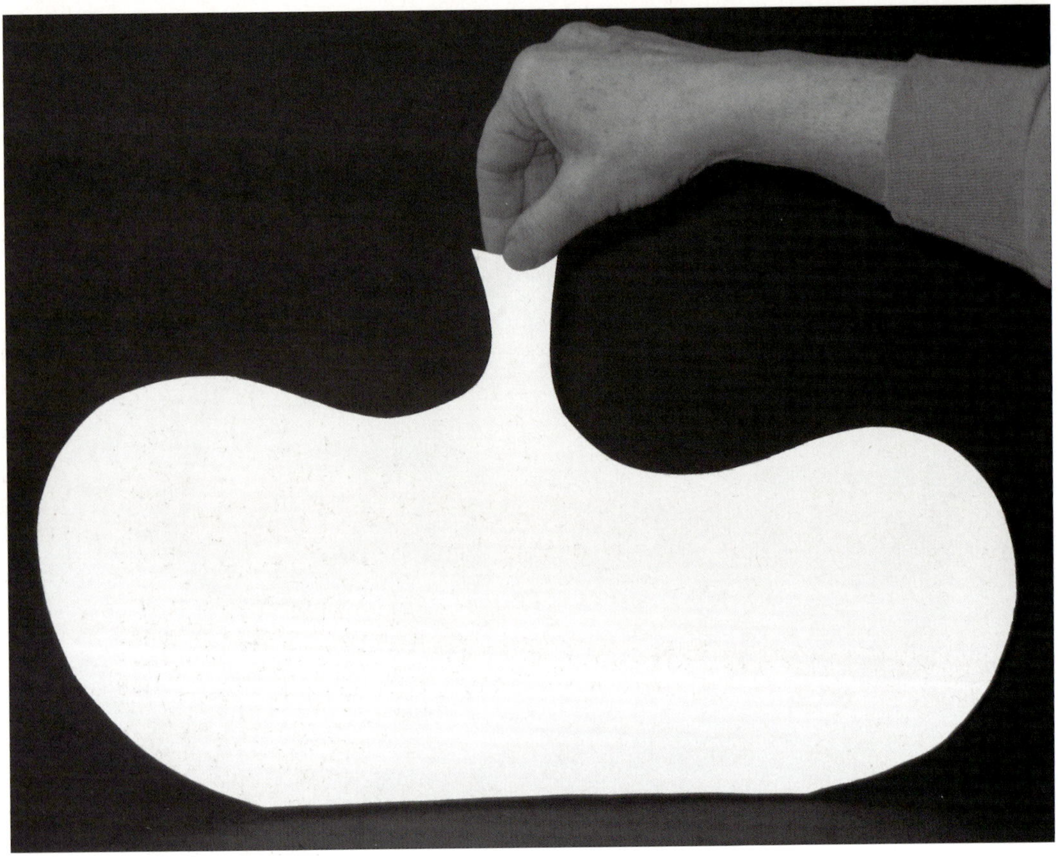

Fig. 48: Soft, rubbery shape (paper cutout).

Fig. 49: Below, left, "Blown up" paper cut-out.

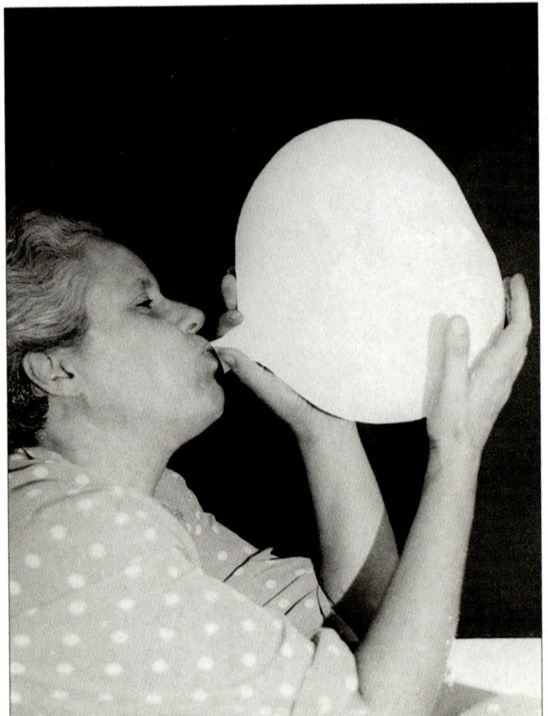

Fig. 50: Below, right, (cutout) "pullable, like taffy."

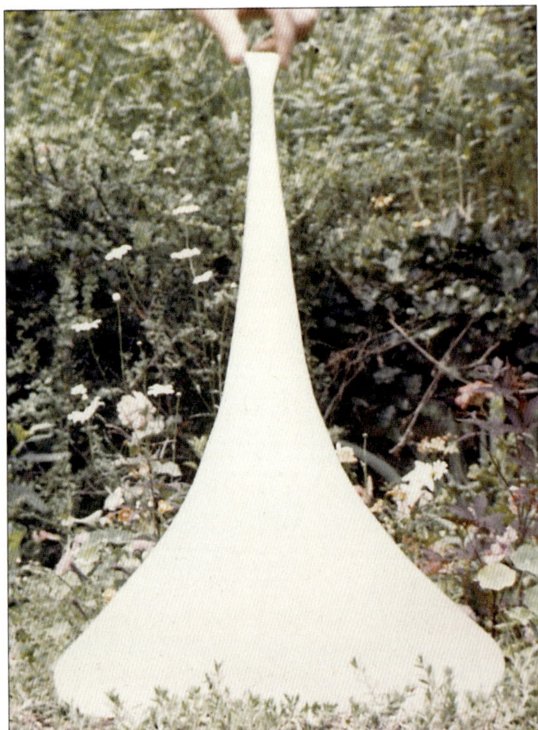

When beginning a design by sketching its outline in two dimensions, you can define its character, even consistency—whether it is soft and rubbery, pokable or squeezable, filled with air, or pullable, like taffy.

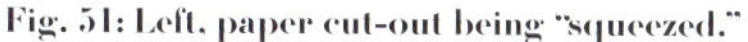

Fig. 51: Left, paper cut-out being "squeezed."

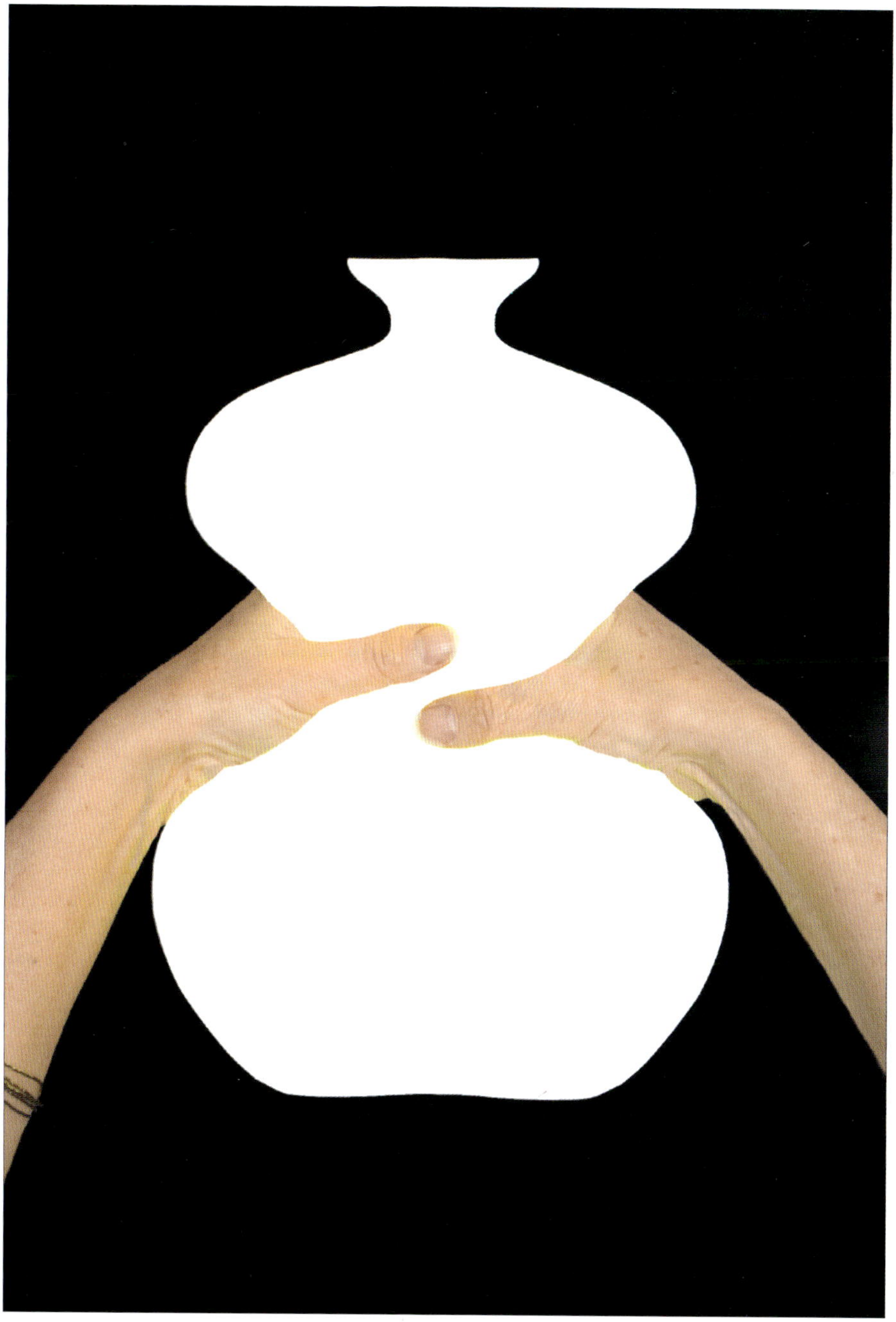

Fig. 53: Gourd shapes, Hyalin pottery, Salisbury Artisans, by Eva Zeisel.

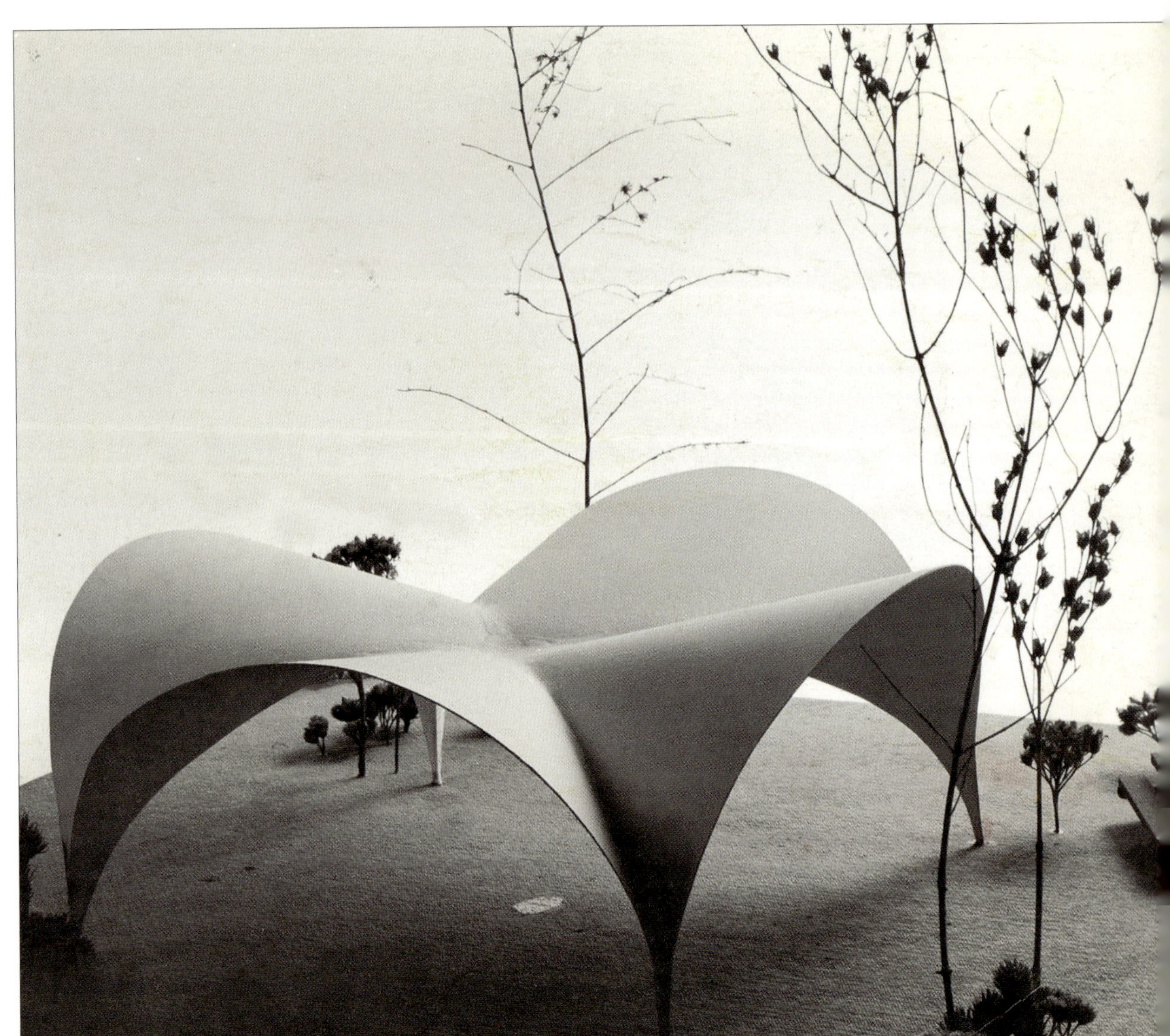

Fig. 52: Architectural model "filled with air," student work, Rhode Island School of Design.

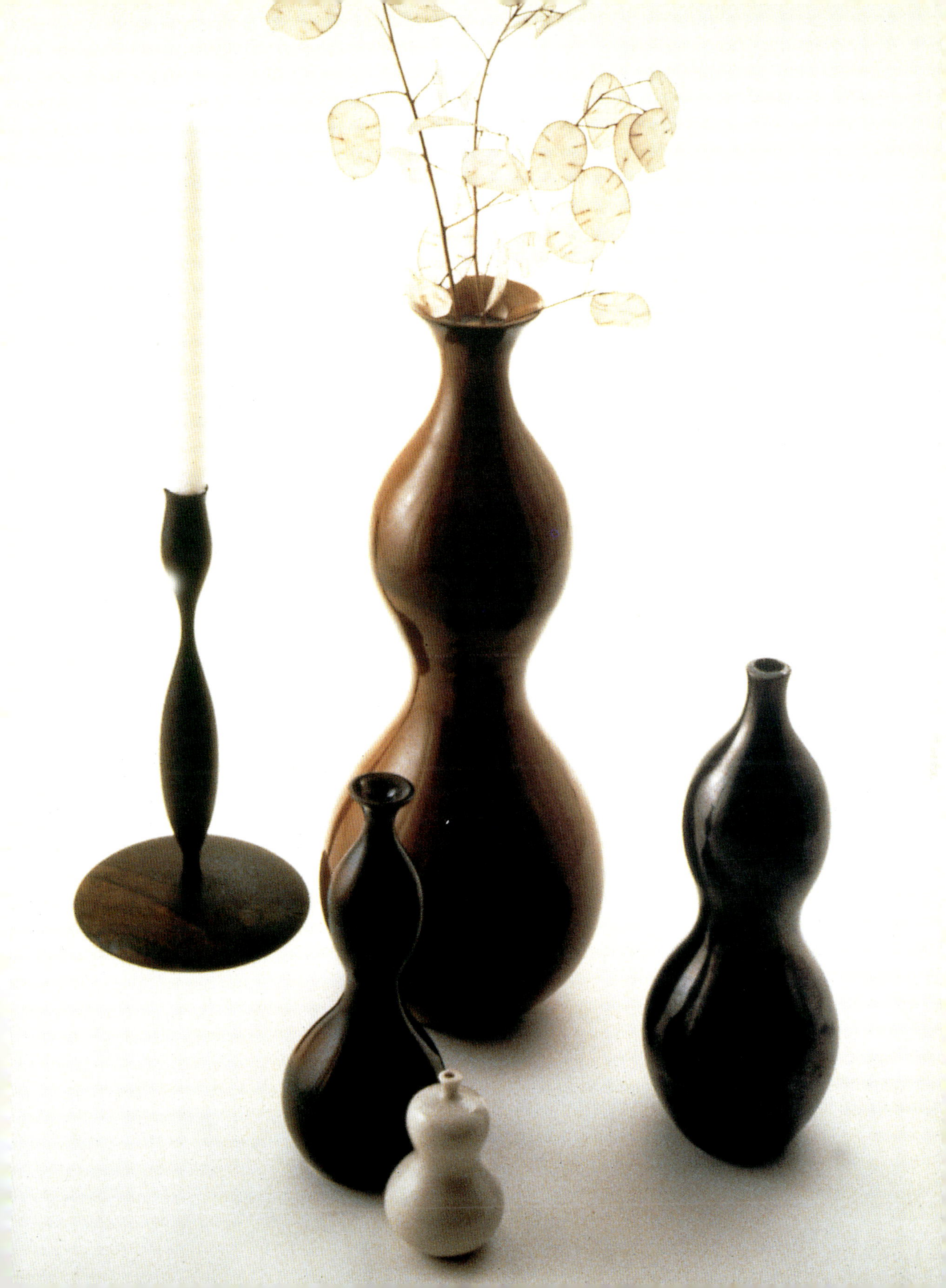

The language of line is general and applies to all things. Whether it is the towers of a castle, glasses for drinking wine or liquor, or an ornamental, painted cup, the line conveys the same feeling.

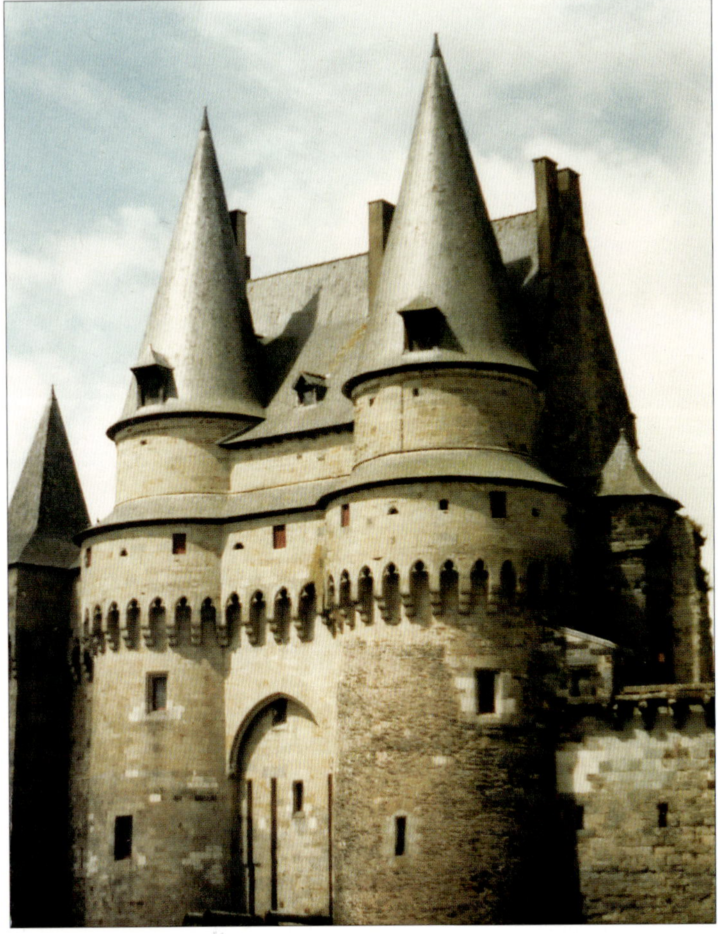

Fig. 54: Castle tower.

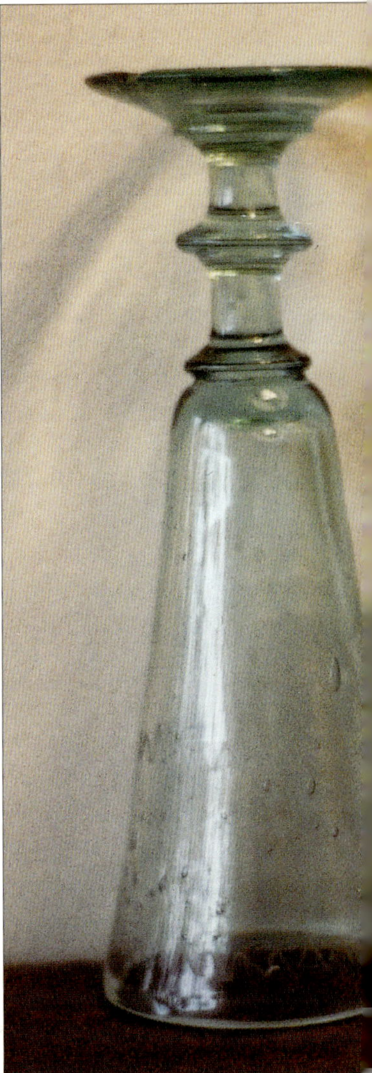

Fig. 55: Wine goblets.

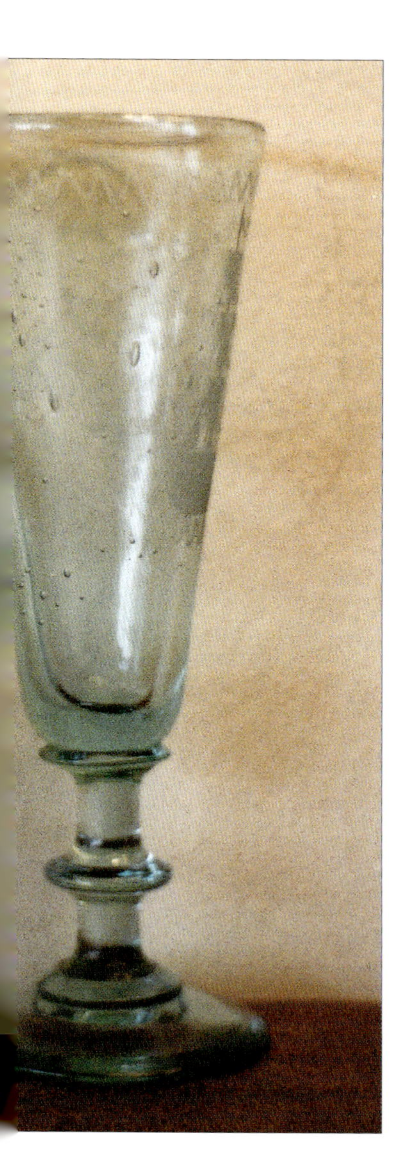

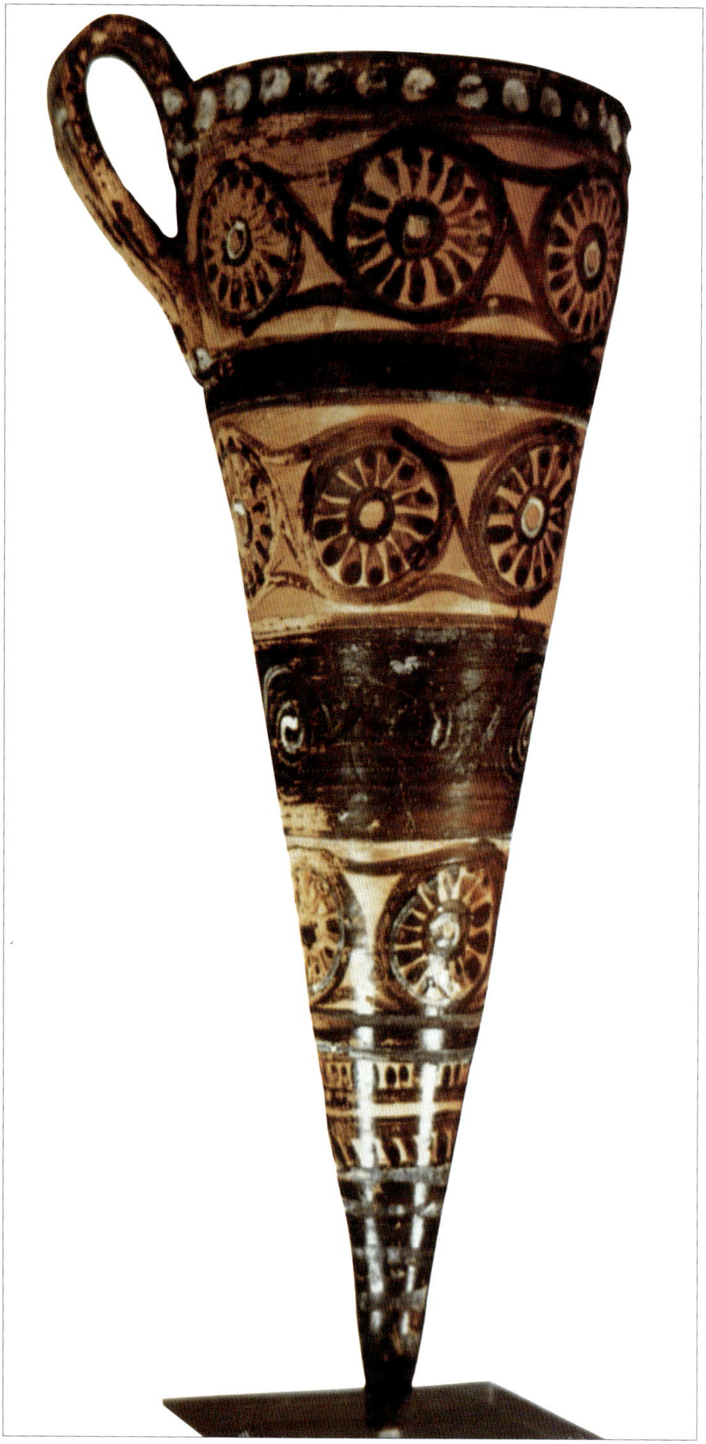

Fig. 56: Painted conical cup.

A braced line consists of a curve fused with a straight line. It makes the form appear stiffened and upright. The braced lines of this dinnerware set go from straight into rounded, giving an elegant, stately appearance. The opposite of a braced line is a flabby line. When considering families of things, take care that the character of line helps to coordinate the group, so that no stranger from another family of lines intrudes.

Fig. 57: "Museum" dinnerware set, Castleton China, 1942-5, Eva Zeisel.

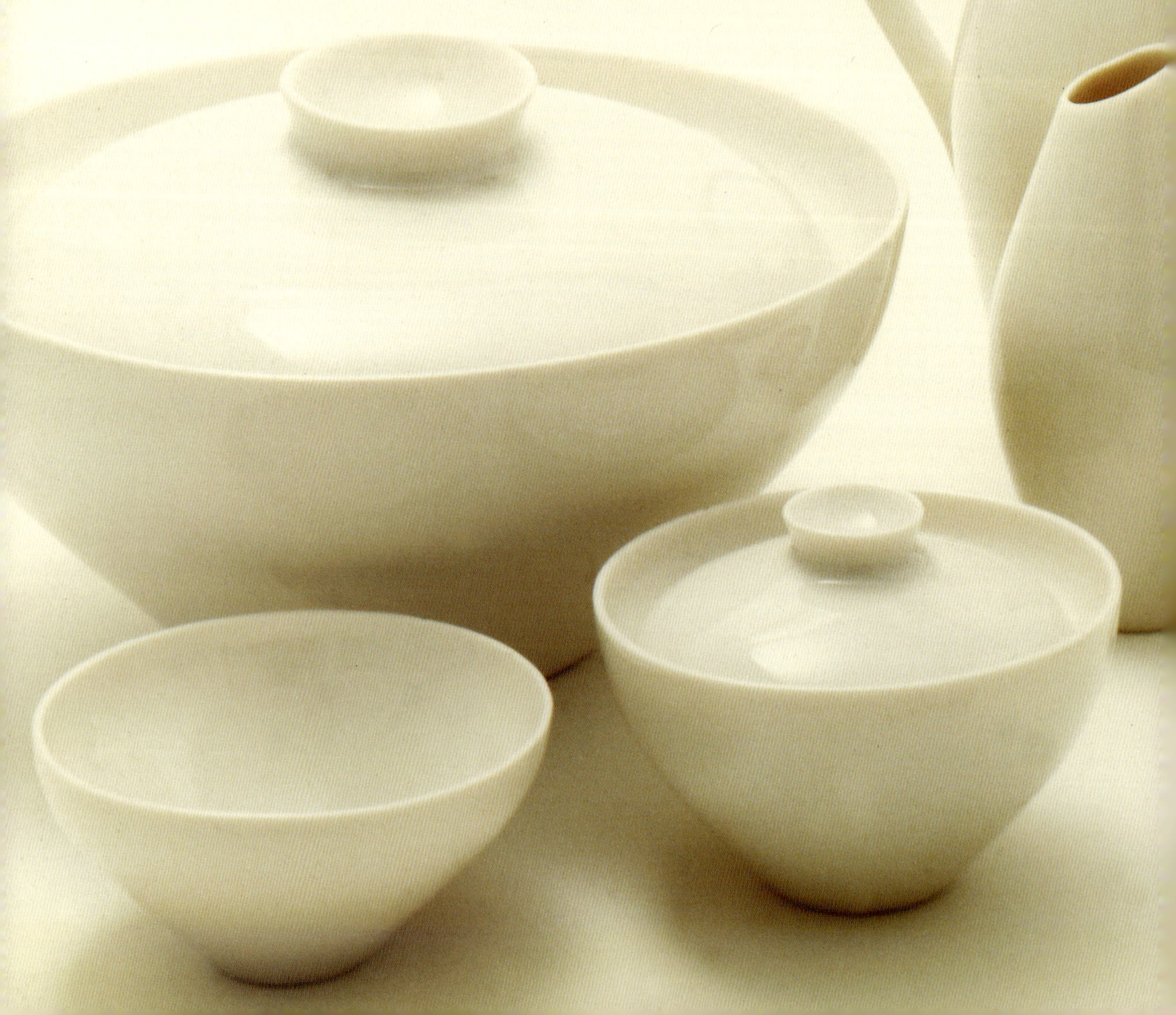

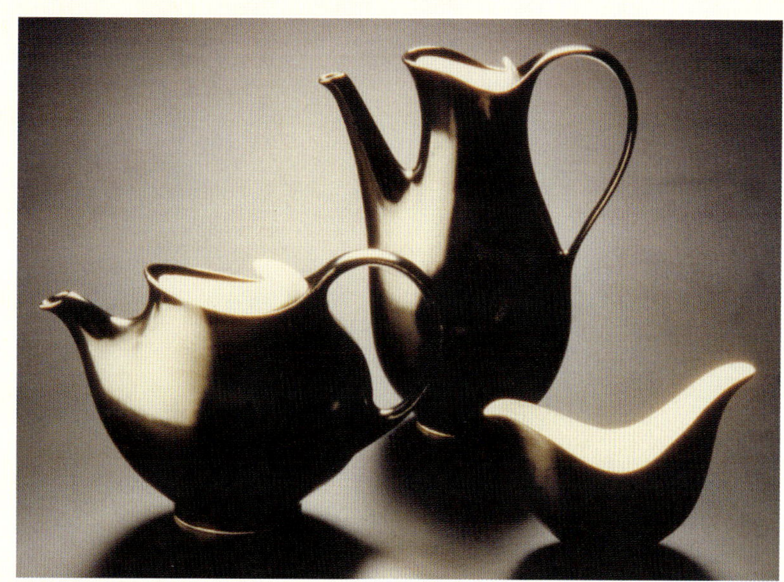

Fig. 58: Hallcraft, Tomorrow's Classic, teapot, coffee pot, open creamer (satin black), 1952. Eva Zeisel.

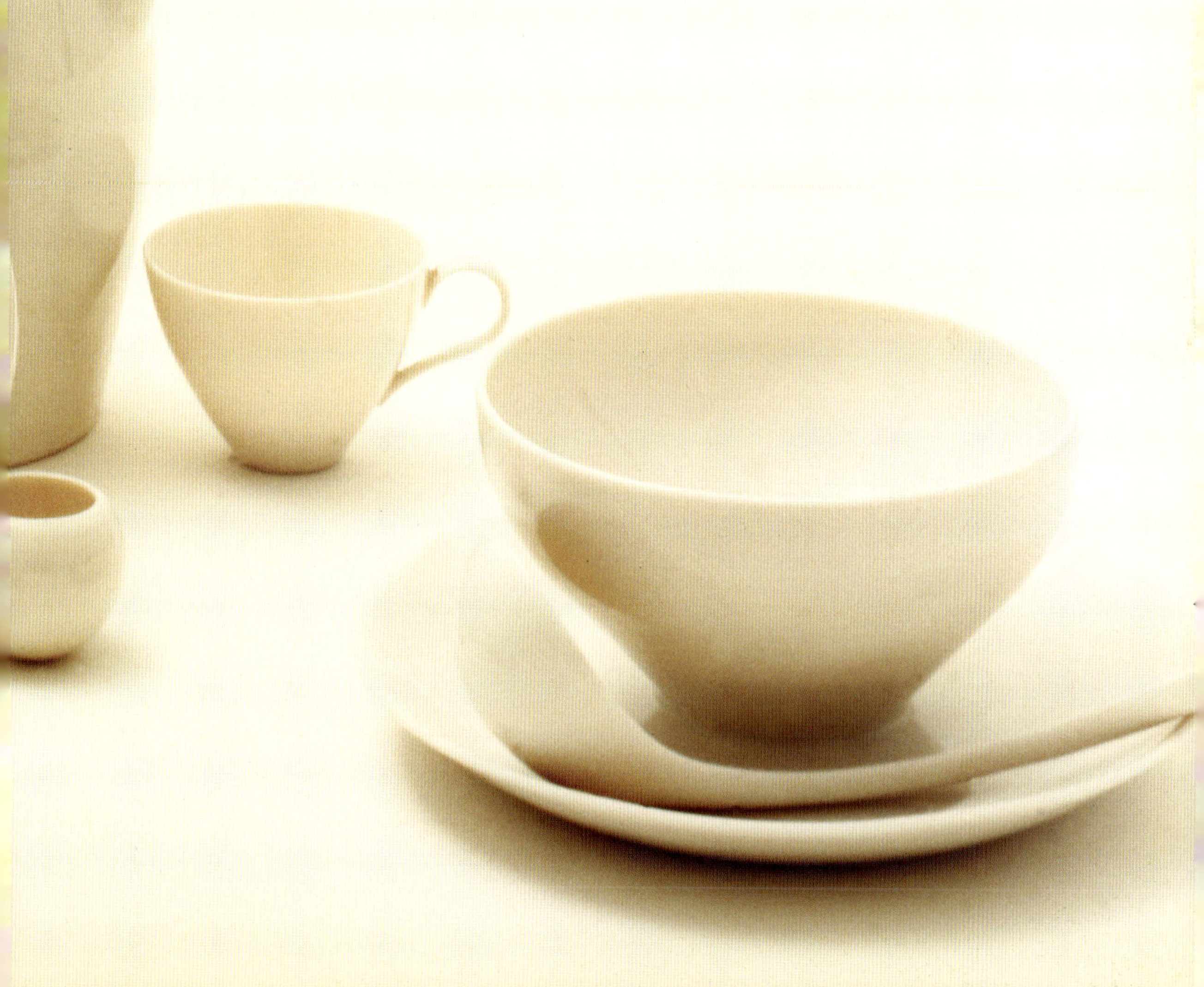

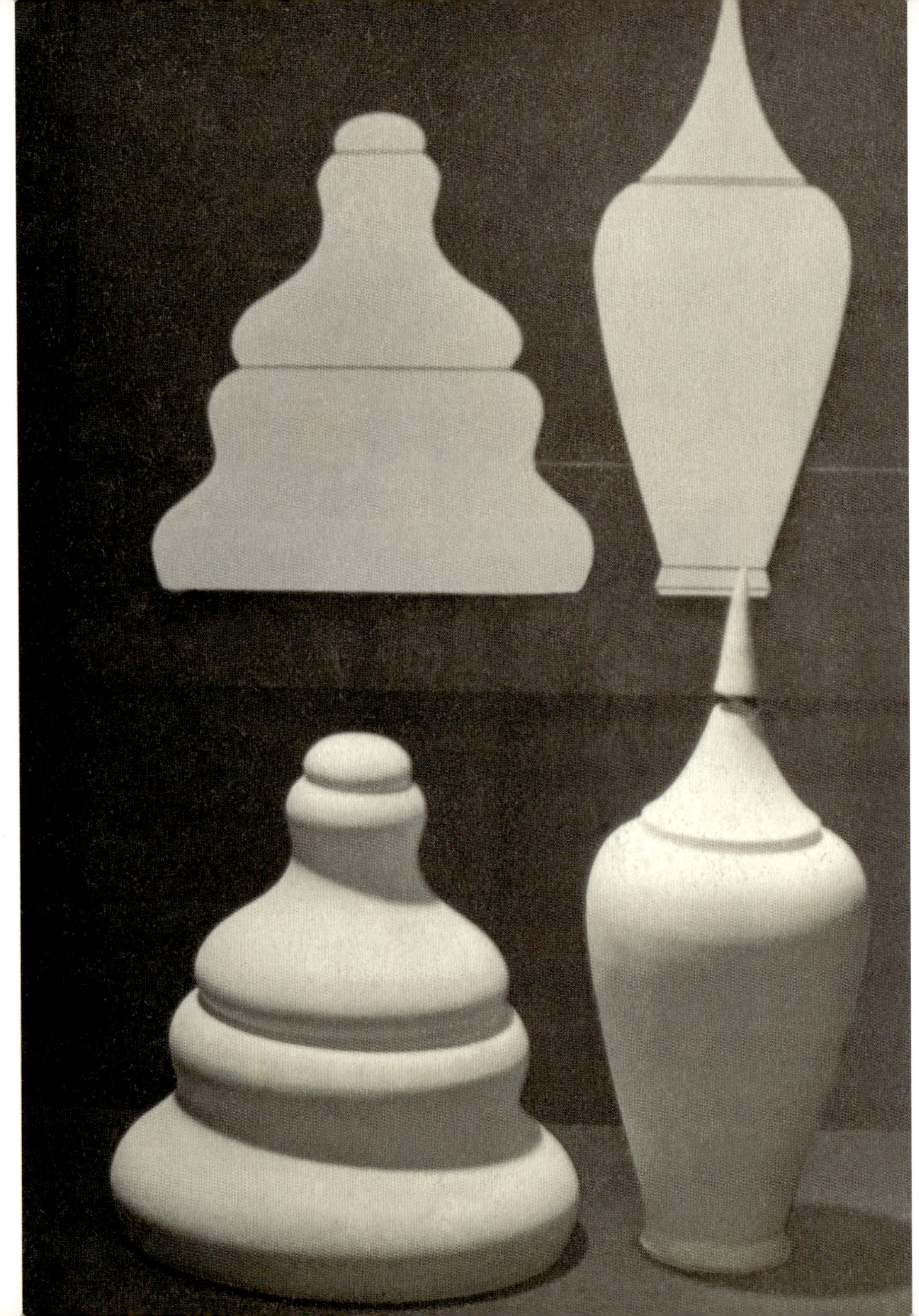

Shading and Shadows

Fig. 59: Paper cut-outs and plaster models.

Shading informs us of three-dimensionality. We explain the shape by means of gradual, wide, shaded areas, or darker narrower areas of shading. Shading can make parts of an object disappear, or things might look thinner than you thought they would when you designed them in two dimensions.

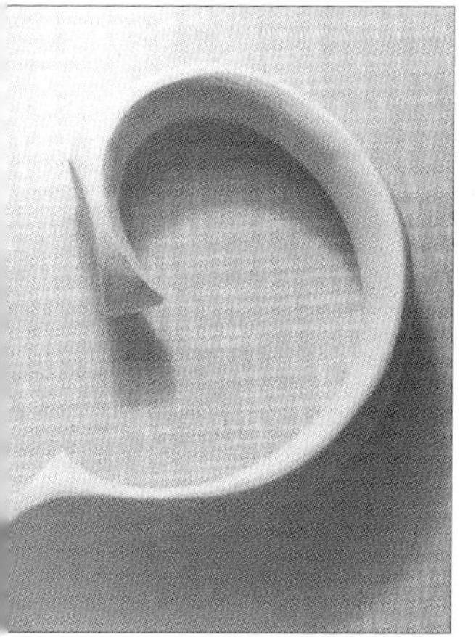

Fig. 60: Plaster model of teapot handle. Eva Zeisel.

Shading might be manipulated to elevate things from their base, or make them cling to the ground.

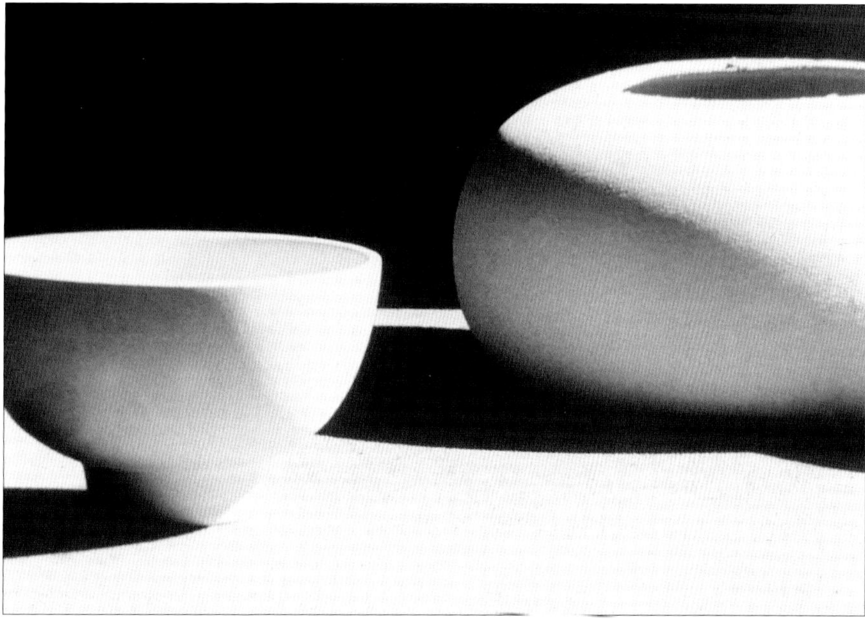

Fig. 61: Footed and un-footed bowls. Eva Zeisel.

Only the gradation of the soft shading informs us of the hills and valleys of the divided dish. Without directional lighting from one side, its subtle modeling would be invisible.

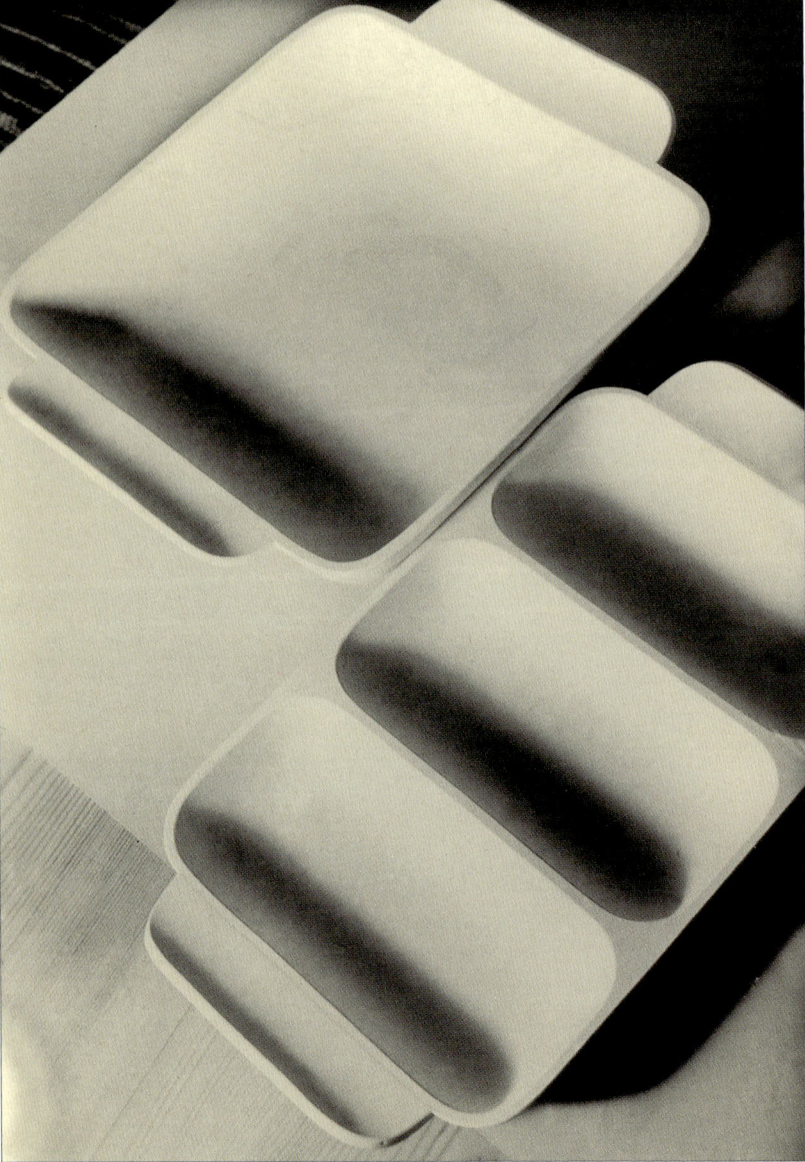

Fig. 62: Divided dish.

When light and dark surfaces meet sharply they form a line that establishes definition and clarification. This line might become the most prominent characteristic of the work

Shading informs us of the indentation. The hardness of the small, round bottle is illustrated by the sharp rim of the indentation at the opening. A soft, gradual shadow here would make it look as if it were made of soft stuff.

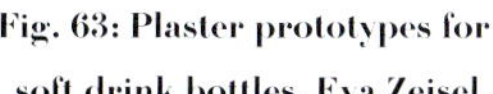

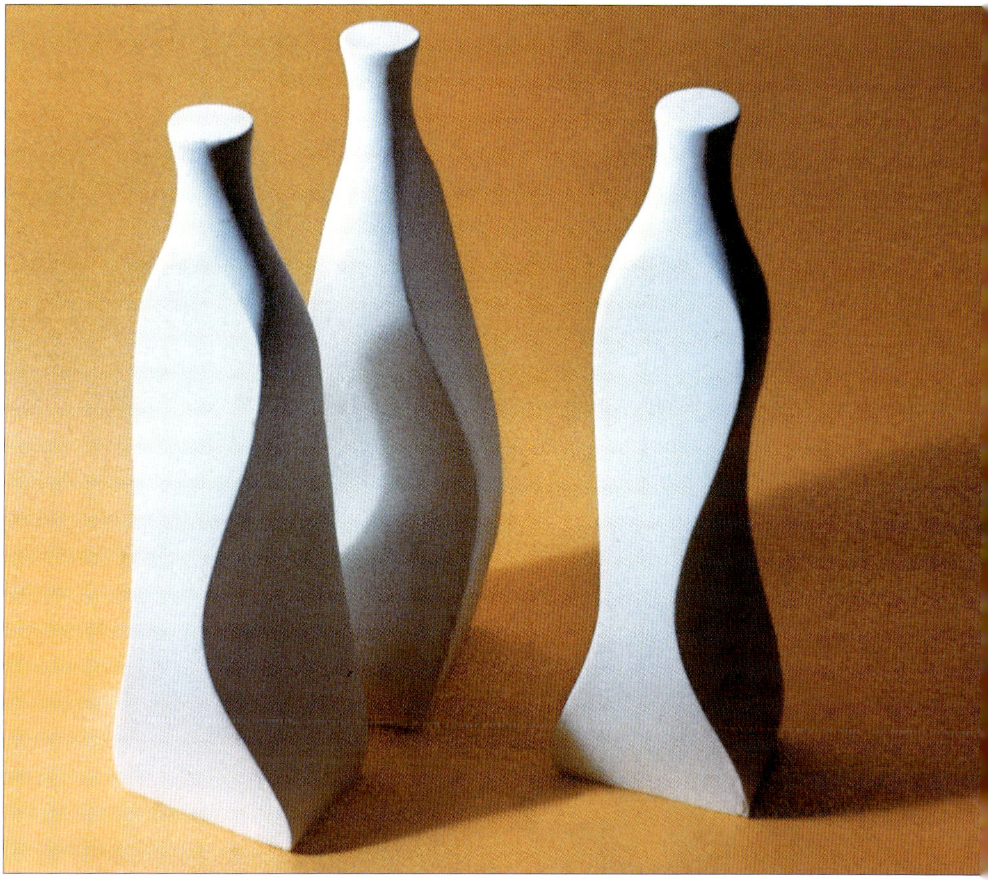

Fig. 63: Plaster prototypes for soft drink bottles. Eva Zeisel.

Fig. 64: Soft bottle.

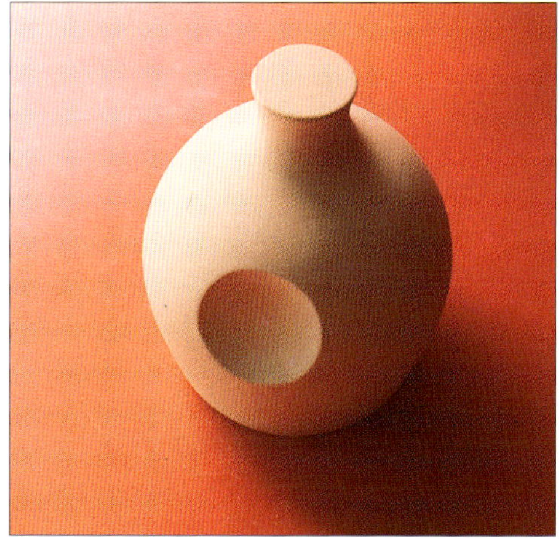

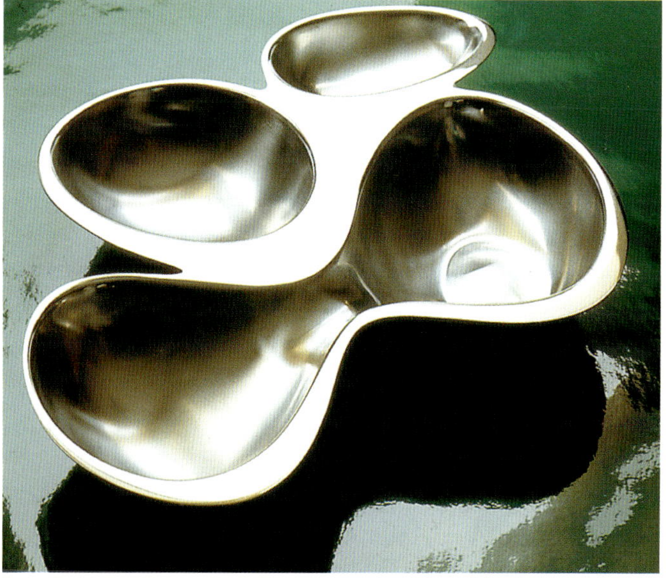

Fig. 65: Babyboop four-section container designed by Ron Arad for Alessi, 2000.

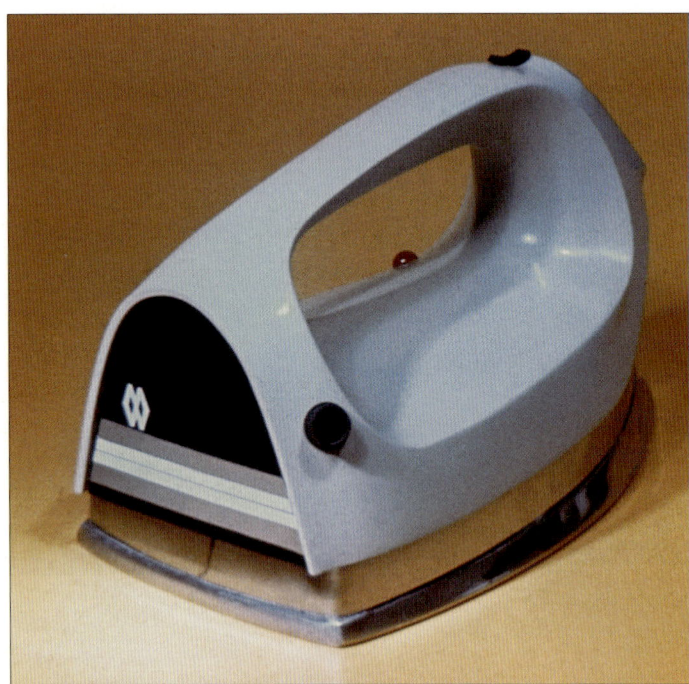

Fig. 66: Blue iron.

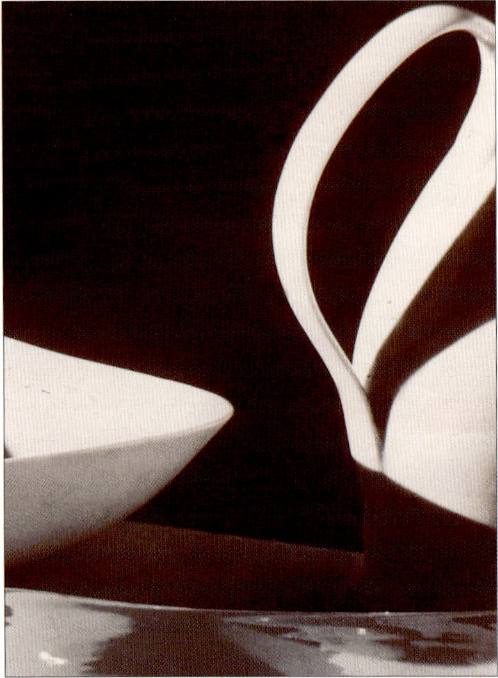

Fig. 67: "Museum" coffeepot handle, Castleton China, Eva Zeisel, 1942–45.

Shadows cast by shapes on themselves can be planned and might make the object more interesting.

The shadows on this adobe building in Arizona, and the sweet lacy shadow of the verandah railing in Mississippi, define the characters of their respective buildings.

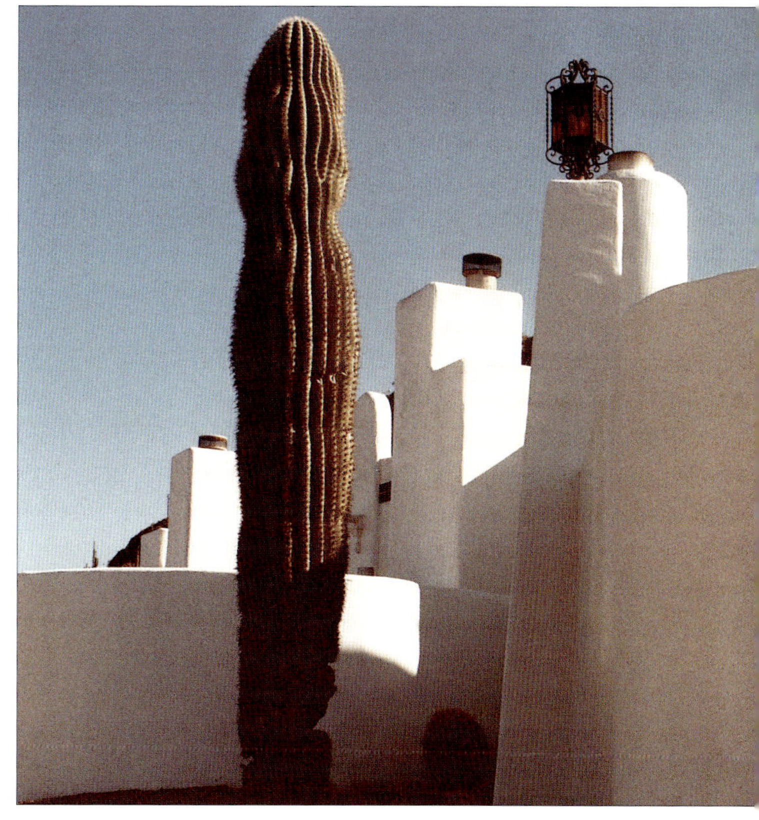

Fig. 68: Adobe building, Arizona.

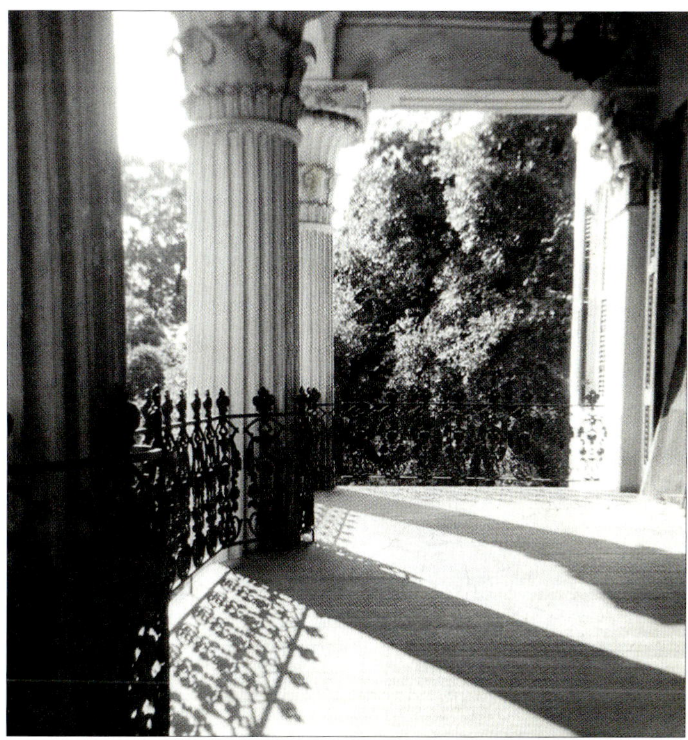

Fig. 69: Cast iron railing, Mississippi.

The many different two-dimensional contours that we find when viewing a single shape from various points of view do not tell us the most critical facts about how the pitcher looks. Its full shape is only conveyed by shading.

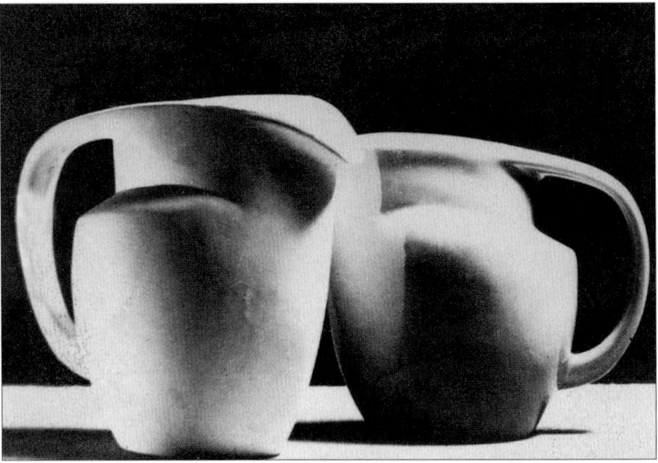

Fig. 70: Models of pitchers, ca. 1941.

Fig. 71: Multiple silhouette views of same pitcher.

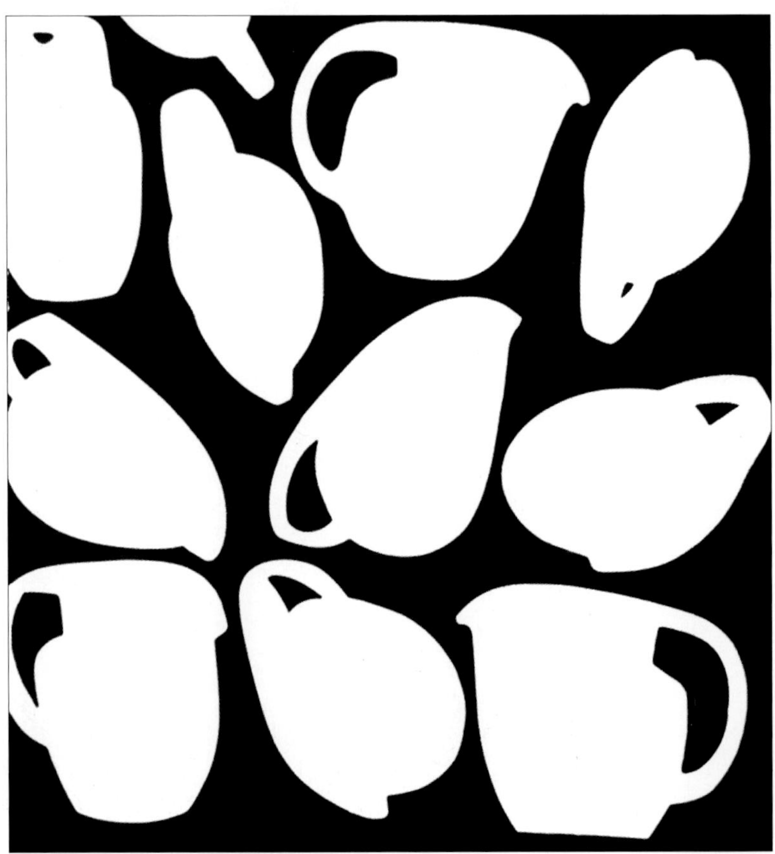

Surfaces: Textures & Reflections

The surface of a thing can be scratchy or smooth to the touch. It can invite the hand to stroke it or wrap around it. It is also important to be able to imagine how a surface would feel when the object is beyond our reach. Though we may see a glass building from afar, we still "touch" it with our eyes, sensing its cool flatness.

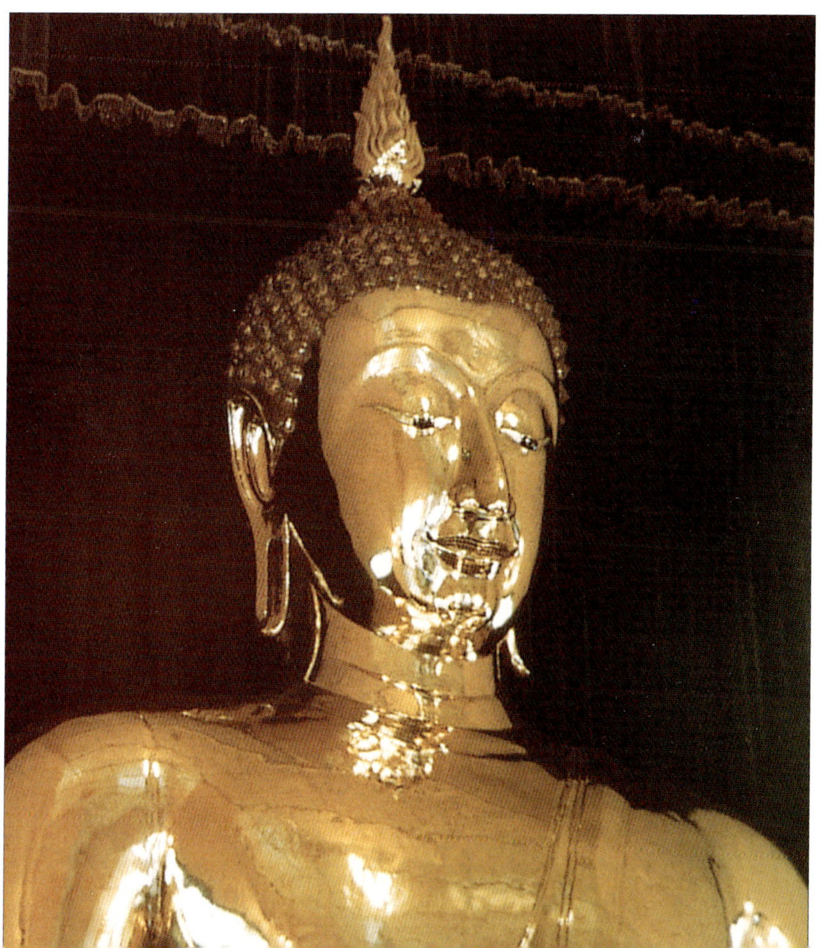

Fig. 72: Smooth, gilded Buddha.

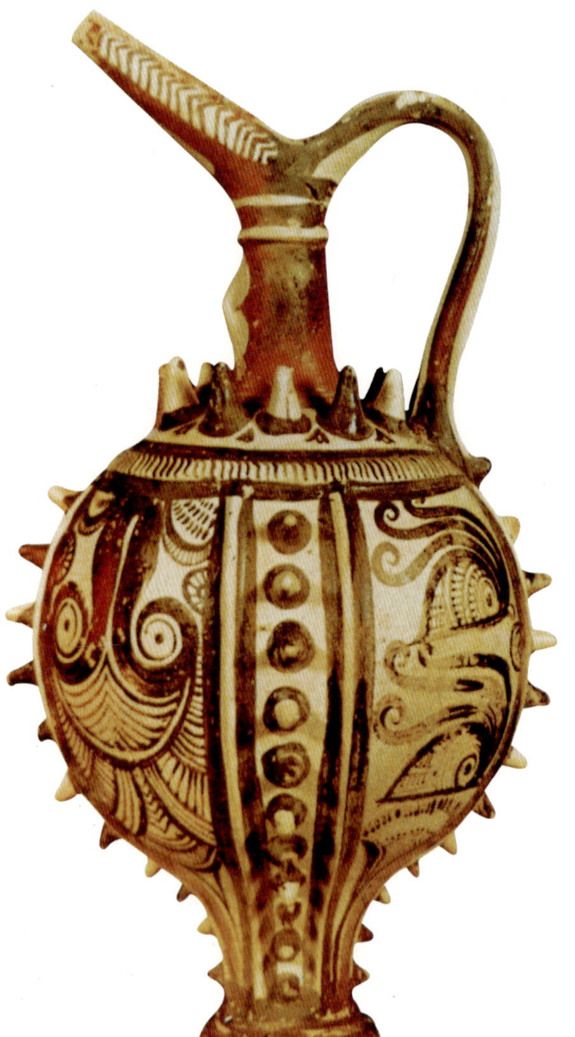

Fig. 73: Spiky pitcher.

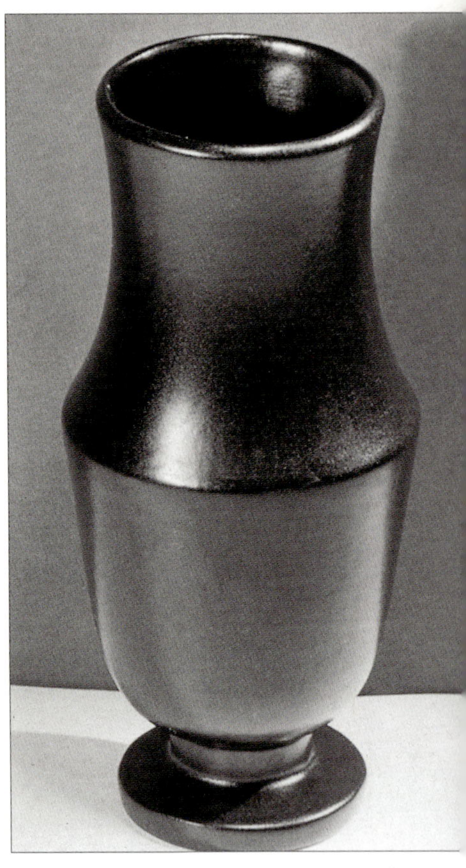

Fig. 74: Vase with smooth surface

When we press on a thing, it might give way to pressure with a feeling of elasticity or softness. It might be warm or cold, depending on the material: a fork made of plastic compared to one made of silver. A plastic champagne flute and a metal chair convey different sensations than a crystal glass or wooden chair.

Texture is not the only attribute that can destroy the agreeable sensation of touching a rounded form. So might decoration, which seems to dress the shape in a garment.

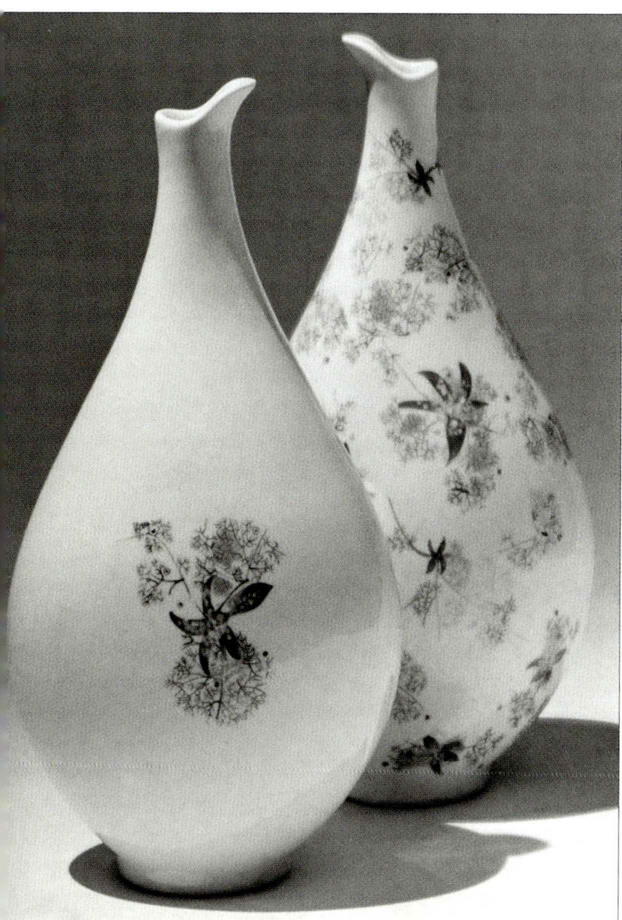

Fig. 75: Hallcraft/Tomorrow's Classic cruets.
Eva Zeisel, 1952. Frost-flower decoration by Irene Haas.

Fig. 76: Ancient jug with octopus decoration.

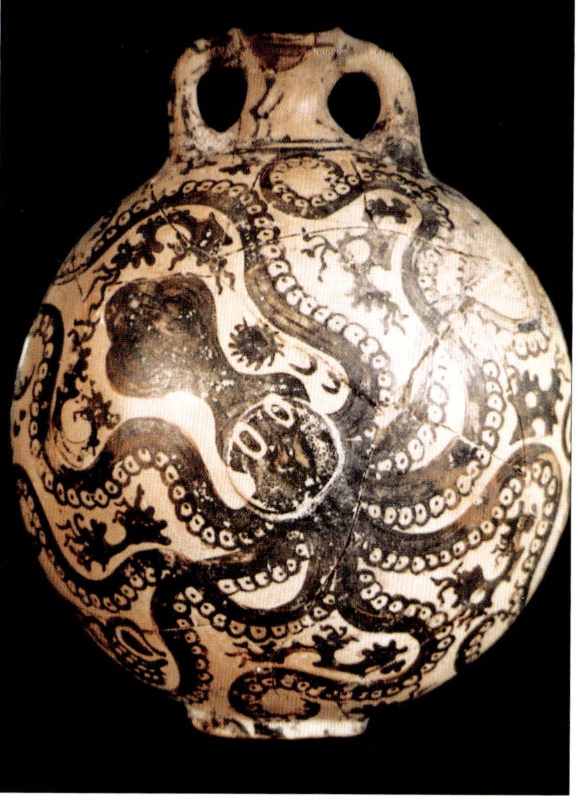

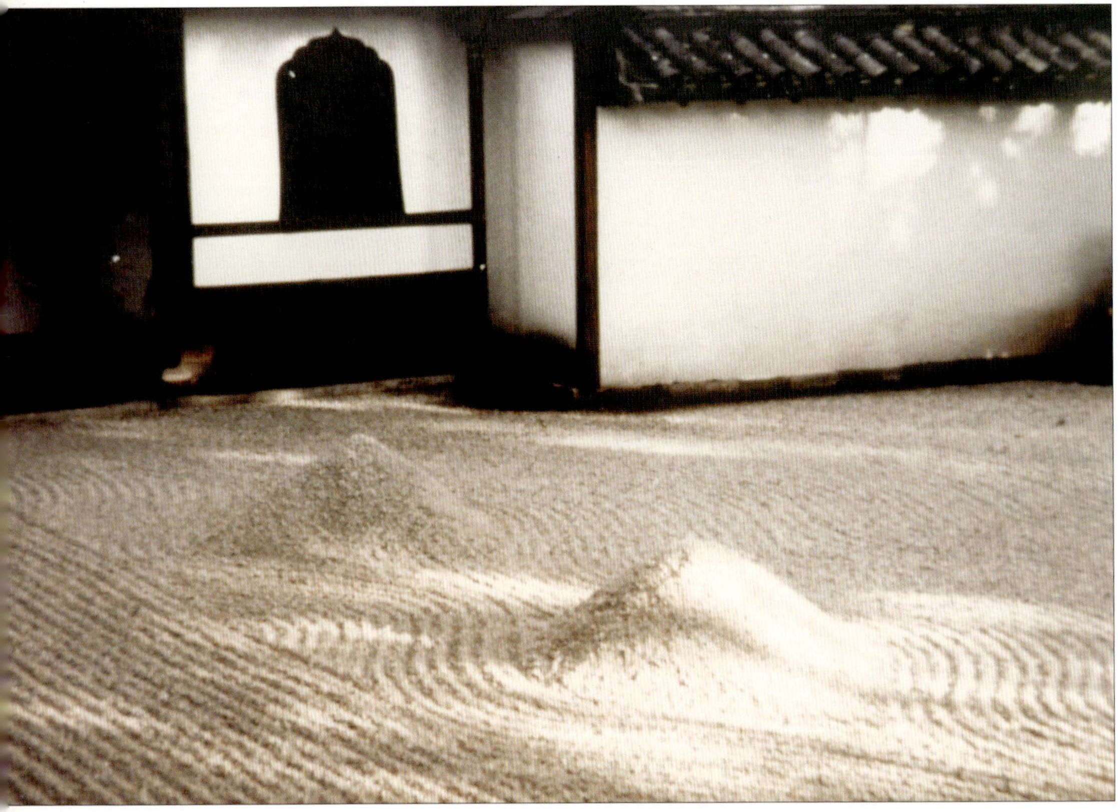

Fig. 77: Japanese courtyard with raked gravel.

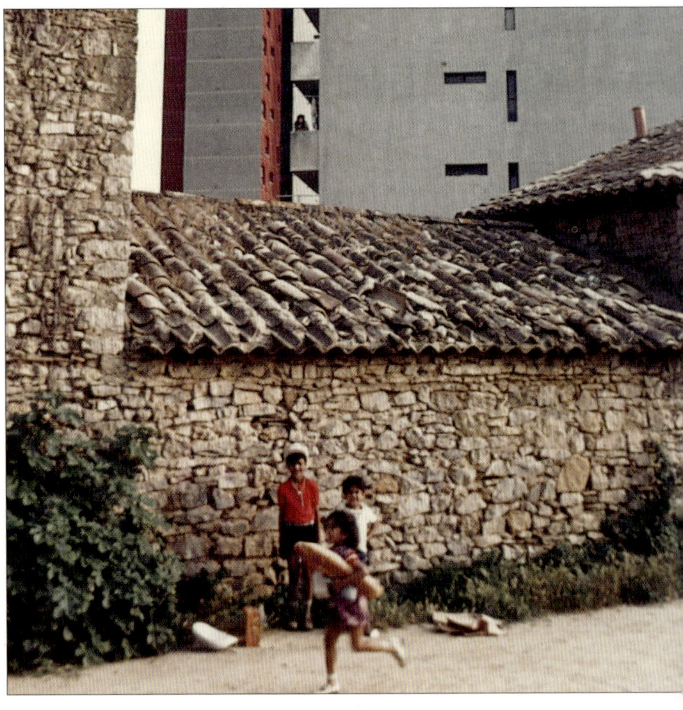

Fig. 78: Stone wall, tile roof, concrete fence, France.

Facing page: Fig. 79: Spiky arch, The Alhambra, Grenada, Spain, 1338–90.

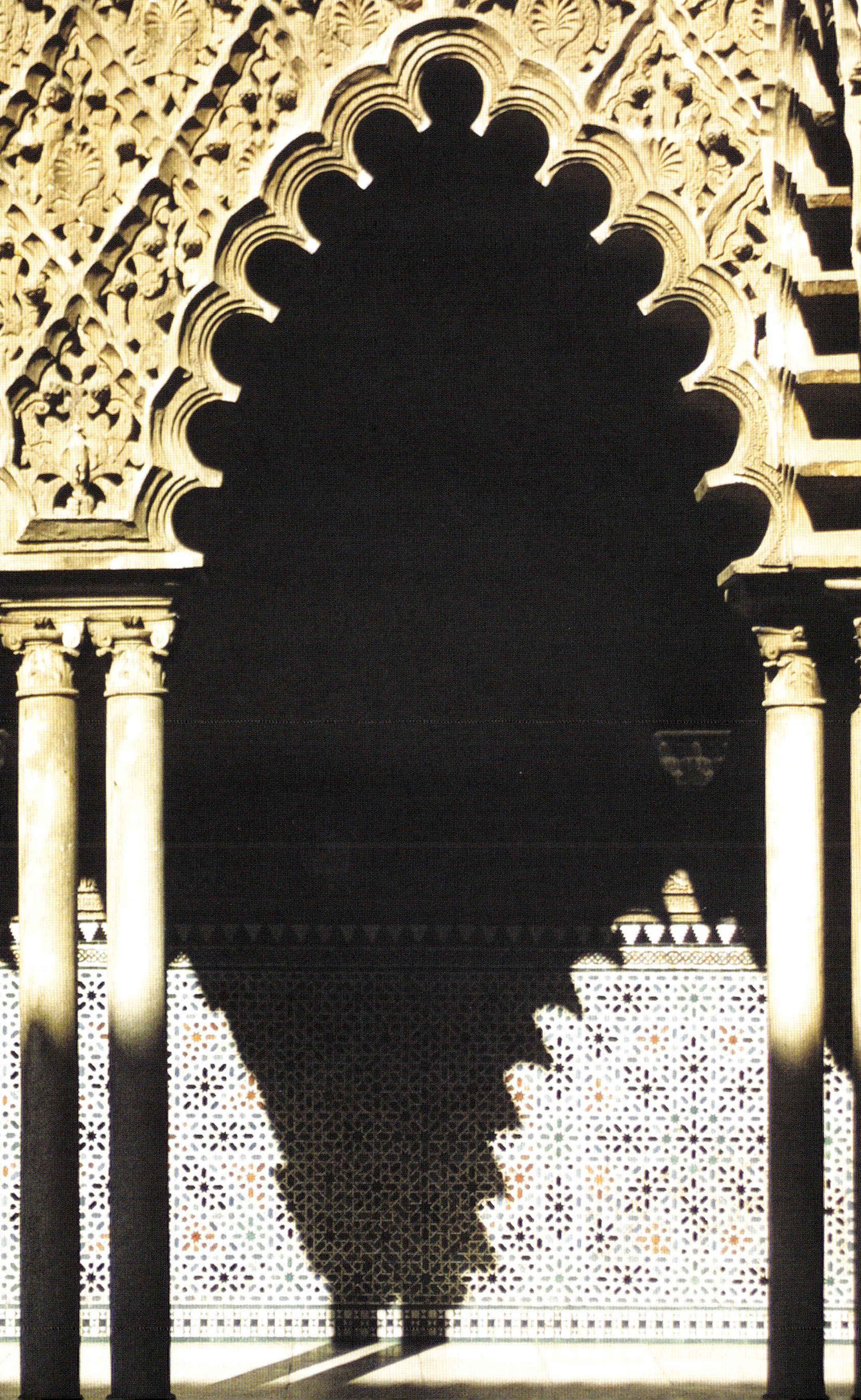

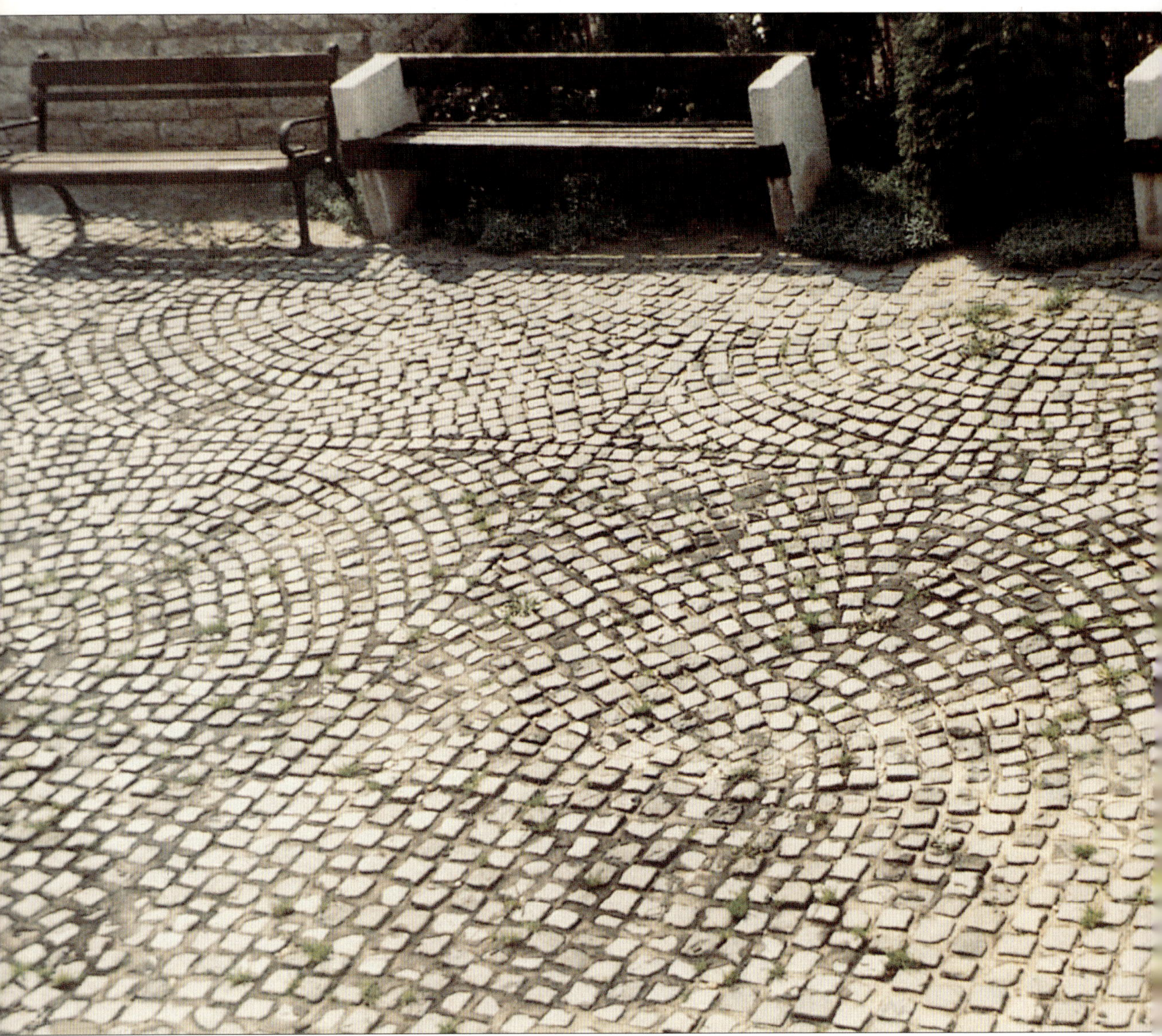

Fig. 80: Paving stones, France.

Fig. 81: Medieval stone building, France.

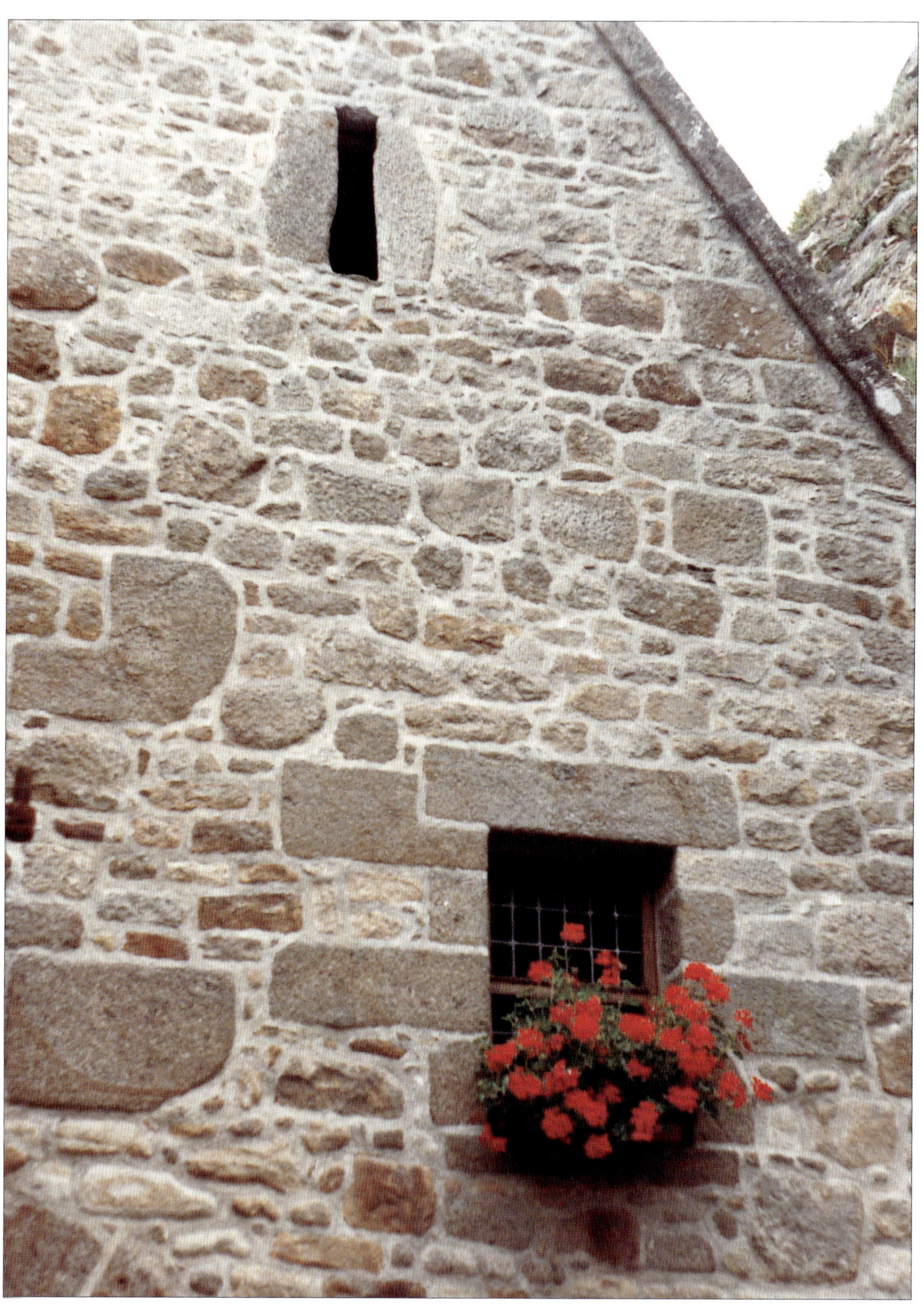

Color and reflections might also be part of our designs, and often surprise us by the way they can destroy—or enhance—the surfaces.

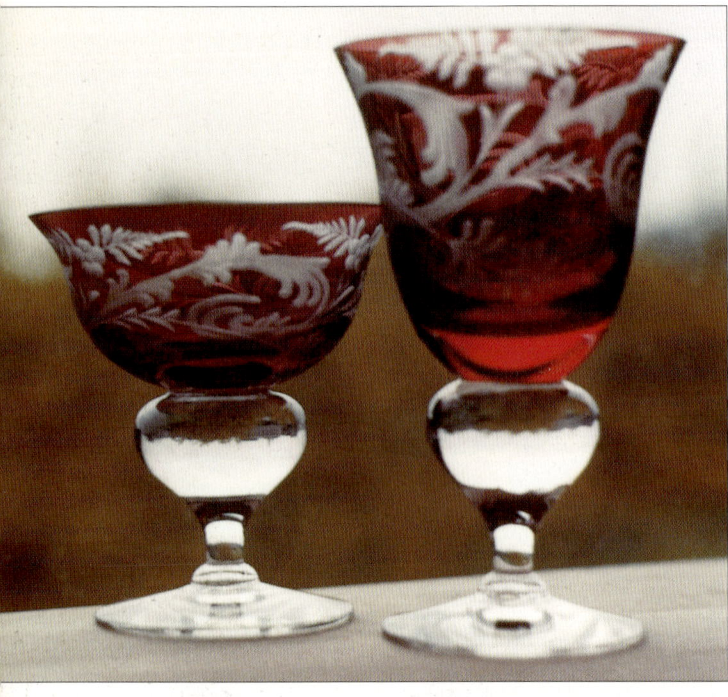

Fig. 82: Red, etched-glass goblets.

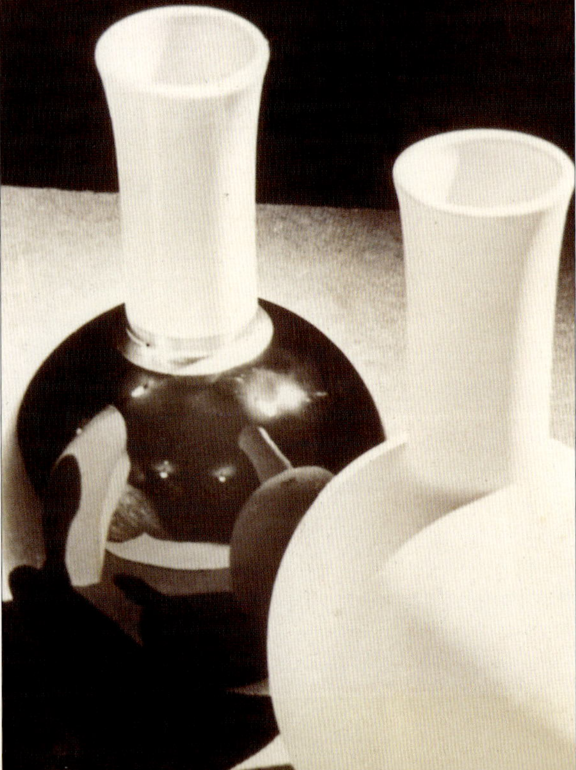

Fig. 83: Shiny, spherical decanter, Eva Zeisel.

Fig. 84: Reflection in skyscraper façad

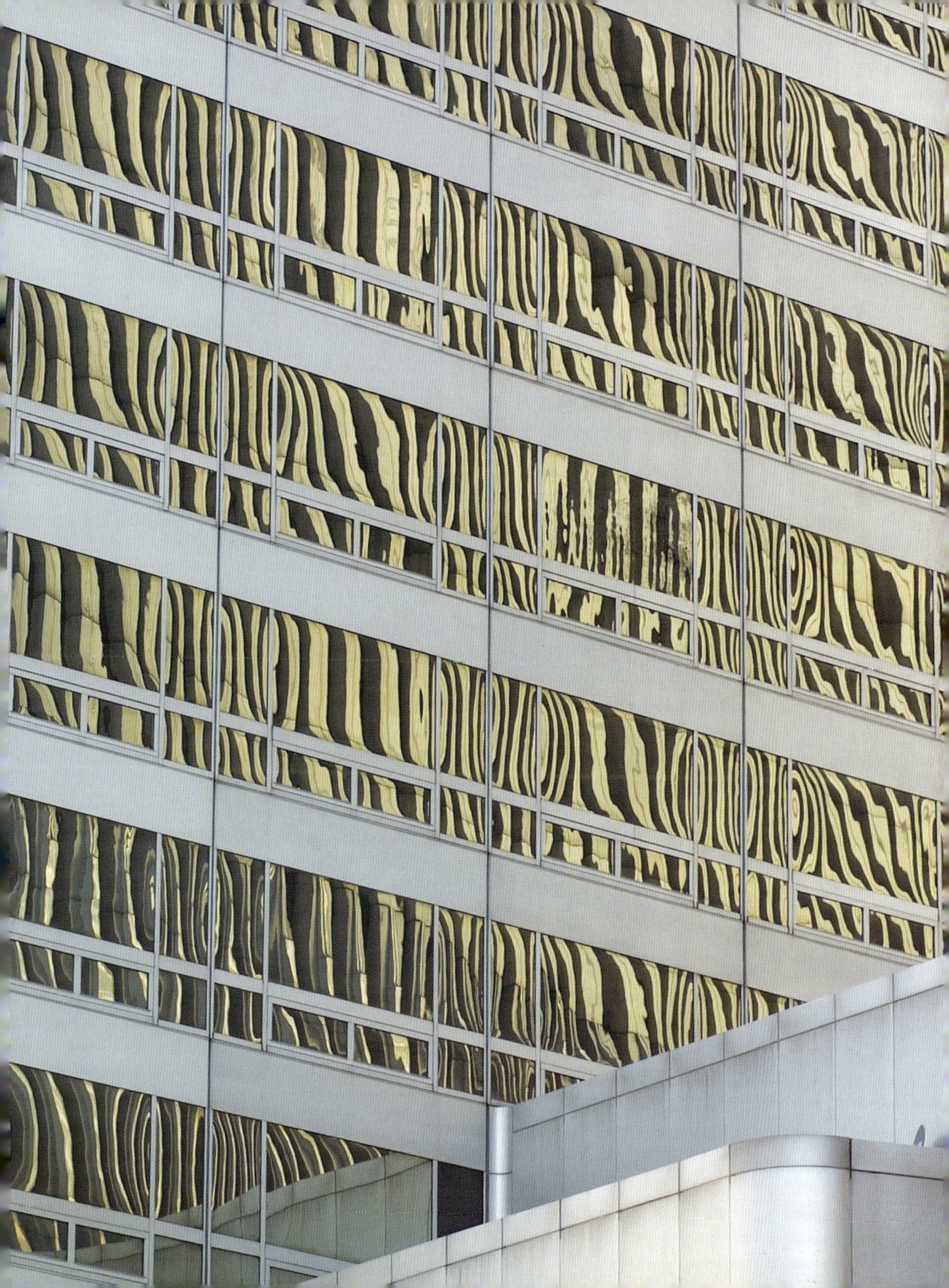

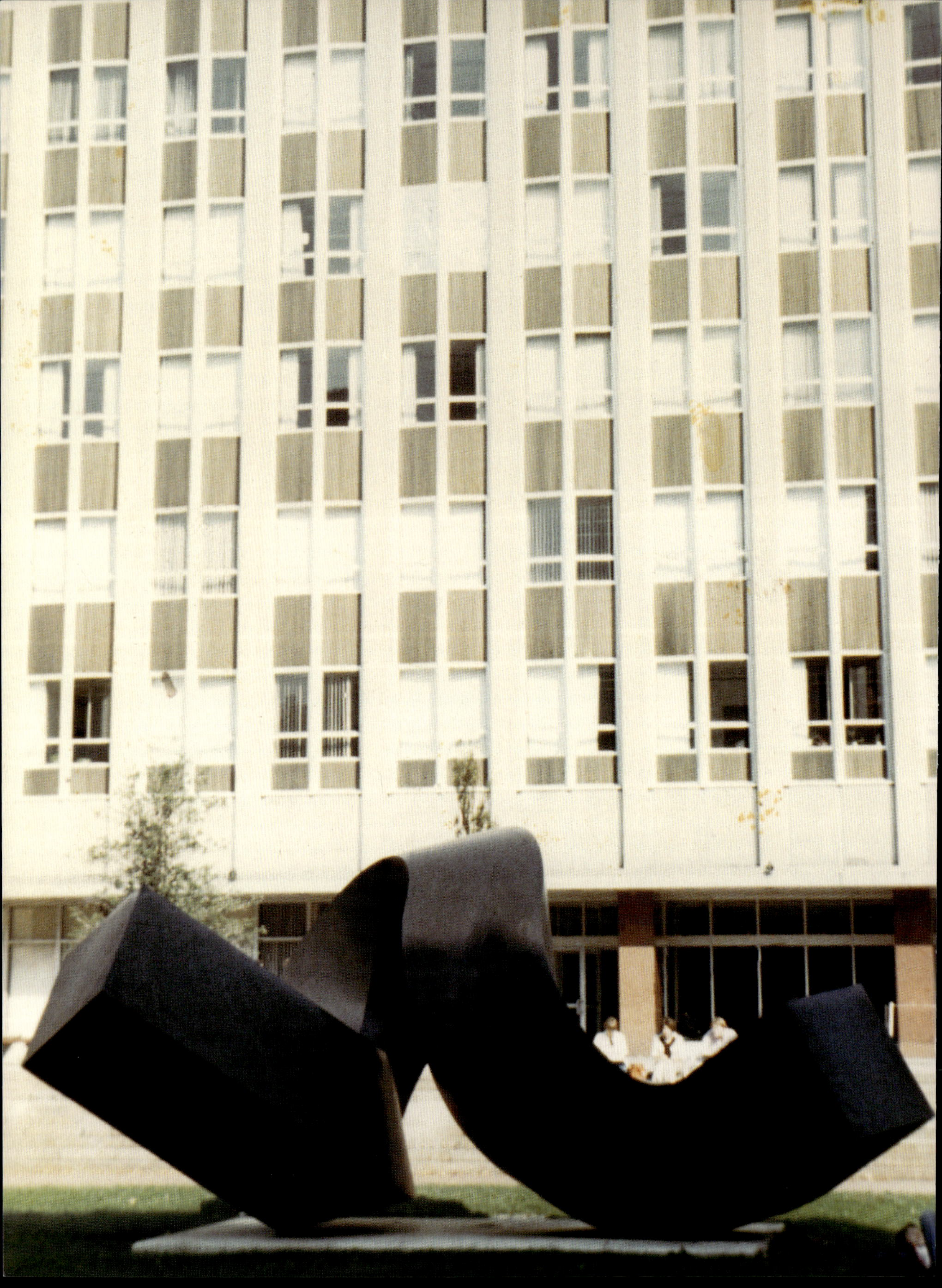

Scale

Scale is one of the most important aesthetic elements, particularly where it reaches its extremes. The pyramids have hardly any other aesthetic quality to hold us but our fascination with their size. Stepping into the nave of the Chartres Cathedral we feel its awe-inspiring height.

The miniature accoutrements of a doll house rivet our attention to their details. The human size becomes the measure of the grandeur or cuteness of the things around us. The monumental ornament shown here seems to me to be the result of an aesthetic misunderstanding. What might have been a casual, even delicate ribbon when seen at the size that it was most probably originally modeled, becomes instead a disturbingly crude object when enlarged to monumental size.

Fig. 85. Outdoor sculpture, New York City, Curb Clement Meadmore, 1968.

The same object, a sphere in this case, evokes different responses at different scales.

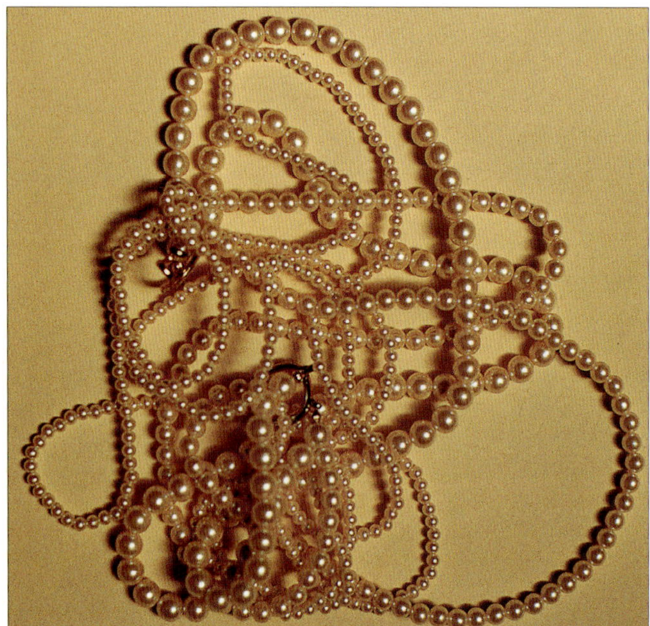

Fig. 86: Small spheres (necklace).

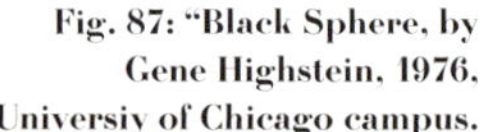

Fig. 87: "Black Sphere, by Gene Highstein, 1976, Universiy of Chicago campus.

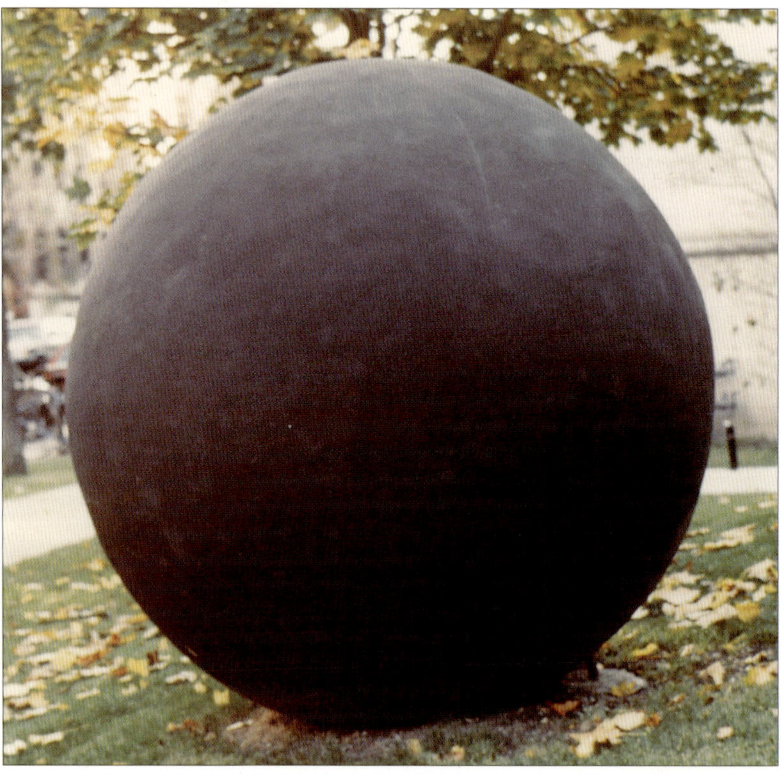

Scale can be deceptive. Consider these two teapots. Is the large one huge and the small one normal size? Or is the smaller one a miniature?

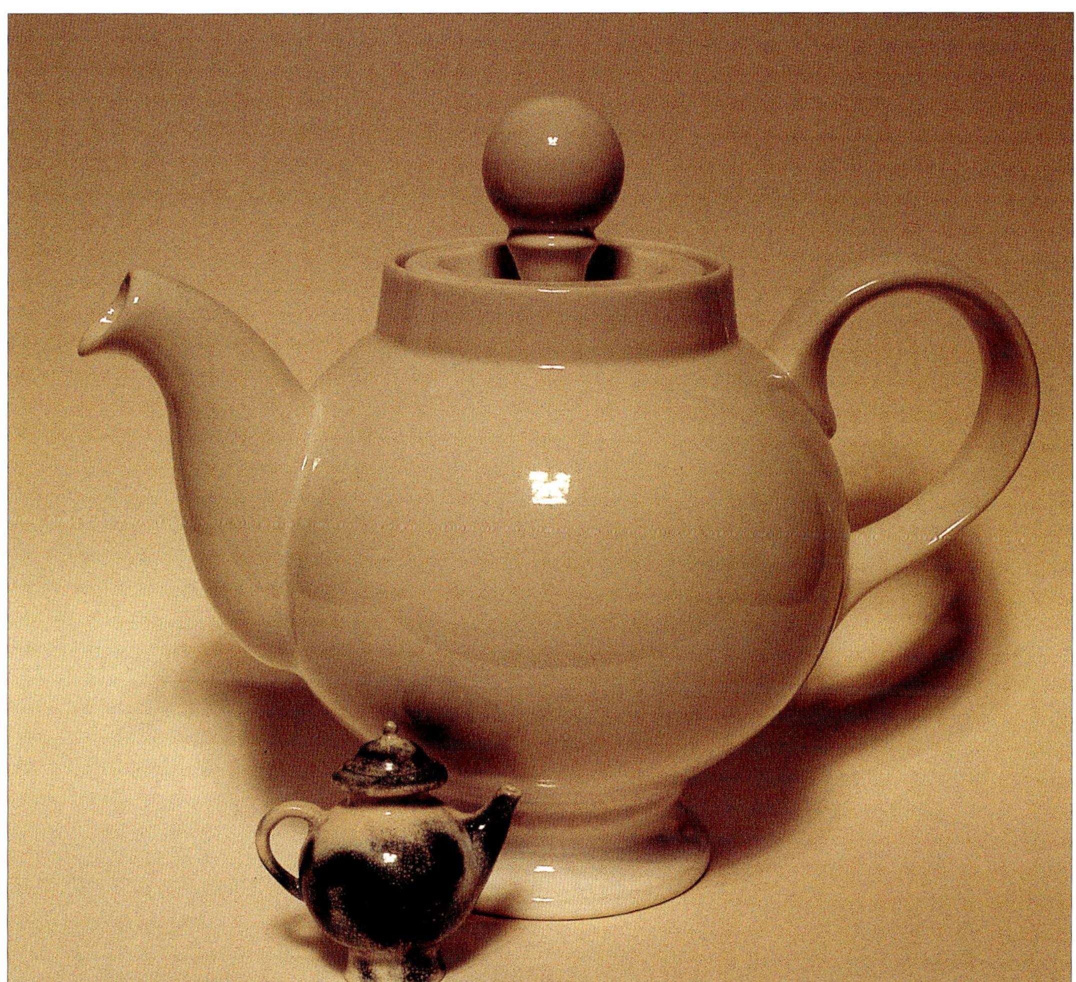

Fig. 88: Large and tiny teapots.

And is the pitcher in this picture used by Godzilla, or are the facades merely toys?

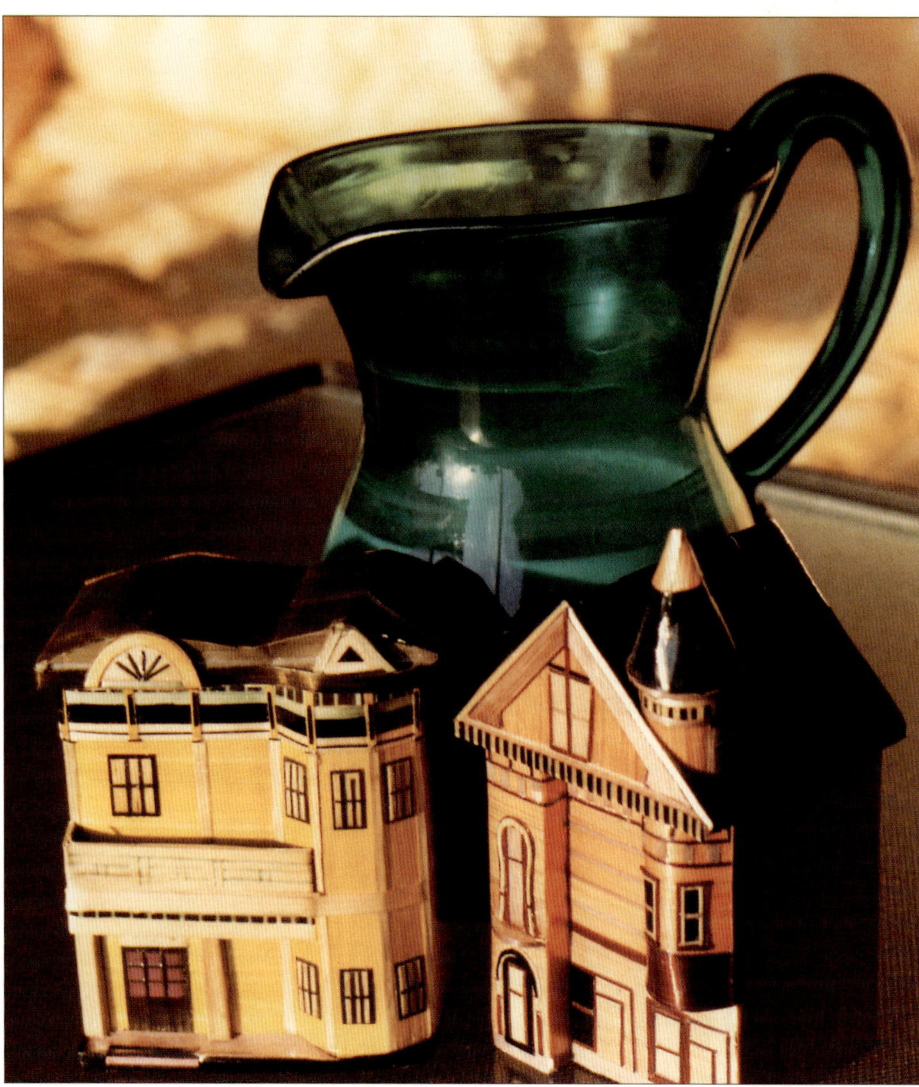

Fig. 89: Pitcher with houses.

We understand the size of two things in relation to each another. Of course the newsprint identifies the dishes as doll furniture. The hand does the same.

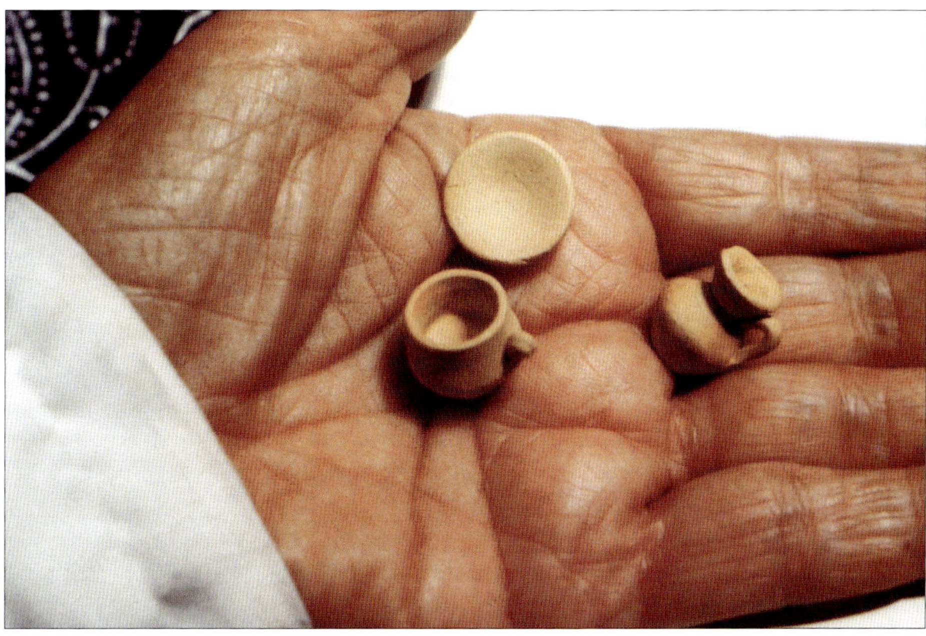

Fig. 90: Tiny pots in a hand.

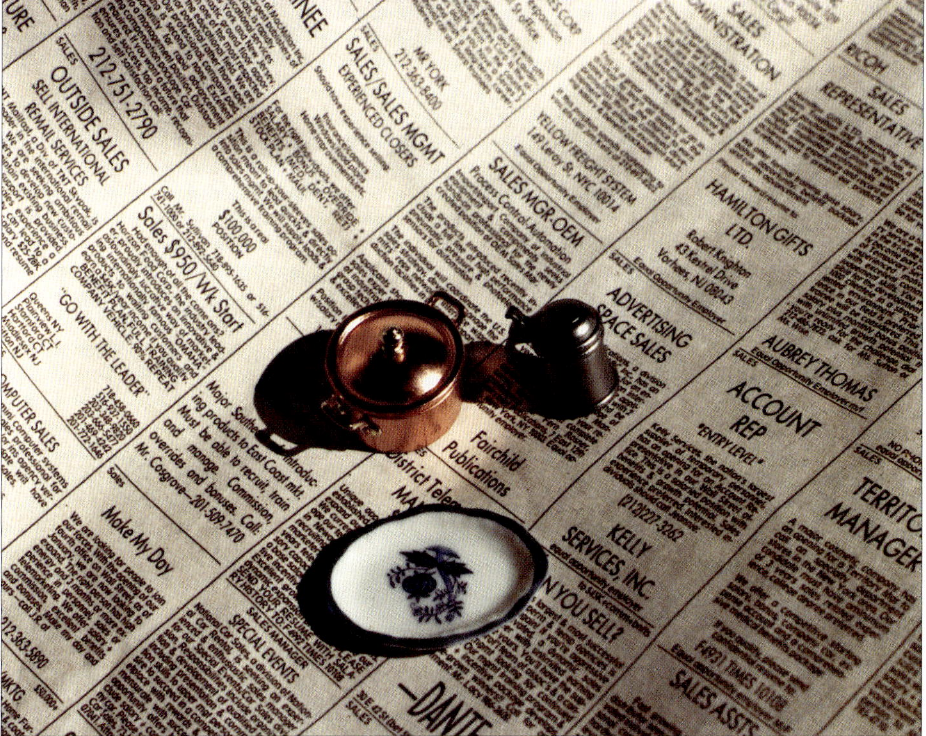

Fig. 91: Doll house dishes on newspaper.

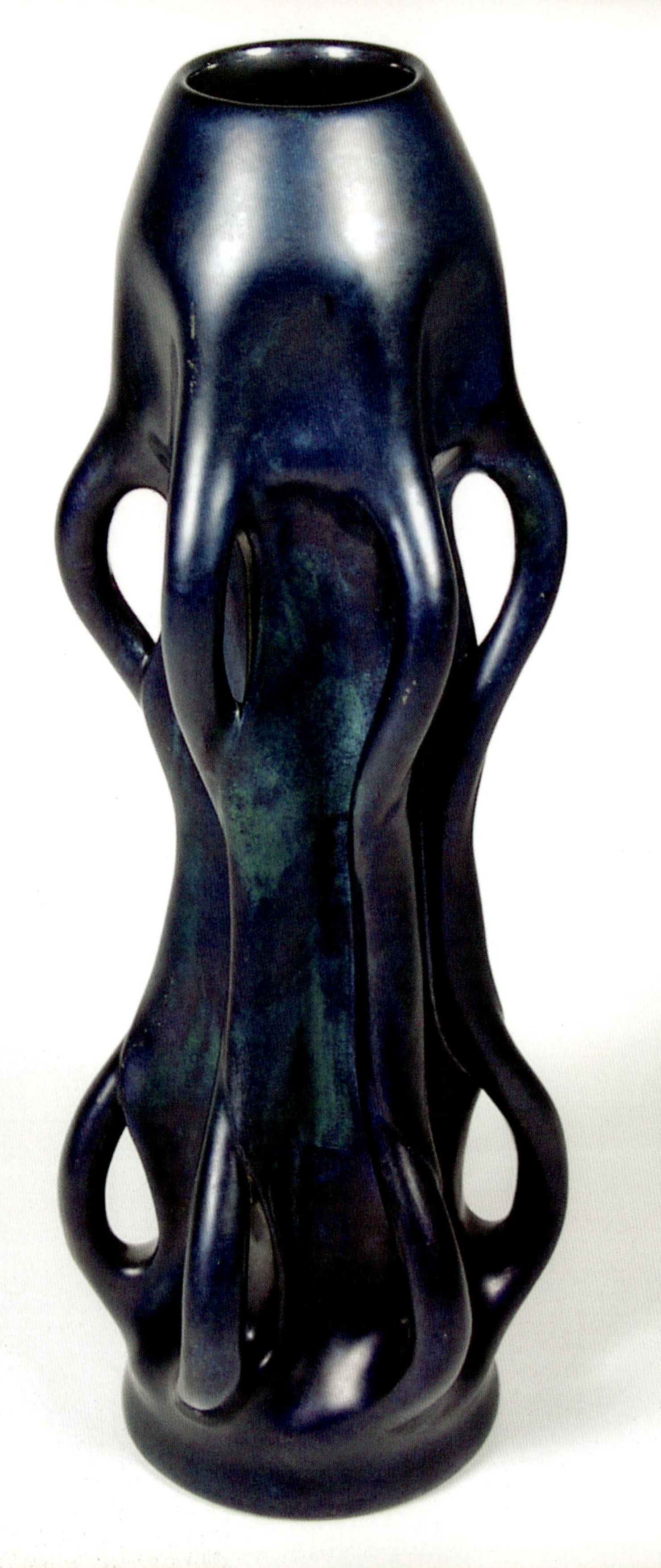

Crisp or Soft

92: Art Nouveau vase.

Whether it is a building wing or a teapot handle, when one part is joined to another the designer faces a delicate problem. Designers must decide how to join the different parts of a design—by having them seem to grow from one to another, for example, or by creating a crisp demarcation line. The former was the Art Nouveau fashion, the latter, that of the Modern Movement.

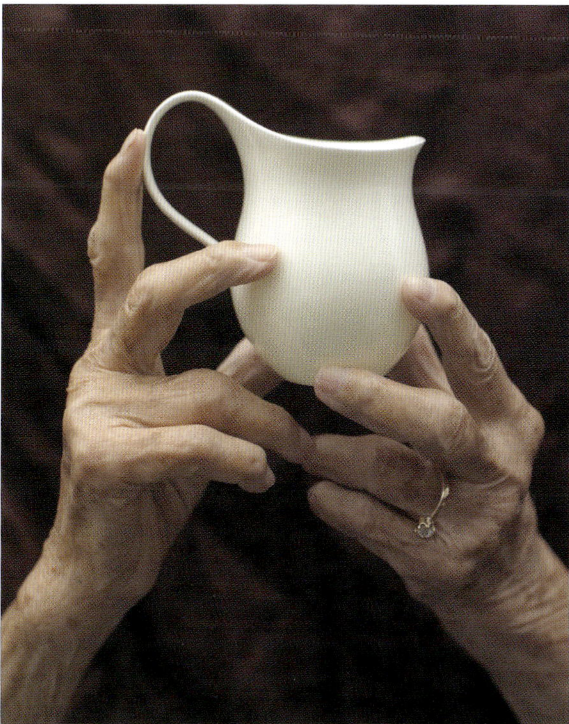

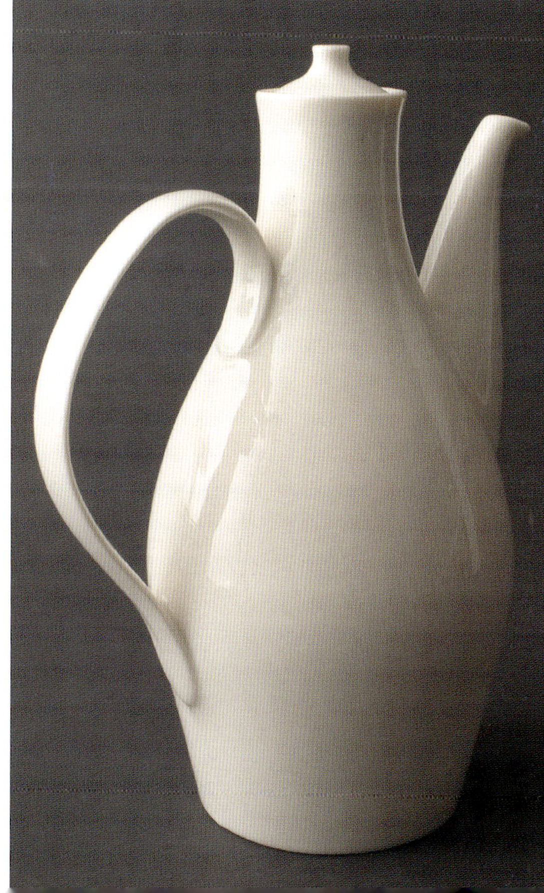

Figure 93: Lomonosov cup, held by author, 2003.

Fig. 94: "Museum" coffeepot with attached handle, Castleton China, Eva Zeisel, 1942–45.

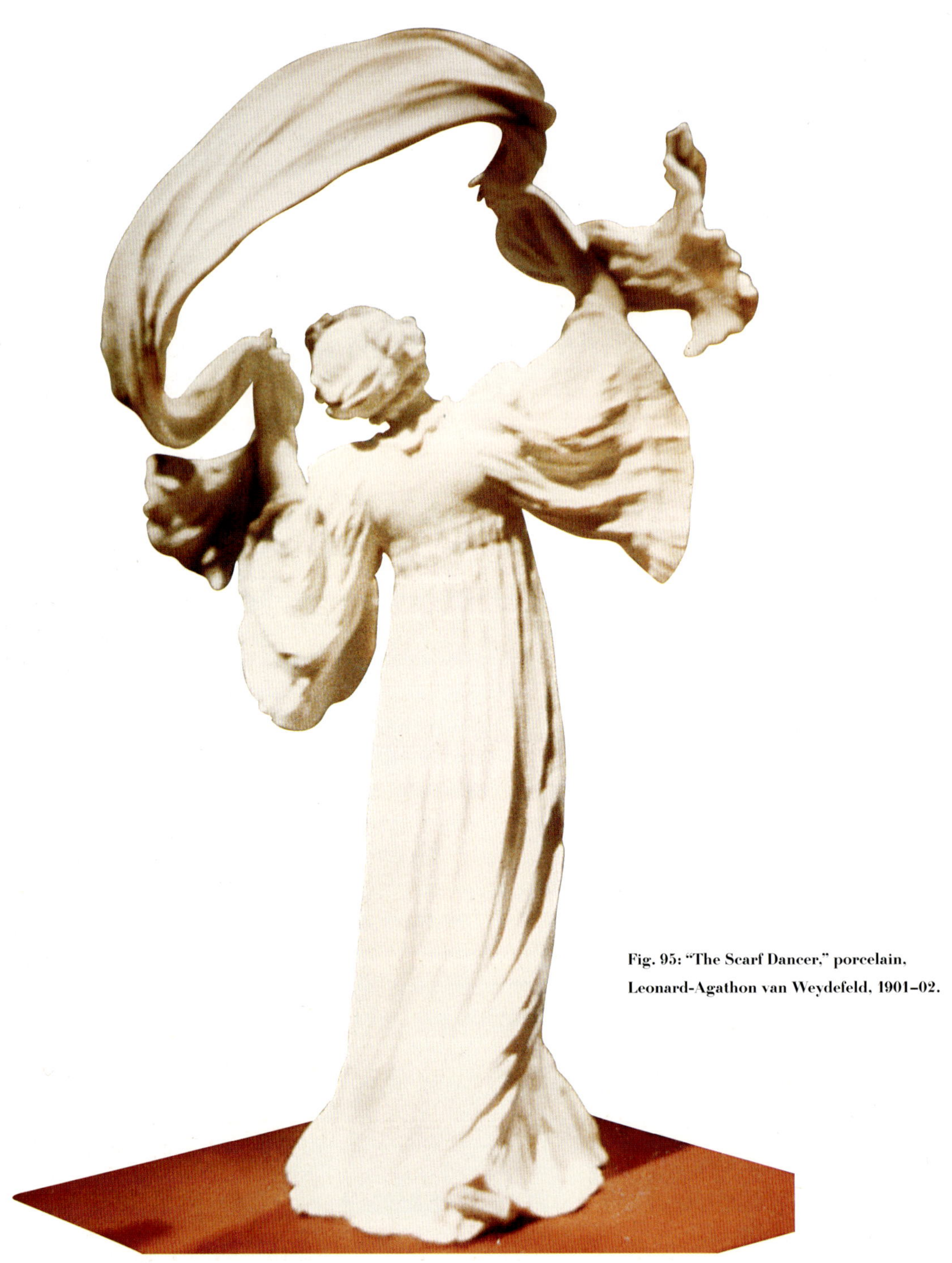

Fig. 95: "The Scarf Dancer," porcelain, Leonard-Agathon van Weydefeld, 1901–02.

To the Limit of the Material

Modernism spoke of "honesty" of materials—implying that there are certain ways of using a material that are "correct" while others are "incorrect." But there are no correct or incorrect usages, only performances with more or less virtuosity.

Fig. 96: Porcelain figurines.

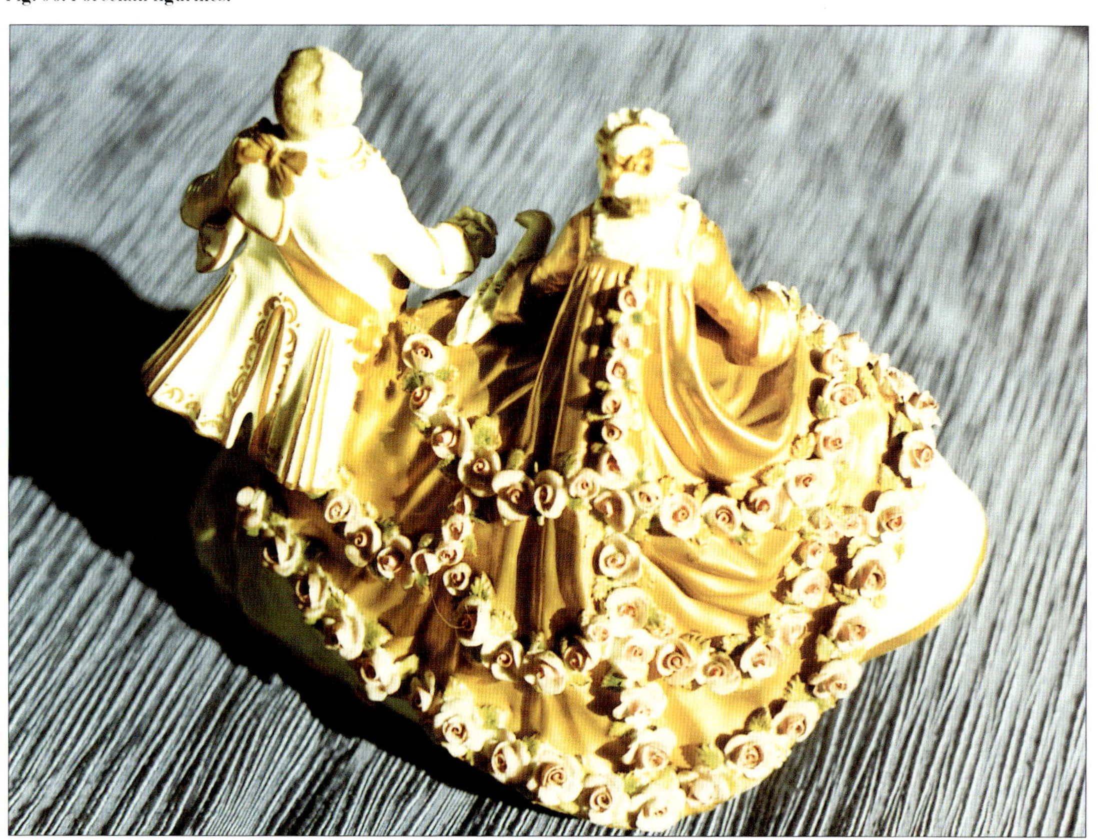

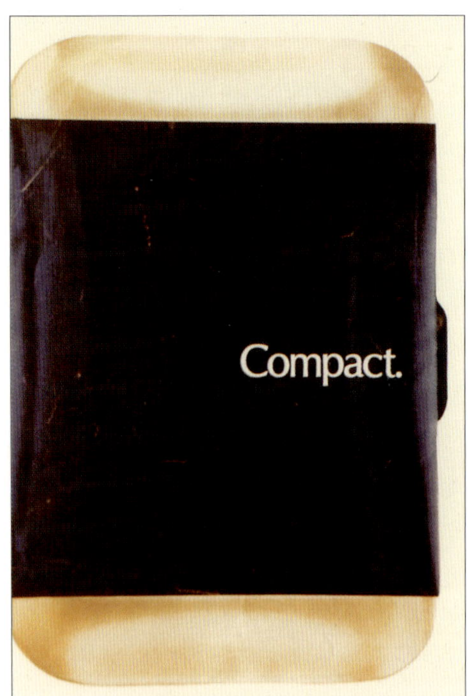

Fig. 97: "Compact."

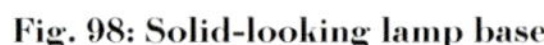
Fig. 98: Solid-looking lamp base.

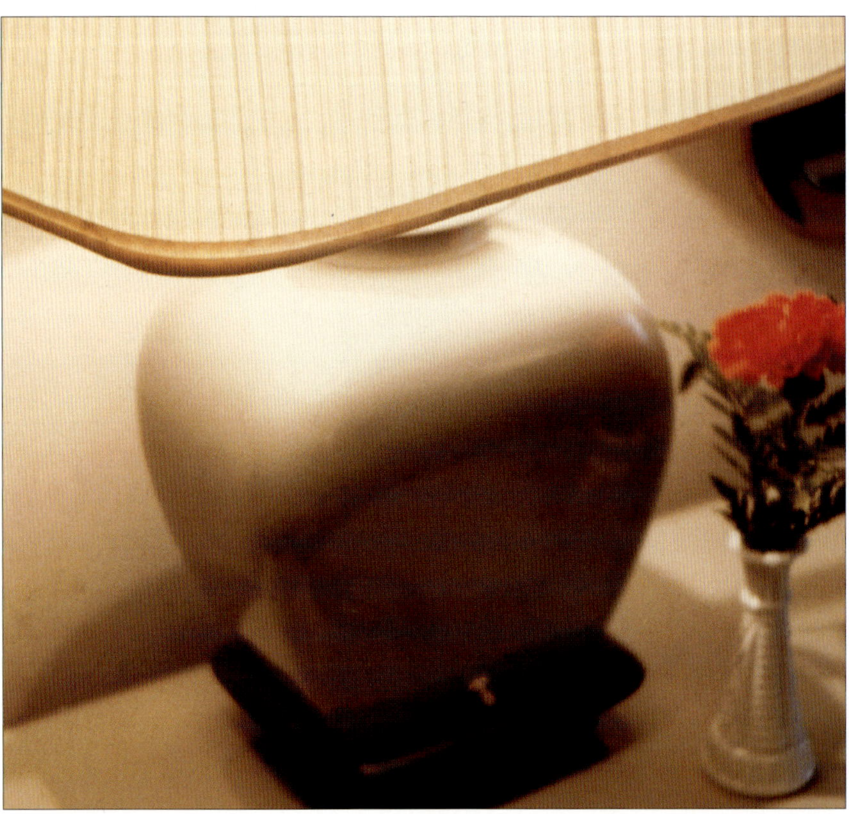

Compact to Lacy

A compact shape expresses solidity. It is comforting by its steadfast presence.

Shapes like these look larger than they really are. If you want to give the customer the feeling he is drinking more coffee than you actually served him, you will use this sort of shape for the container. It's not a chic shape, but a motherly one, sedate and ample, reliable, here to stay.

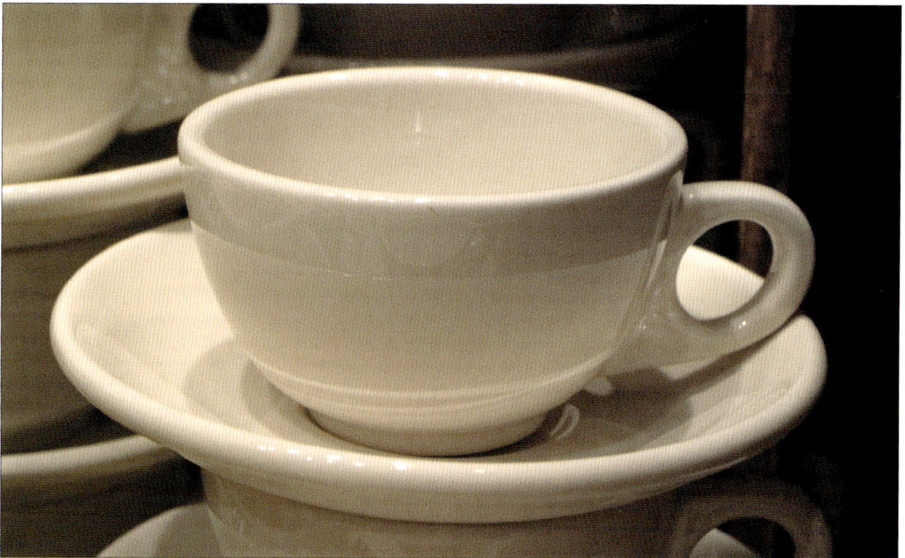

Fig. 99: Restaurant cup, compact form.

However, you might like to make a graceful, light shape, one which does not seem to squat on the ground, one which looks lighter than its actual weight, which seems to poke into the sky, even to fly away, weightlessly. You might play with the object's edge.

Break up the rim and let it meet its sky with a ragged contour. Or a lacy contour. Frail-looking, fine lacey ornaments break up the compact bulk of the buildings.

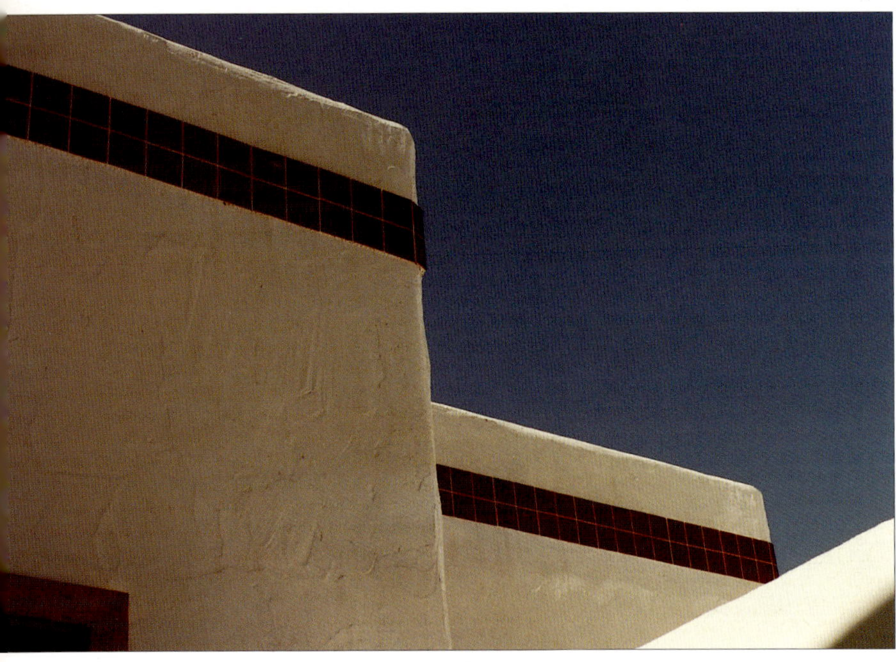

Fig. 100: Adobe building with compact form.

Fig. 101: Wall with broken contours, Iranian village.

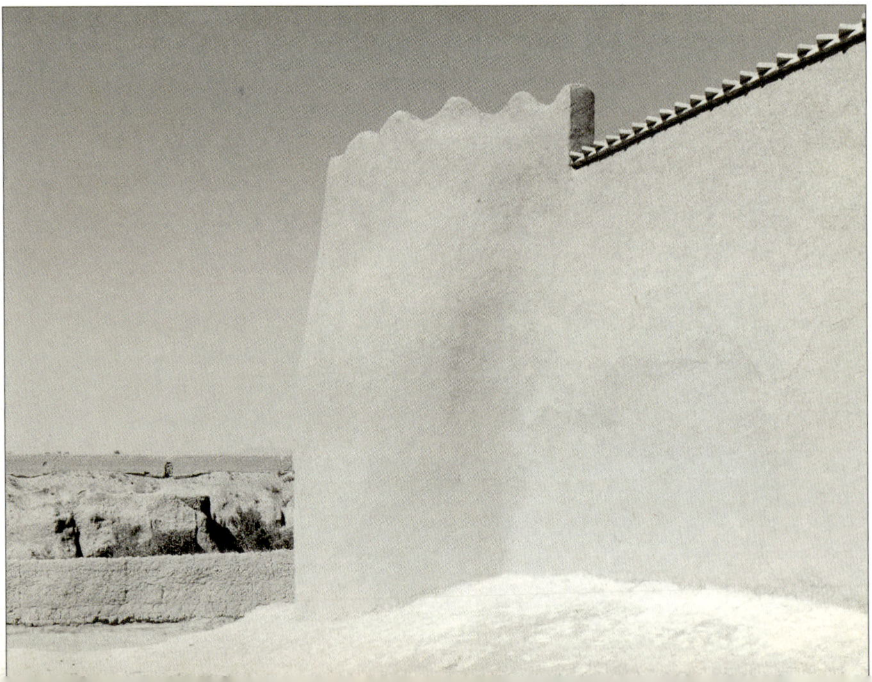

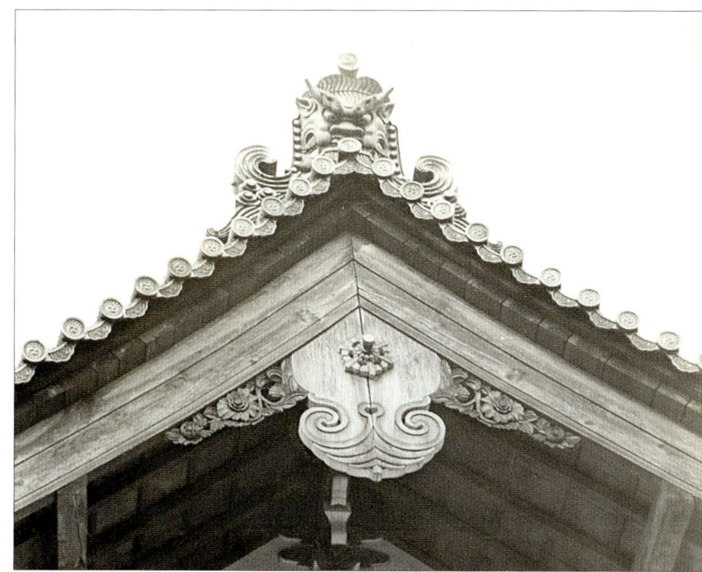

Fig. 102: Gable of Japanese tiled roof.

Fig. 103: Folk Gothic, Brittany.

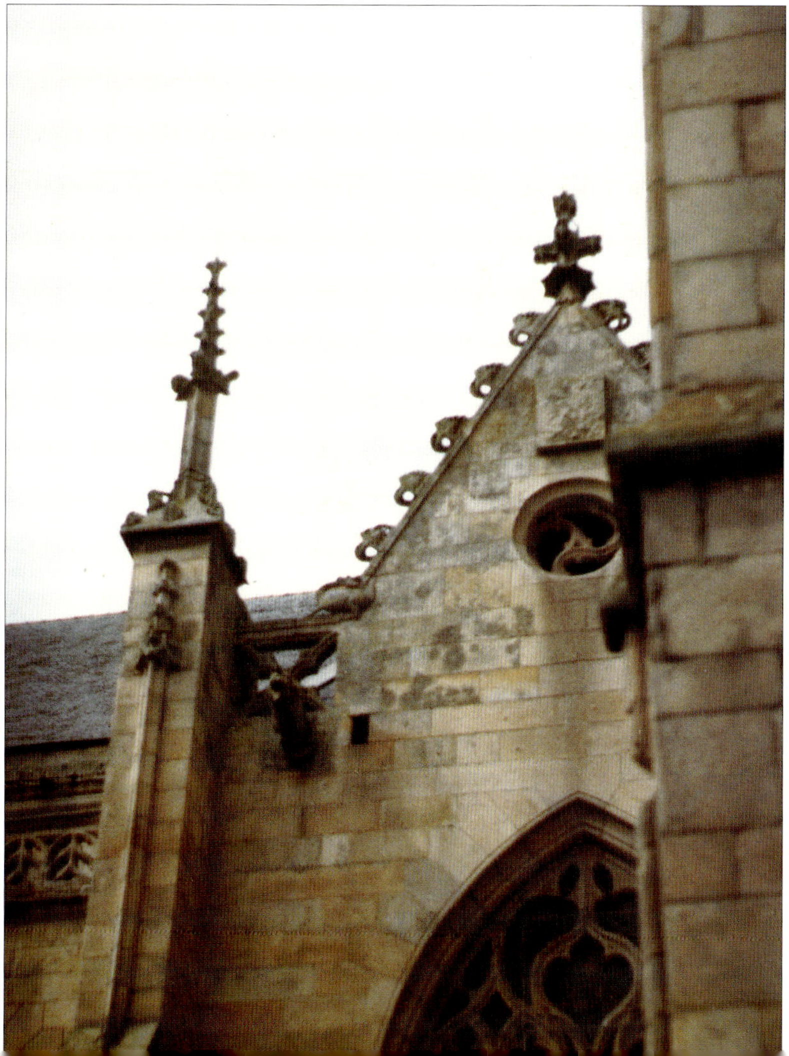

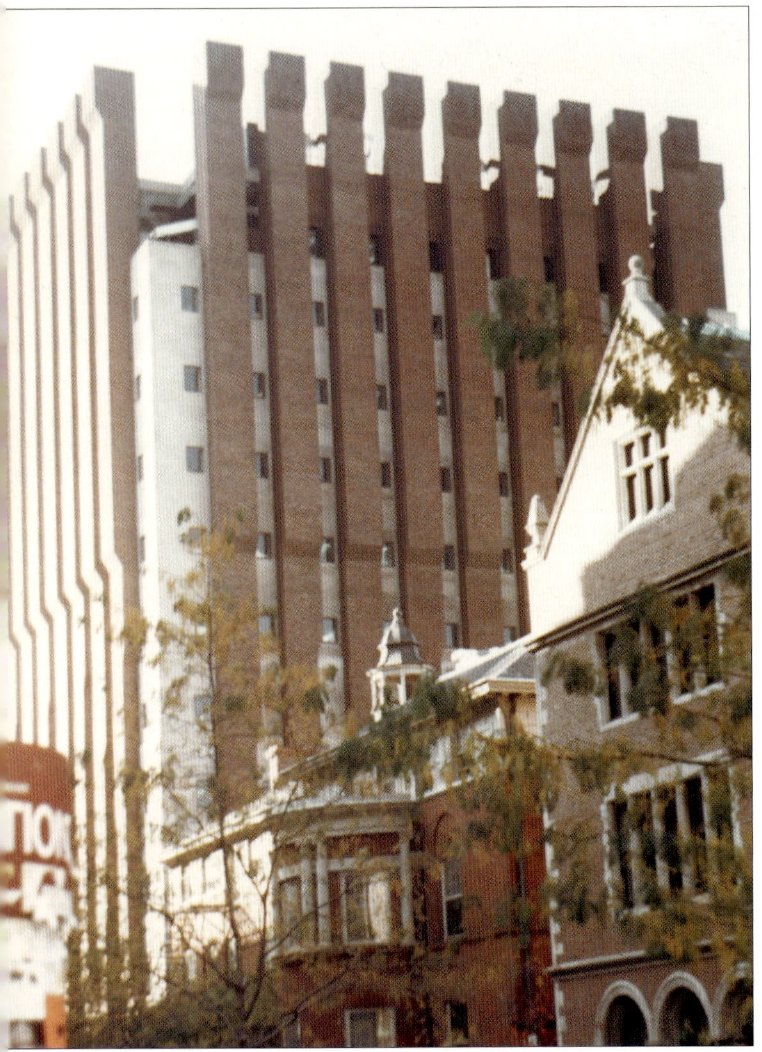
Fig. 104: Cummings Life Science Center, University of Chicago.

Fig. 105: Lion sculpture on column, Franc

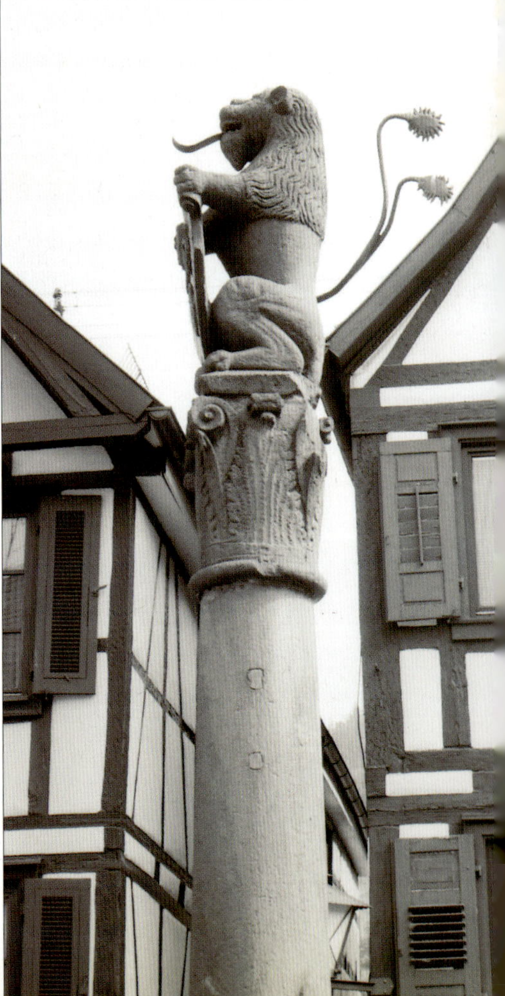

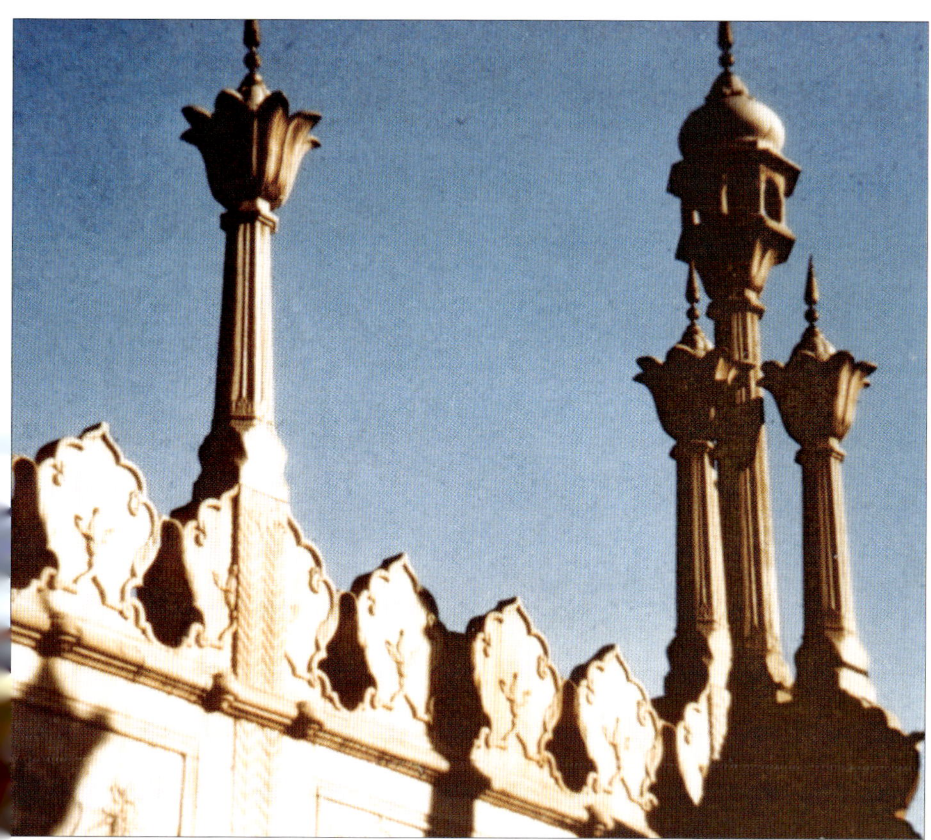

Fig. 106: Mogul architecture, India.

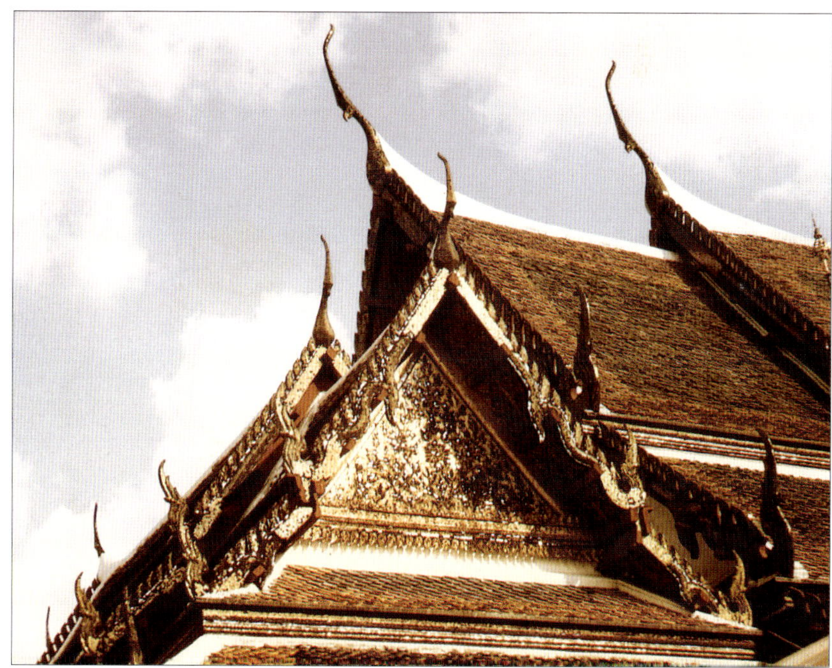

Fig. 107: Temple roof, Thailand.

Still playing with the contour, you might help your shape's ascent to the sky by giving it wings to fly. Still, it is only the contour of the solid shape that you manipulate.

Fig. 108: Bathtub faucet with "wing" handles, student work.

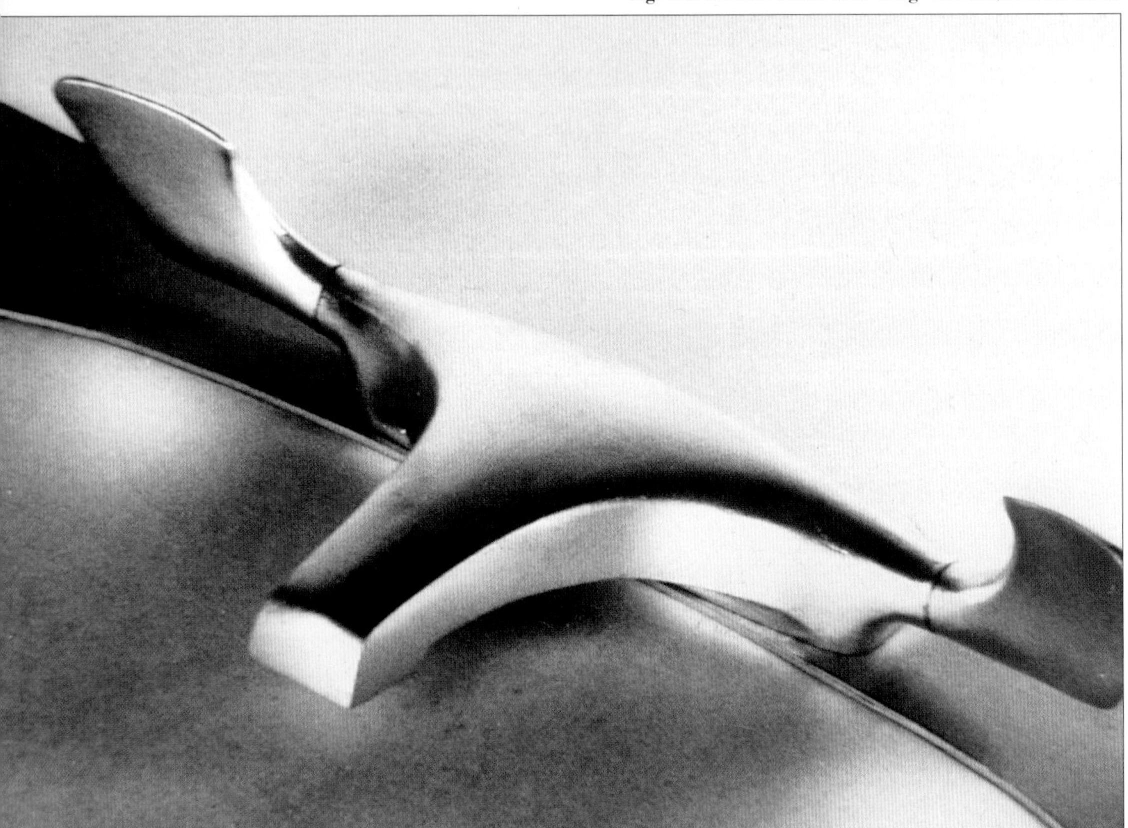

However, you might make the shape seem lighter, reducing its earthbound solidity, by lifting it up from the ground like many of the buildings by the architect Le Corbusier.

Fig. 109: City University, Paris. Le Corbusier.

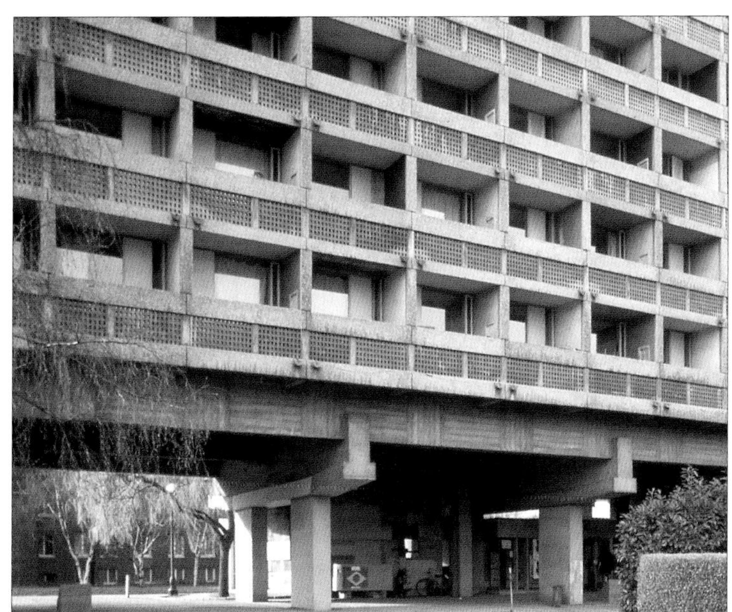

Or even by poking holes into it.

Fig. 110: Palladio's Basilica, Vicenza, Italy.

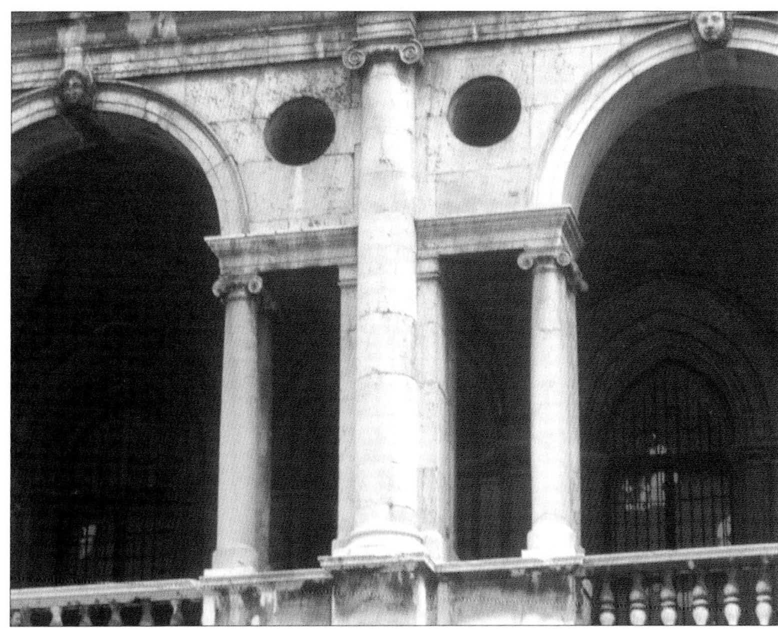

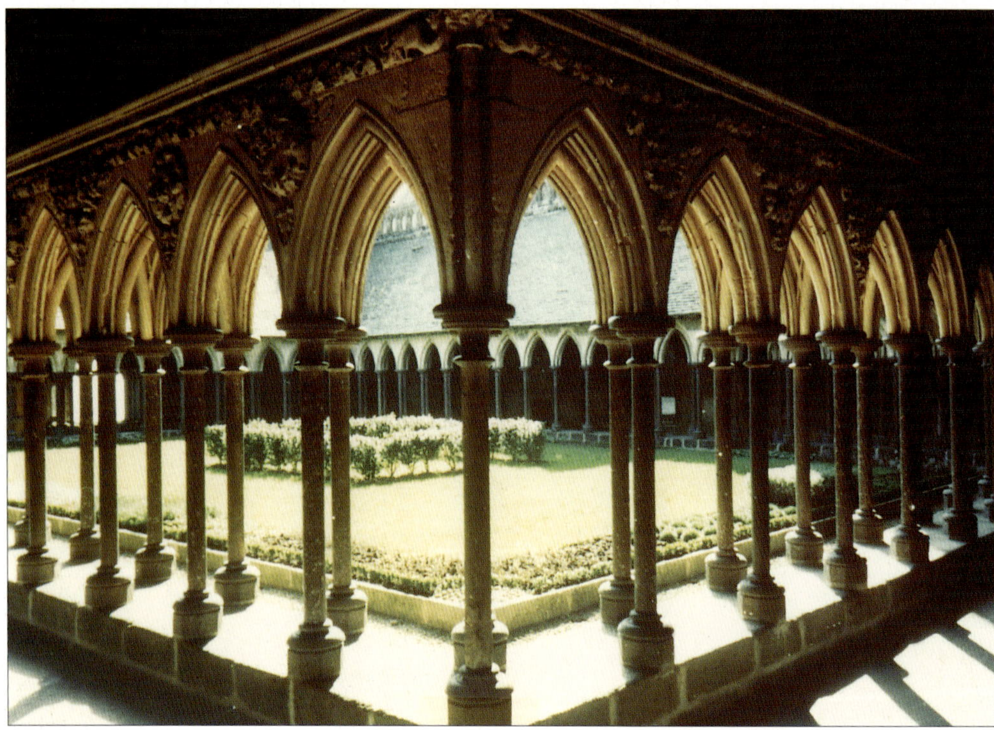

Fig. 111: Medieval cloister.

Intruding into the bulk of buildings make them look lighter than if they were solid walls.

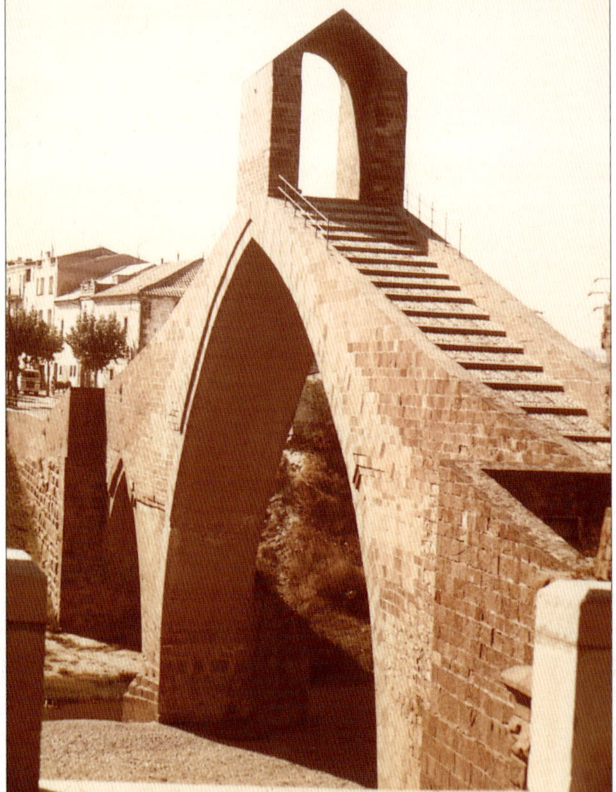

Fig. 112: Stone pedestrian bridge, France.

***Facing page*, Fig. 113: Roman aqueduct, France.**

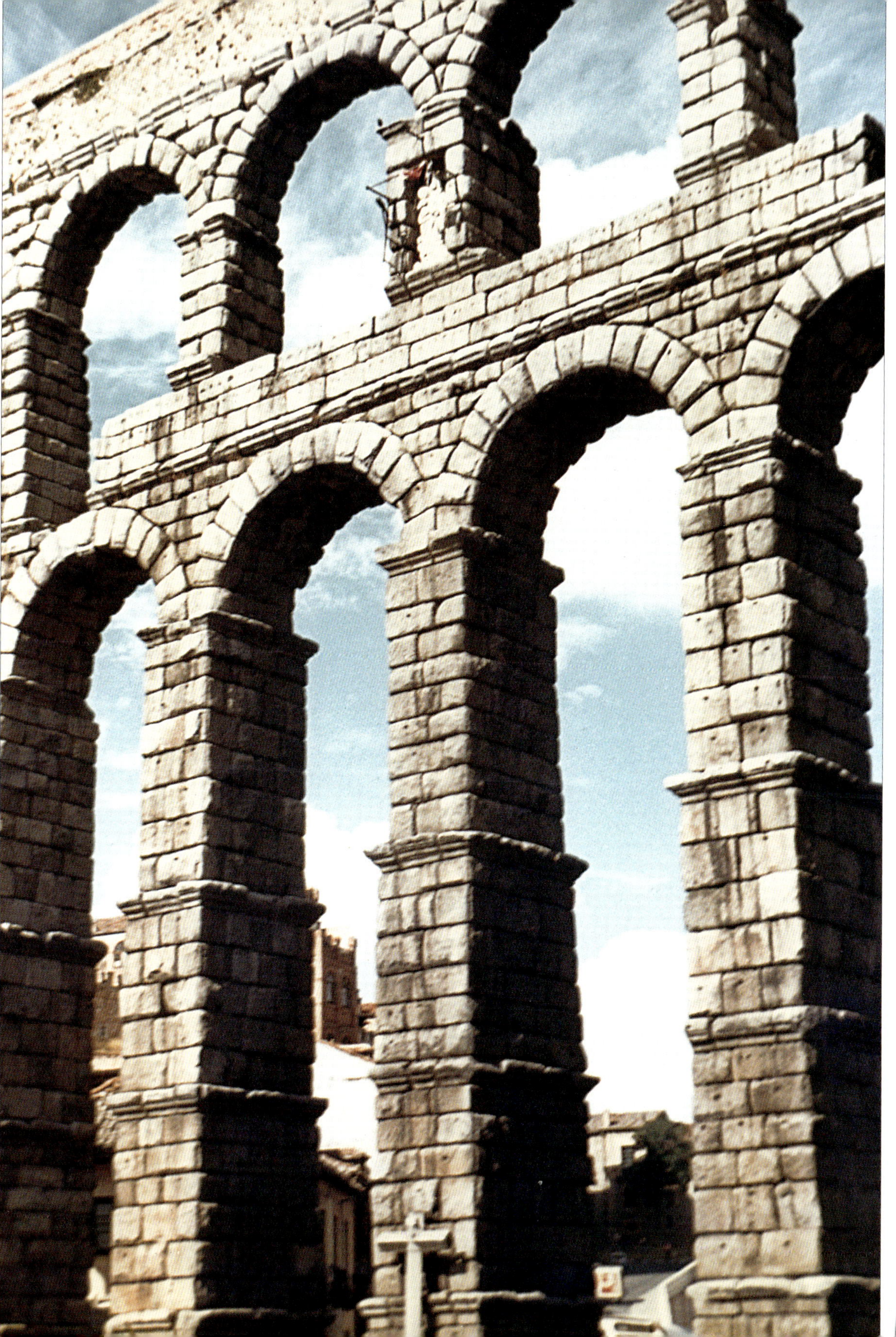

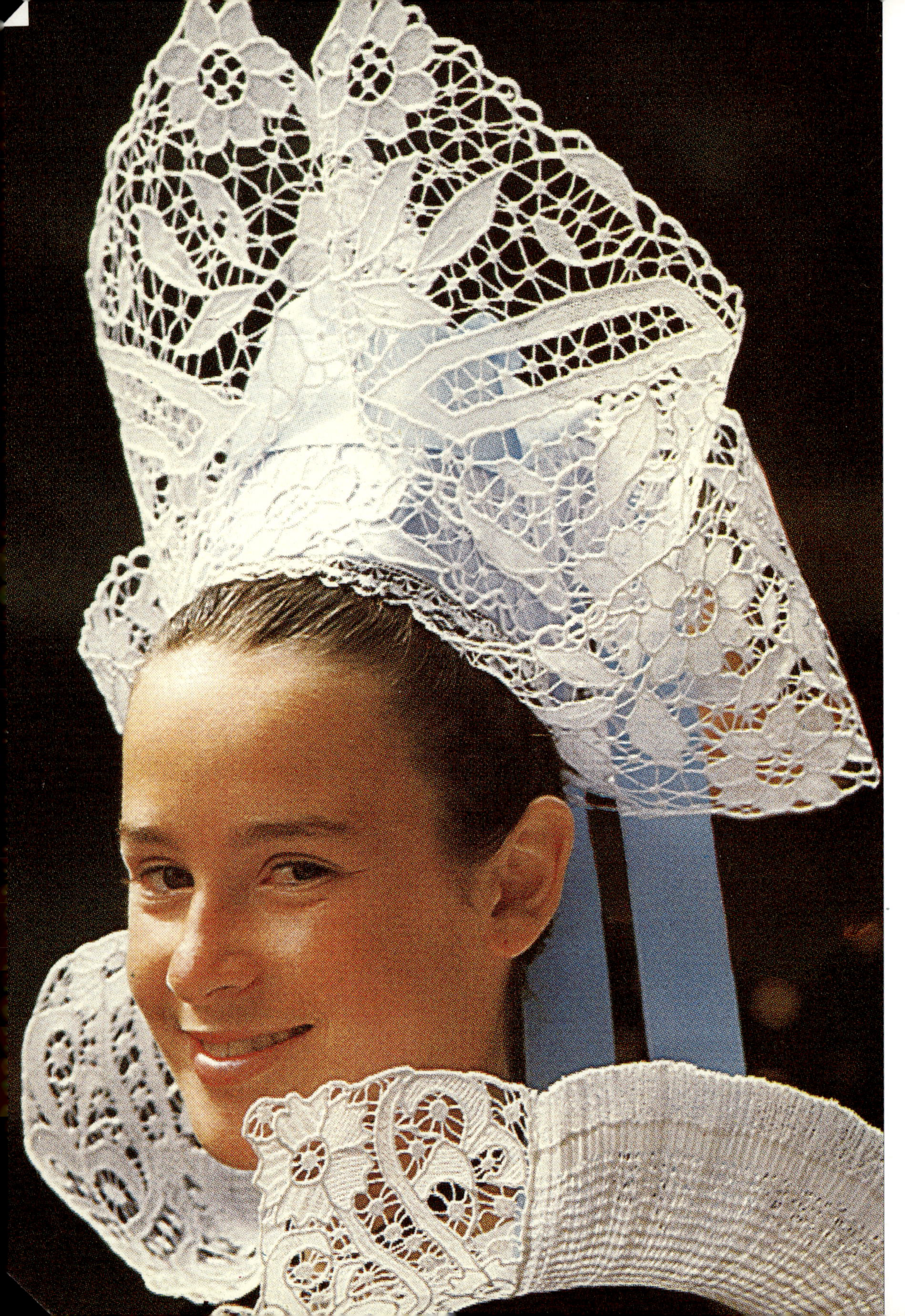

Fig. 114: Woman wearing a Fouesnant folk costume, from Brittany.

Lacy ornaments make the lady and the glassware look precious.

Fig. 115: Etched glass vase.

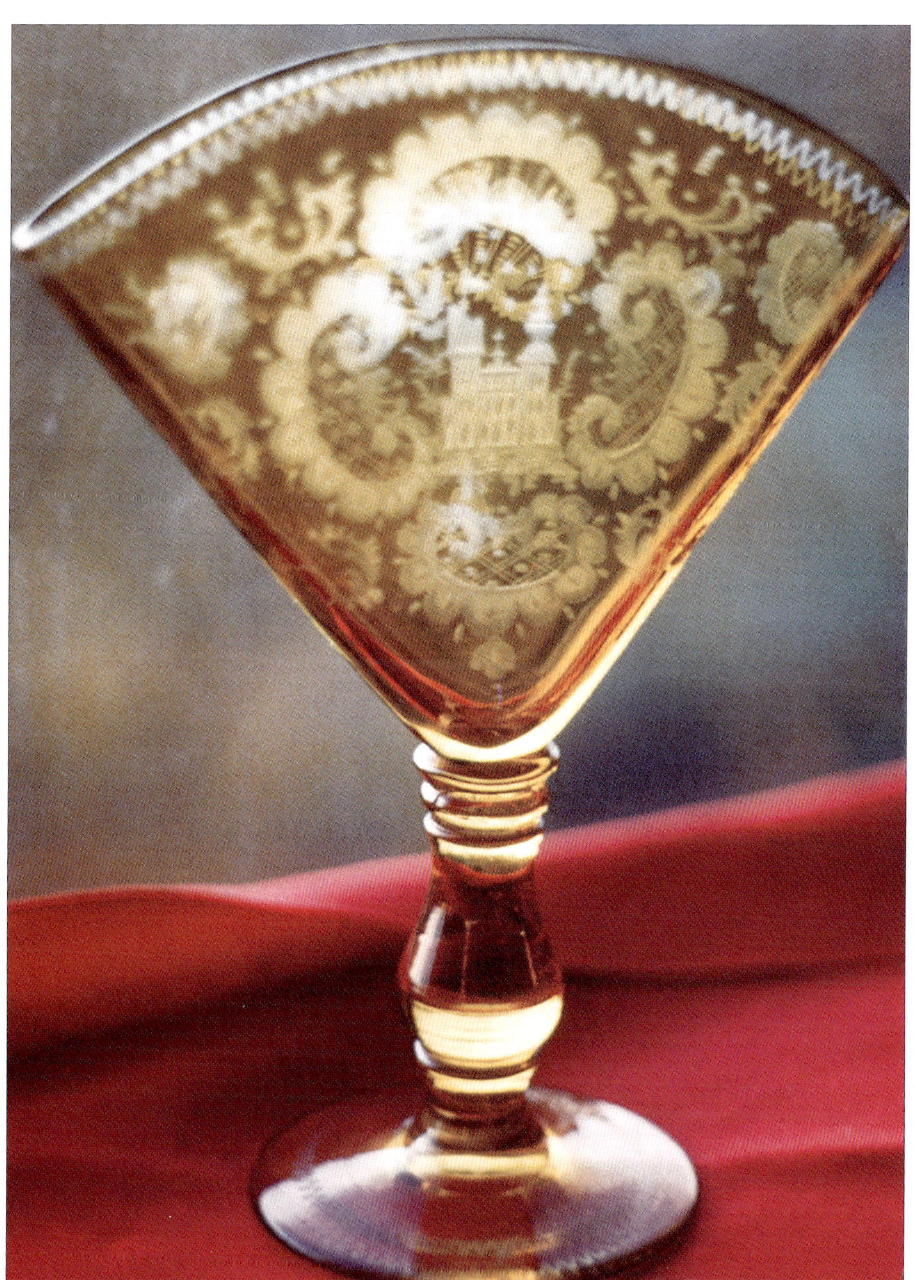

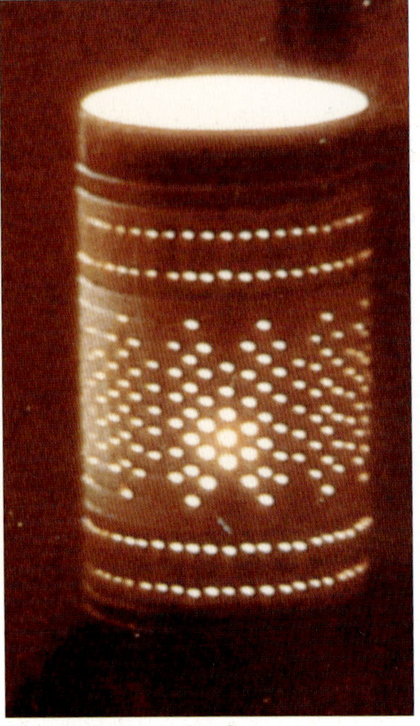

Fig. 116: Perforated tin lamp.

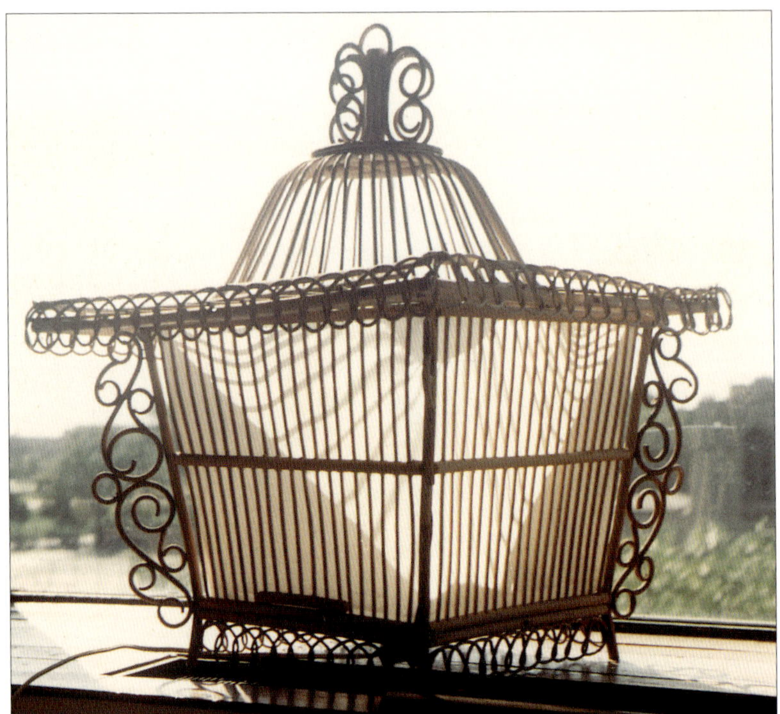

Fig. 117: Bird cage lamp.

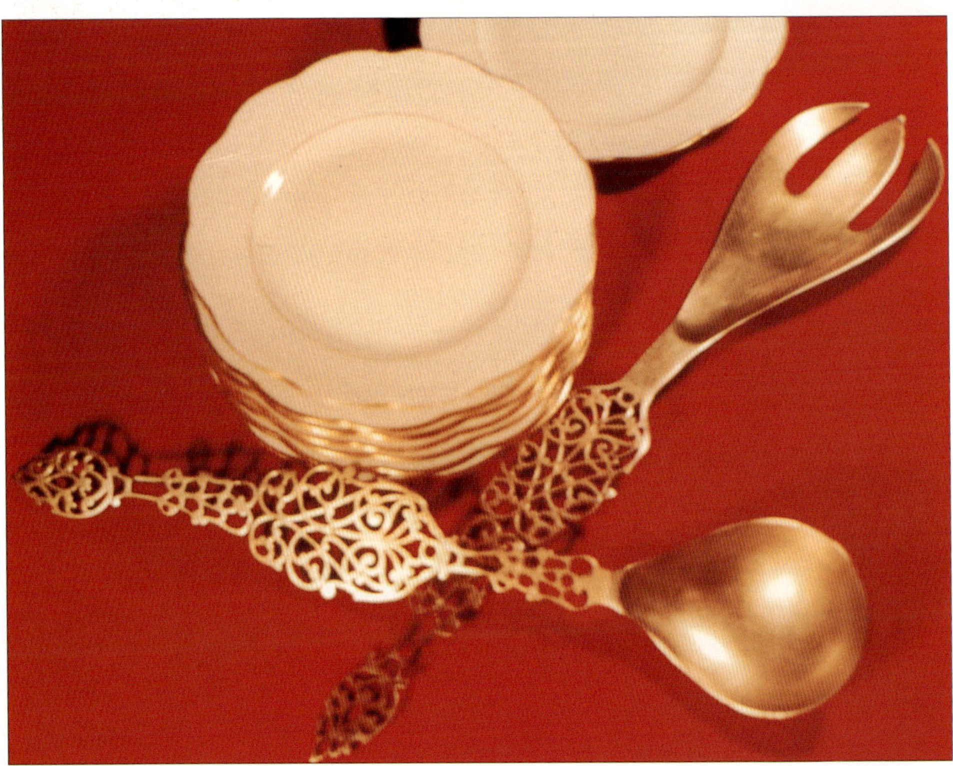

Fig. 118: Perforated serving utensils.

These are shapes broken through by many little holes to look like lace.

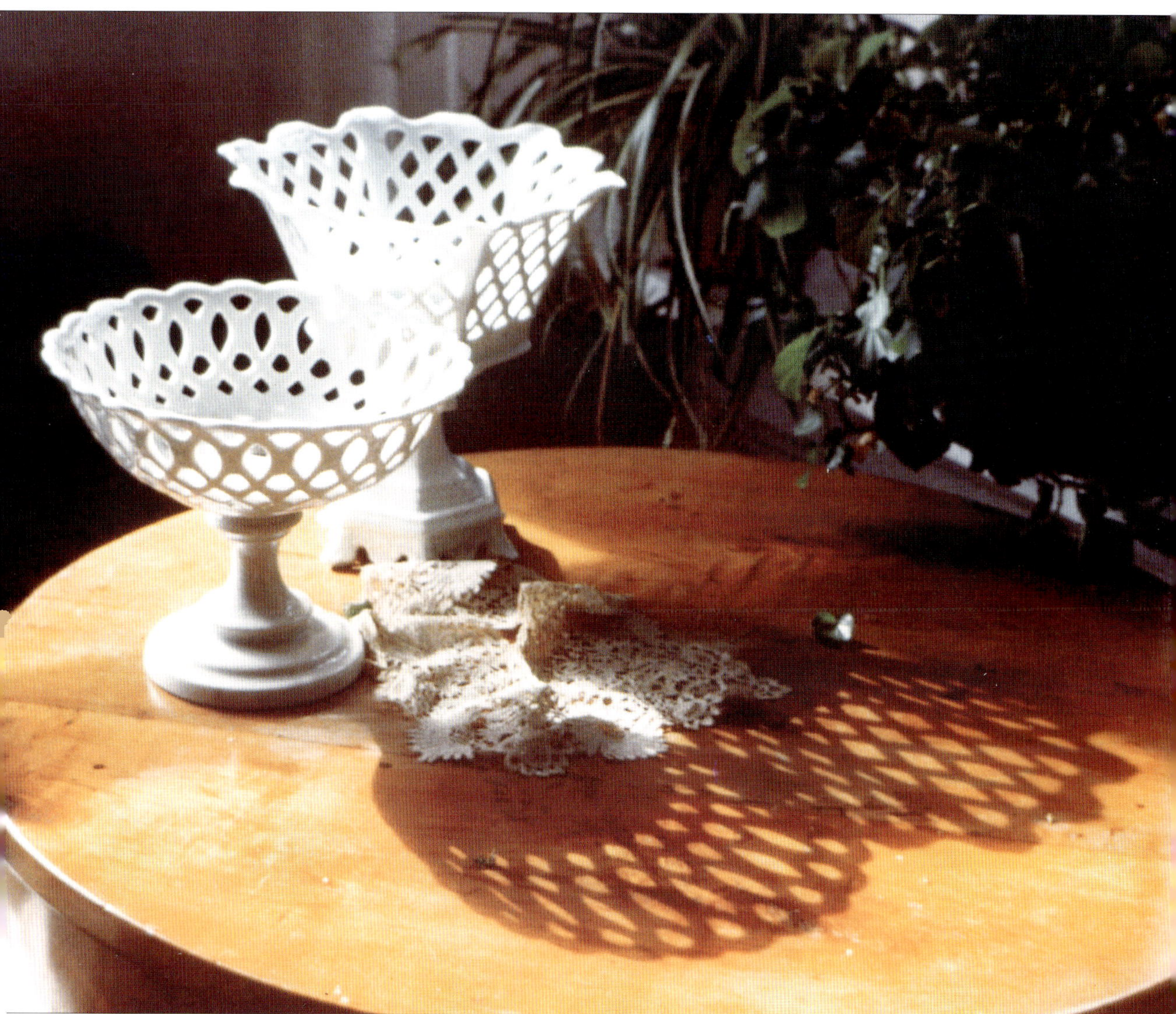

Fig. 119: Perforated porcelain bowls.

Contours: Complete and Incomplete Forms

When shapes culminate in lively upper contours, like parts of the whole,

objects feel like growing things—seashells, pods or flowers. Imagine these objects with their tops cut off; they would no longer have as intimate a relationship to natural forms.

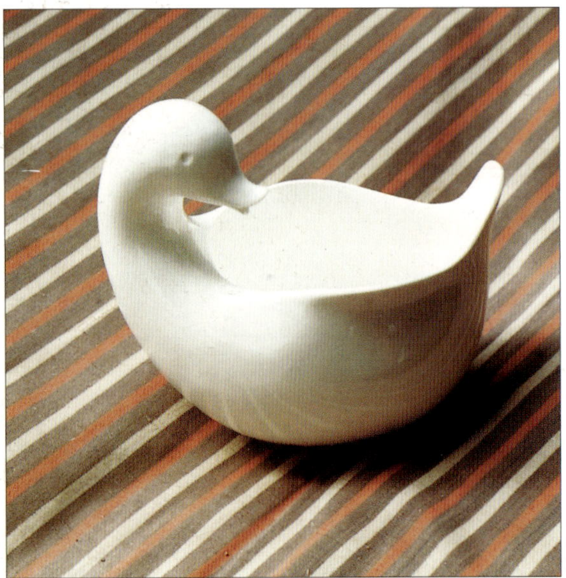

Fig. 120: "Bird" serving dish.
Western Stoneware, Eva Zeisel, 1953.

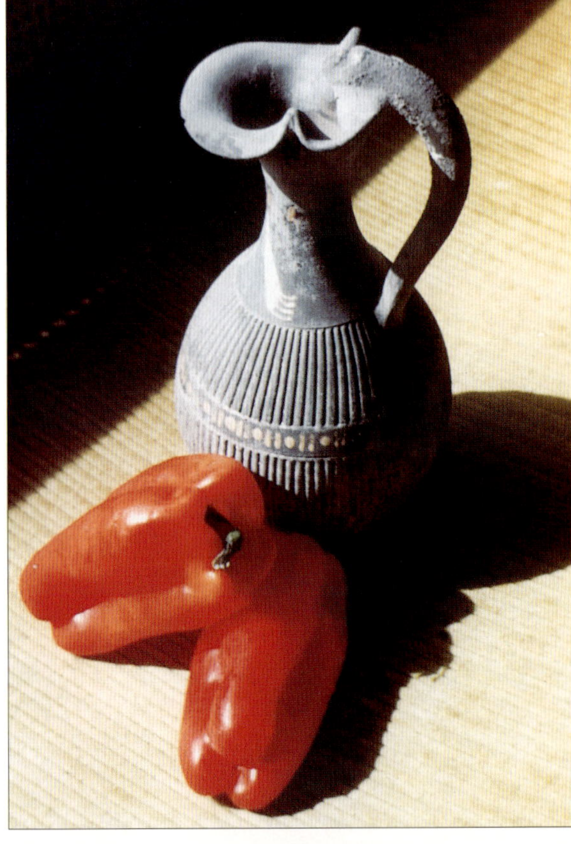

Fig. 121: Etruscan vase.

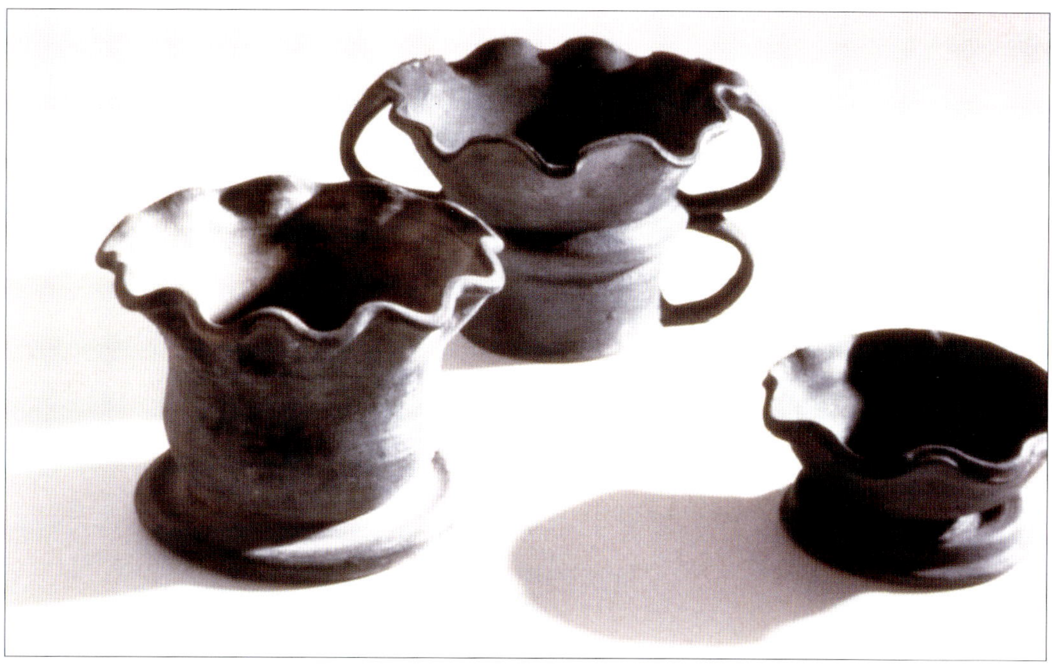

Fig. 122: Pottery bowls with wavy edges, Eva Zeisel, Budapest, 1926.

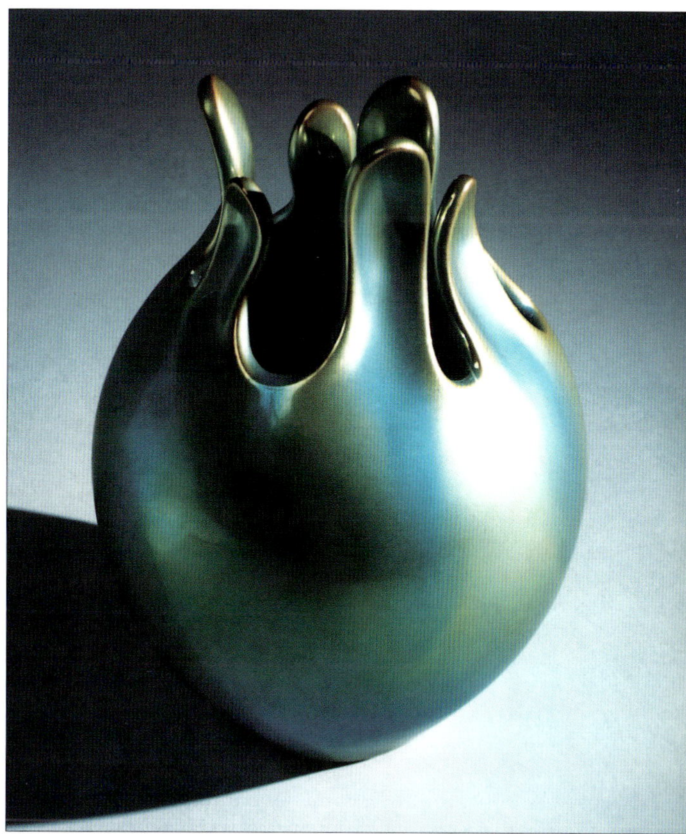

Fig. 123: Zsolnay vase, Eva Zeisel, 1983.

When buildings are conceived and created as complete sculptures or compositions, we know where they begin and where they end.

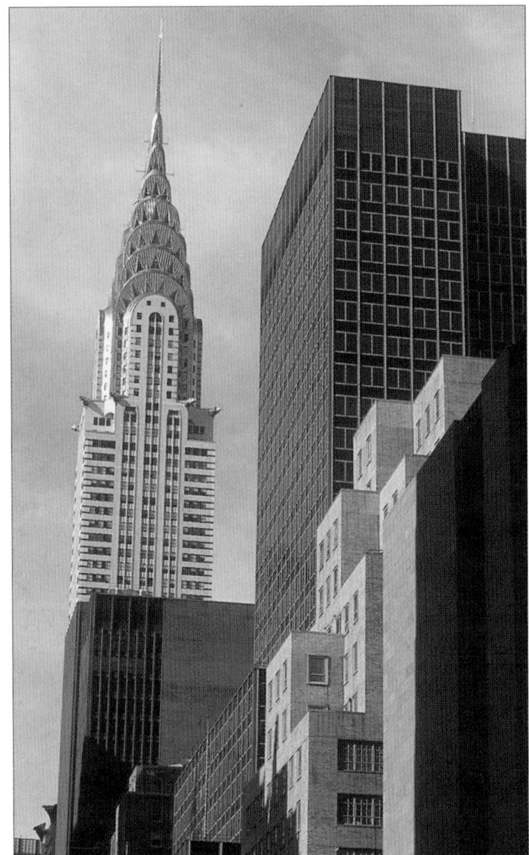

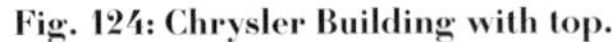

Fig. 124: Chrysler Building with top.

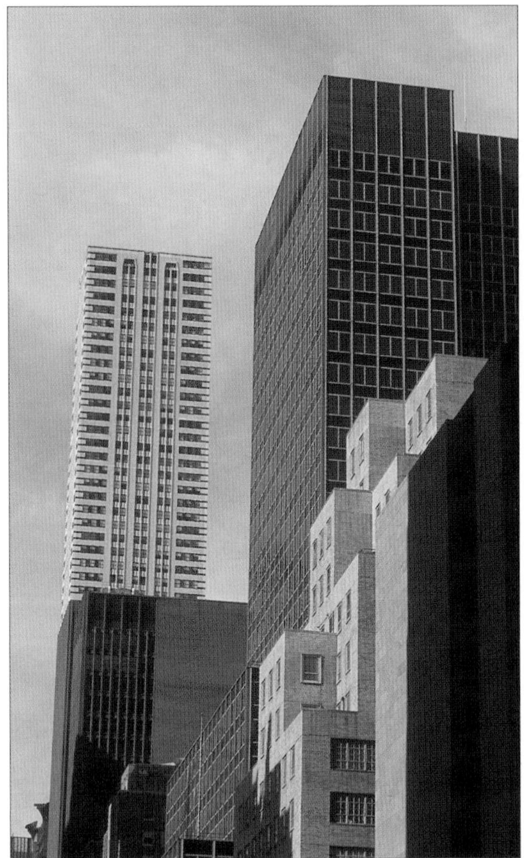

Fig. 125: Chrysler Building without top.

Buildings or inkwells or vases or pitchers which look as though they were cut off haphazardly seem incomplete, unfinished, unsatisfactory.

When vessels are rounded at the bottom, and not cut off, they too look complete, like fruits plucked from a tree. Sometimes the contents of a vessel complete its form.

Fig. 126: Apple with Riverside China sugar bowl, Eva Zeisel, 1946–47.

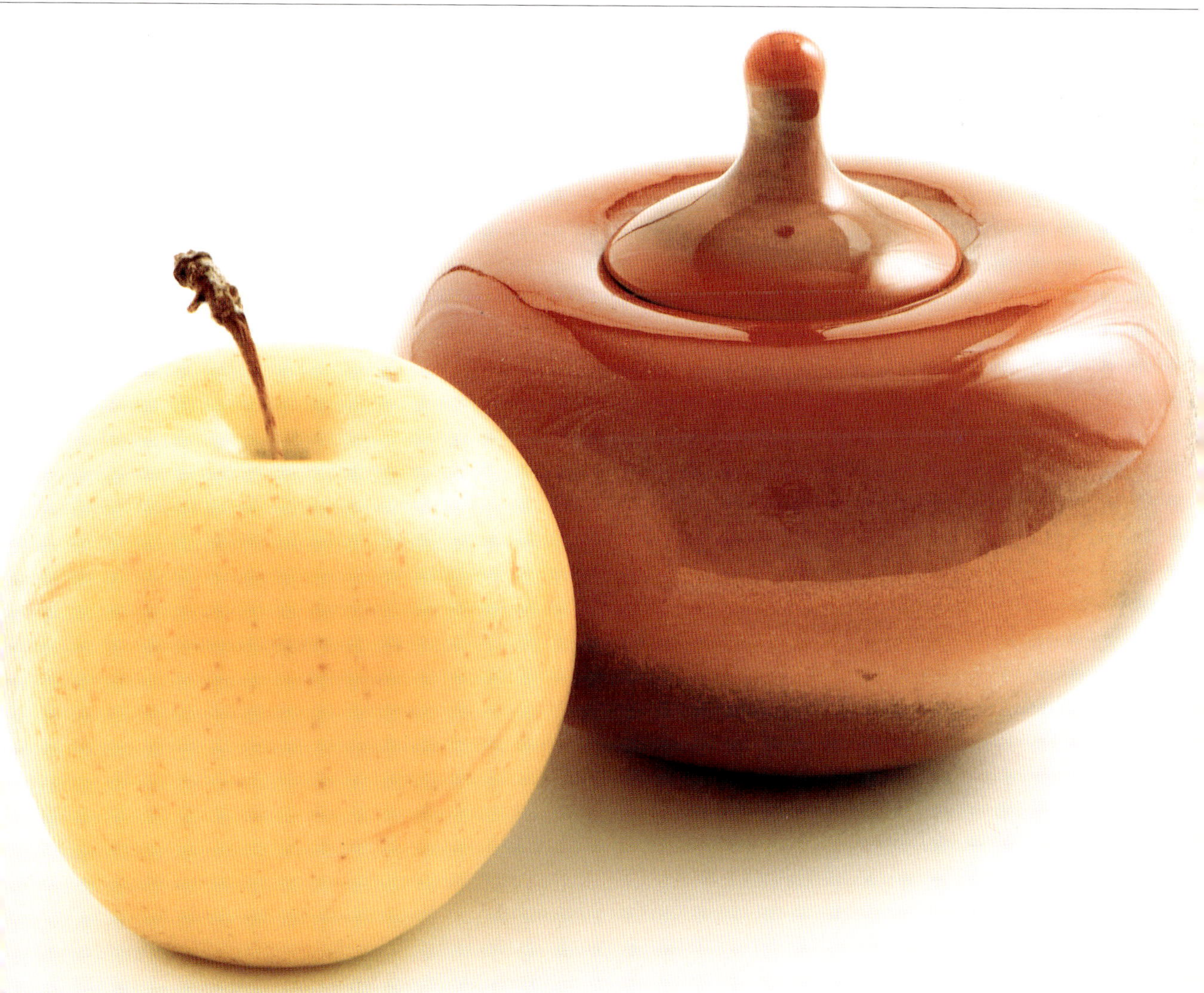

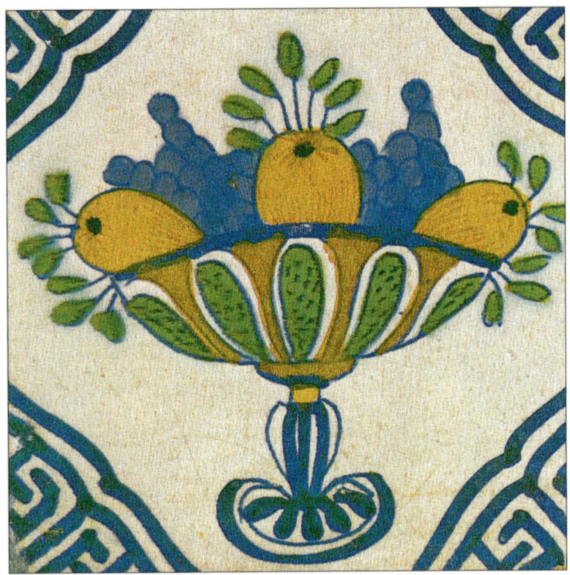

Fig. 127: Bowl painted on tile.

The contour of the fruit completes the form of this bowl, painted on a tile.

The empty glass bowl speaks clearly of emptiness. Its content completes it.

When designing an open bowl, the inside shape must be modeled so that it does not show a gaping emptiness.

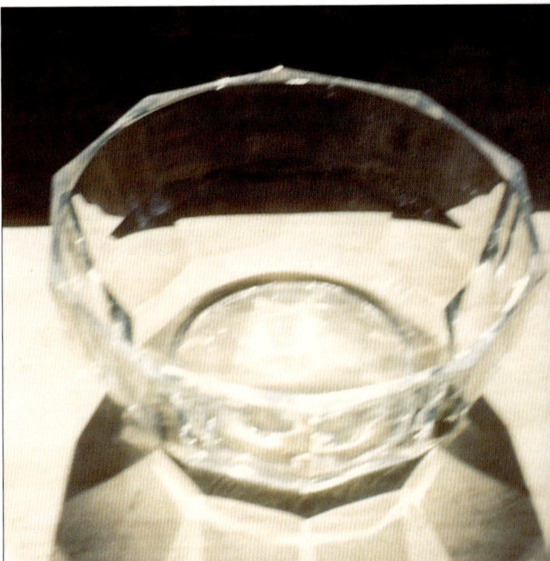

Fig. 128: Empty glass bowl.

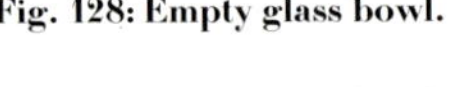

Fig. 129: Filled glass bowl.

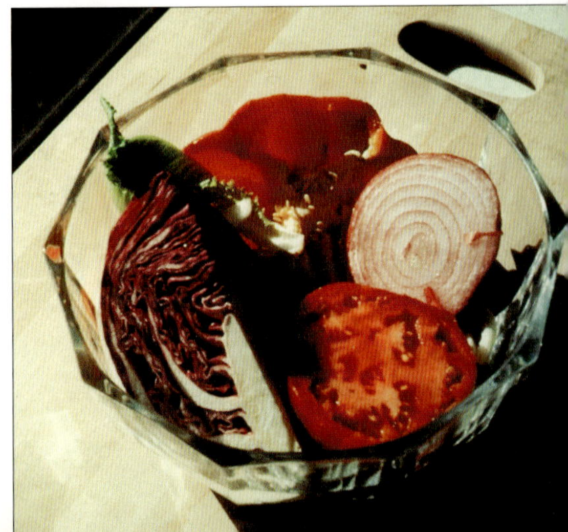

Togetherness

I have noticed in my long working life that I have never photographed an object alone, but always with others that are sympathetic to it. I have rarely designed objects that were meant to stand alone. My designs have family relationships. They are either mother and child, siblings, or cousins. They might not have identical lines, but there is always a family relationship.

Many things come in pairs, groups or sets, like salt and pepper shakers, vinegar and oil cruets, dinnerware, or furniture. Other forms should fit together, such as the buildings in a street or town square. In any case, objects are never alone, except, perhaps, in museums. There is always something nearby, and if no other object is around, there is always a natural or artificial horizon, where the "sky" meets the object.

Fig. 130: Family relationship:
Hallcraft/Tomorrow's Classic.
open creamer, cruet, ladle.
Eva Zeisel, 1952.

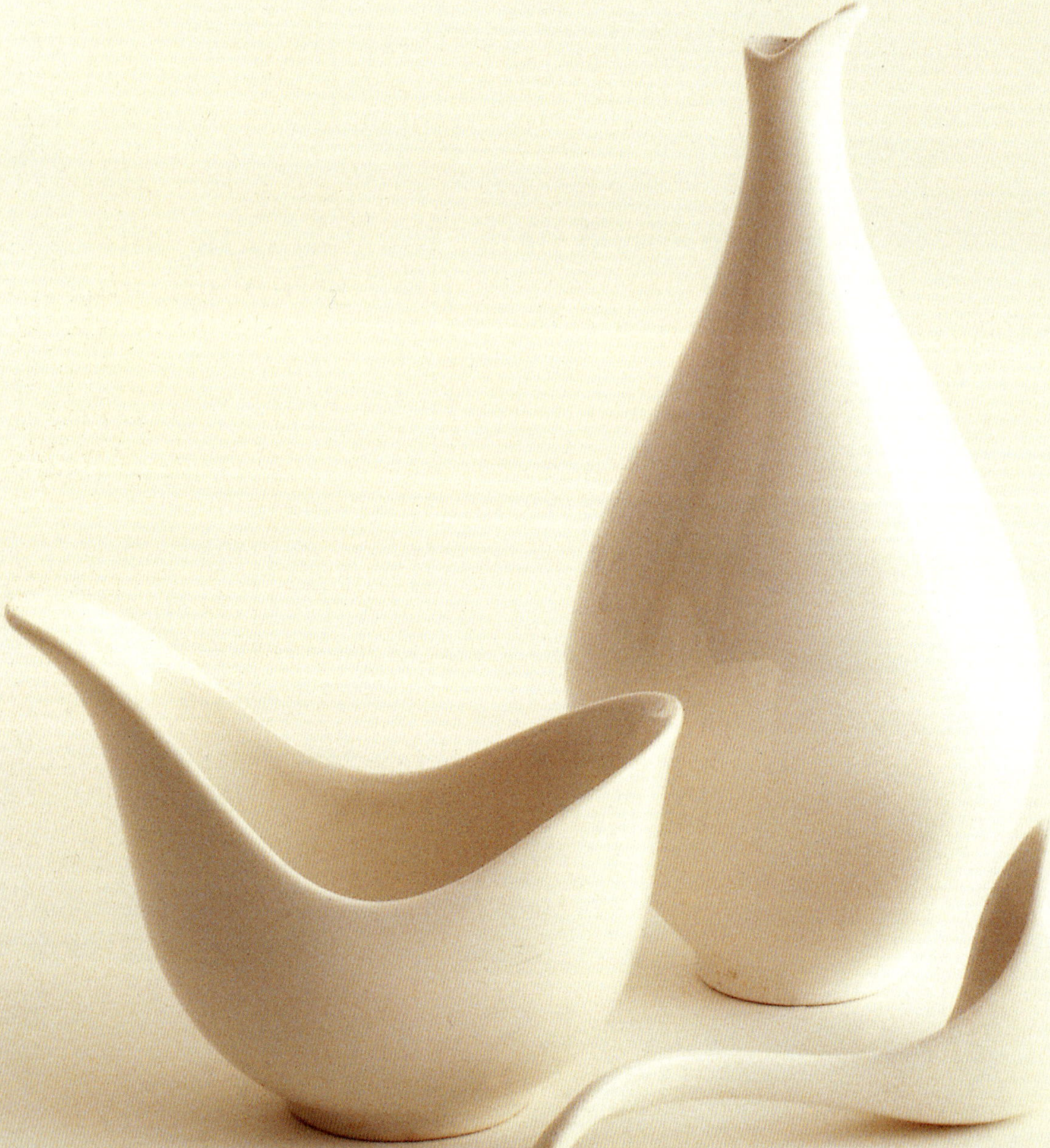

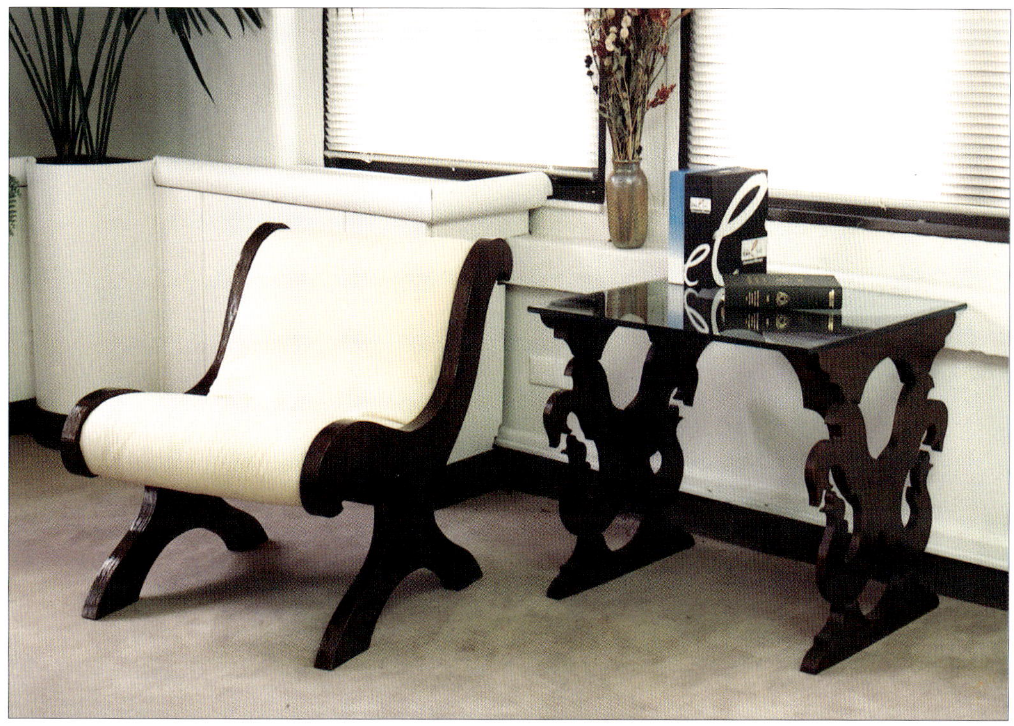

Fig. 131: Furniture designed for Brownstone Publishers by Eva Zeisel, 1990s.

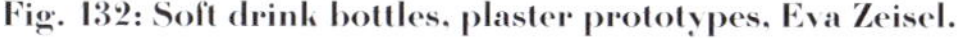

Fig. 132: Soft drink bottles, plaster prototypes, Eva Zeisel.

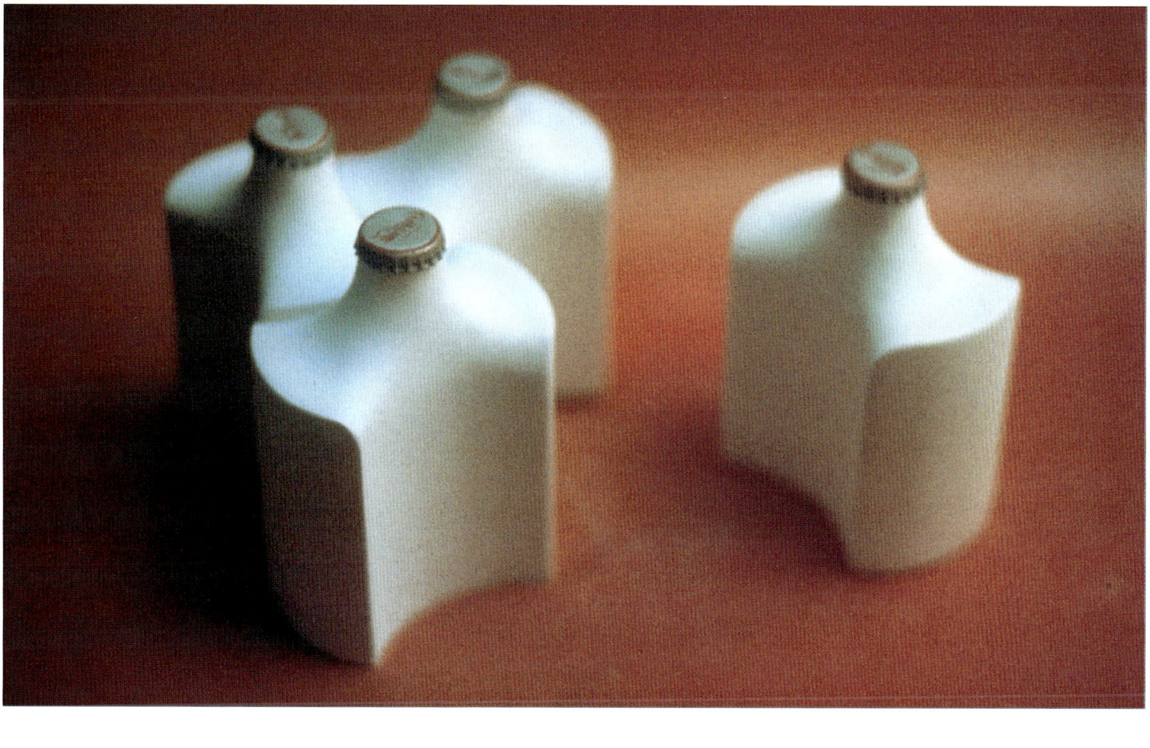

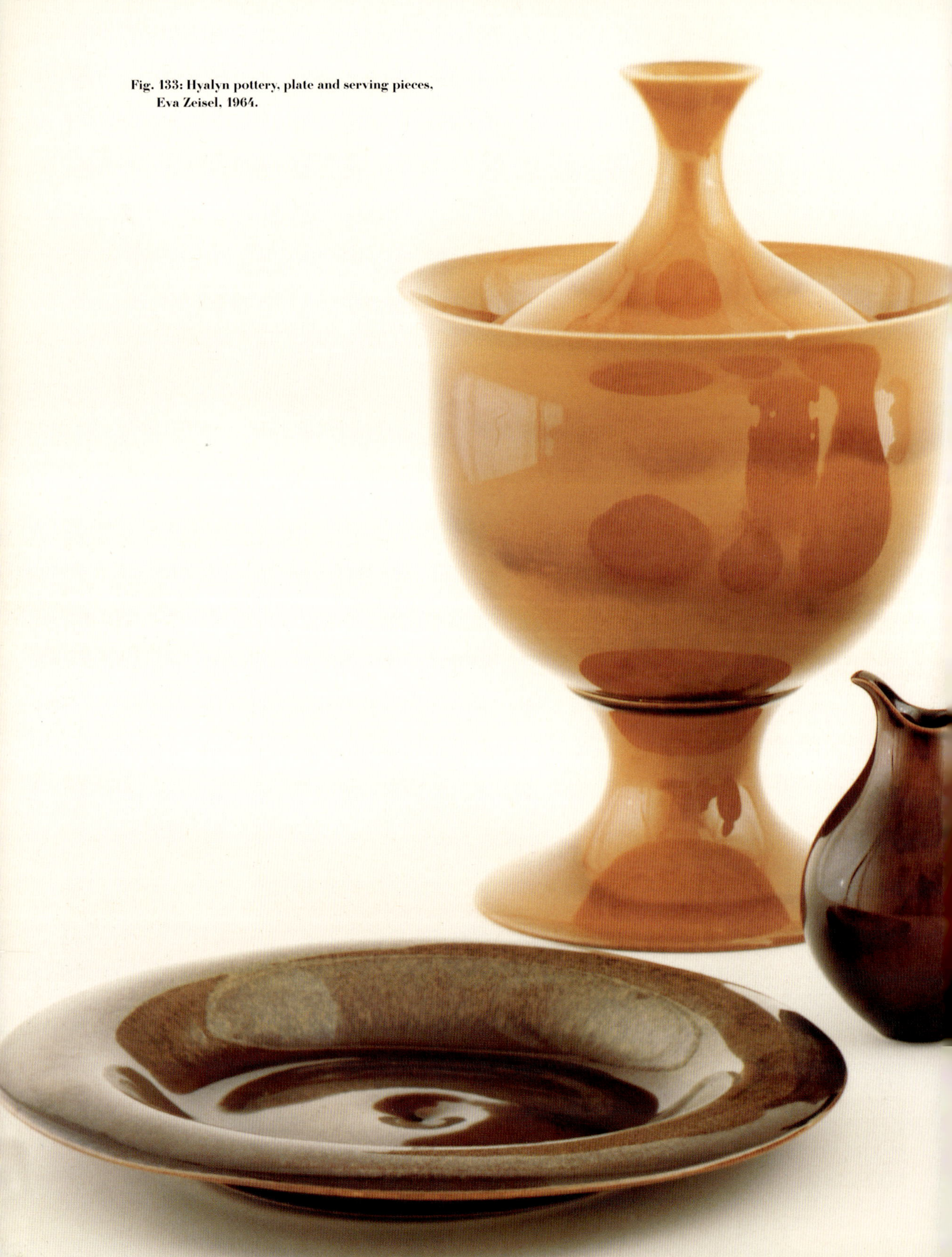

Fig. 133: Hyalyn pottery, plate and serving pieces, Eva Zeisel, 1964.

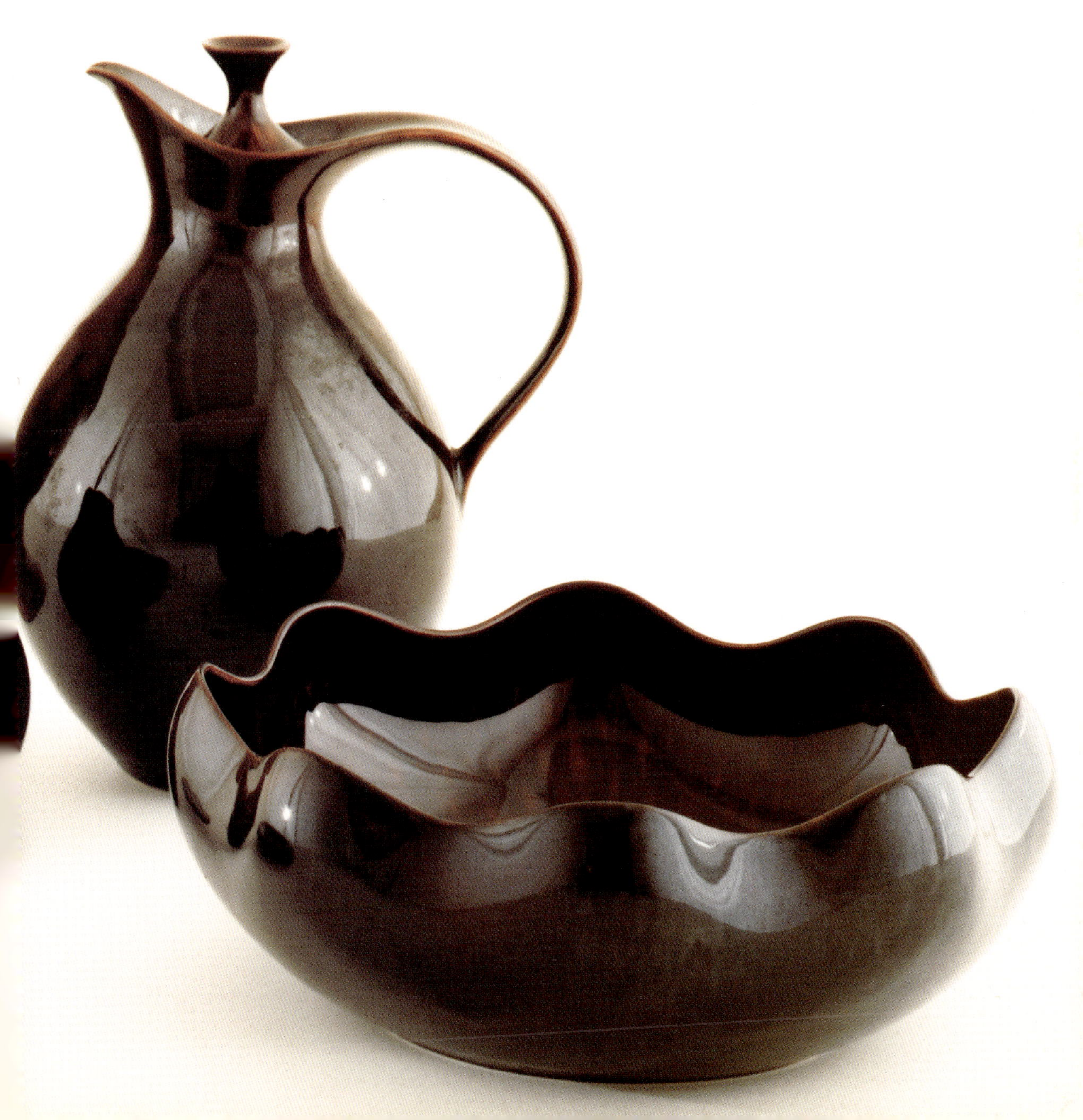

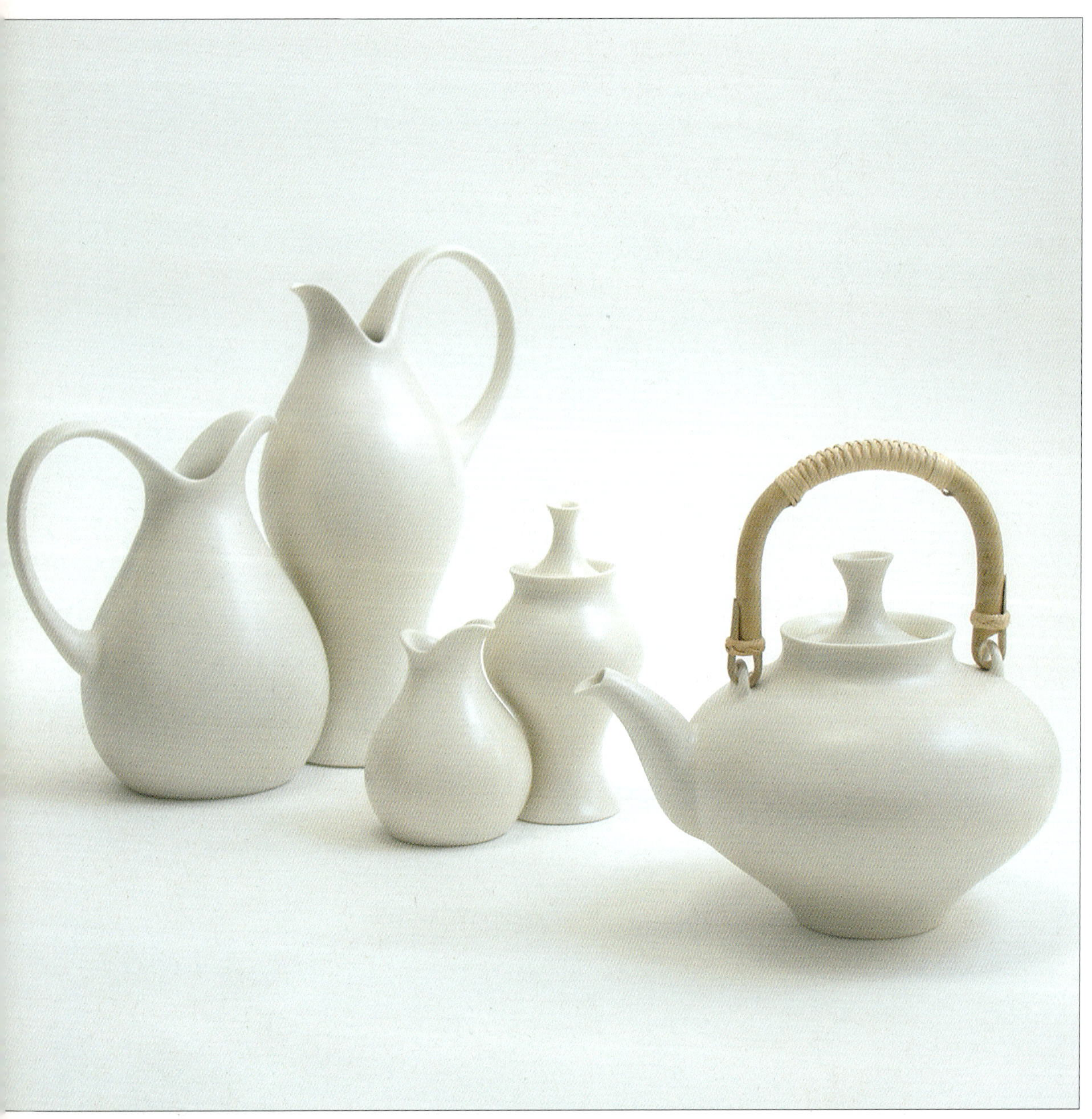

Fig. 134: "Eva" pitcher and tea set for KleinReid, 2002.

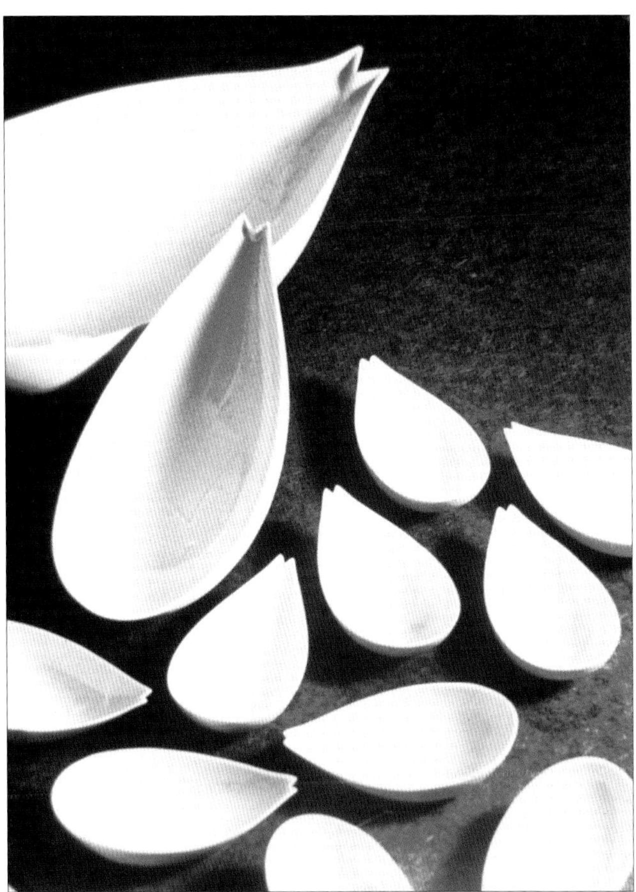

Fig. 135: Riverside China bowls. Eva Zeisel, 1946–47.

Fig. 136: Hallcraft/Century, serving bowls. Eva Zeisel, 1957.

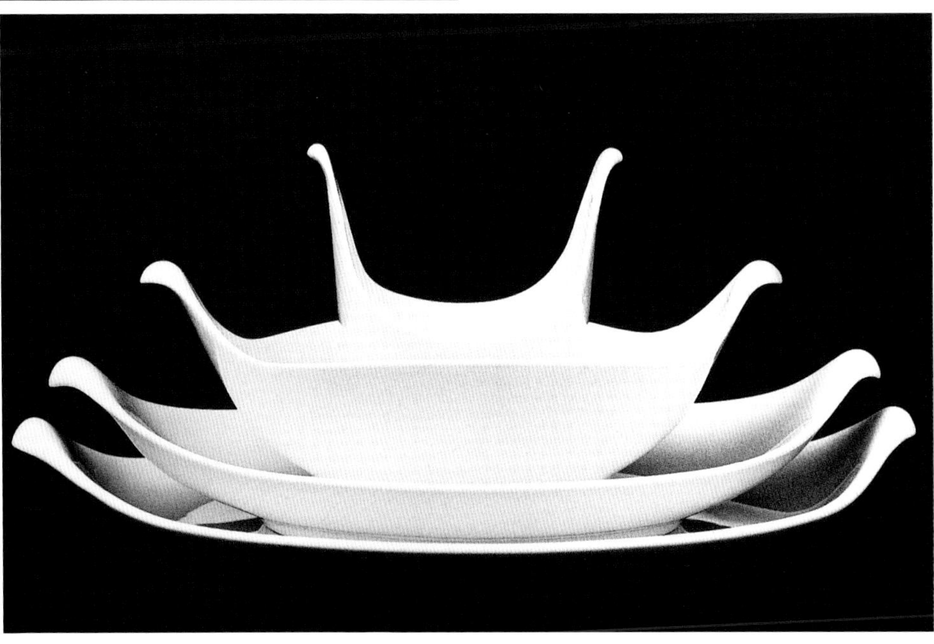

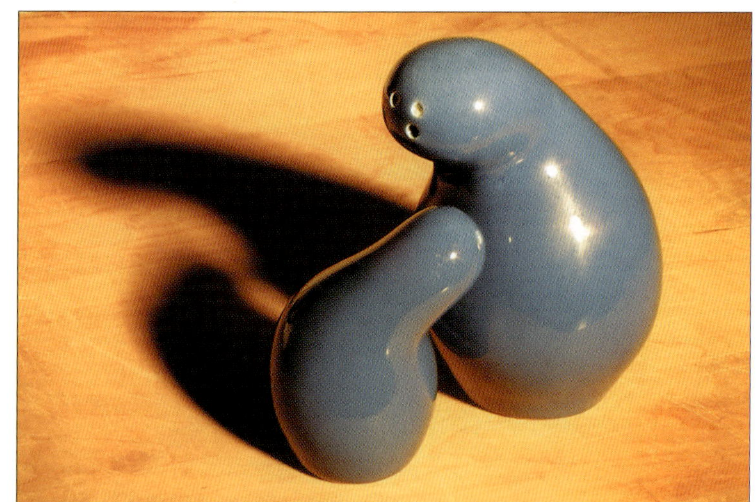

Fig. 137: Town and Country, salt and pepper shakers (Red Wing), Eva Zeisel, 1946.

Fig. 138: Town and Country cruets, Eva Zeisel, 1946.

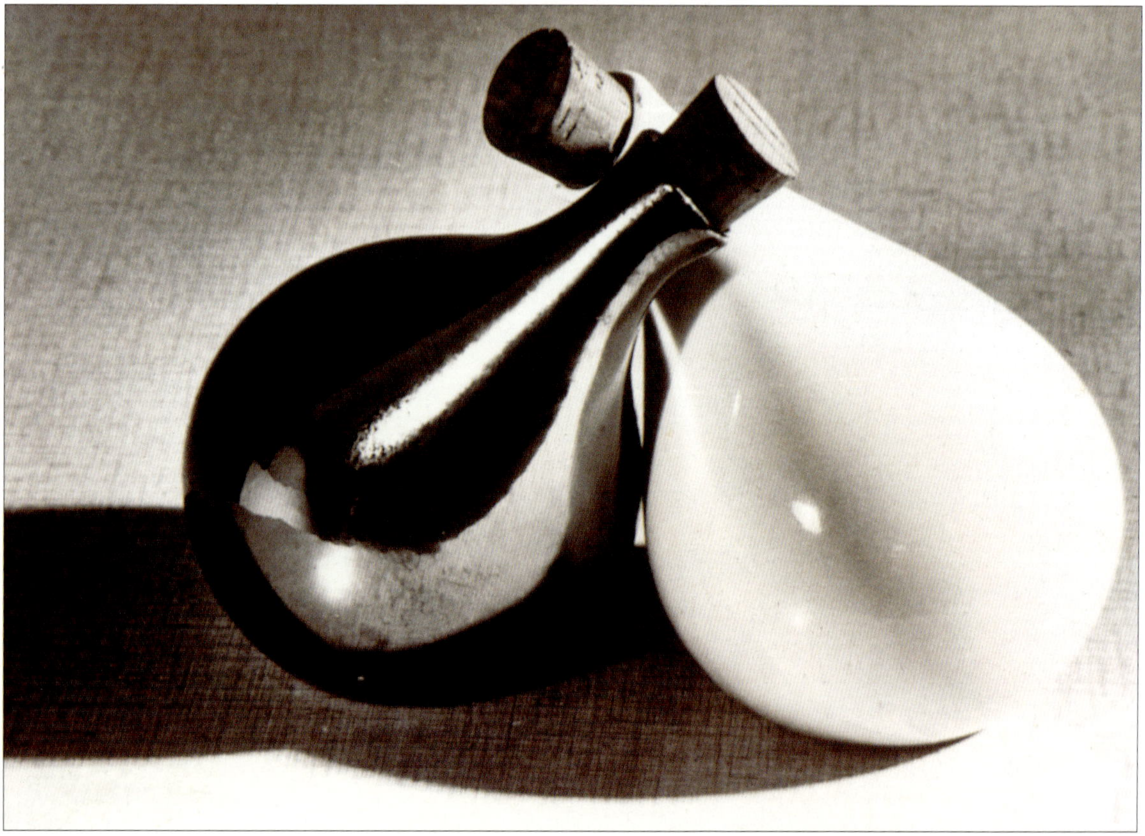

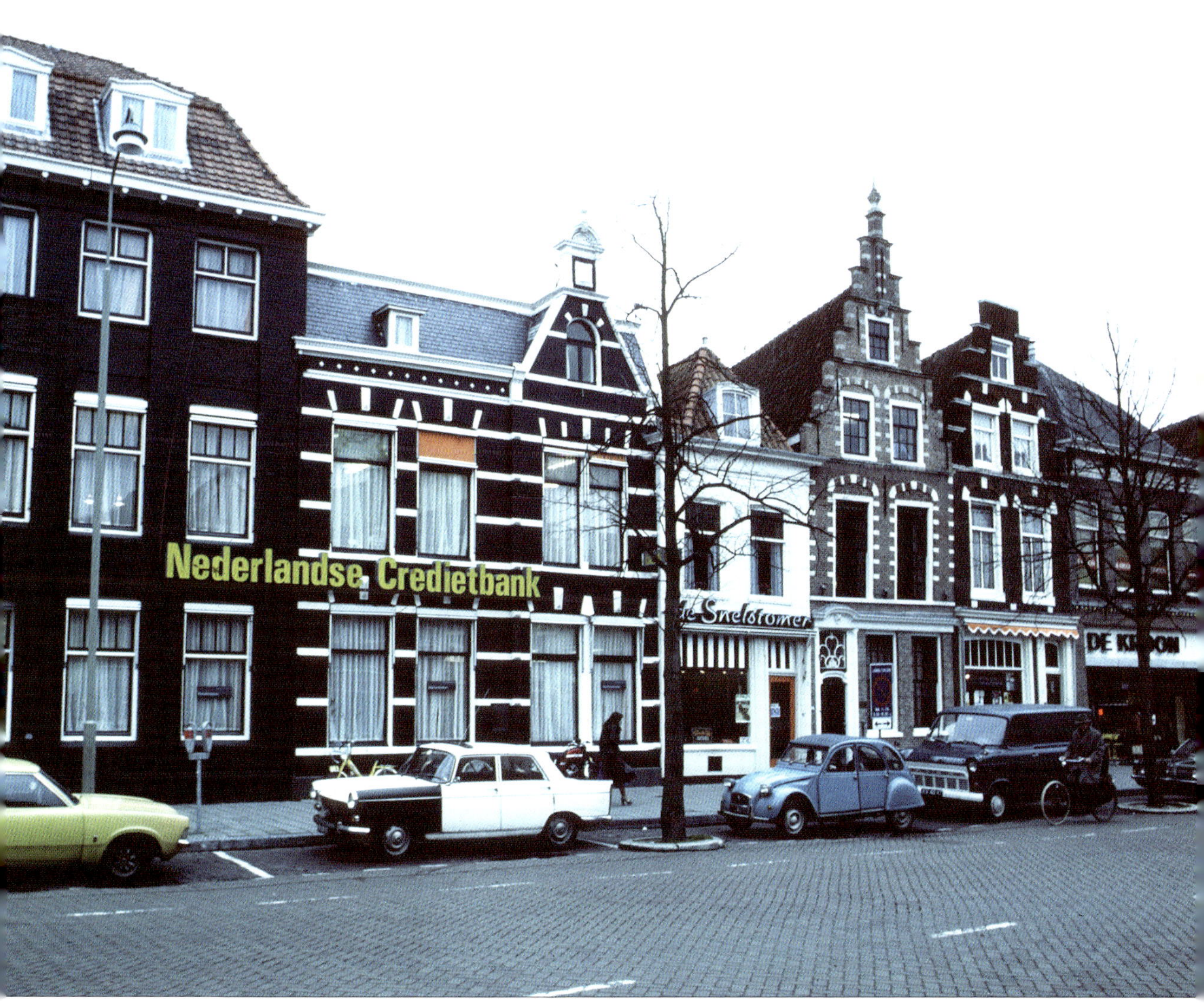

Fig. 139: Dutch street.

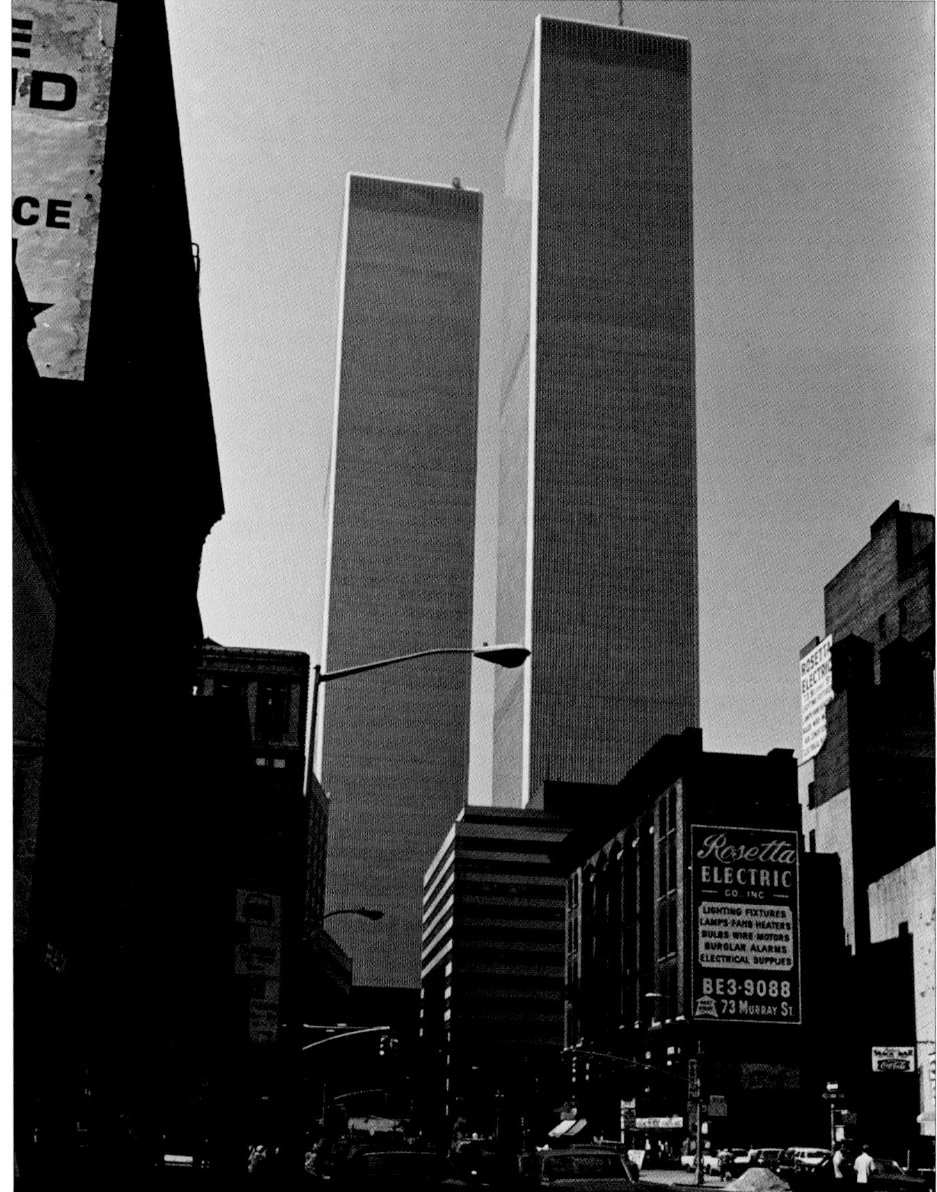

Fig. 140: World Trade Center.

There is also a spatial relationship between the object and its neighbor or neighbors. The two World Trade Center towers were often separated by a narrow, elegant bar of light. The two towers also seemed to keep each other company, as if each would be lonely without its twin.

Forms that one sees in relation to others may be made to appear disturbing and hostile, such as when a modern building or other object seems to want to demonstrate its newness, its modern style, or when its maker wants to make a statement, perhaps declaring his or her displeasure with older, neighboring styles.

When we make a thing and work on it without considering where and with whom it will ultimately live we often forget to tone down its over-interesting features, its novelty, because we are thinking primarily of ourselves as designers, because we want to show our skill. Buildings and other objects made under these circumstances are often disturbingly out of harmony with the context into which they are finally placed.

When you make something and want to put it into a specific place, it is often difficult to make its lines and form share the character of its companions.

Fig. 141: Detail from cover of *Architecture in Context: Fitting New Buildings with Old*, by Brent C. Brolin.

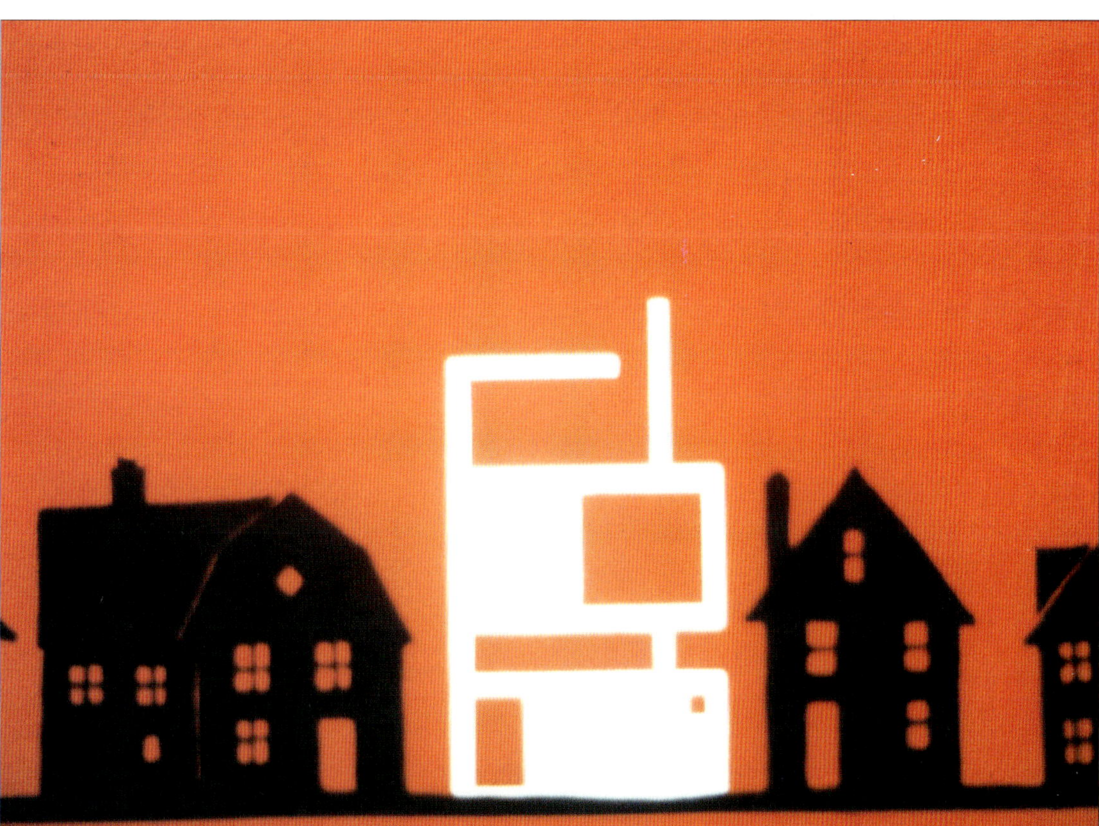

Functional Objects

Before starting our project, we should define the purpose of our work. The aim of a design might be to give pleasure to the eye, comfort to the body, or ease of use. Of course, handles, spouts, and other such aids should do what they are supposed to do, but a fine designer might add elegance, refinement, and pleasure to the handling of plates or eating utensils—the pleasure of touch or balance, the feeling of bulk or the finesse of thinness—whatever game the designer devises to play with the audience's senses.

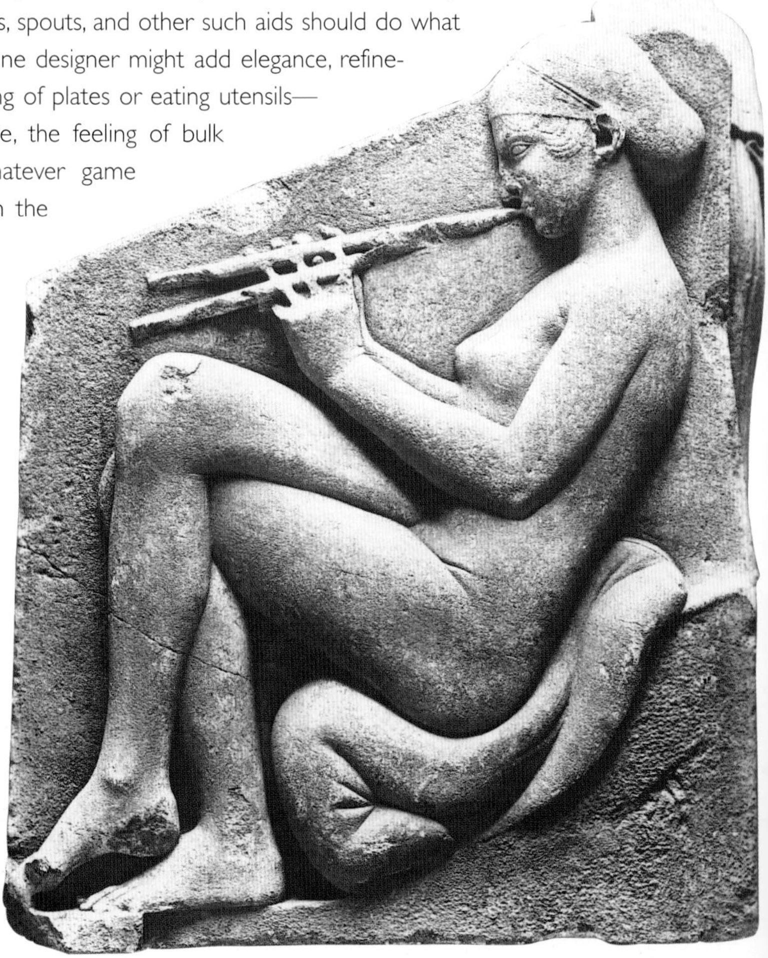

Fig. 142: Comfort to the body: classical flute player resting on cushion.

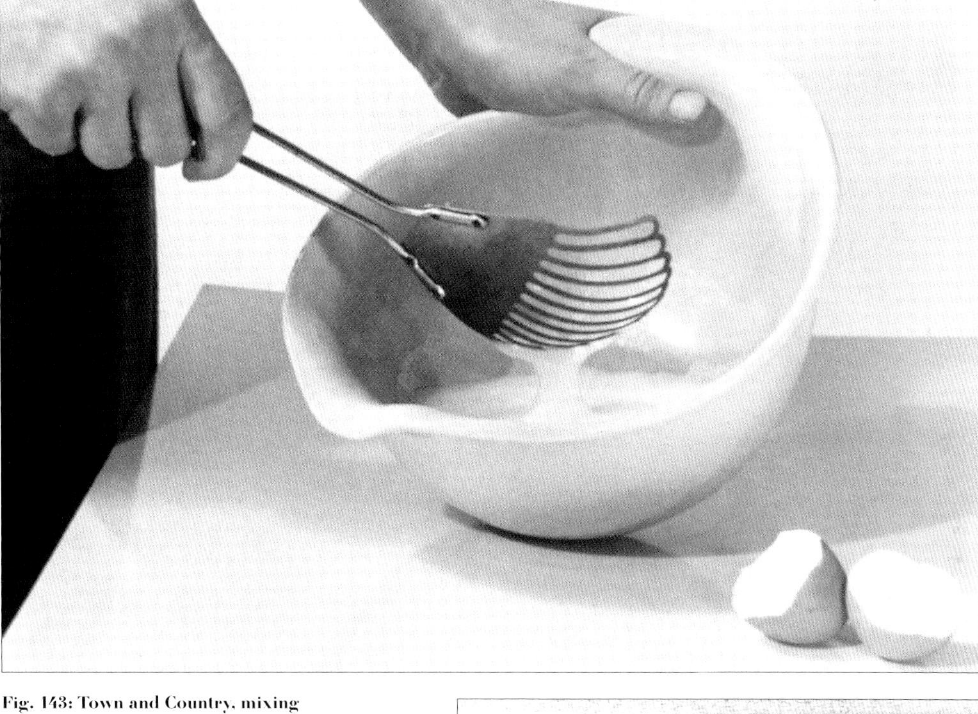

Fig. 143: Town and Country, mixing bowl (Red Wing), Eva Zeisel, 1946.

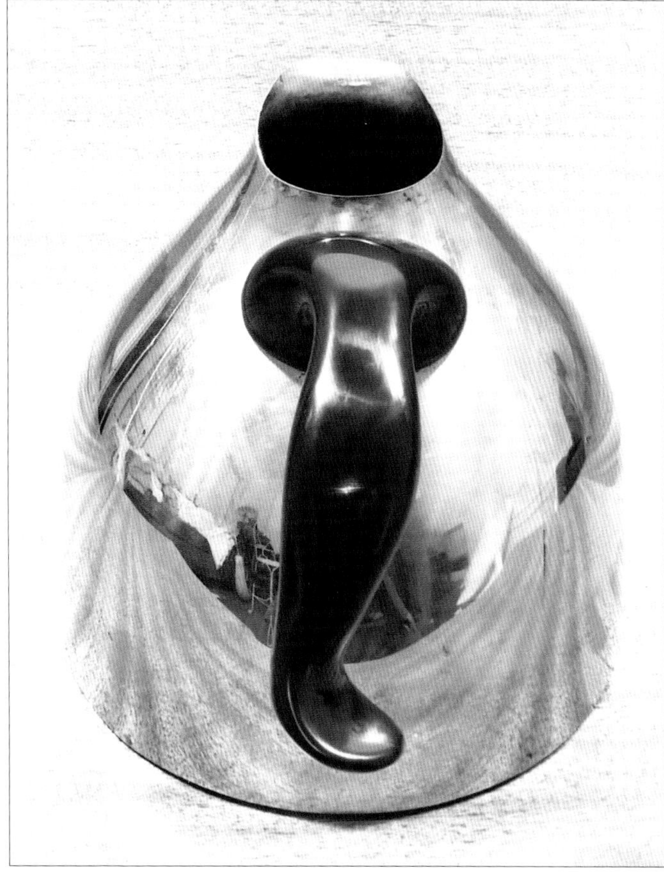

Fig. 144: Prototype stainless steel pitcher for General Mills, Eva Zeisel, 1948.

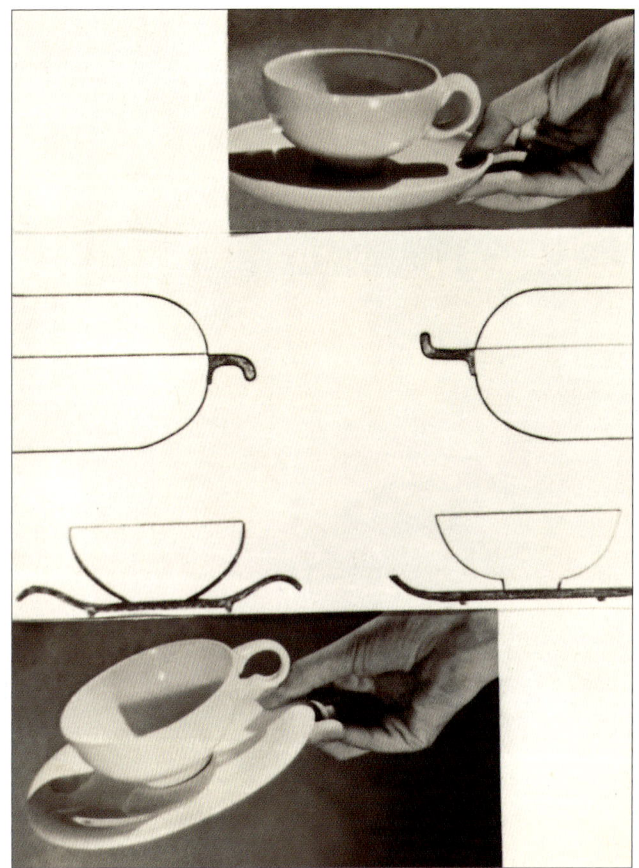

Fig. 145: Drawing and inset photo of easy-to-handle saucer.

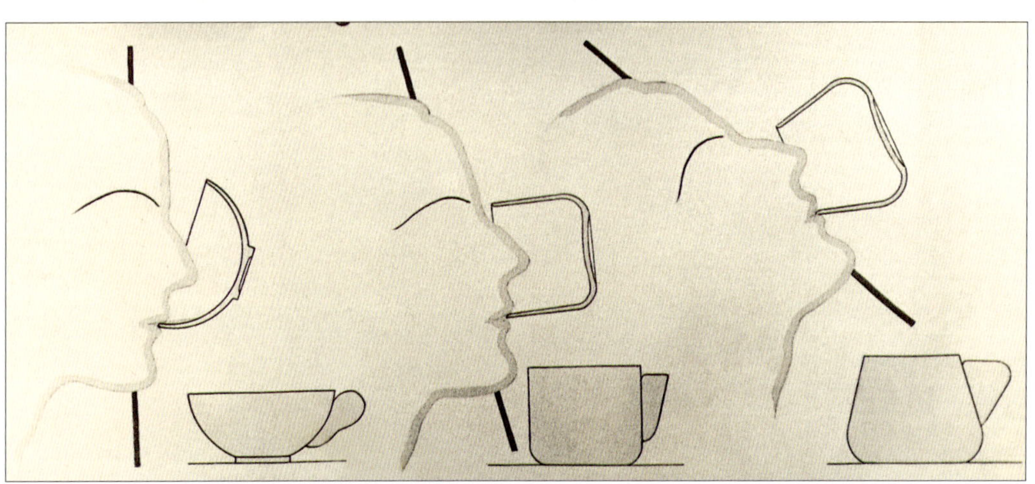

Fig. 146: Shapes that make cups easier or harder to drink from.

The designer's task is not always primarily the obvious usefulness of his project. It might be its visual appeal, novelty, process of its production, price, mechanism, etc. Keeping the aim of the project in mind, the designer's attitude is that of giving a gift of her or his work to the client. Whether beauty or function is the primary purpose of our task depends on the intent of the designer and/or client.

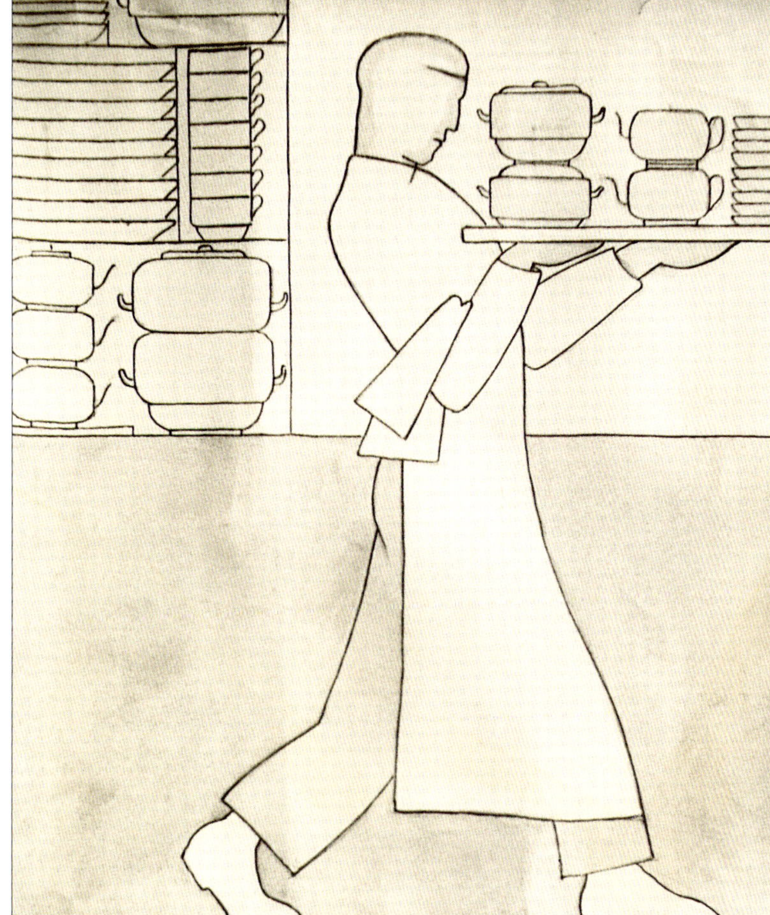

Fig. 147: Stackable dishes.

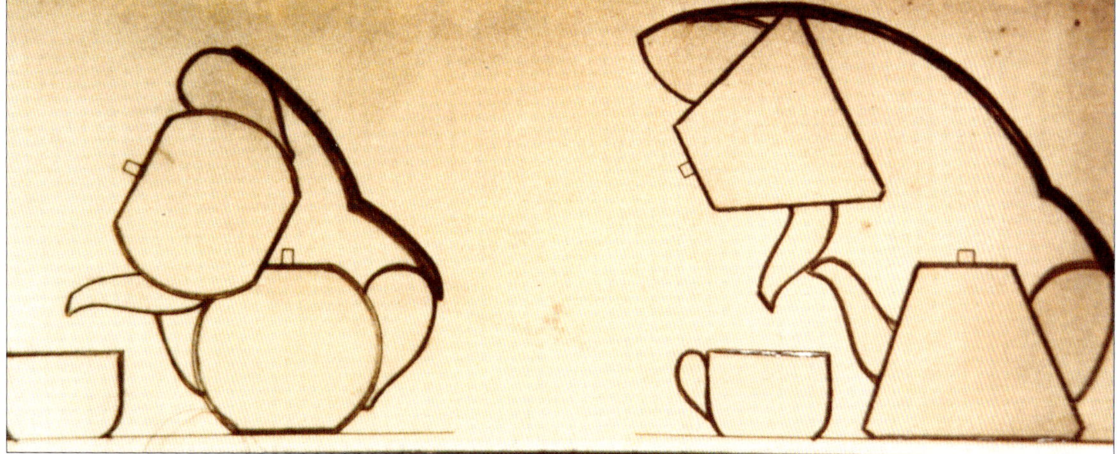

Fig. 148: Teapot more and less easy to pour from.

Since the beginning of the twentieth century, a style has developed in Europe and America that could be called "functional" style. This style is a popularization of a principle of the modern movement. One recognizes the style by its geometric forms, clean, uncluttered lines, and what appears to be a clear delineation of structure.

The buildings and objects designed in this style are not as a rule easier to use than buildings or objects of other times or other styles. They are, however, generally referred to as "useful objects," and their usefulness is considered their beauty.

Yet, hardly any useful objects are truly necessary. In fact, most people do not even use what we consider such "useful" objects as forks and knives and beds. Such useful items are certainly not self-explanatory, nor are they always understood outside of our own culture: Yemenite Jews, when offered beds in Israel, lay down under them. And, in Japan, I was stunned to be given chopsticks to eat fried eggs.

Most people do not sit on chairs or eat with forks, and the taboos connected with the use of knives far outnumber their "proper" uses. In fact, the use of useful objects, even in our own culture, must be carefully taught in childhood, as they are often instruments of proper manners rather than strict utility, and therefore their faulty employment exposes social incompetence.

It seems clear, then, that the so-called useful objects surrounding us are not so much needed for daily use as for cultural accoutrements. Designers of useful objects take into consideration the direct physical contact between the user and the object. The comfortable accommodation of the palm around a handle, or glass, or when raising a vessel was the purpose of many functional designs. But we do not wrap our hand around the body of a glass when we propose a toast. We hold it daintily, by its stem. The polite elegant handling of things in social intercourse is an age-old function of most utensils associated with food. Designers of the "functional" tradition frequently fail to understand that one function of an object can be its ceremonial use.

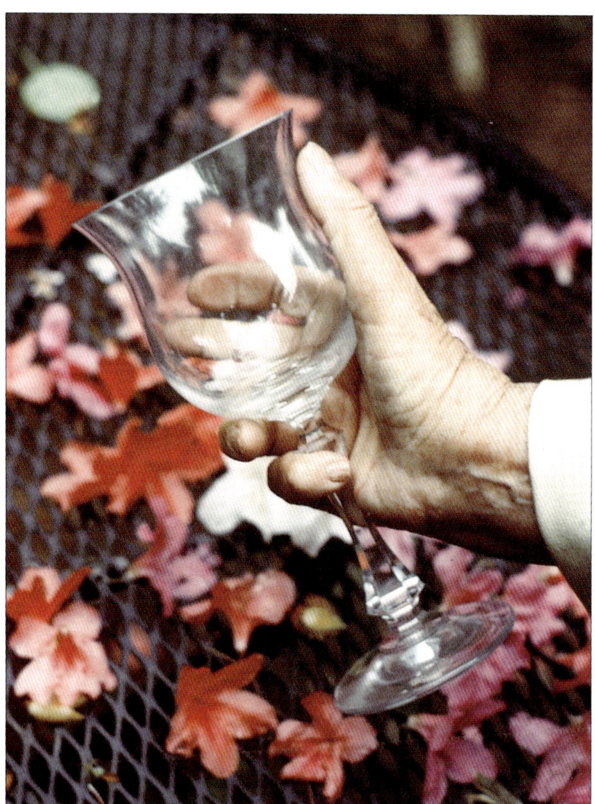

Fig. 149: The wrong way to hold a wine glass.

Fig. 150: Serving sake.

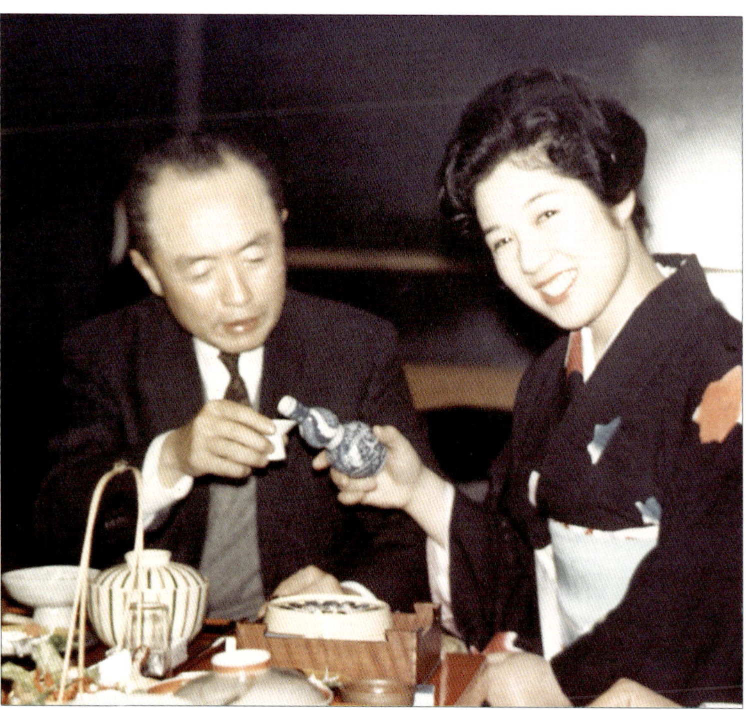

Functional design considerations can also help direct or refine our social behavior. We read in Atheus, a fourth century B.C. writer on social customs, that it would be impolite to serve a country dweller from a vessel meant for a city dweller, or that a cup which you cannot put down might be conducive to longer social contact than one which has a base on which it can rest. There are many social situations in which the form of the object induces conversation, and other situations in which privacy, closeness, etc., can be influenced by design.

We should by now be past the more primitive notions of "functional" style and should think of elegance, charm, grace and the tender use of objects, the soft-spoken relationship between things and us. Although designers frequently have to decide between considerations of use and harmonious design, objects should be so designed that one can use them without any particular attention and without giving much thought to them.

These objects are truly and specifically functional. The halberd is designed for the efficient dispatching of the enemy. The famous Kothon, the use of which is described by Herodotus and other ancient writers, was used by campaigning soldiers to filter mud and other impurities from river water.

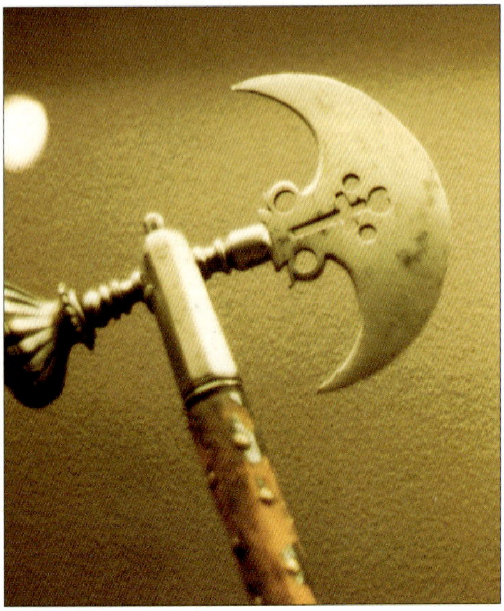

Fig. 151: Halberd.

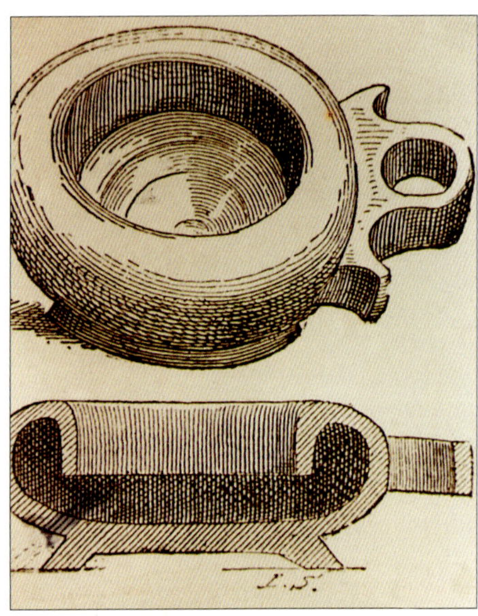

Fig. 152: Kothon cup.

Function can be played with when making gadgets. The little stand for the fork was necessary to protect the tablecloth. This necessary object has since become unnecessary.

Fig. 153: Fork on f

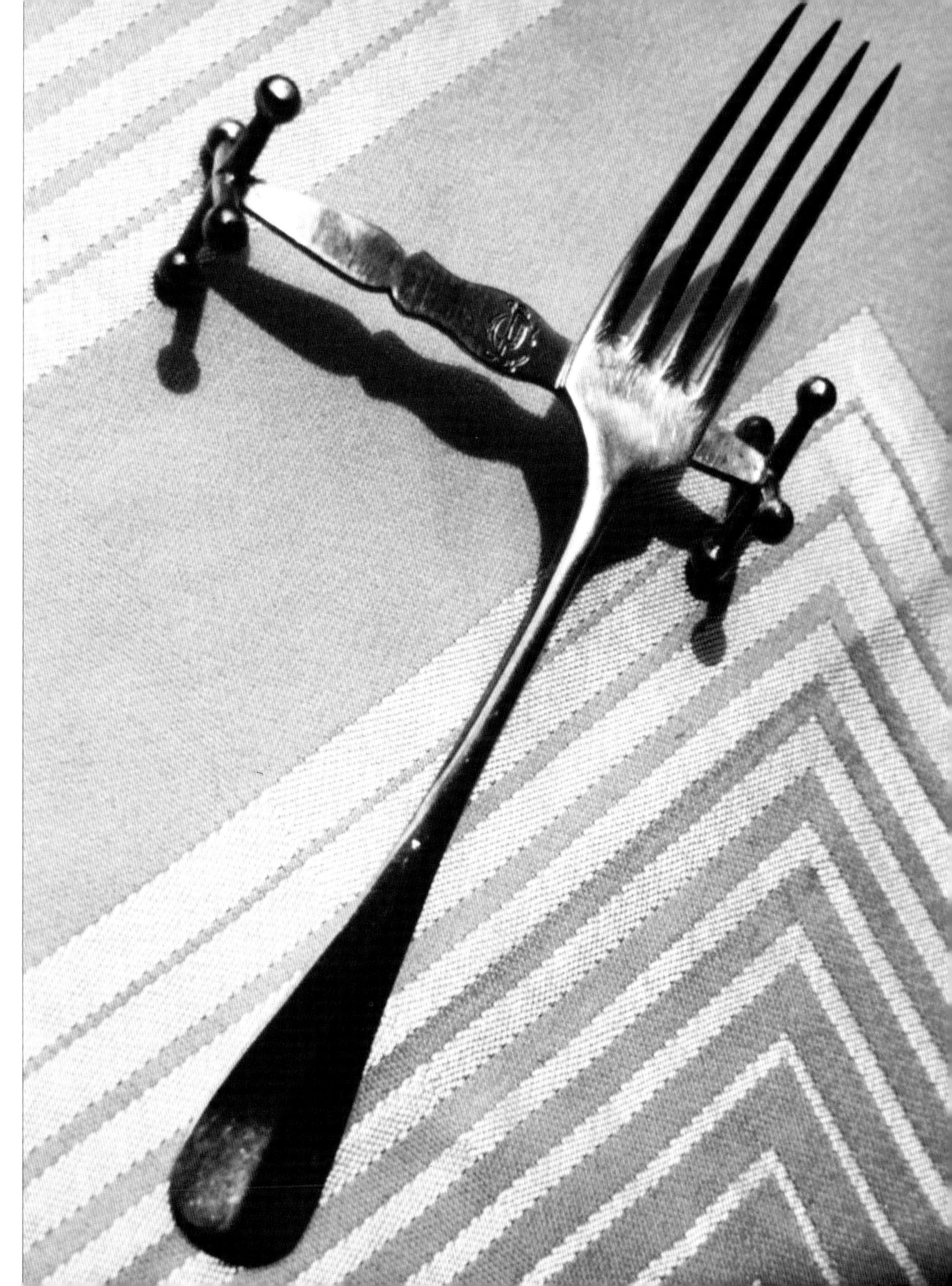

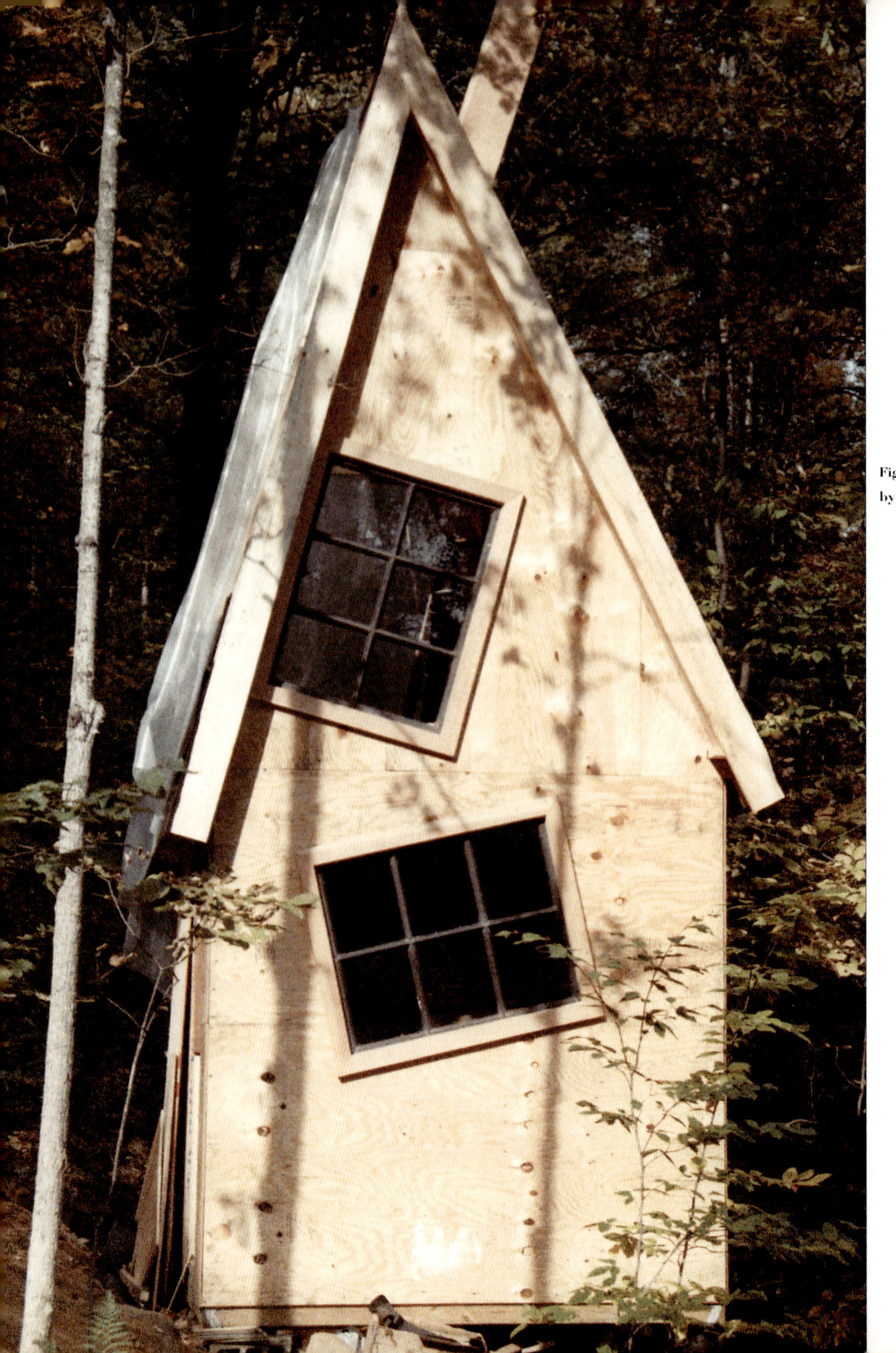

Fig. 154: Silly hous
by Ross Miller.

Fun

We have spoken for so long now about design in terms of industrial design, in terms of making useful things, that we have forgotten good humor, an attitude of lightheartedness, of frivolity, of *joie de vivre*. It might be useful to mention that we must not take ourselves so seriously, in following the strict rules and principles of Puritan order and restraint preached by the modern movement, that we forget about making lovely and funny things, including jokes and toys.

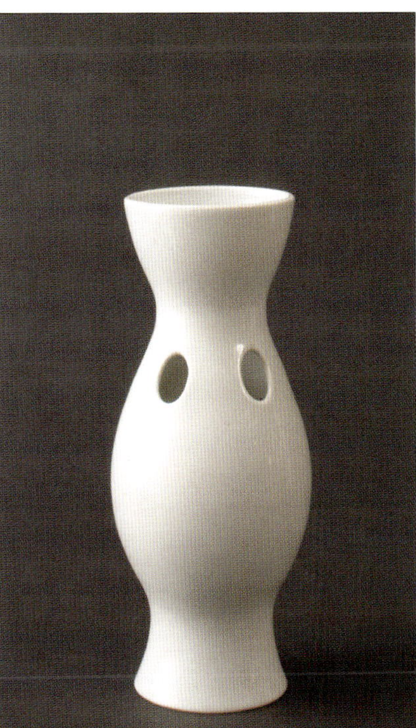

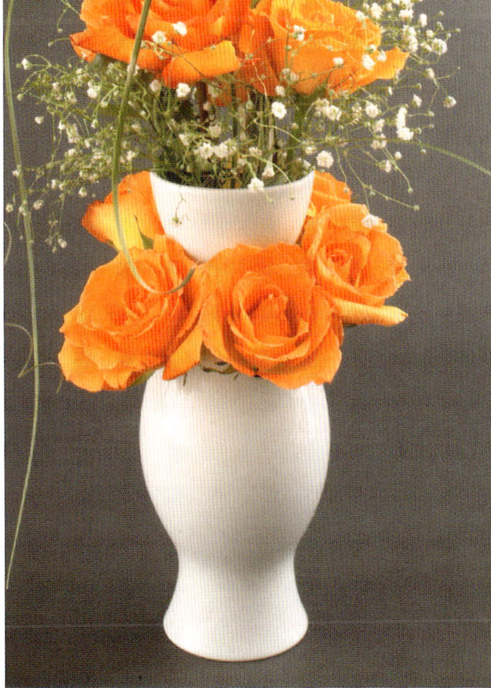

Fig. 155: Peekaboo Vase (Nambé) with and without flowers, Eva Zeisel, 2003

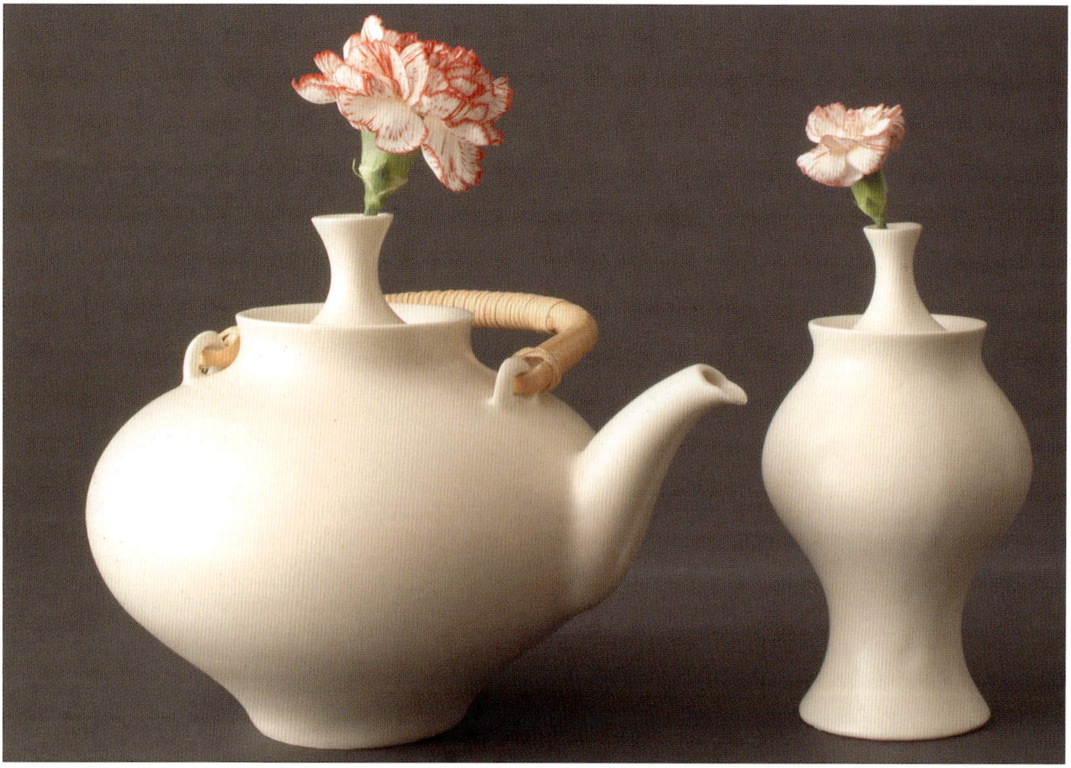

Fig. 156: "Eva" teapot and sugar bowl for KleinReid, Eva Zeisel, 2003.

Fig. 157: Animal jug from Honduras.

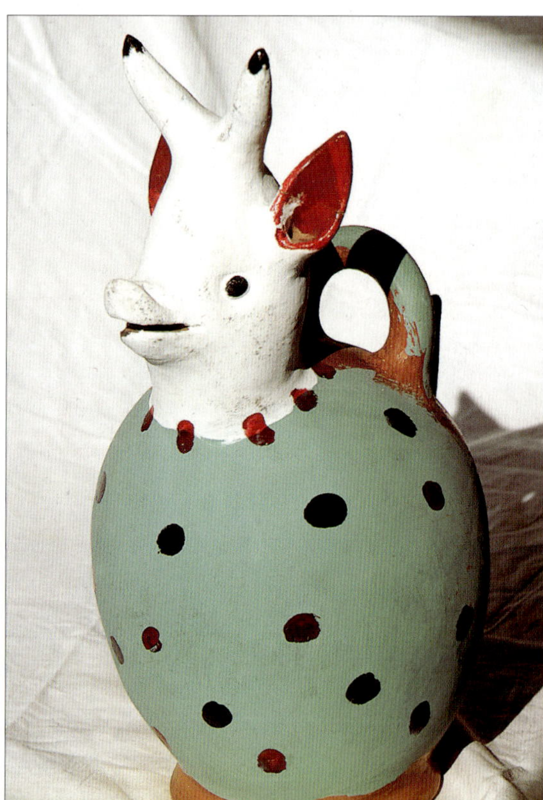

Fig. 158: Old toy (15th century B.C.).

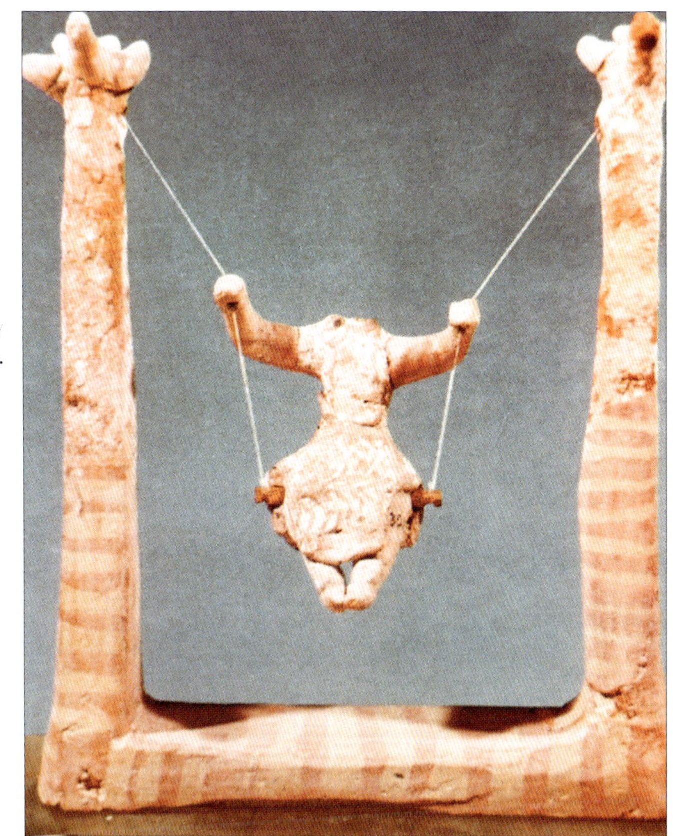

Fig. 159: Invitation/card designed by Milton Glaser, 1984.

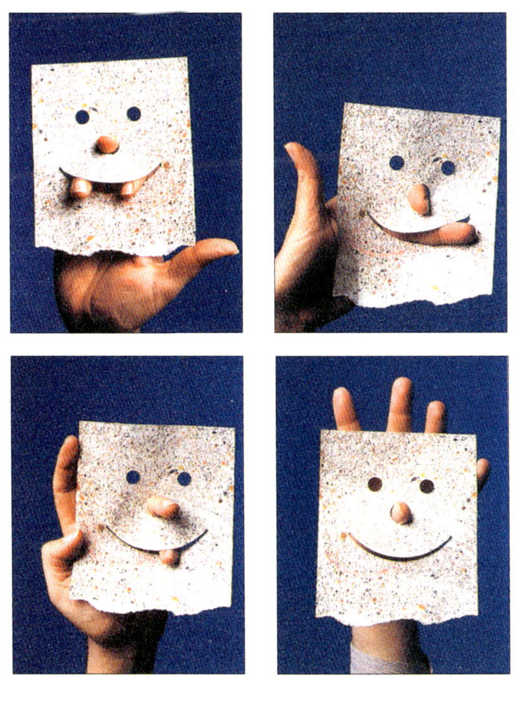

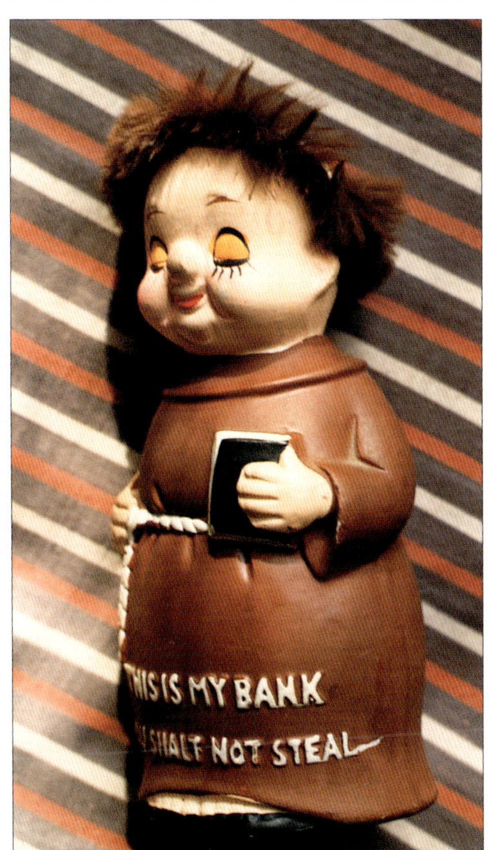

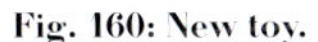

Fig. 160: New toy.

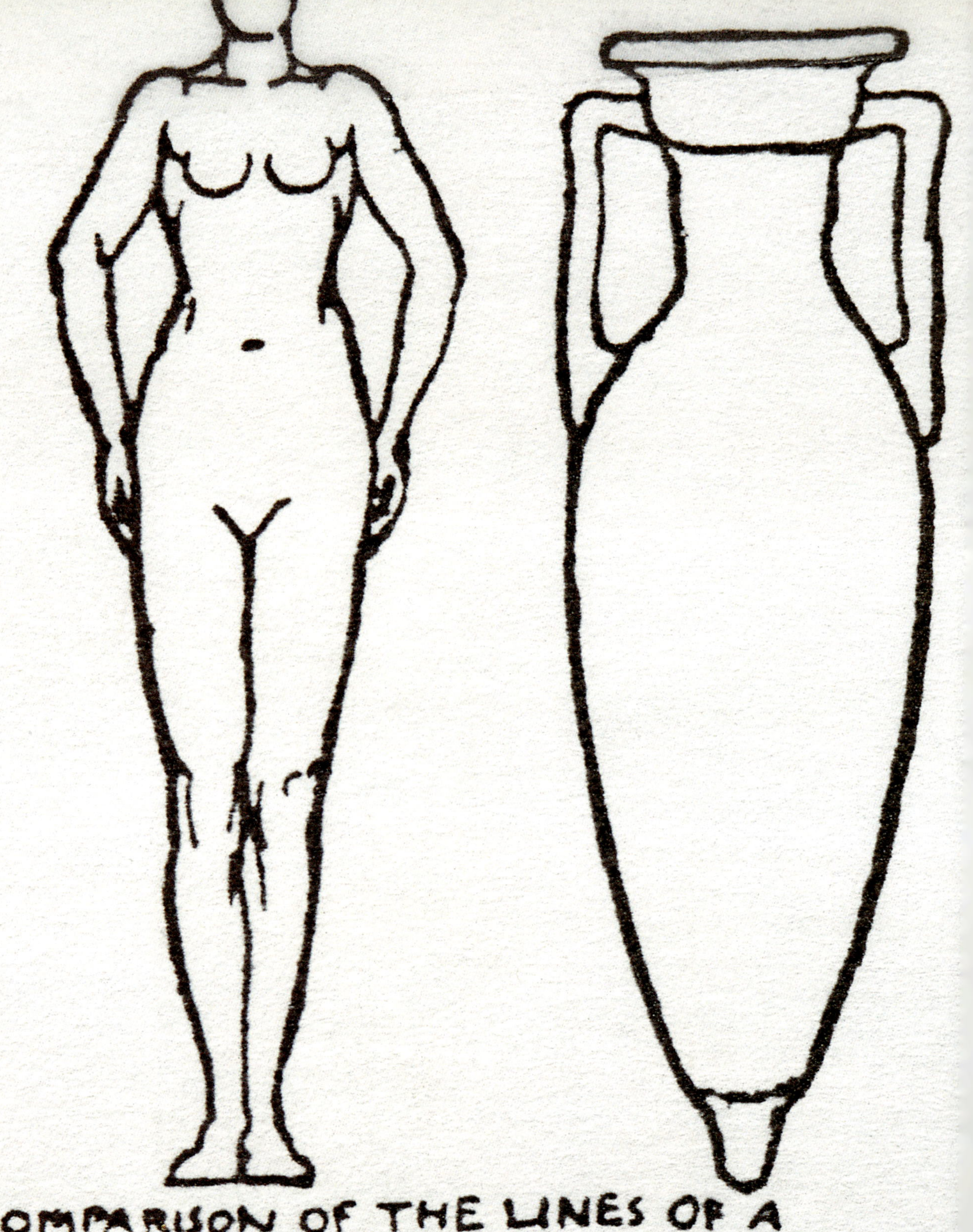

COMPARISON OF THE LINES OF A FEMALE FIGURE & THOSE OF AN AMPHORA

Associations with the Human Body

ig. 160: Drawing of body and mphora by Walter Crane.

In this picture, Walter Crane compares the proportions of an amphora to that of a human body, suggesting that when we look at things we unconsciously compare their heights and widths to our own proportions. Whether something seems too high, or hunchbacked, or incomplete, is based on our subconscious expectations, which are rooted in the proportions of the human shape.

Through these associations, it is in our power to put others at ease, but also to make them uneasy. Deviation from symmetry of form in this bottle and silhouette evoke a disagreeable sensation.

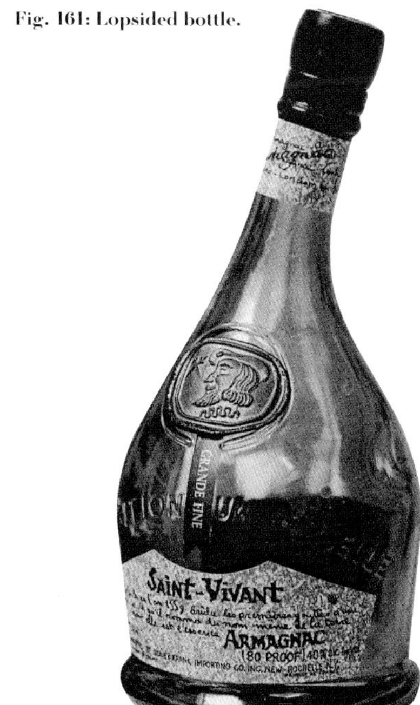

Fig. 161: Lopsided bottle.

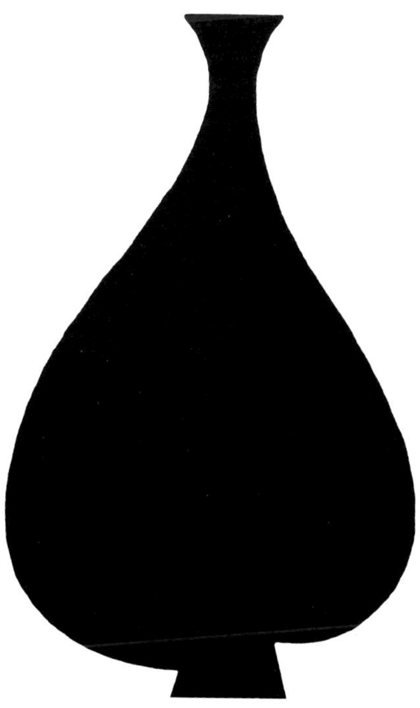

Fig. 162: Asymmetrical silhouette.

The crooked picture urges us to put it straight and so conveys a sense of suspense. So does the tipsy vase.

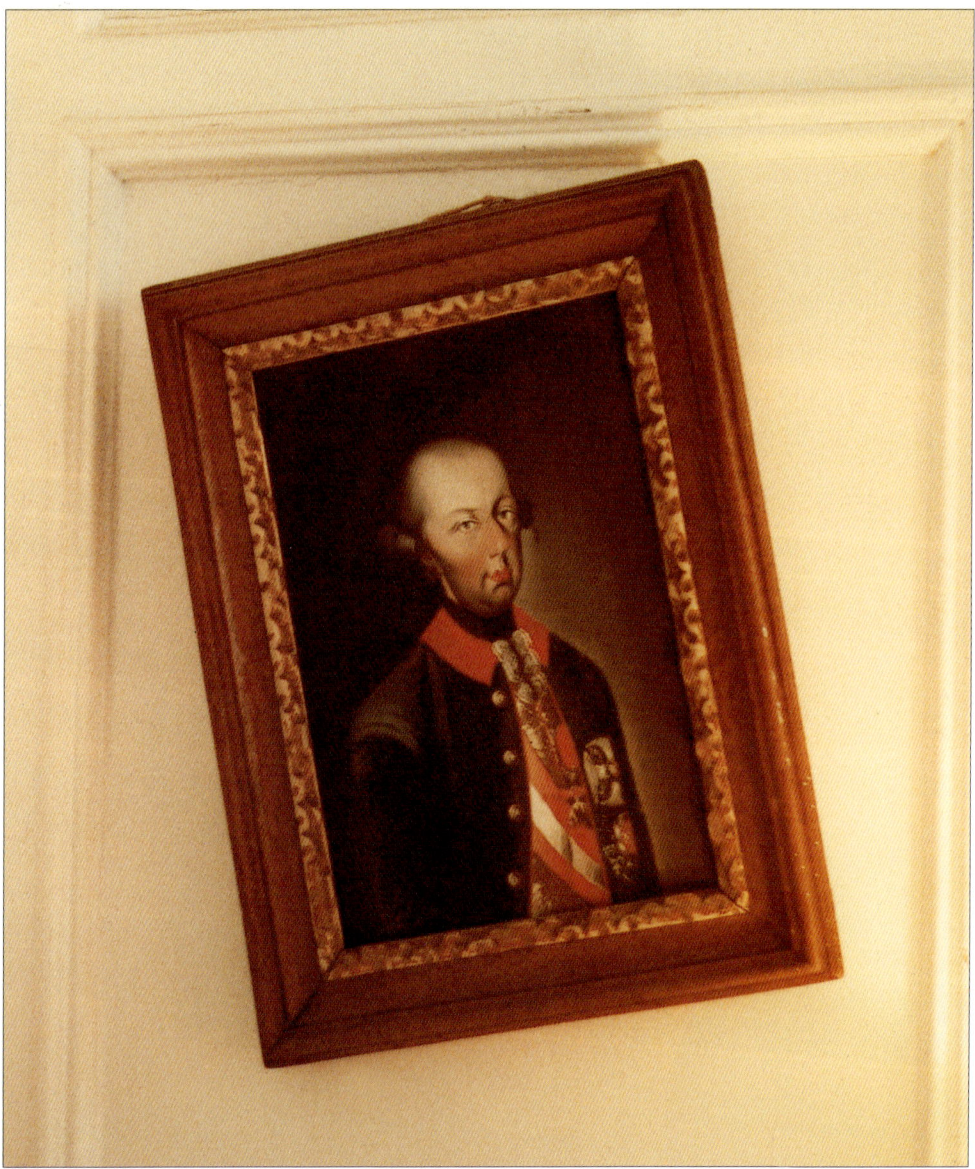

Fig. 163: Crooked picture.

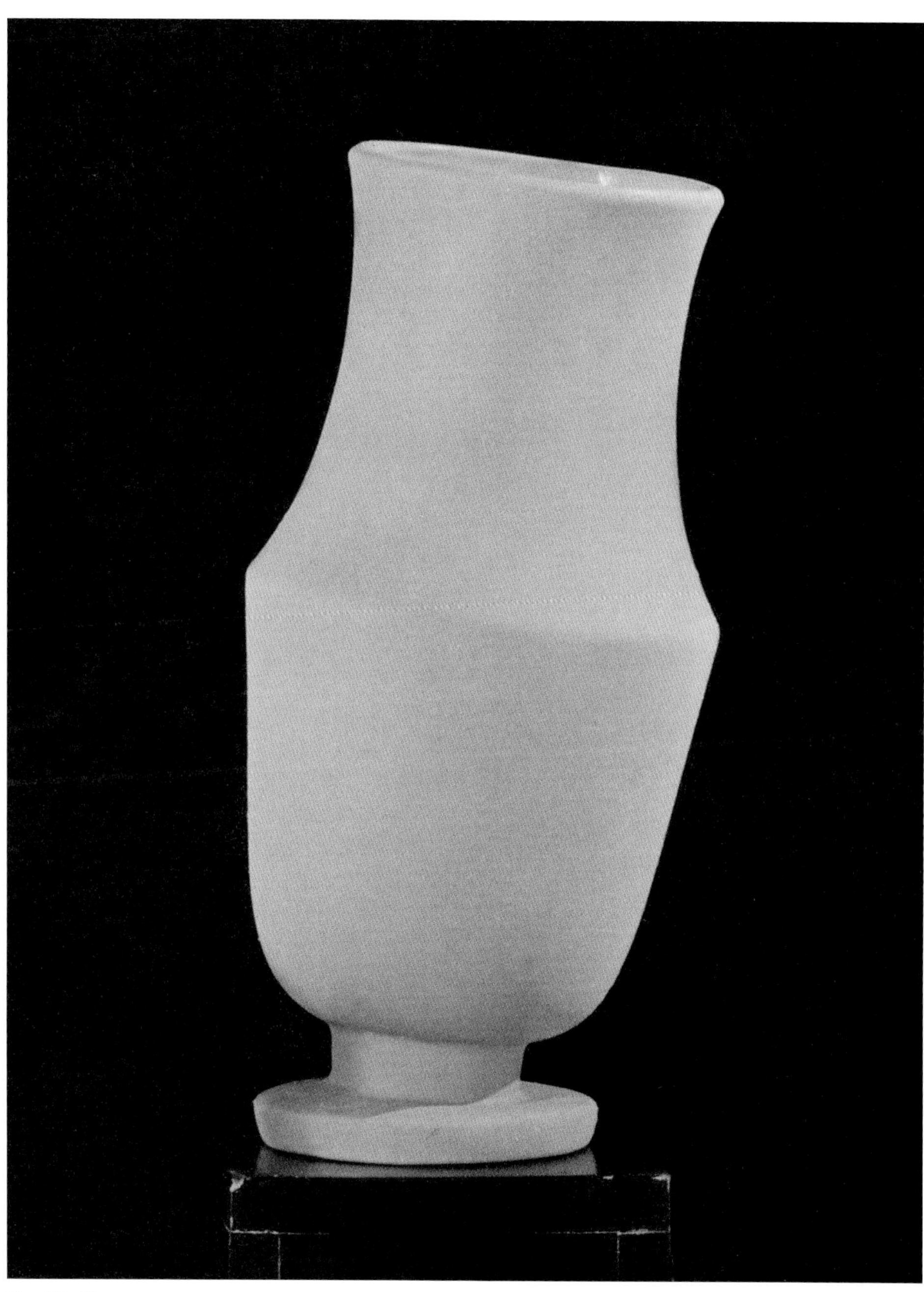

Fig. 164: Tipsy vase.

Fig. 166: Leaning Tower of Pisa, Italy.

Alone, this teapot would make us feel ill-at-ease, off kilter. Together, the teapots seem to be dancing.

Fig. 165: Porcelain teapots. Scott Dooley, 2001.

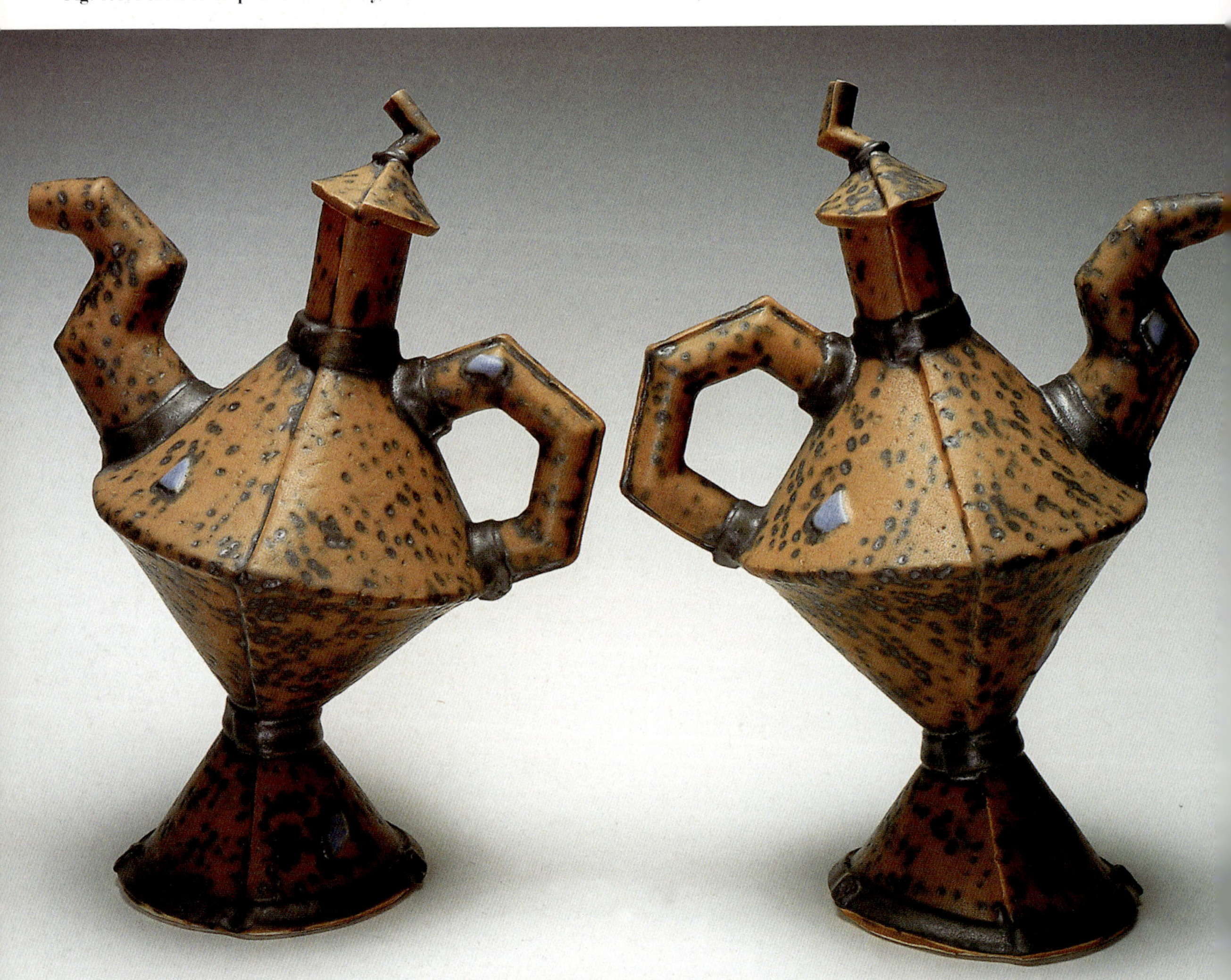

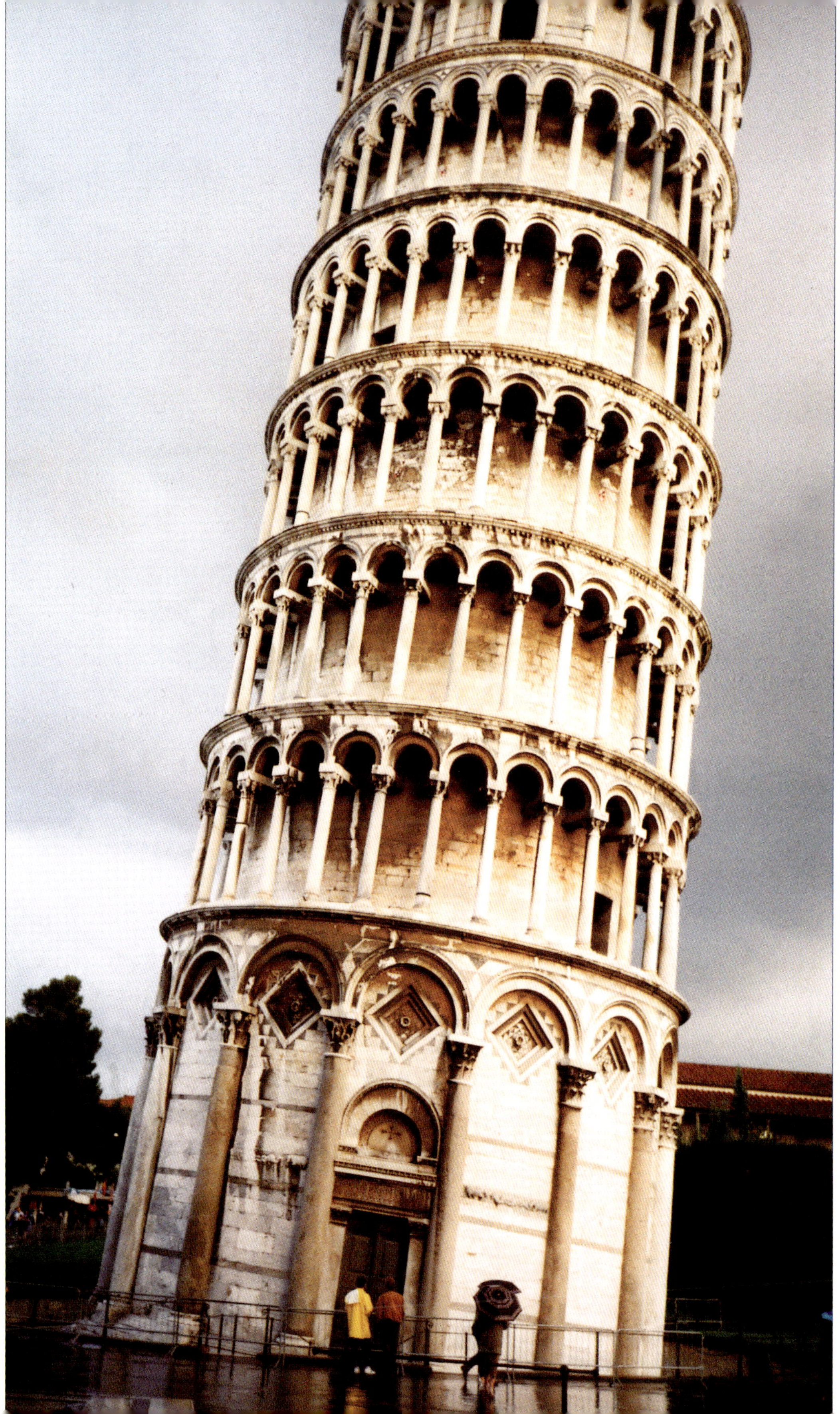

If we see a row of young ladies—instead of a line of amphorae—is it surprising that things we make are often vaguely related—or sometimes not so vaguely related—to the shapes or proportions of the human body? It seems difficult to deprive them of bosoms and eyes. Or, if they are pitchers, we cannot resist the temptation of using the nose as a spout.

Fig. 167: Goose-necked lamp, 1940s.

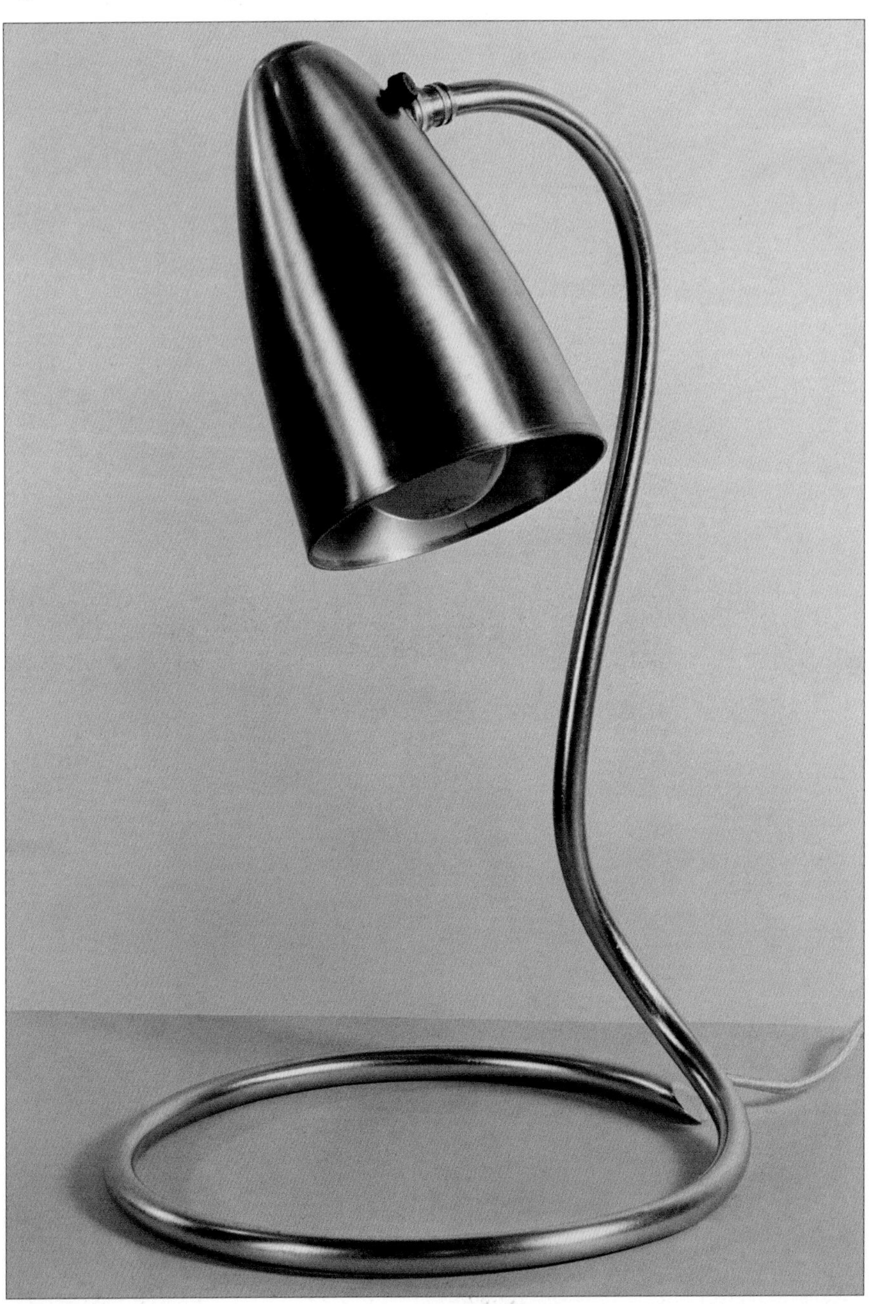

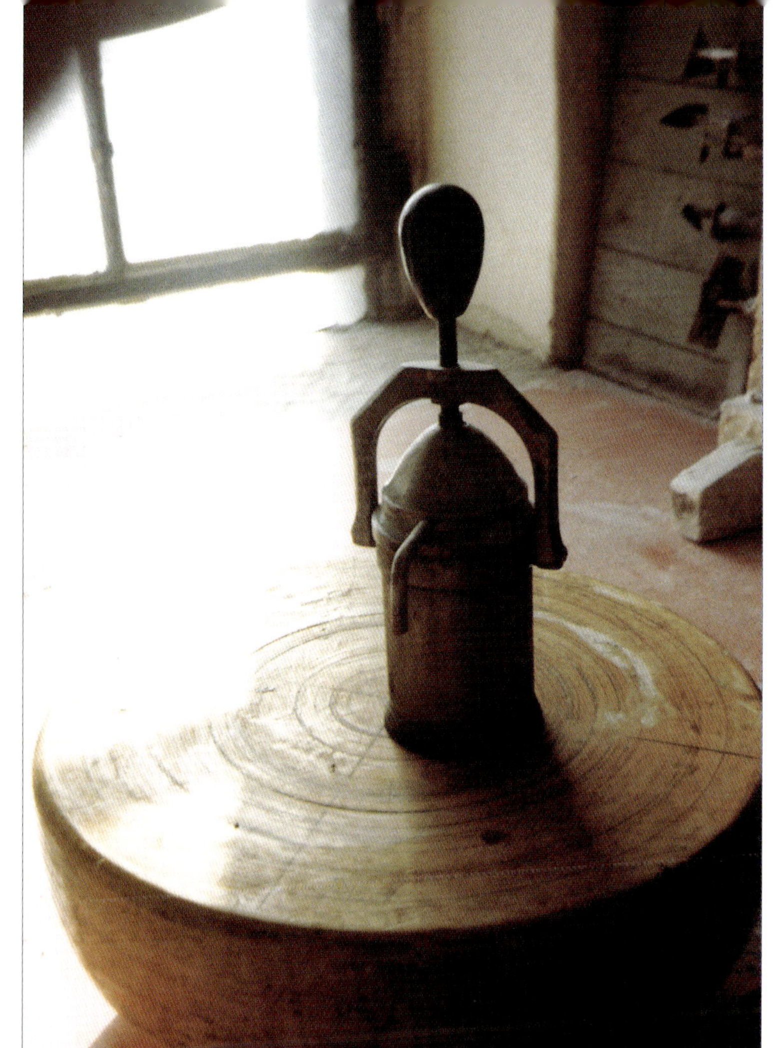

Fig. 168: Bell on a potter's wheel.

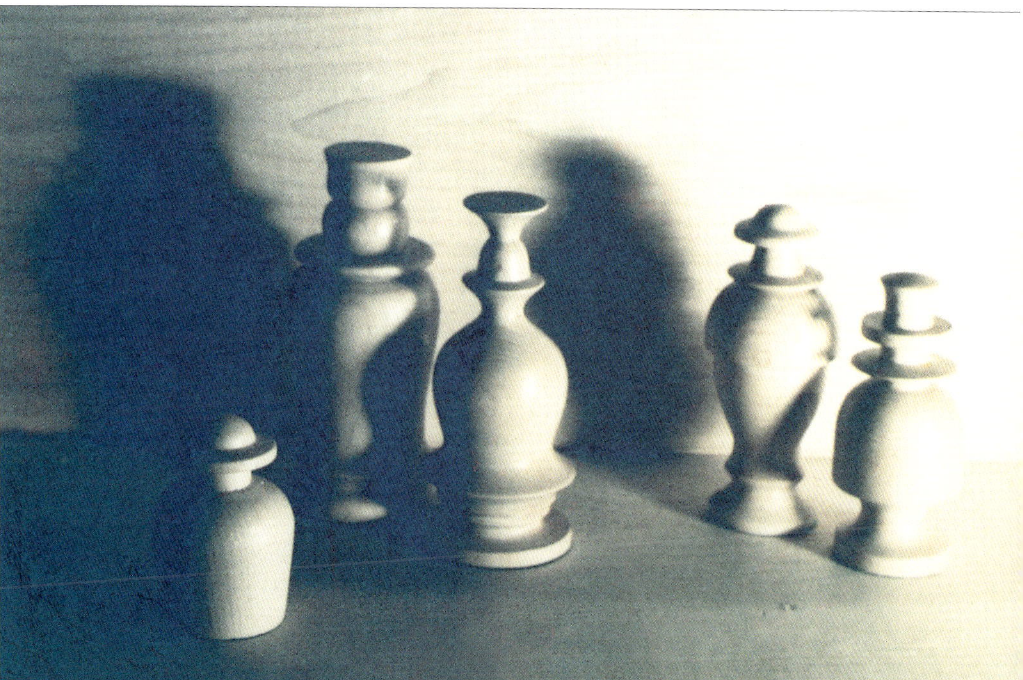

Fig. 169: Wooden chess set. Eva Zeisel, 1970s.

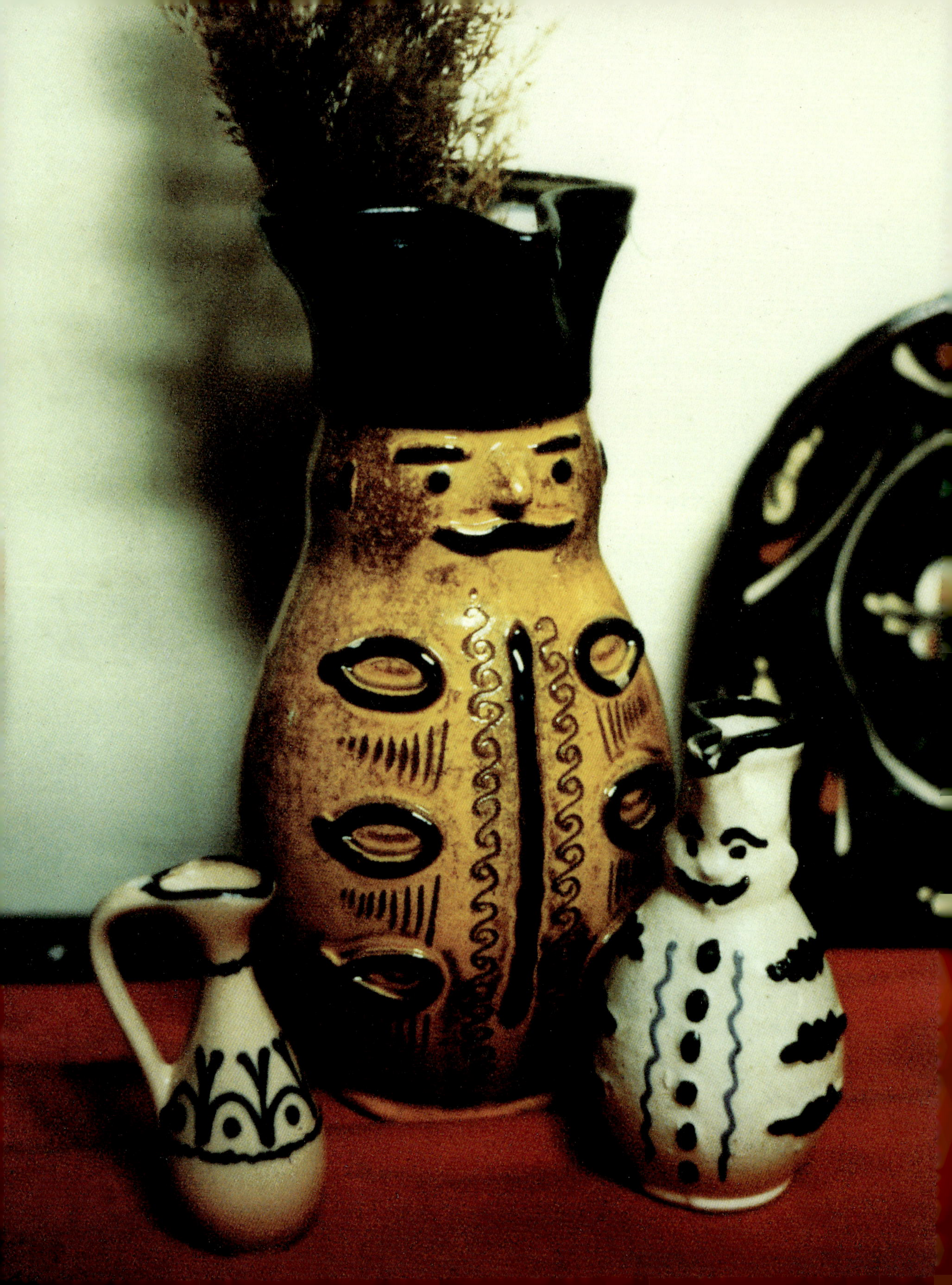

Fig. 170: Traditional Hungarian vases.

Fig. 171: Pitcher by Erik Blegvad, for Rosenthal, Studio Line, ca. 1958.

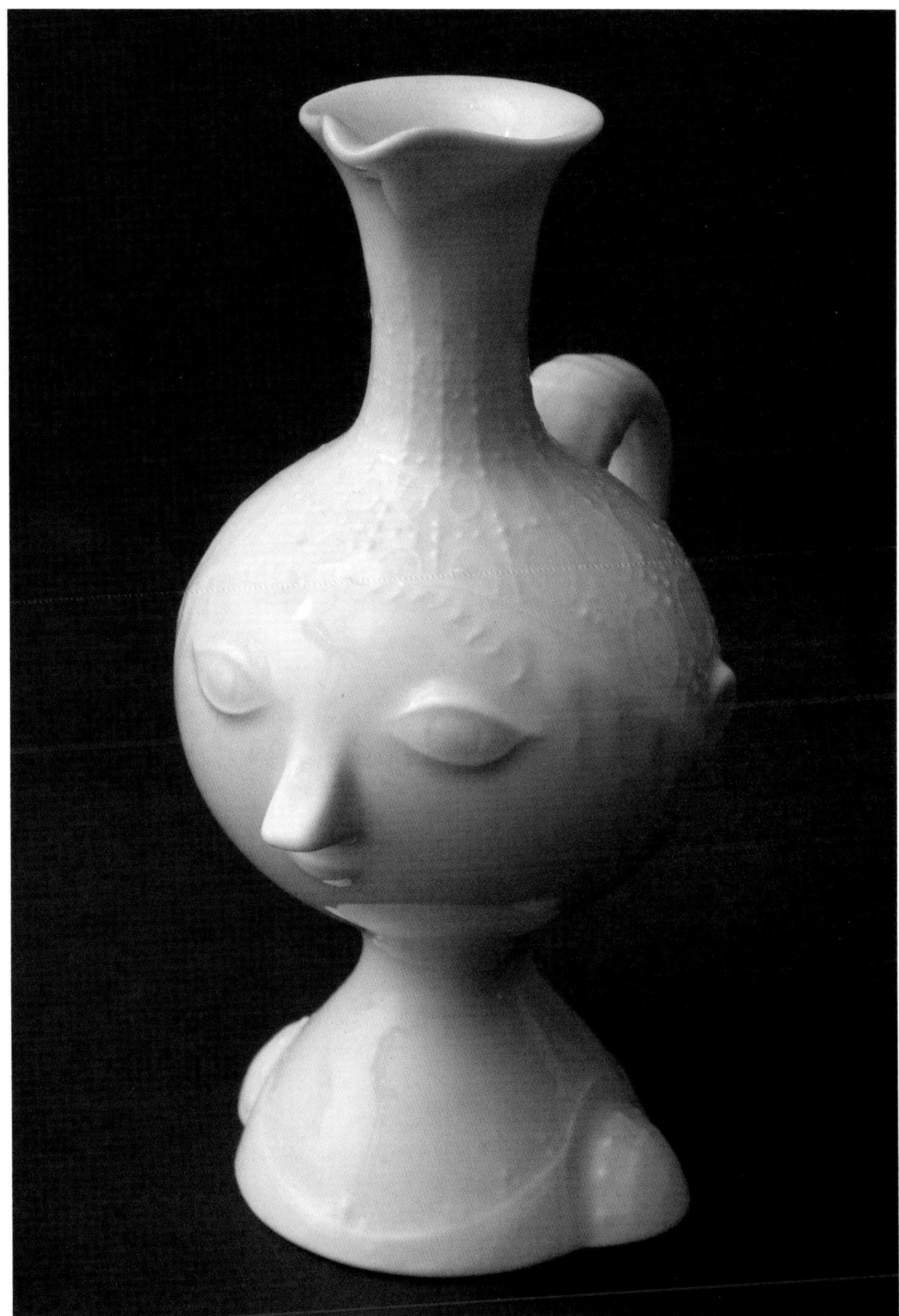

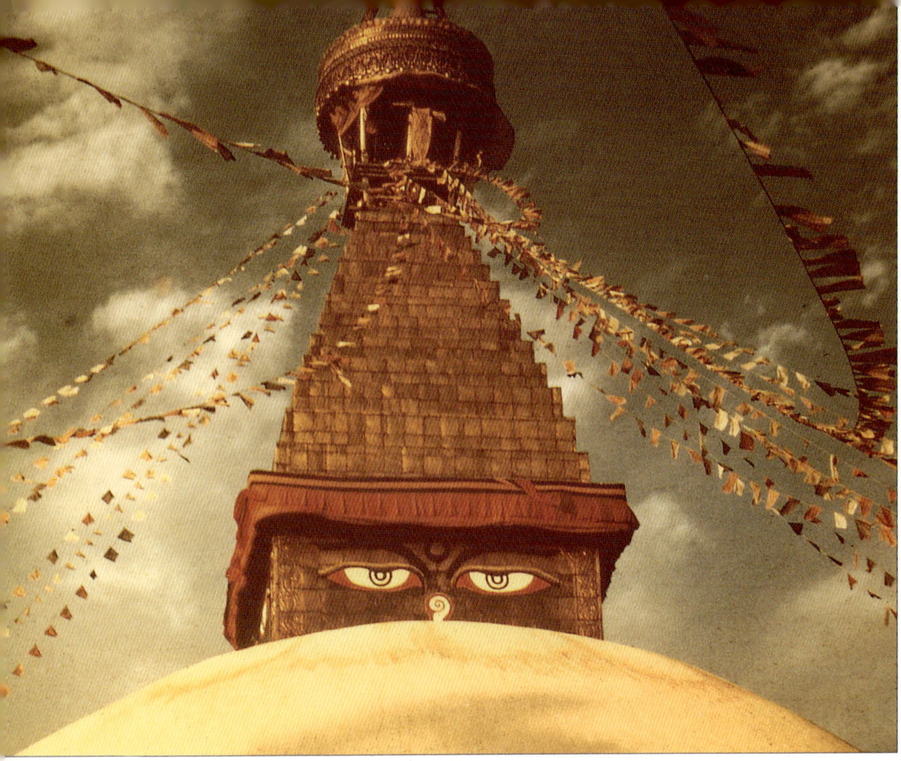

Fig. 172: Buddhist stupa, Nepal.

Fig. 175: Ancient pitche
with breast

Fig. 174: Pitcher by
Edmund Ashby.

Fig. 173: Camille vase,
by Jonthan Adler.

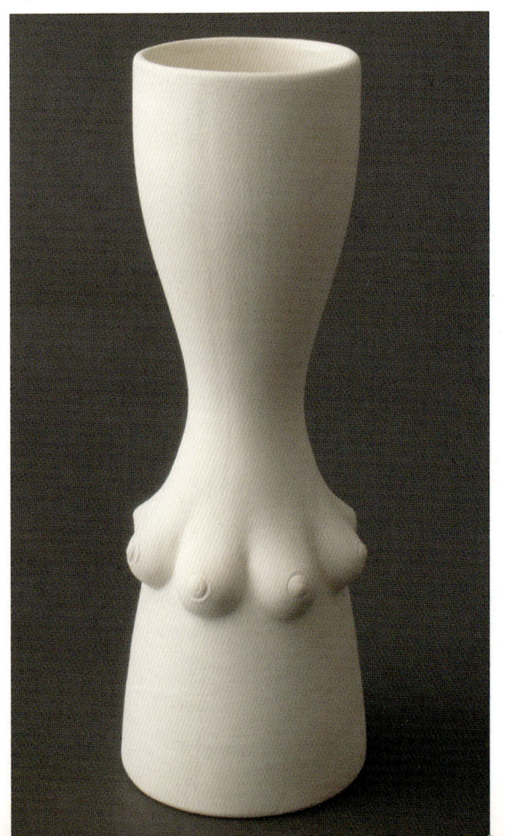

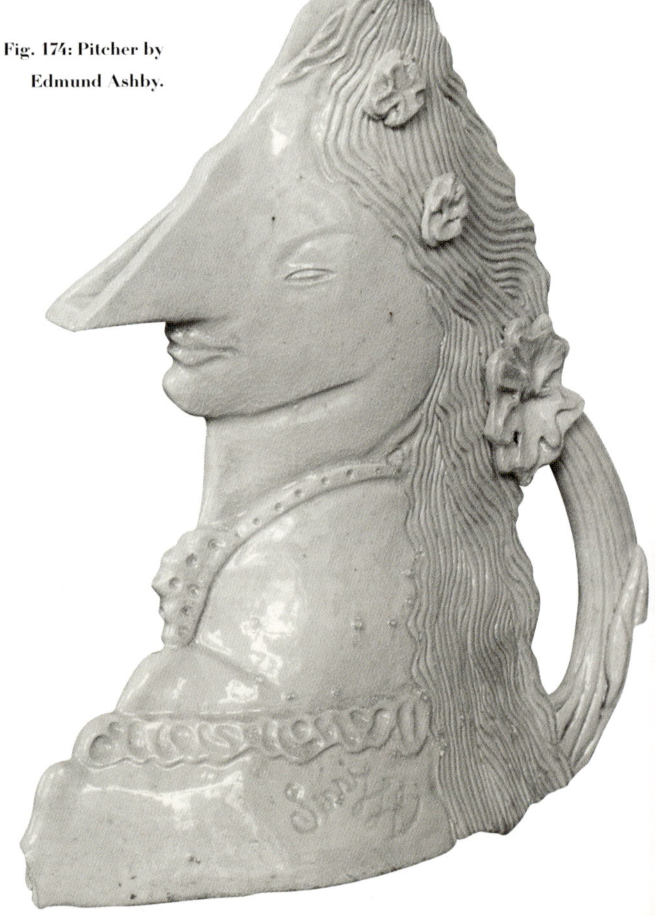

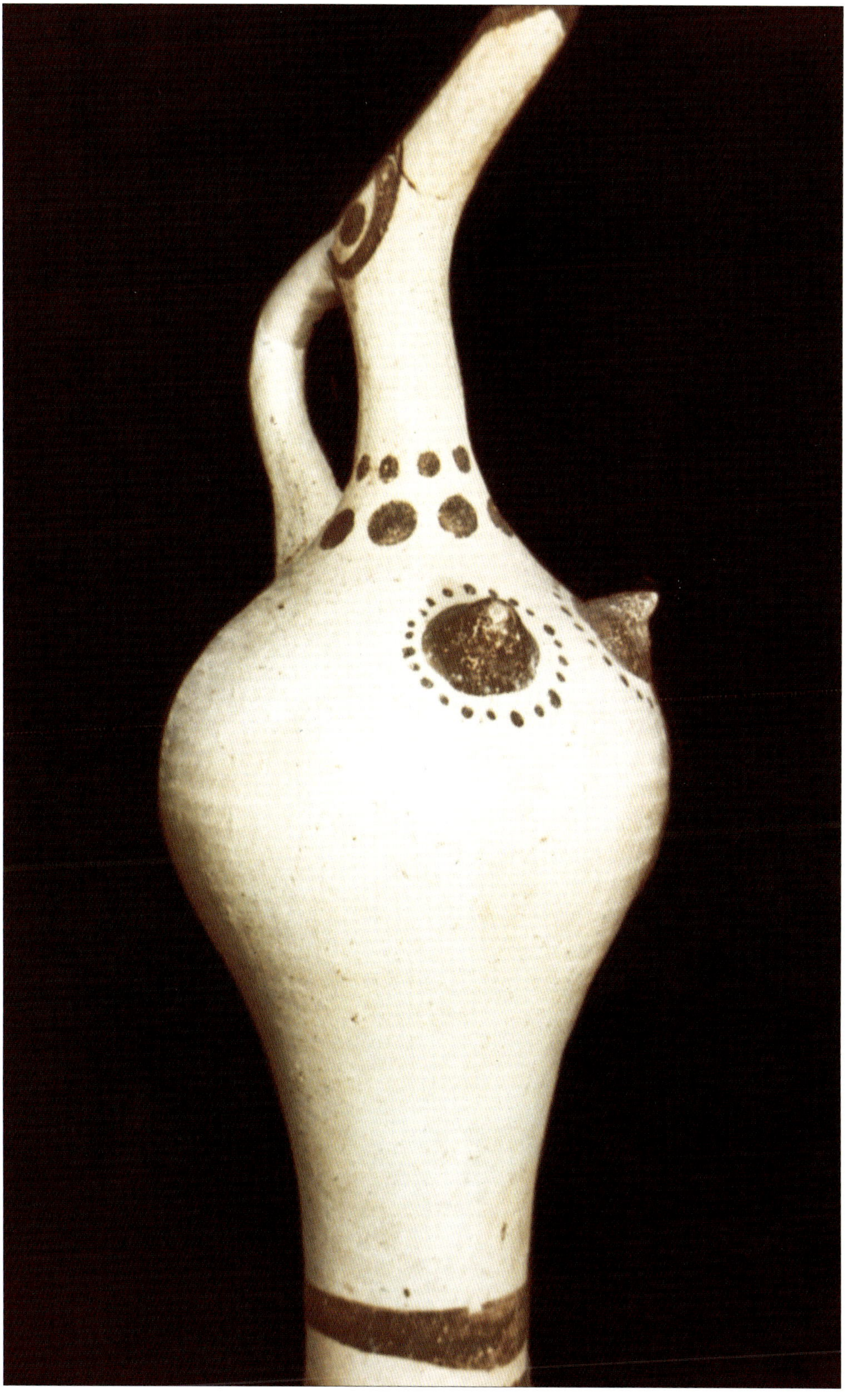

151

Or is it surprising that spirits often live in things and trees and look at us surreptitiously, or even gesture towards us and stare as we pass by? Sometimes they look at us because they were intended to do so by their designers.

Fig. 176: Carved wooden chair back with face.

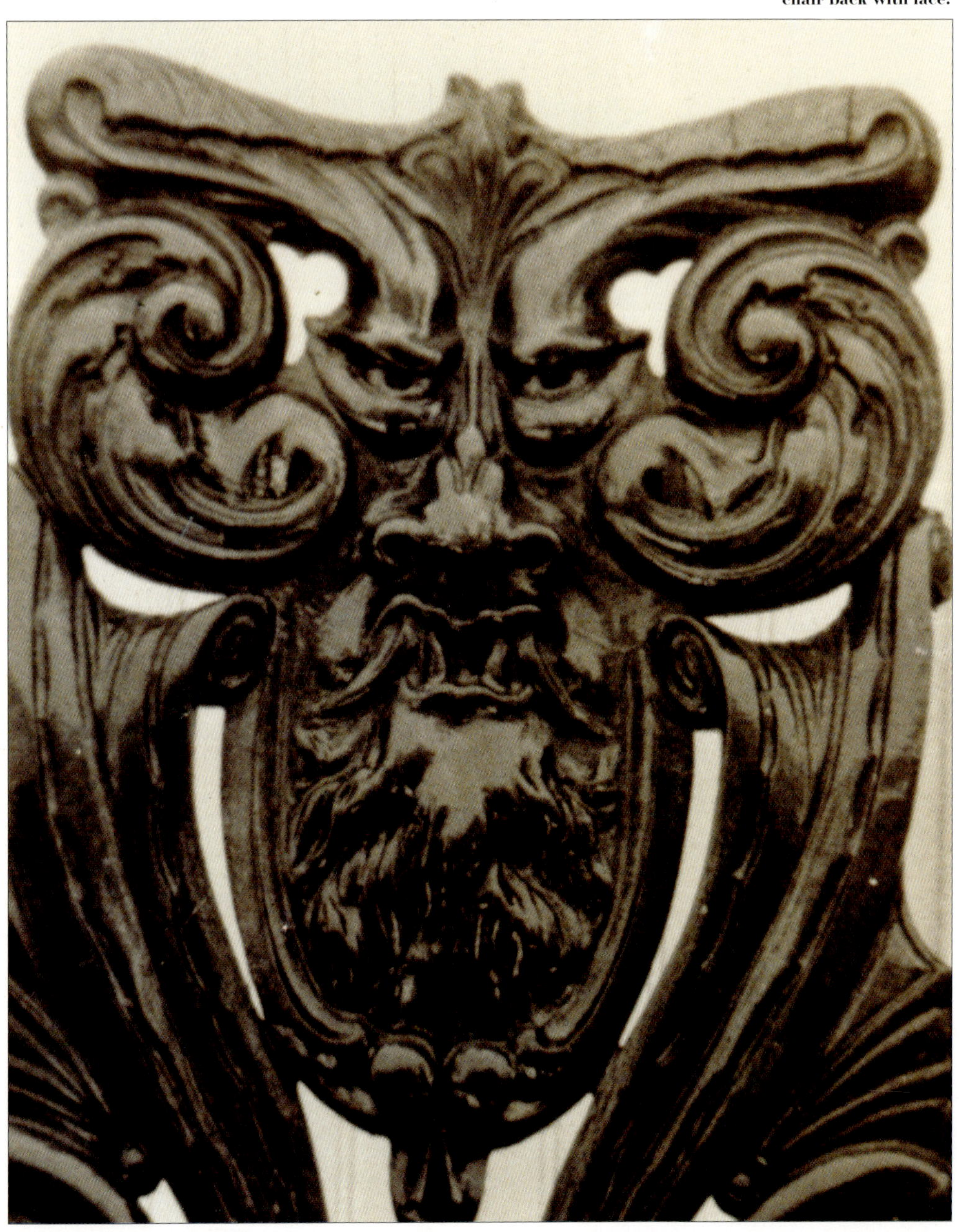

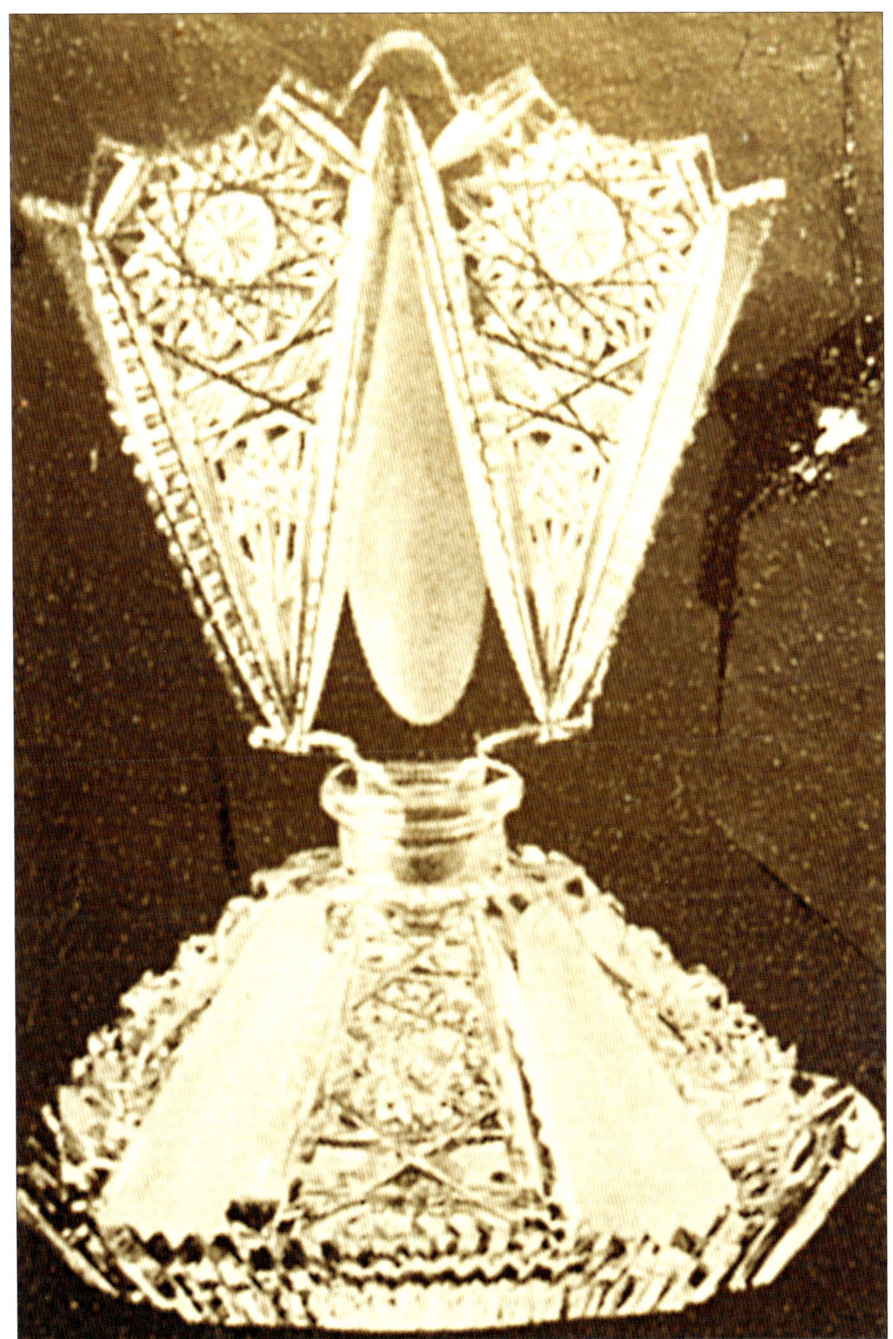

Fig. 177: Cut-glass bottle with attachment.

But even if things don't really have eyes, they communicate and we respond.

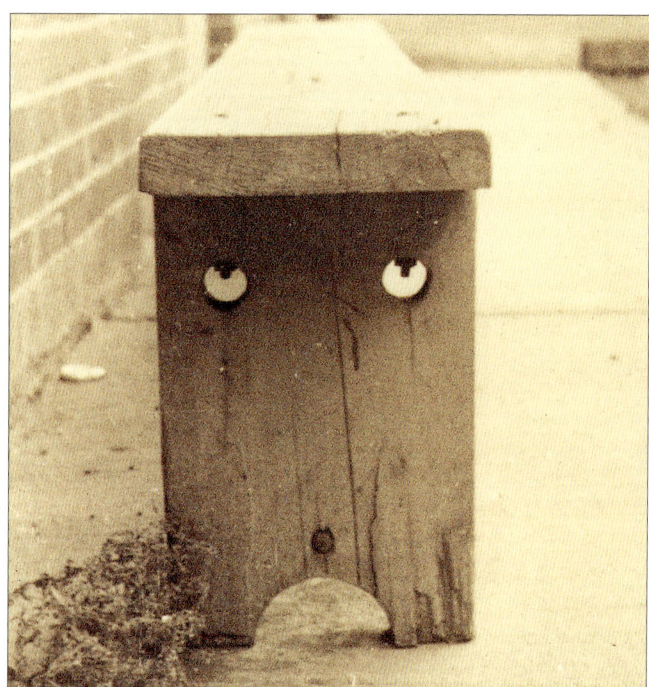

Fig. 178: End of wooden bench.

Fig. 179: Bathtub fixtures.

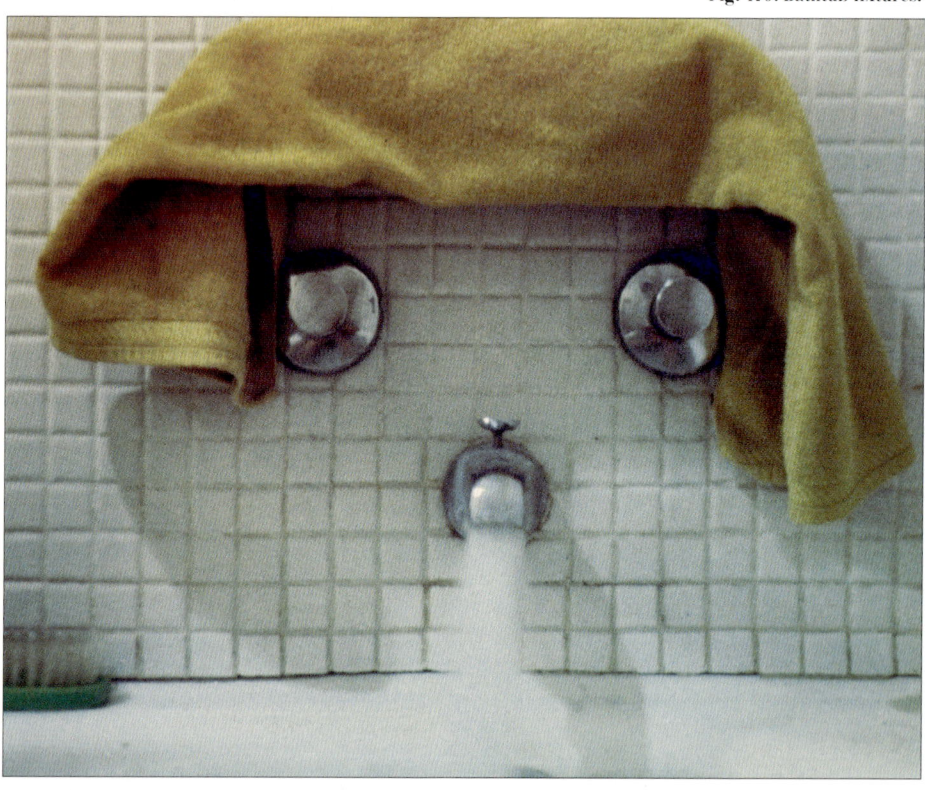

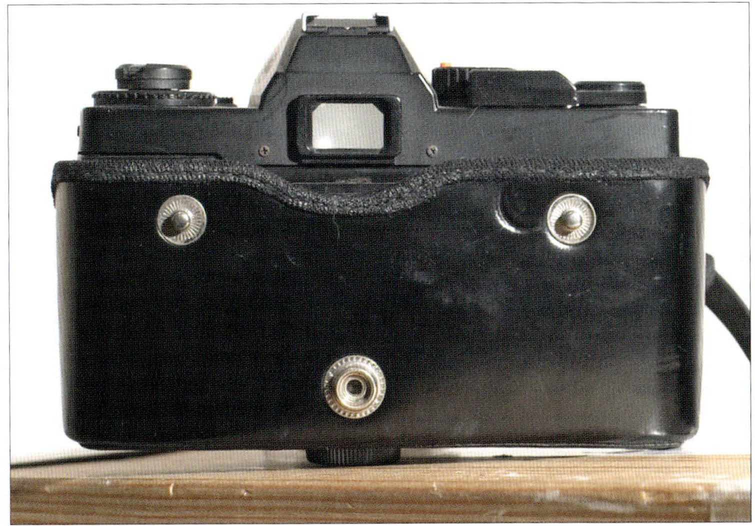

Fig. 180: Back of camera case.

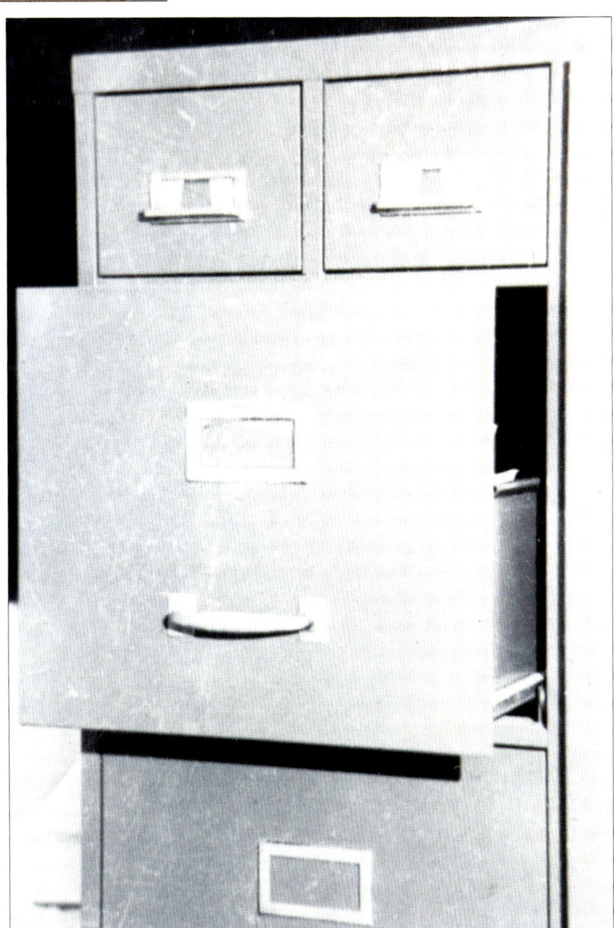

Fig. 181: File cabinet.

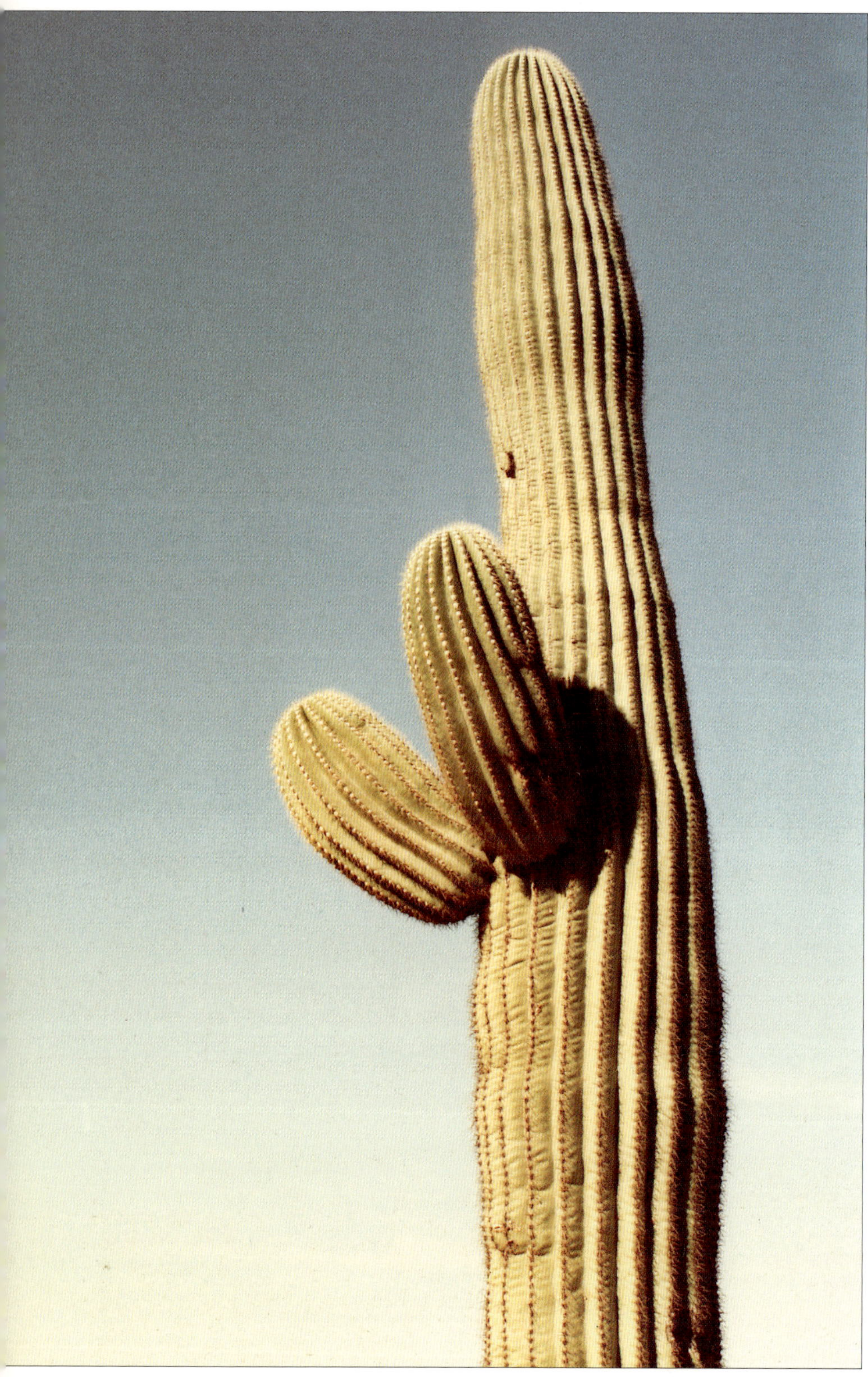

Fig. 182: Cactus.

Influences

We are, of course, fascinated by things we see, and I can trace several such fascinations as they are reflected in the work of designers. When we designers started to work in factories, we were fascinated to see huge quantities of mass-produced goods that, in the outside world, usually appeared singly or in small groups. Photographs of these ranks and files of the same form frequently appeared in the press, and always created a sense of rhythm from their repetition.

Fig. 183: Layout of work for *Die Schaulade*, Eva Zeisel, 1930.

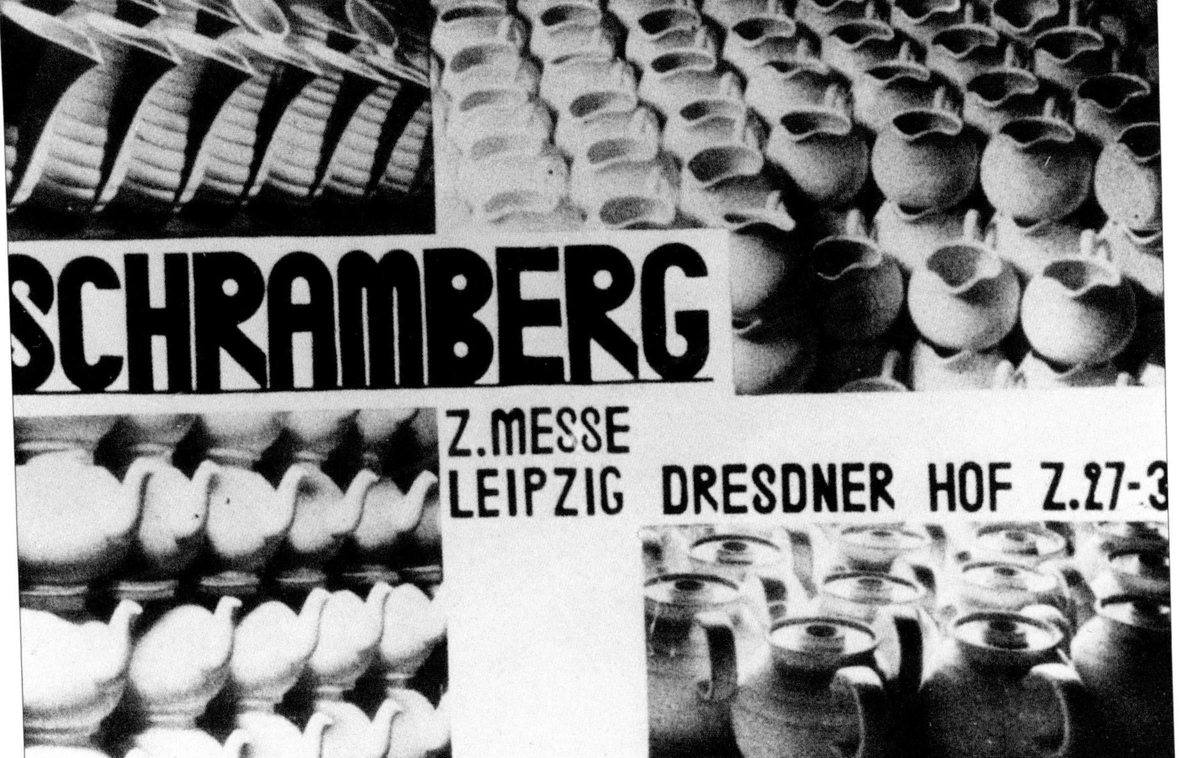

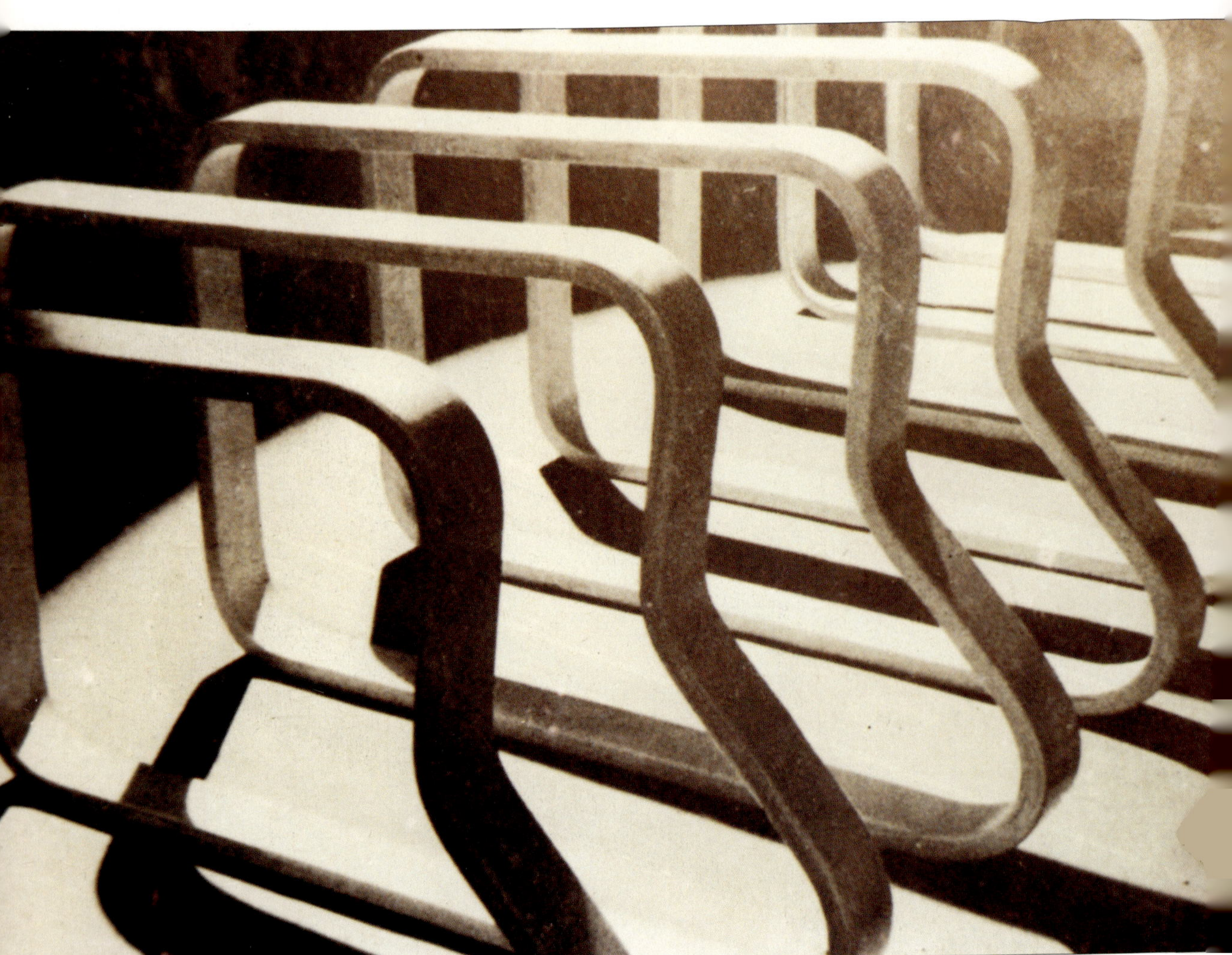

Fig. 184: Molded plywood chair arms.

When Modernist ornamentation appears, it too is generally based on this kind of repetition.

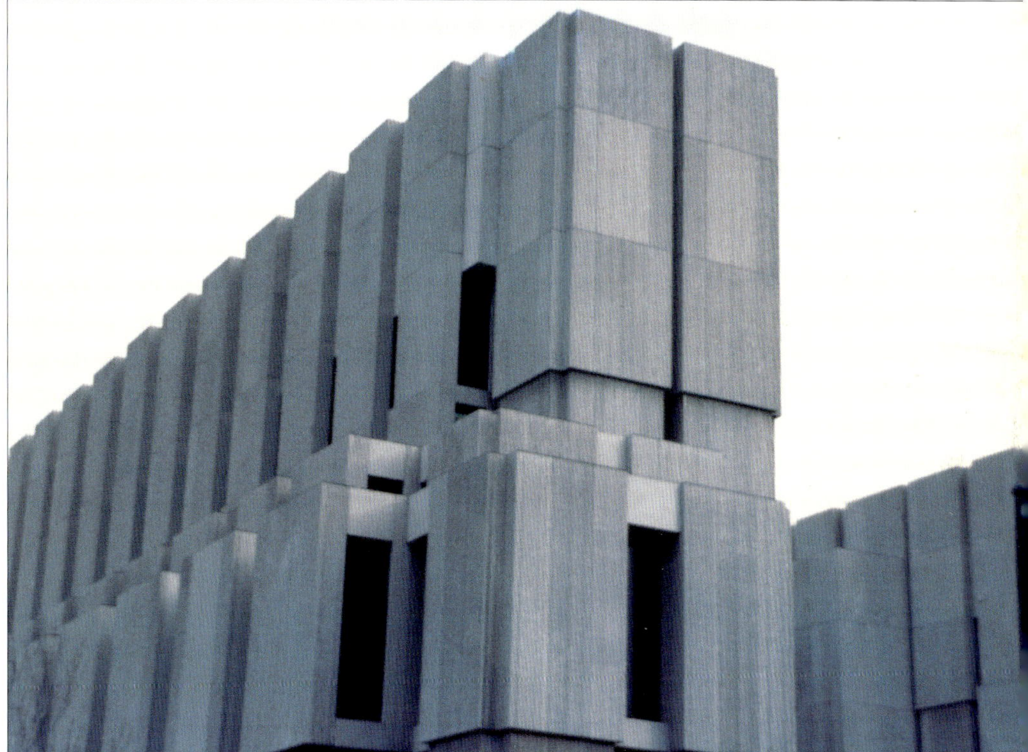

Fig. 185: Joseph Regenstein Library, University of Chicago: Walter Netsch, architect.

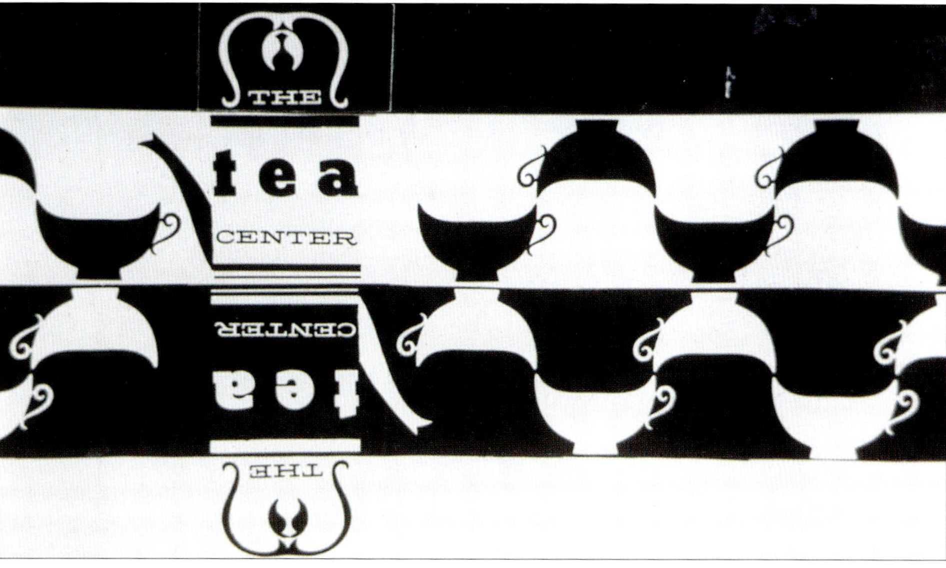

Fig. 186: Logo for The Tea Center, Eva Zeisel, 1954.

Another fashion can be traced to the impact of Spanish surrealist Salvador Dali's melting watch painting and an exhibition called Organic Design, which was held at New York City's Museum of Modern Art in the early 1940s. The exhibition came about because of new techniques in molding materials. All kinds of objects adopted the lines and shapes of kidneys and other bodily organs, giving a dual meaning to the word "organic."

Fig. 187: Salvador Dali, *Persistence of Memory*, 1931.

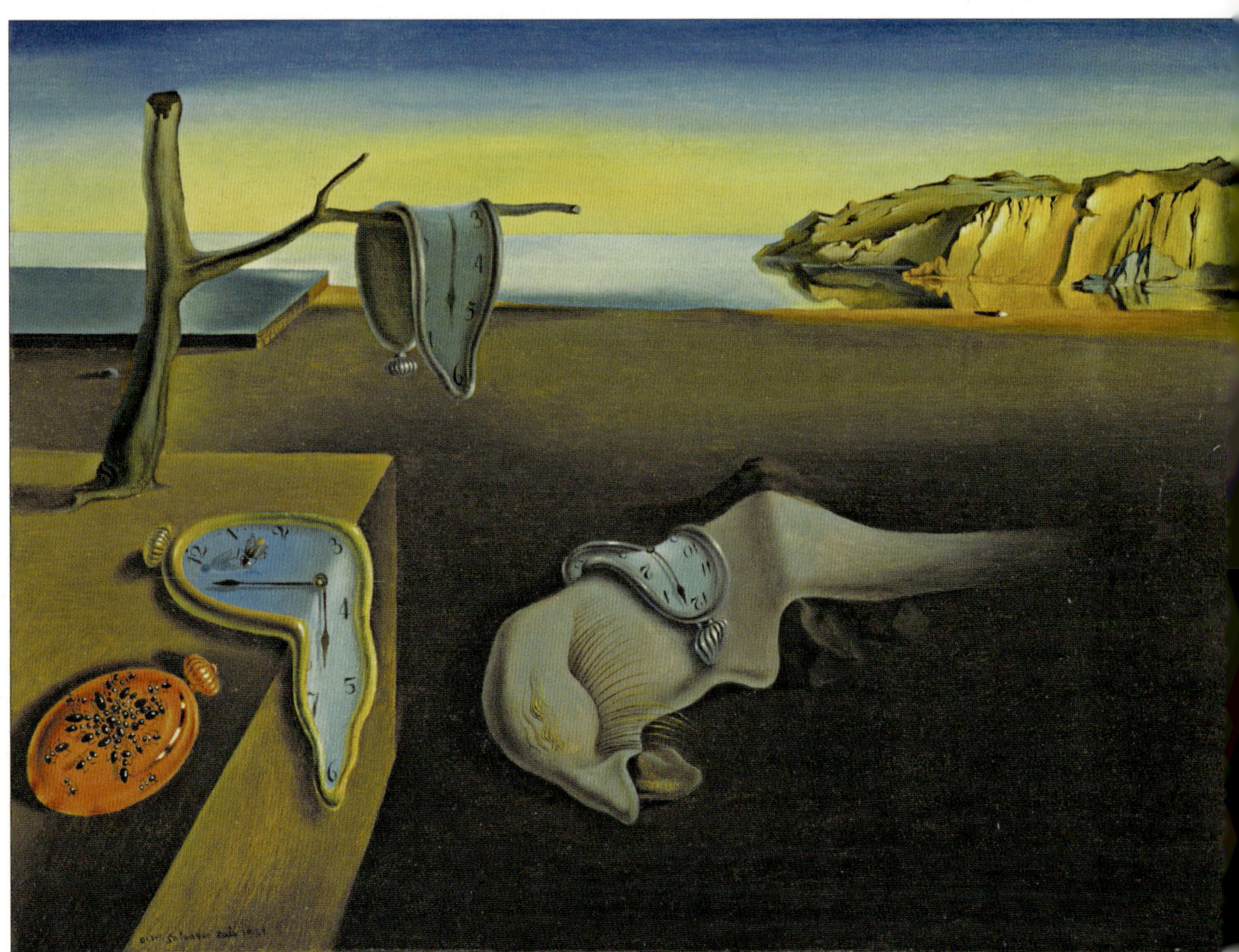

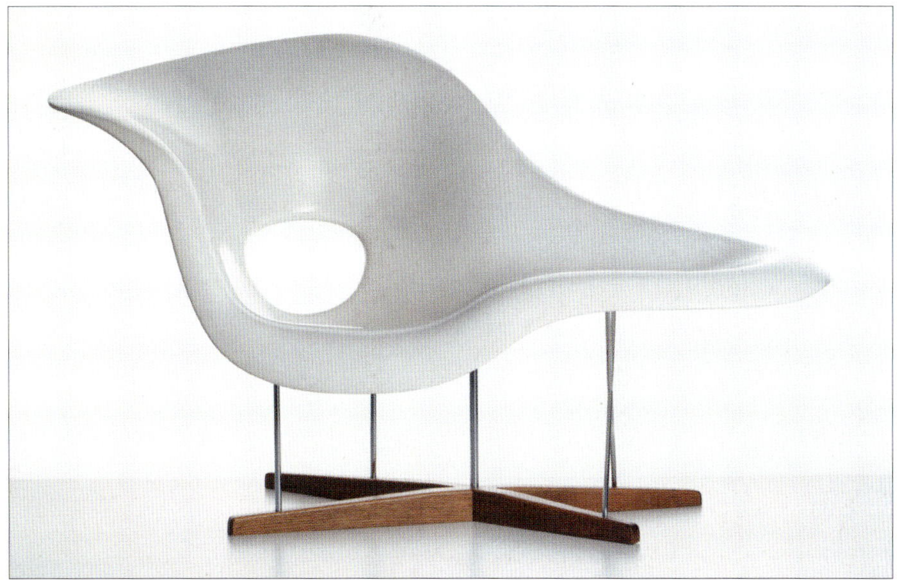

Fig. 188: La Chaise by Charles and Ray Eames, 1948.

Fig. 189: Cloverware plastic salad bowl and nut dish, Eva Zeisel, 1947.

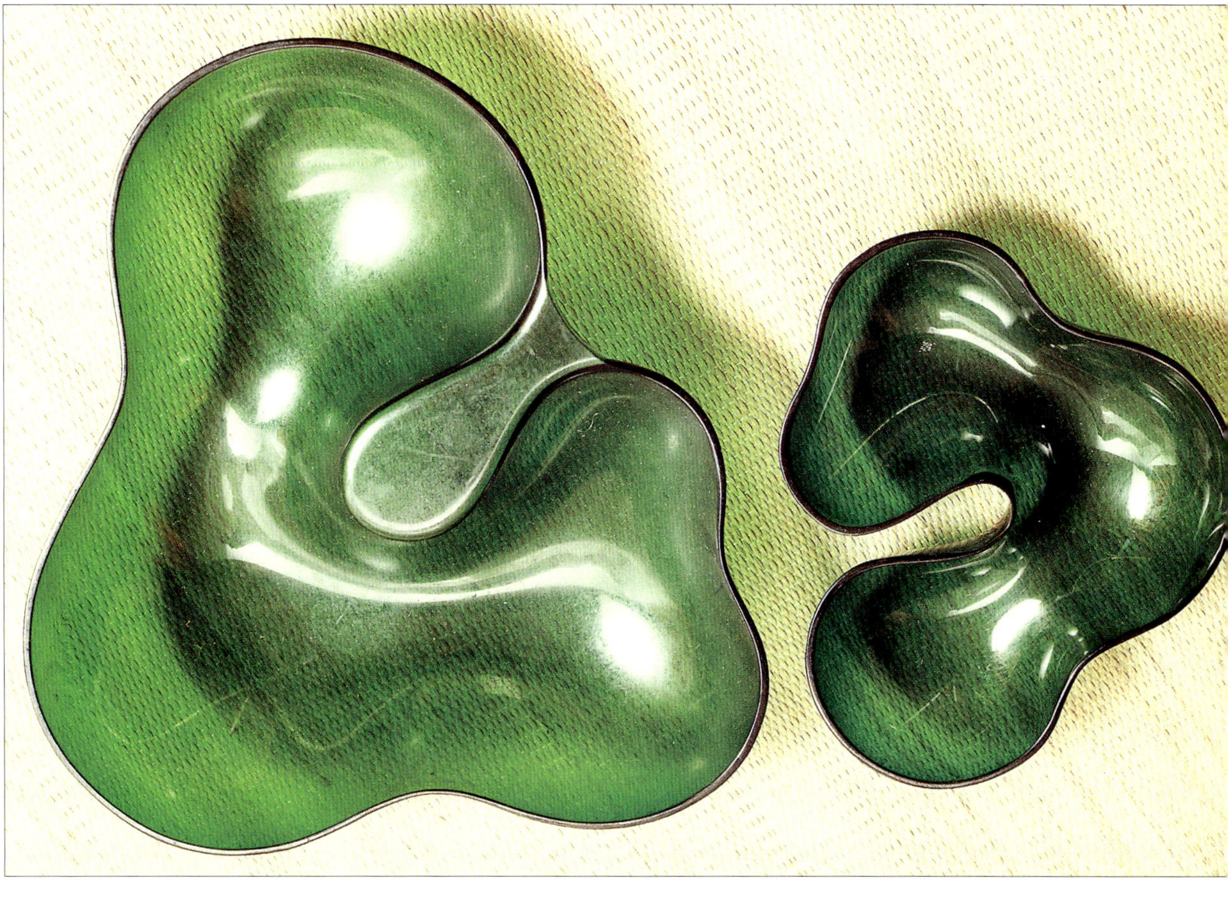

A designer's own body shapes is often reflected in his or her work.

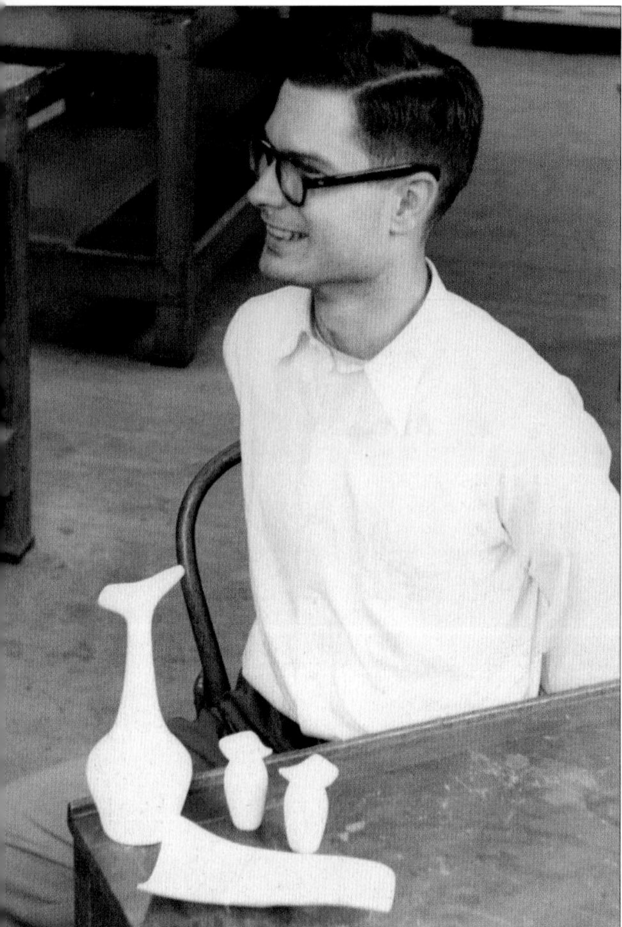

Fig. 190: Pratt student and his work.

Fig. 191: Pratt student and his work.

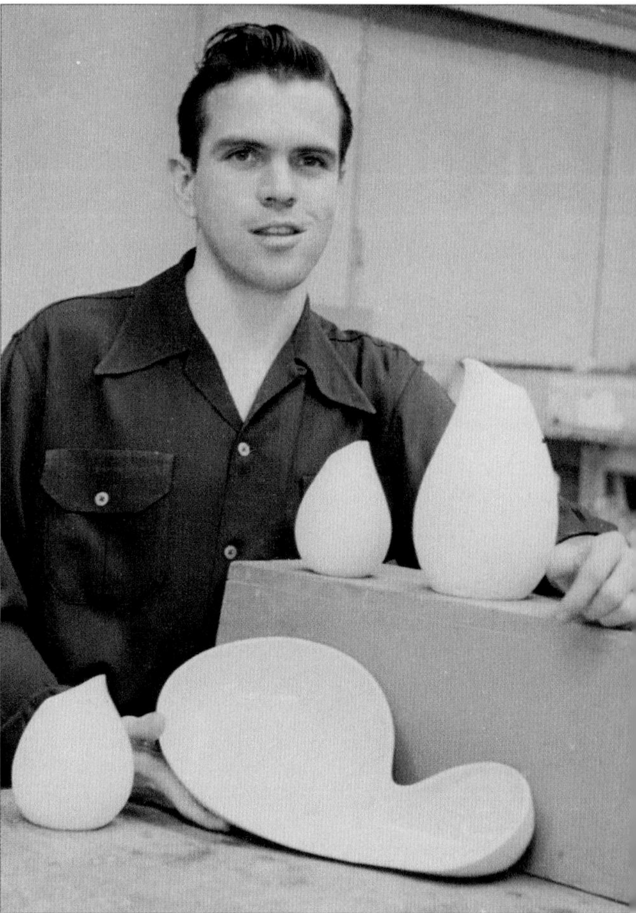

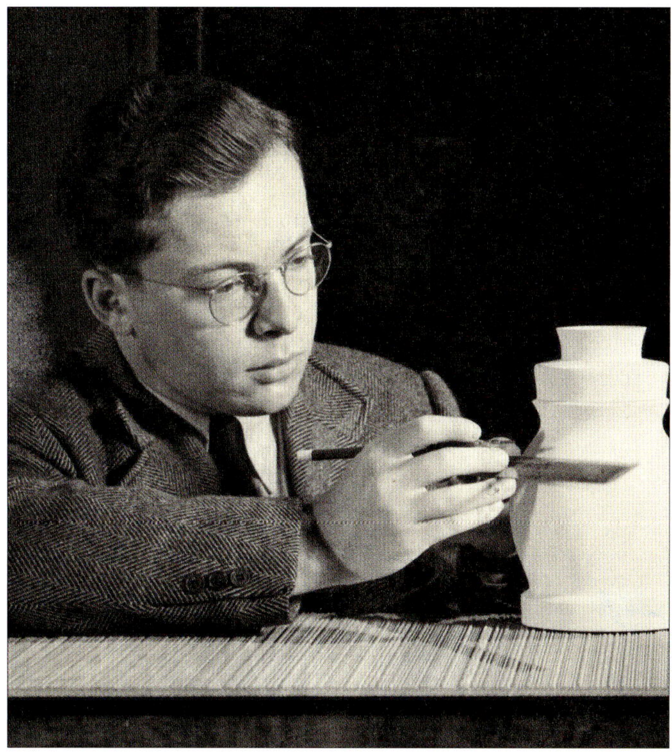

Fig. 192: Pratt student and his work.

Fig. 193: Pratt student and his work.

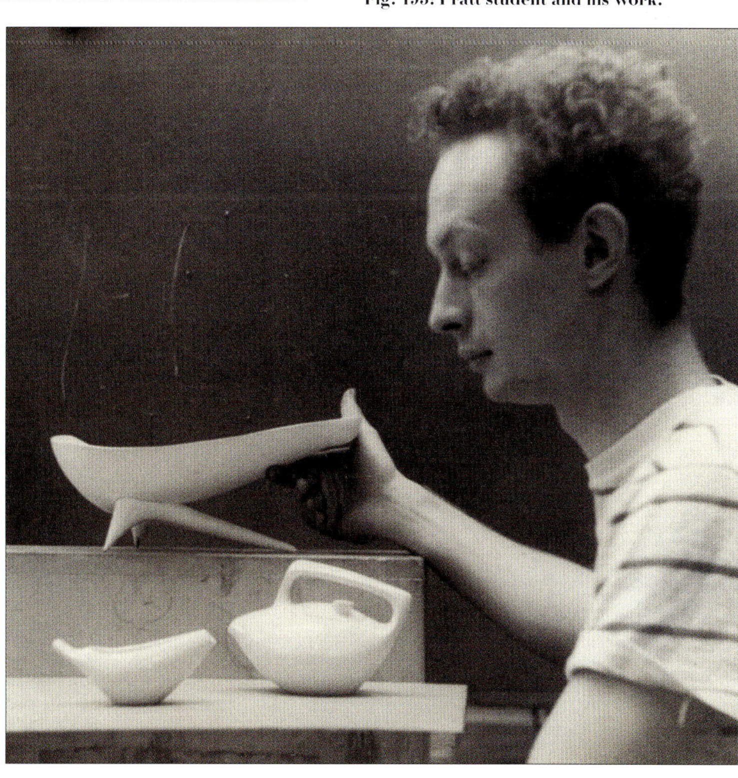

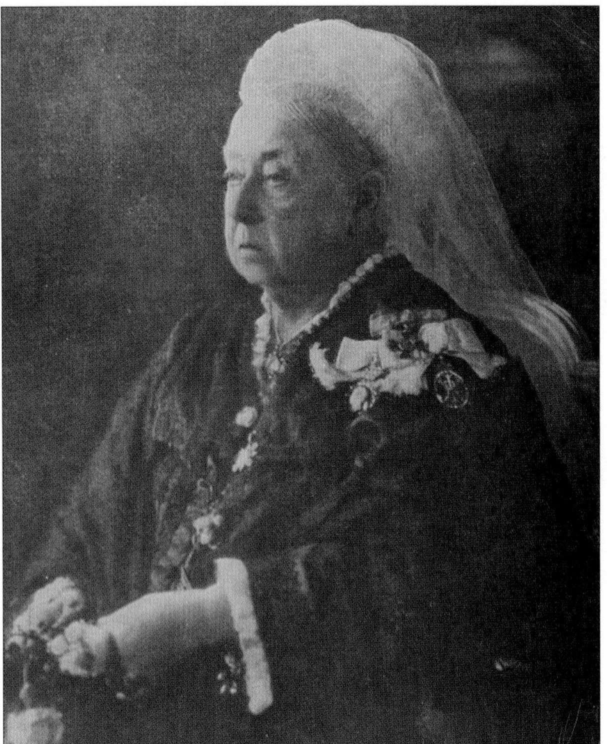

The most general influence can be called the spirit of the time. Queen Victoria, who gave her name to a style, seems in this picture to embody that style.

Fig. 194: Queen Victoria.

Fig. 195: Overstuffed, Victorian chair.

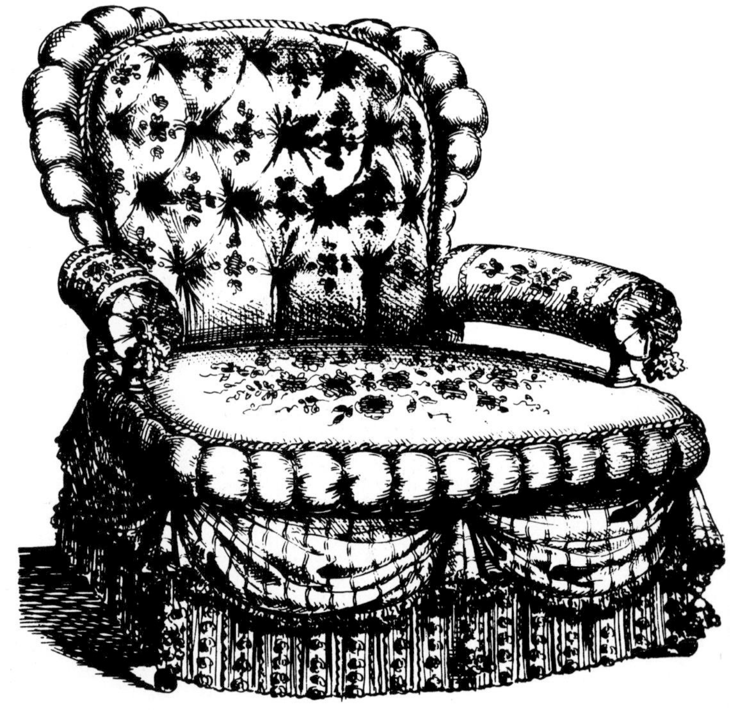

In our own time, the fascination with space, influenced the design of objects such as this "space helmet" radio.

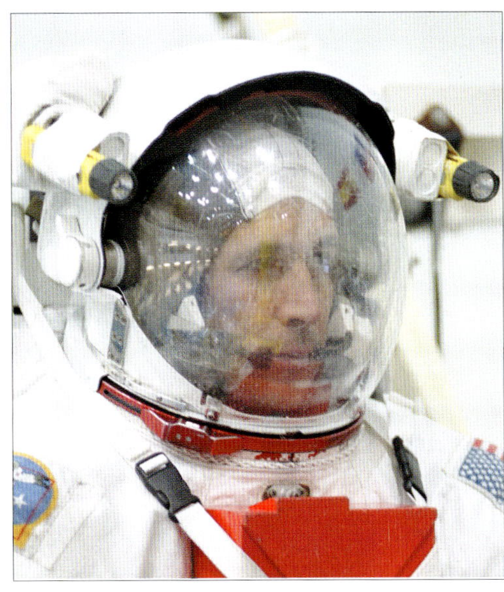

Fig. 196: Astronaut in space helmet.

Fig. 197: Space helmet radio from the '70s.

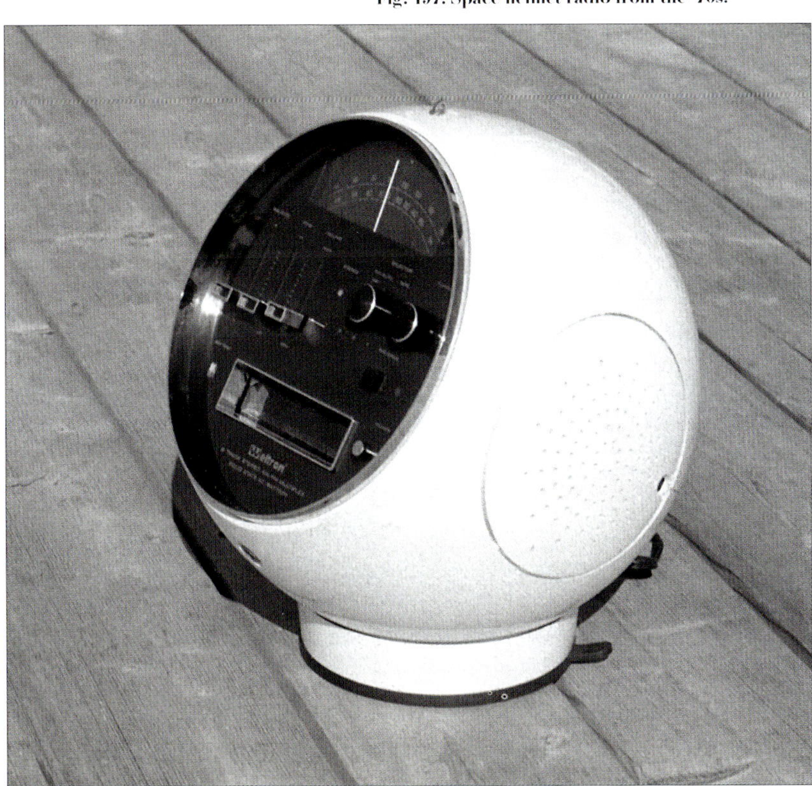

Birds

We are deprived of the many decorative elements of other, more eclectic times.

Yet before you develop the lines and symbols of a new era, before you can be generous in providing variety and pleasure within your own style, why not reach for any lovely element and use it to decorate or inspire your design, for example, flowers, curlicues, shells, or birds? Many cultures have used them as painted ornaments. Or you might search for bells and pomegranates, like the ones embroidered on the hem of the high priest in the Biblical Tabernacle, so that people could hear his steps in the holy precinct. Now that you may use ornament or not, now that you do not have to strain to reach for the "triumph of simplicity," you may adapt anything that seems suitable in order to make your work pretty.

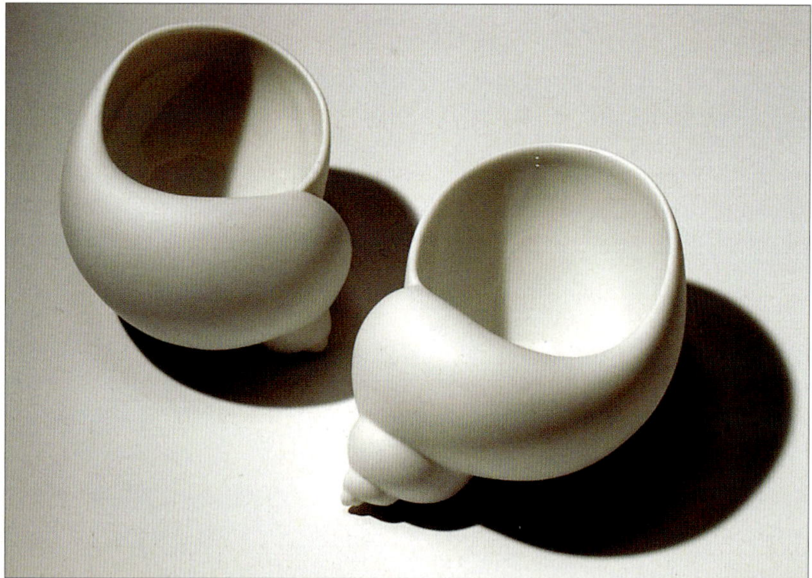

Fig. 198: Snail salt and pepper cellars, Ted Muehling, for Nymphenburg Porcelain.

Fig. 199: Silhouette of vase with double bird-head stopper, Eva Zeisel, 1959.

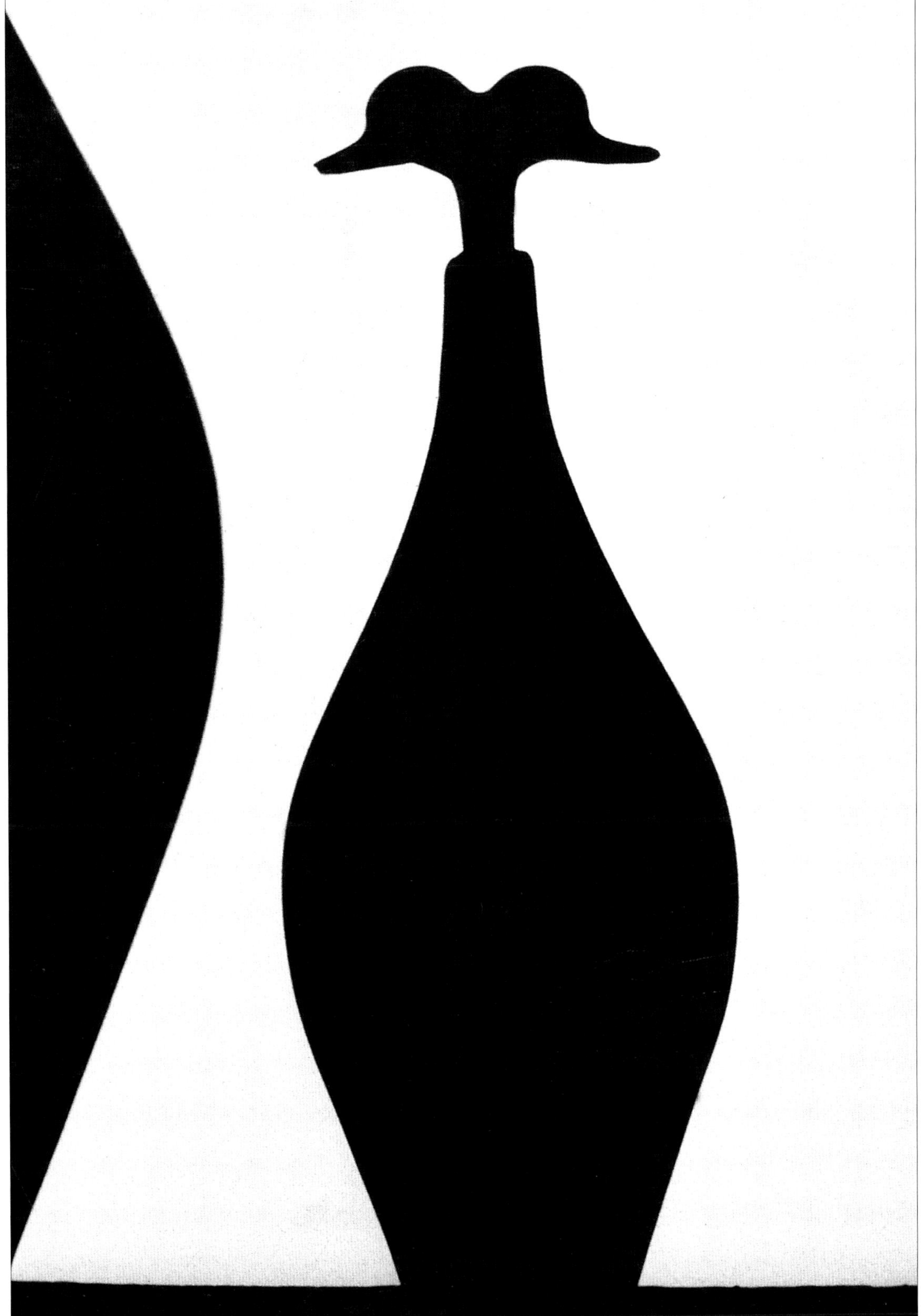

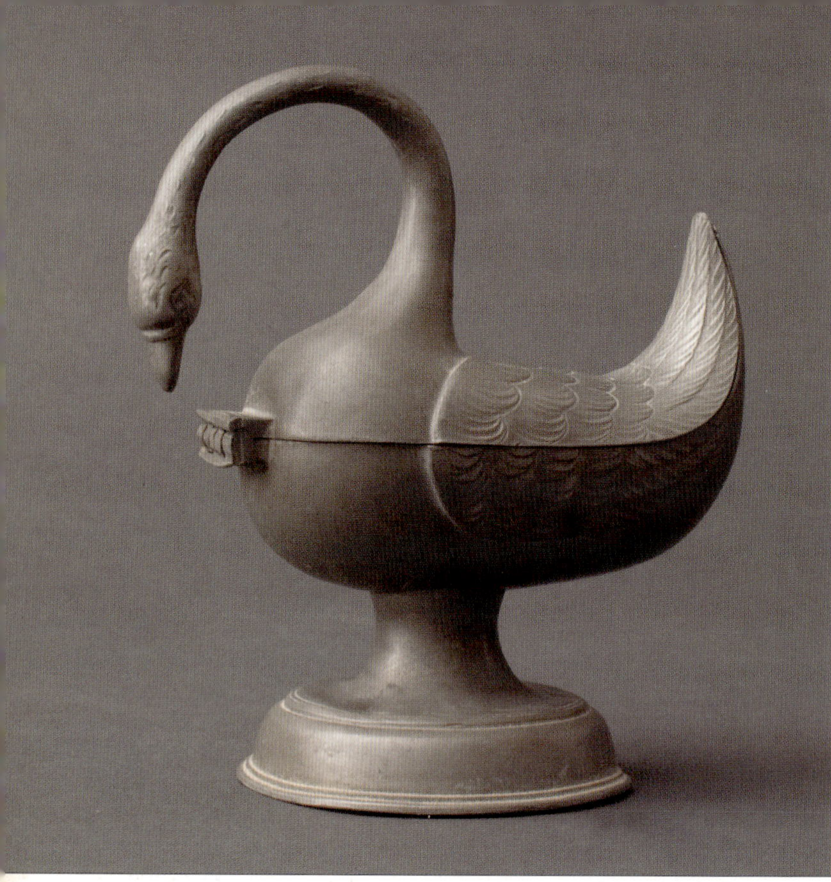

Fig. 200: Pewter bird vessel.

Fig. 201: Brass candelabra with double eagle.

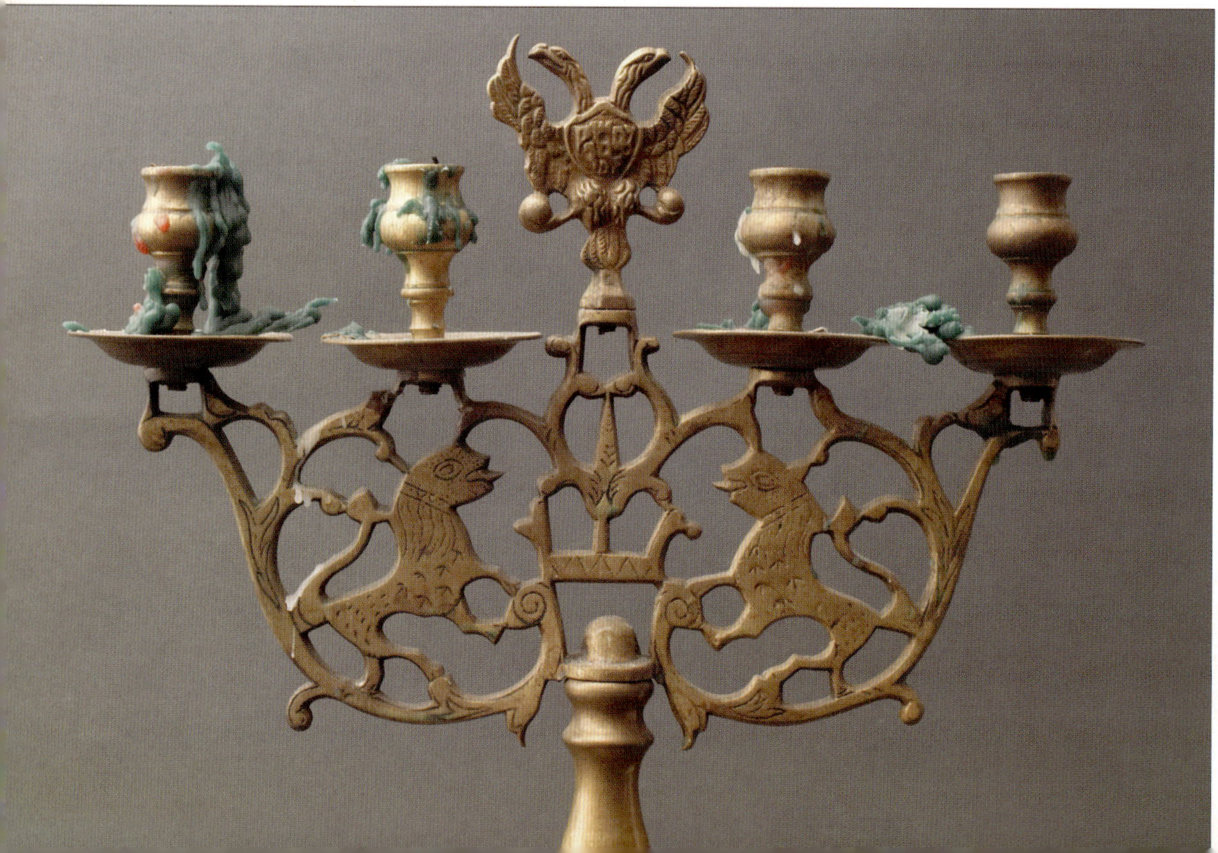

Some of the birds shown here are realistic and some have long ceased to look like birds. They have become ornaments.

Fig. 202: Pattern with birds.

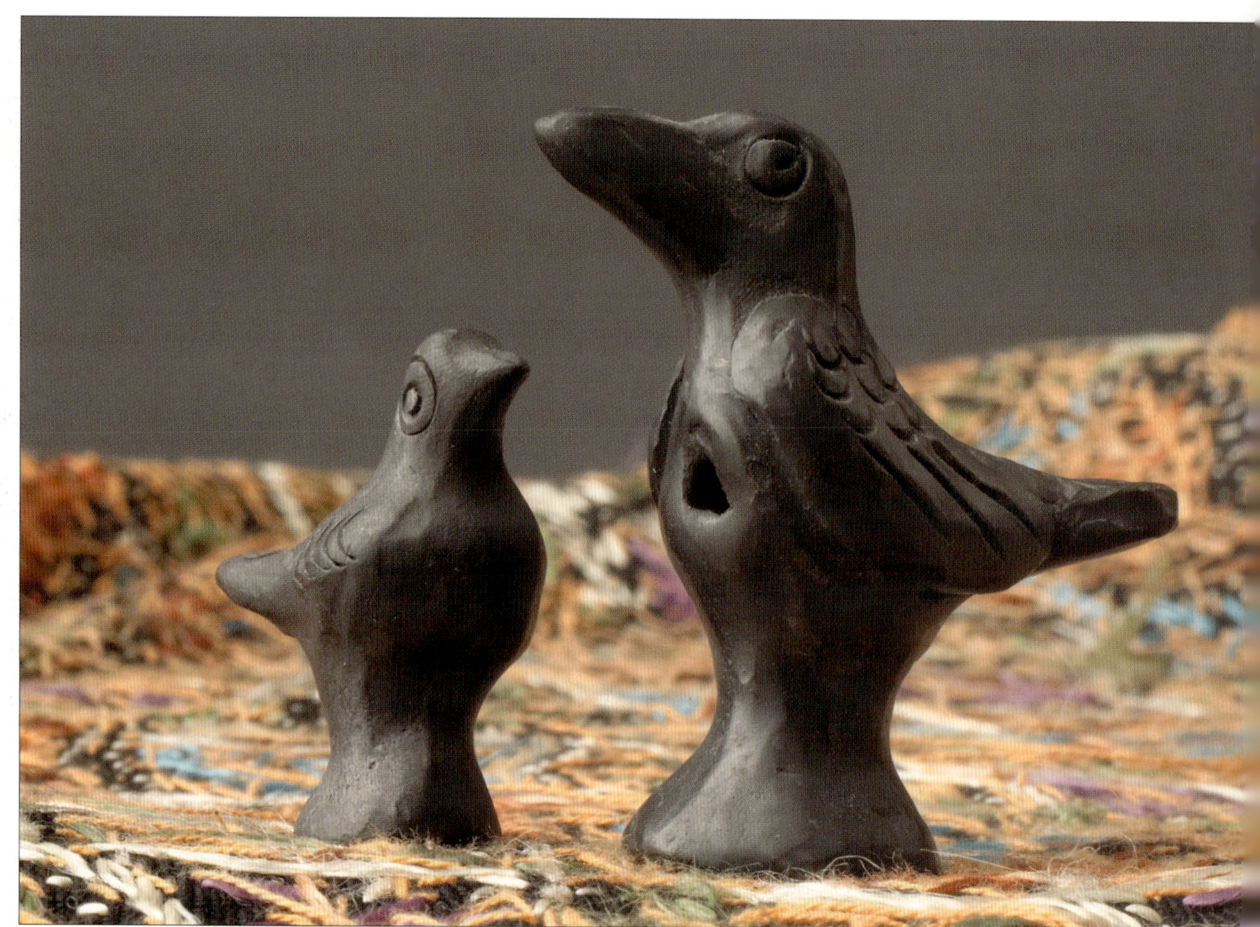

Fig. 203: South American bird whistles.

Fig. 204: Fabric with double eagle.

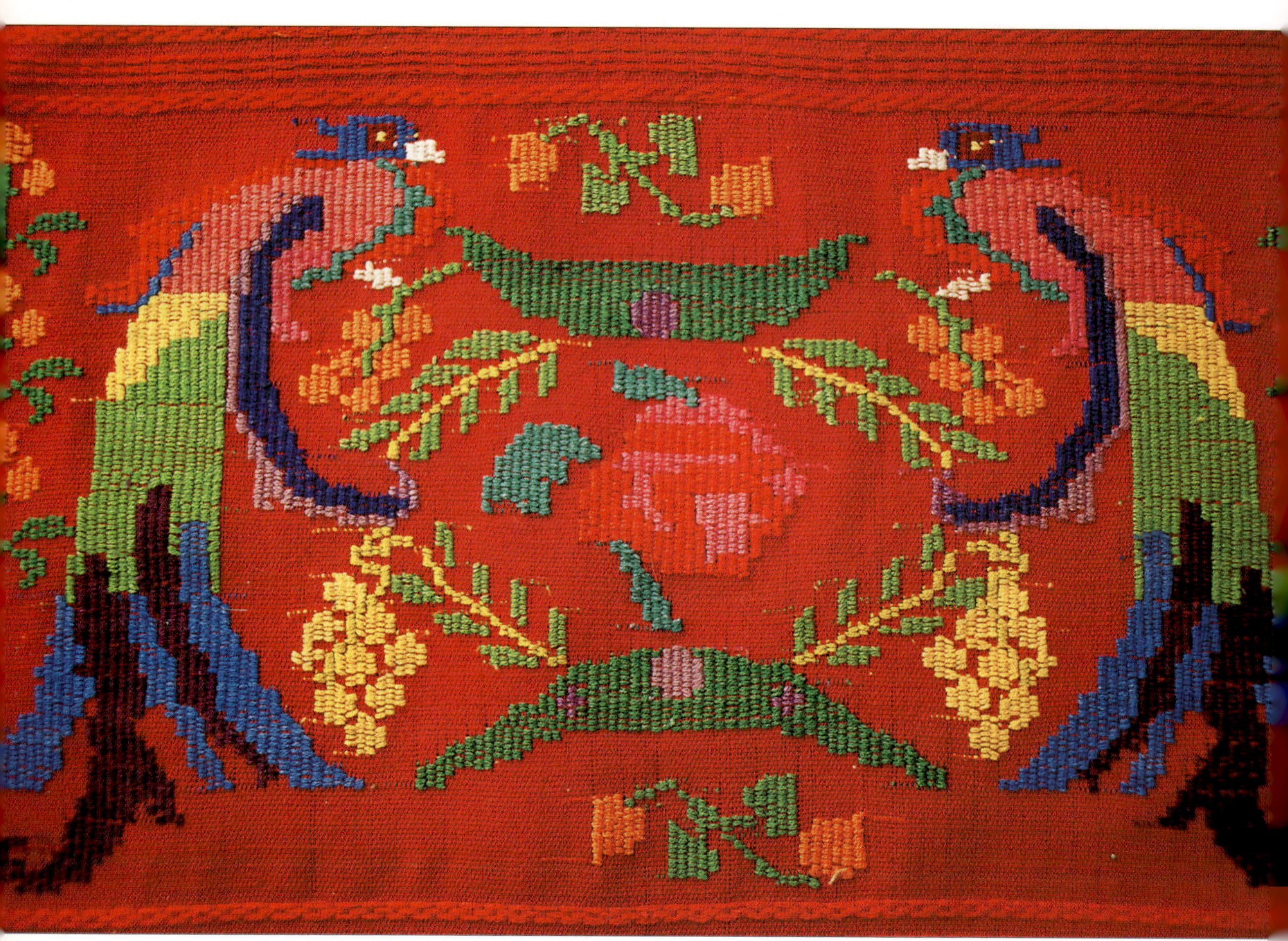

Fig. 205: Native-American weaving with birds.

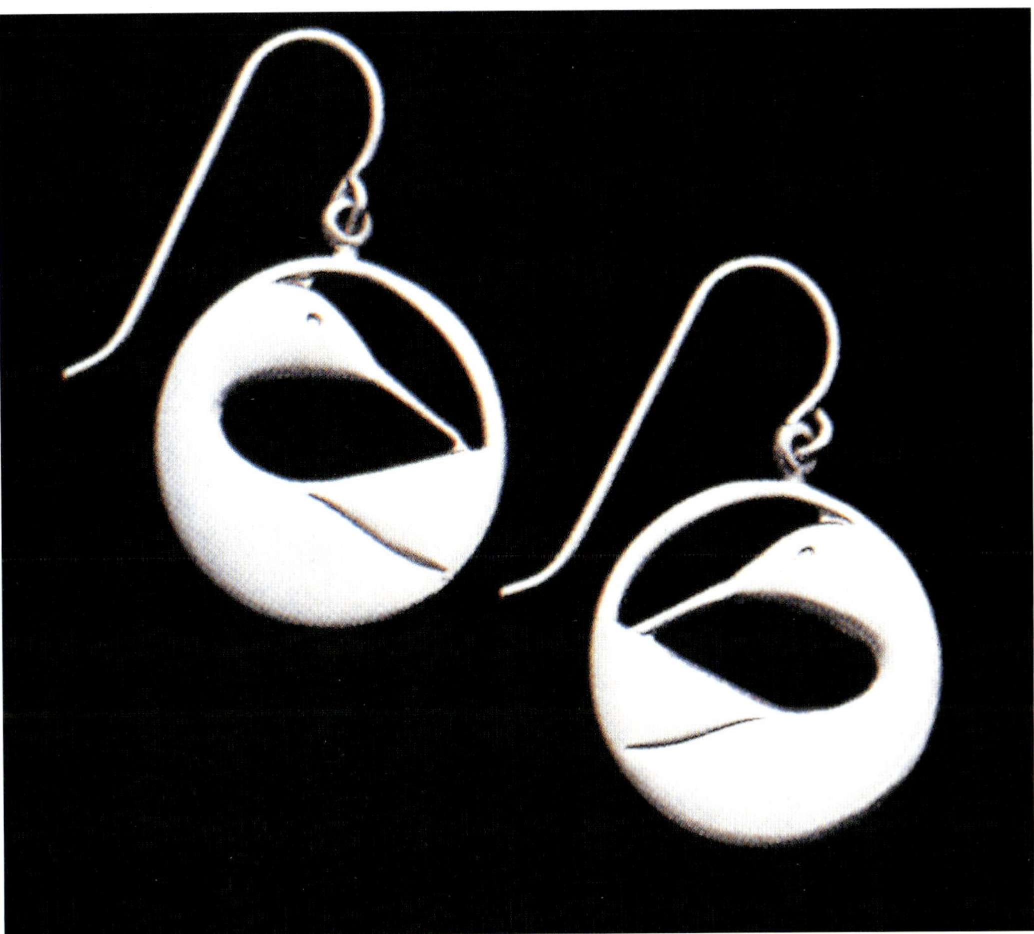

Fig. 206: Bird earrings.

Fig. 208: Bird-shaped casserole and creamer for Western Stoneware Company, Eva Zeisel, 1952.

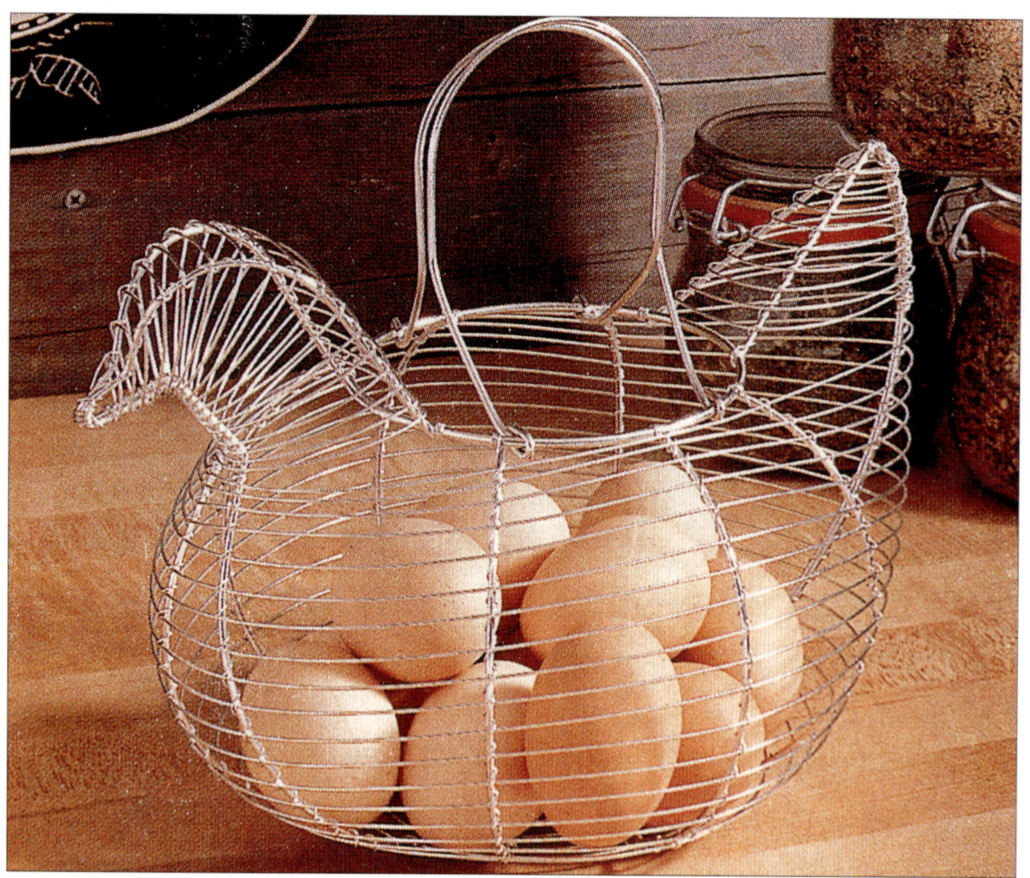

Fig. 207: Bird egg basket.

Fig. 209: Wrought iron gat
designed and fabricated b
Dominic Habsburg, 200

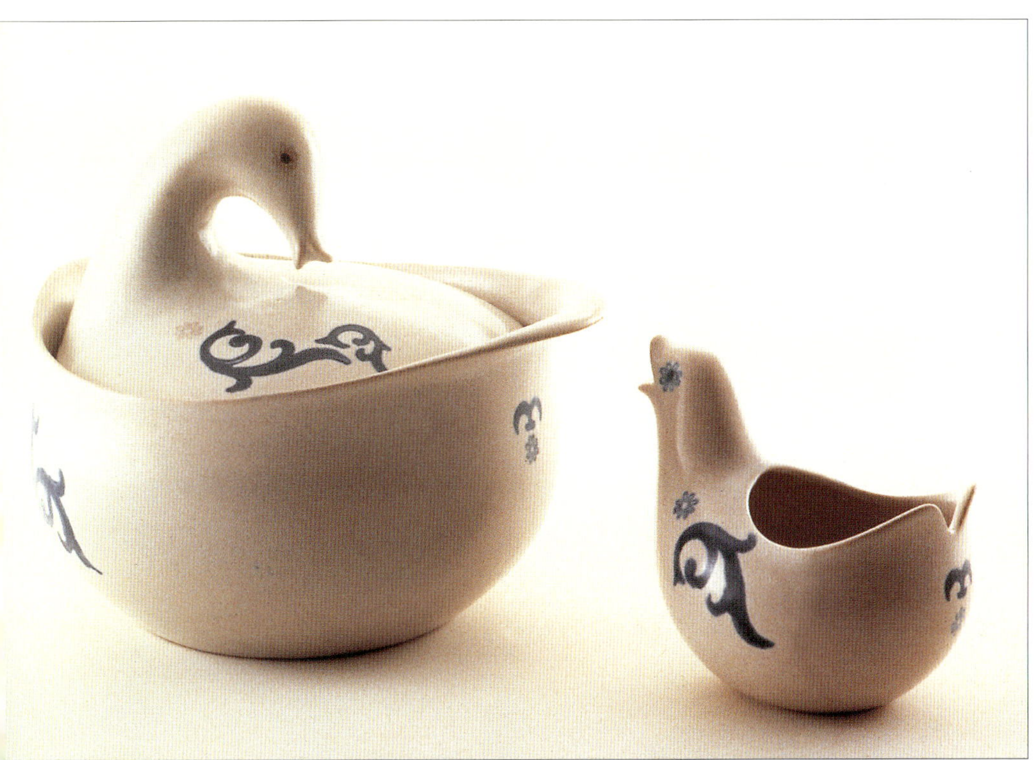

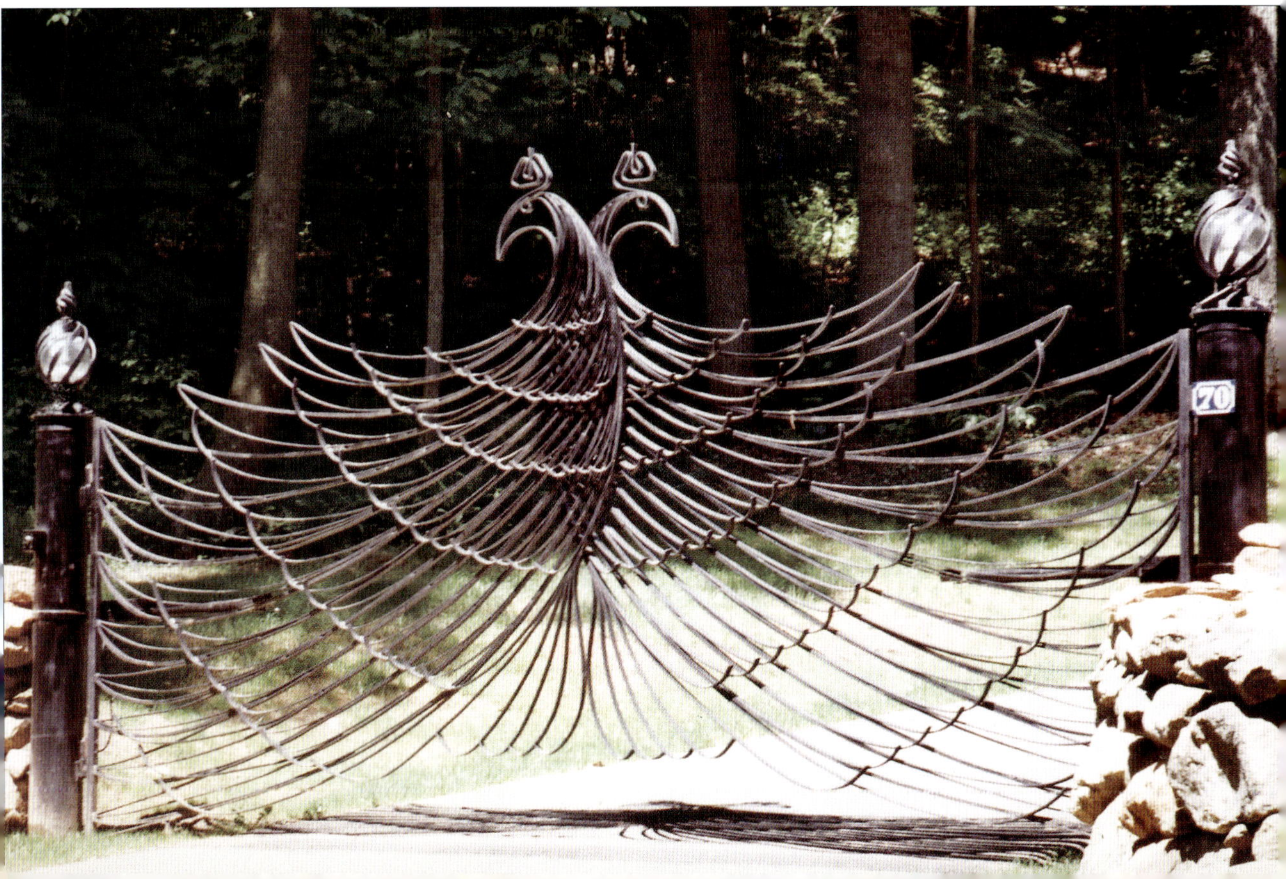

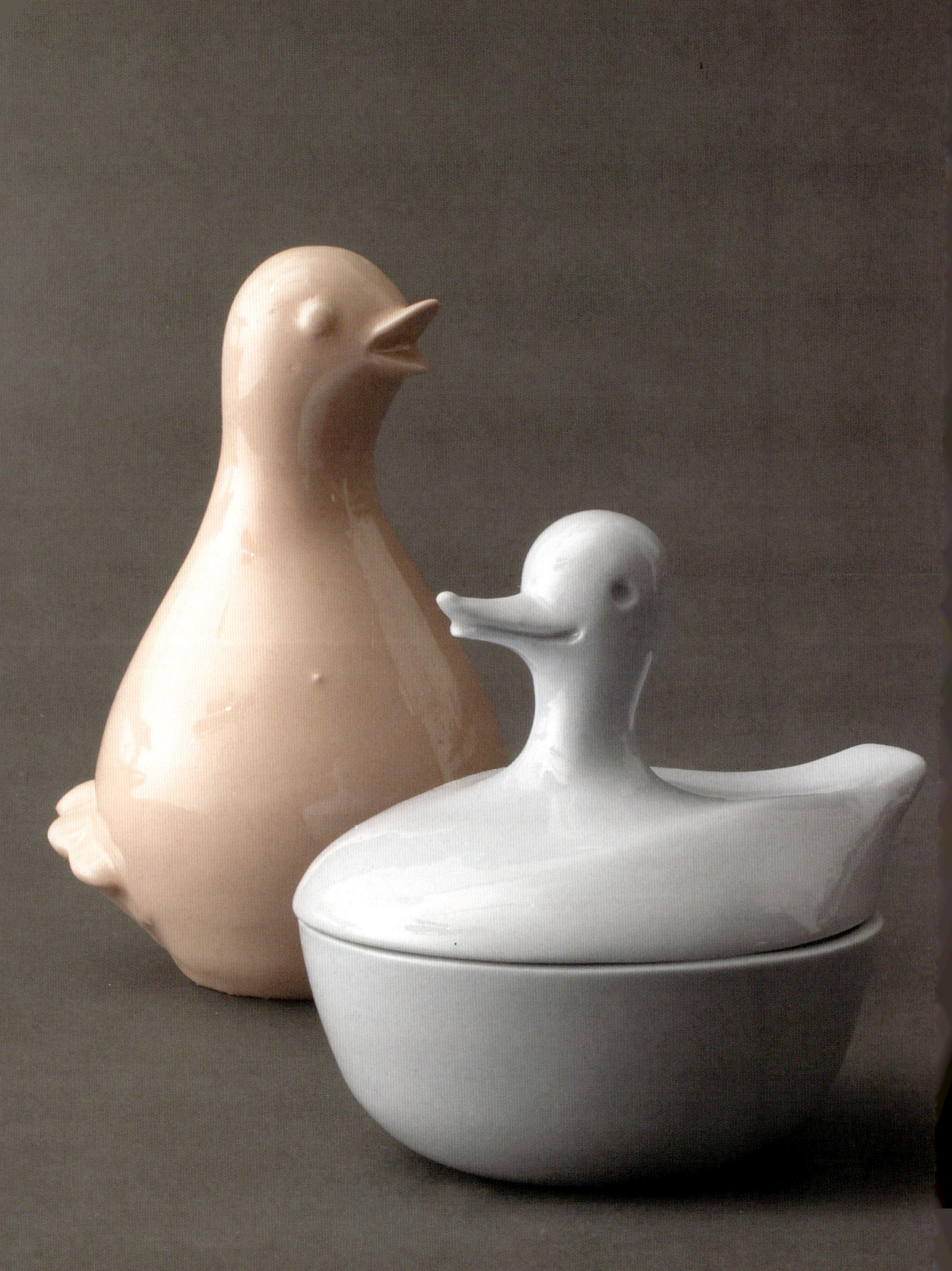

Fig. 210: Baby set, powder dispenser, and covered container, Eva Zeisel, 1950s.

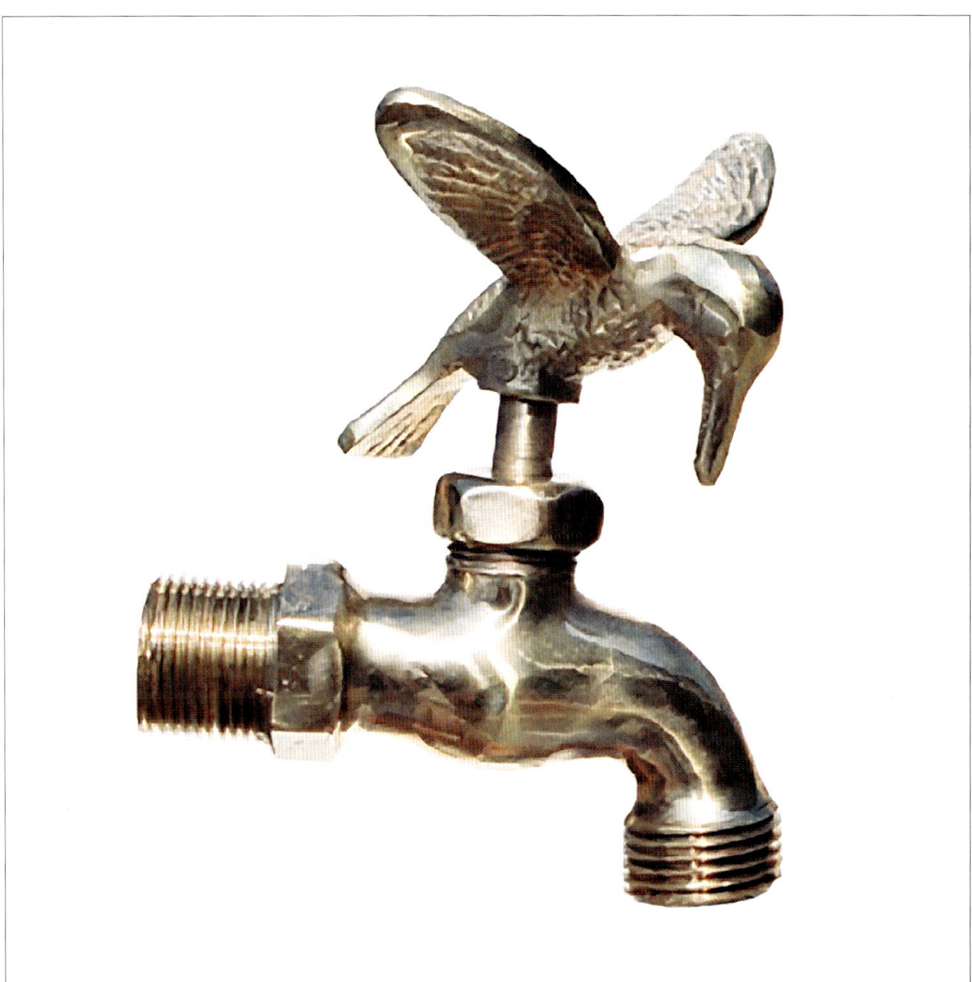

Fig. 211: Bird as faucet handle.

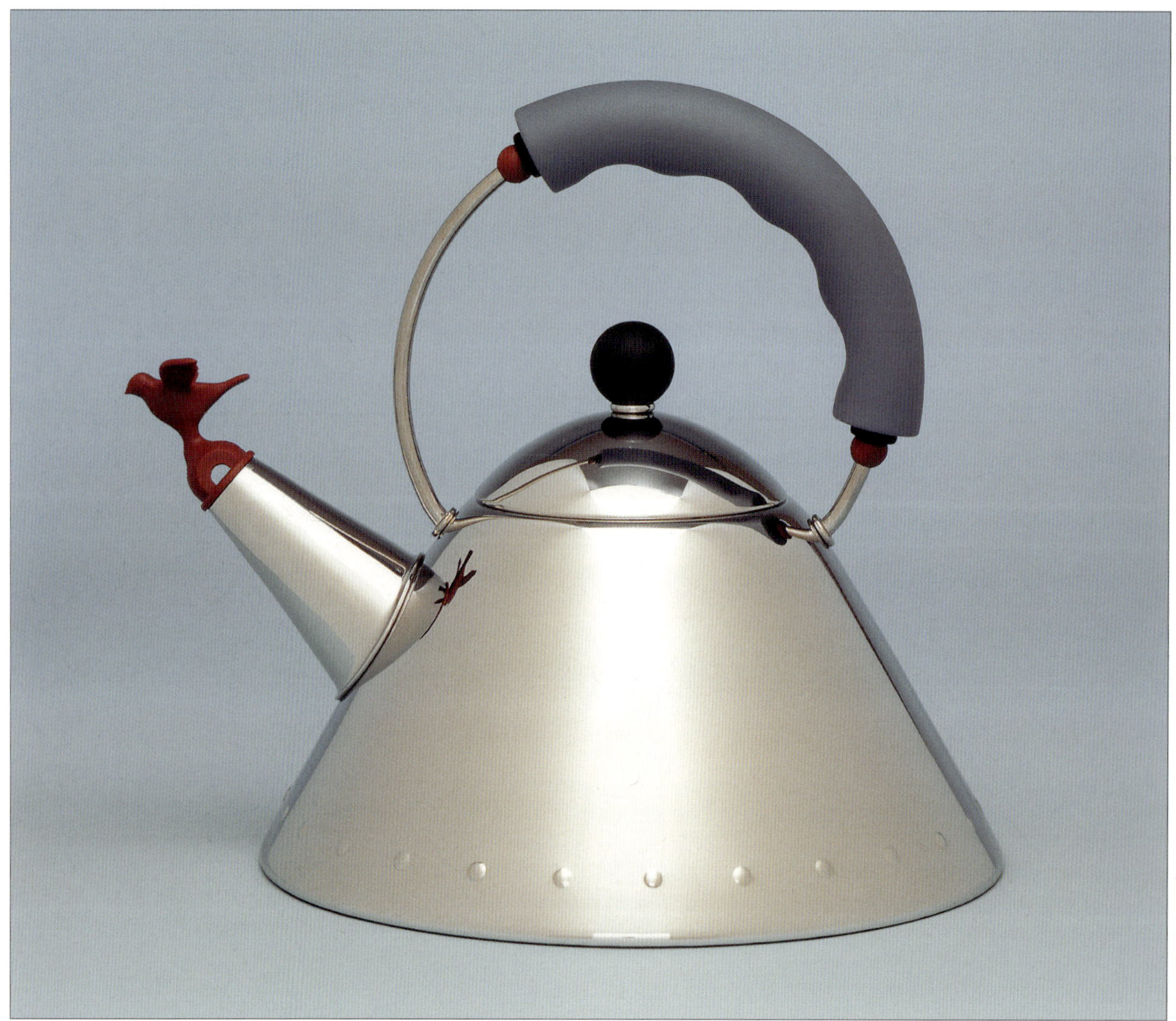

Fig. 212: Michael Graves tea kettle for Alessi.

Visible Structure

The spidery web of steel construction, which is still fashionably chic in the

design, for instance, of public buildings.

Construction forms, both useful and beautiful, have appeared since much earlier times, but they certainly were ubiquitous by the time the new iron monuments, such as the miraculous bridges, intruded upon the vision of the aesthetically sensitive. Their symbolic meaning became acute when industrialization became the preoccupation of the young Soviet Union. The shapes of iron girders were then accepted into the new art movement of Constructivism and simultaneously appeared in the writings of all the greats of the new architecture.

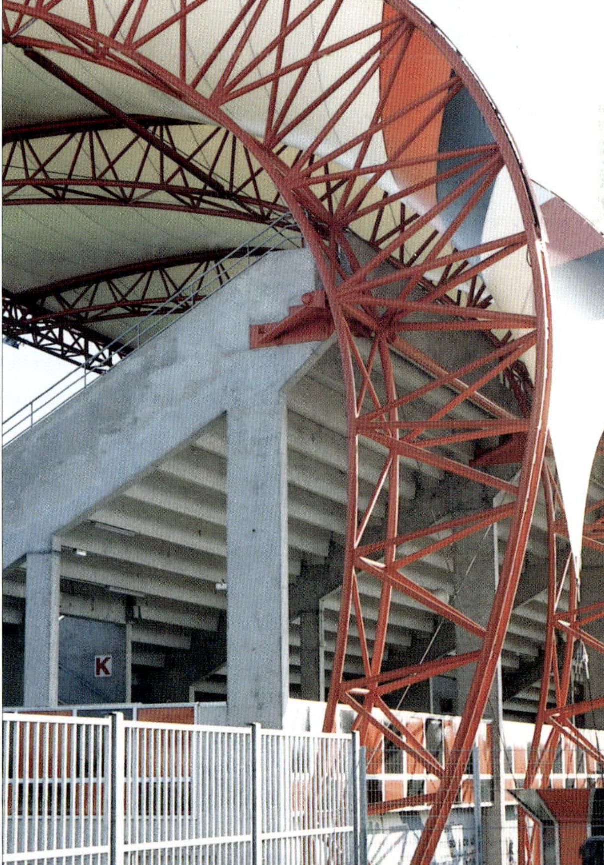

Fig. 213: Racetrack grandstand, France.

Eventually structure became one of the formal elements accepted in the form language of the modern movement.

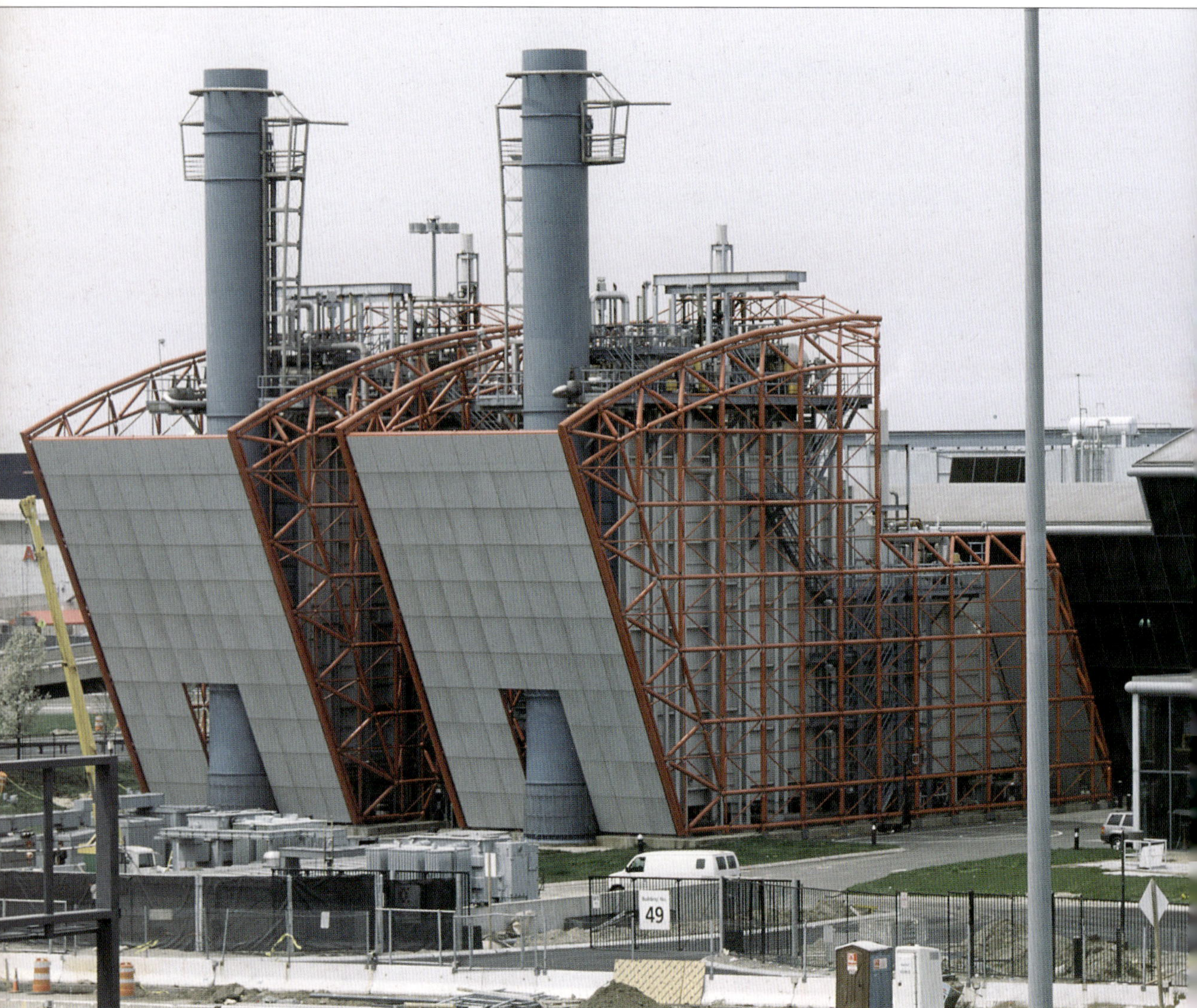

Fig. 214: New York Times printing plant, Polshek Partnership, architects.

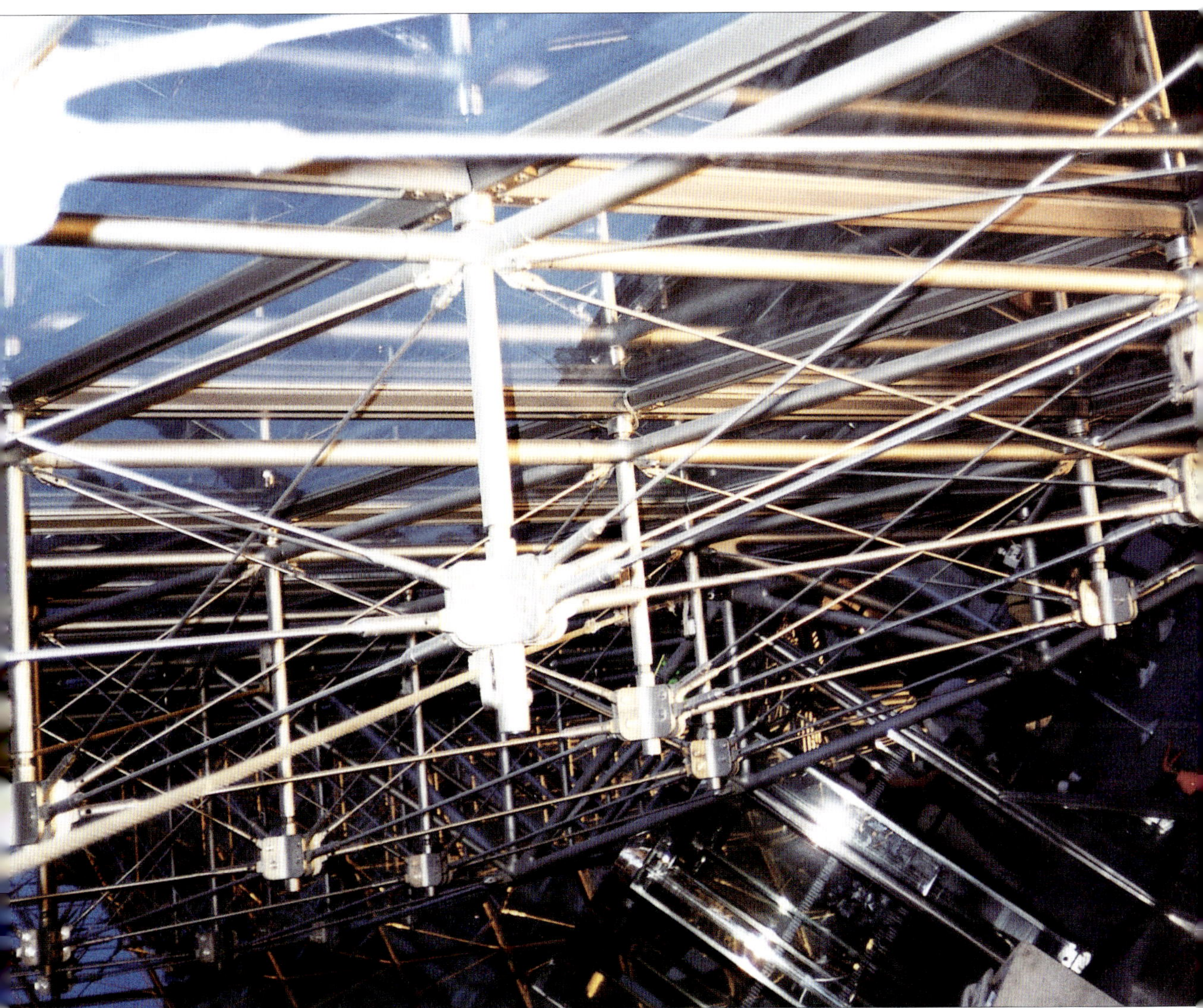

Fig. 215: Interior of Louvre pyramid entrance, Paris, France, I.M. Pei, Architect.

Fig. 218: Temporary park structure, New York City, 125th Street at the Hudson River.

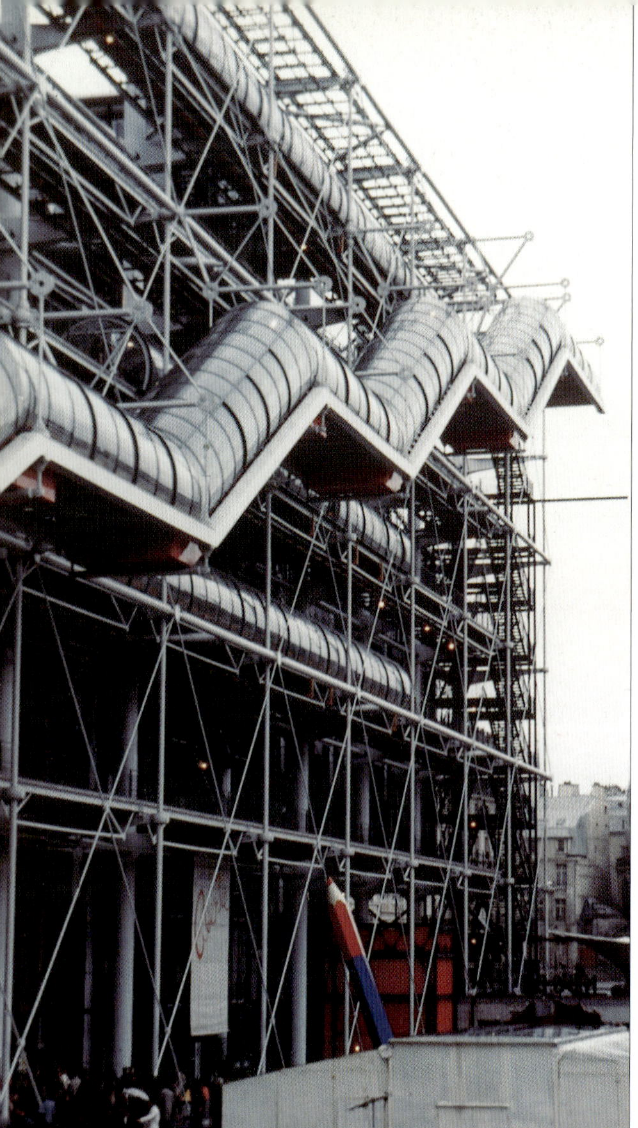

Fig. 216: Pompidou Center, Richard Rogers and Renzo Piano, architects, Paris, France.

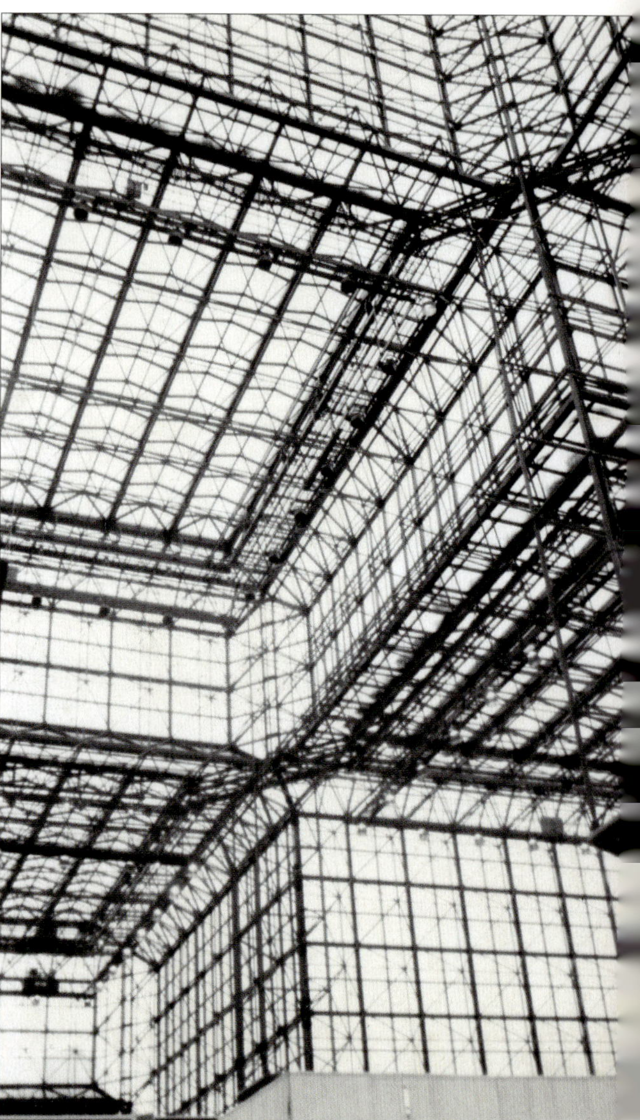

Fig. 217: Jacob K. Javits Convention Center, New York City, I. M. Pei.

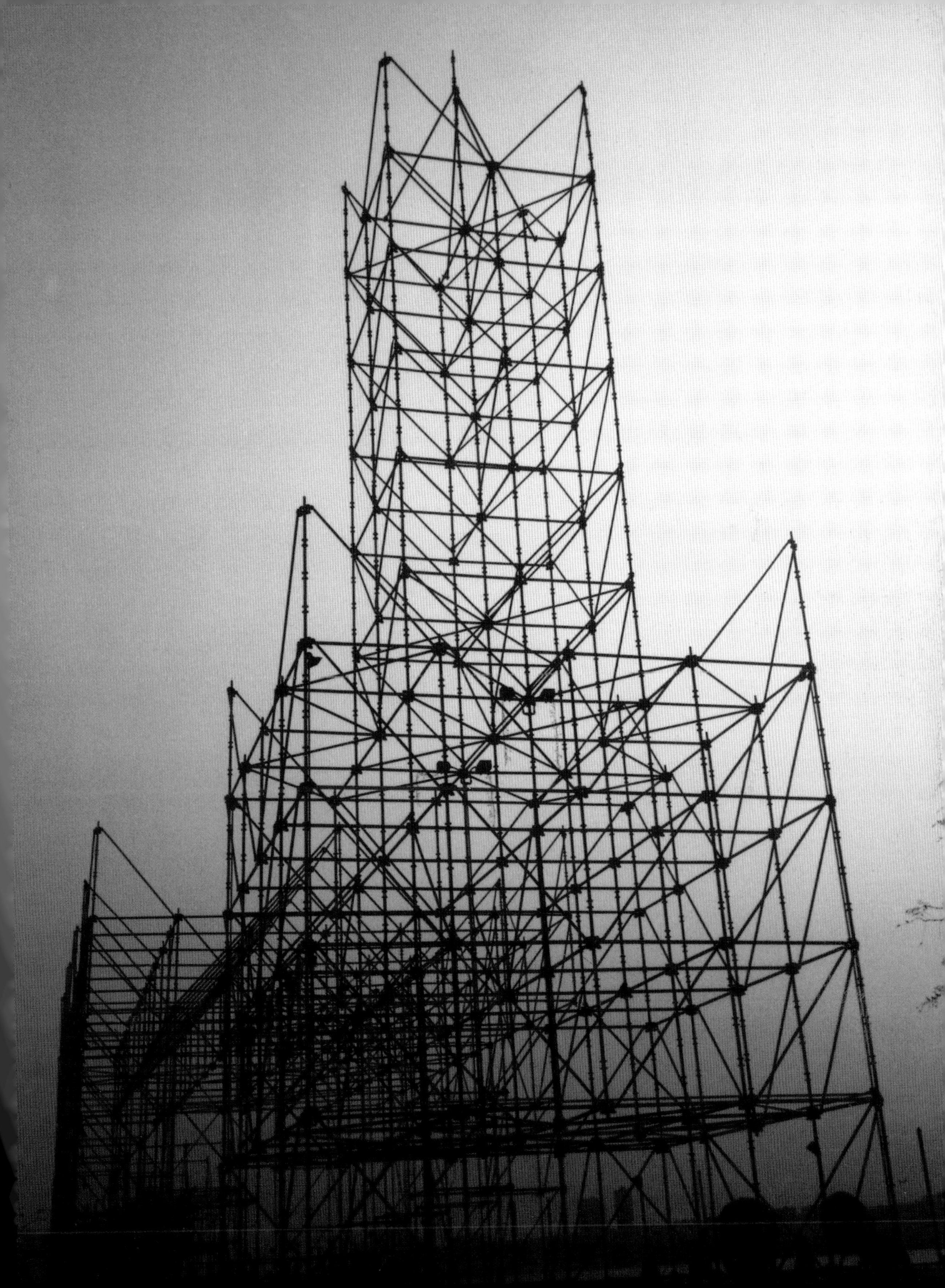

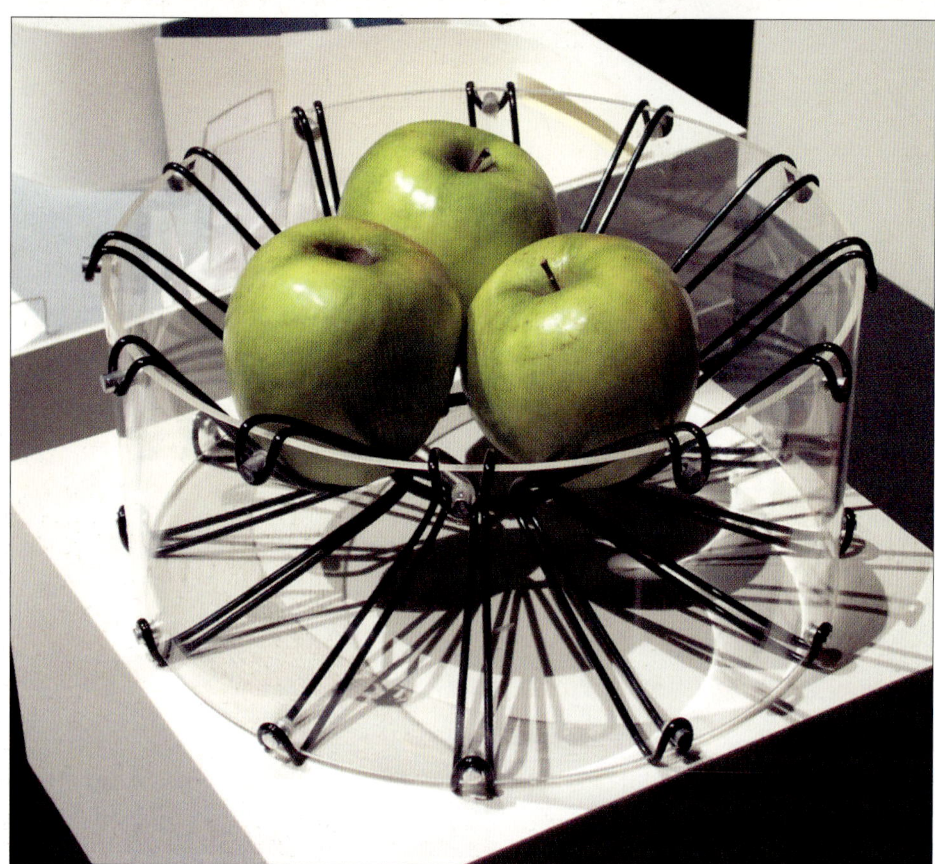

Fig. 219: Fruit basket, Yuni Jie, Pratt Institute, 2001.

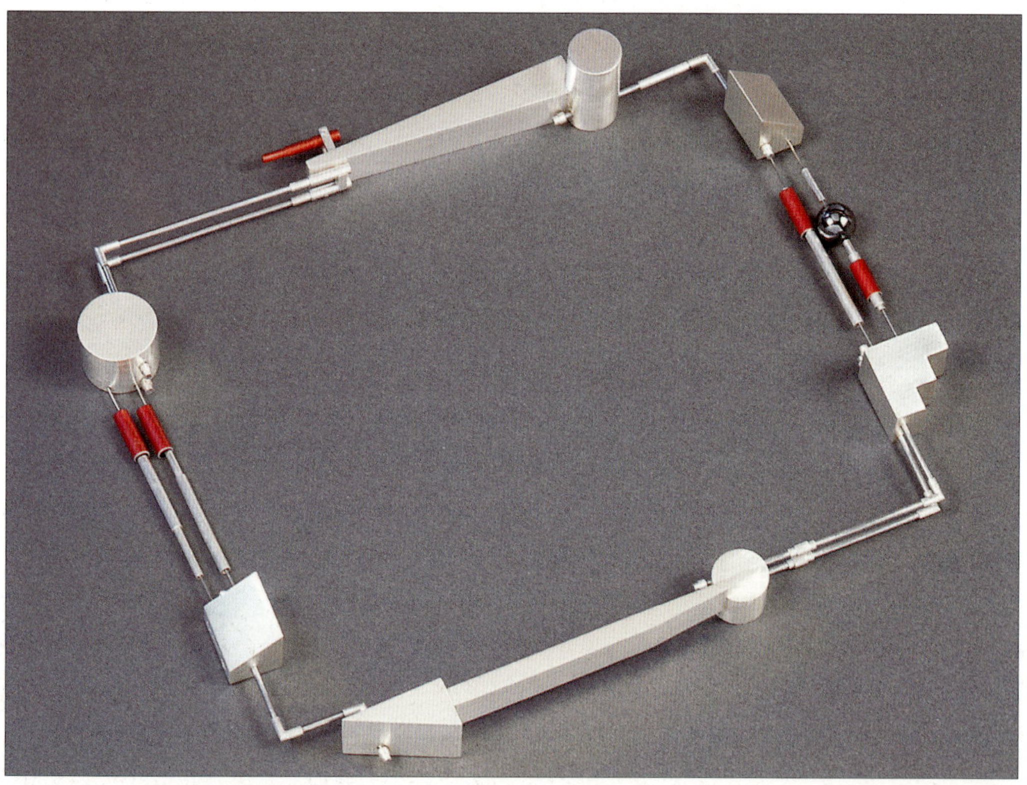

Fig. 220: "Architectural Morphosis" necklace. Designer: Gretchen Raber, 1996.

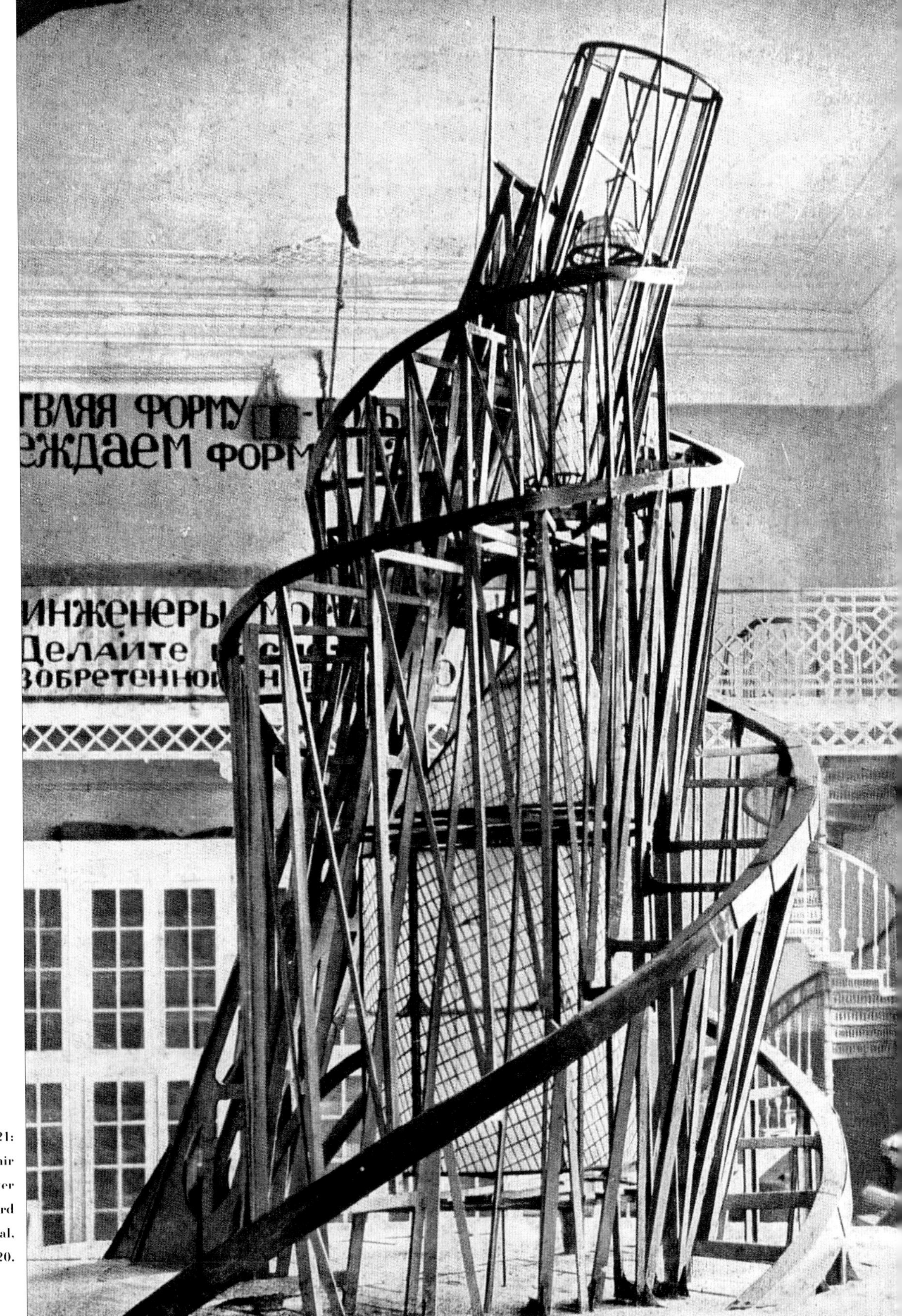

Fig. 221: Vladimir Tatlin, Tower for the 3rd International, 1919–1920.

In the decorative arts, rebel, conformist, and avant gardist have used these elements of construction in demonstratively novel creations. Fortunately, this fashion is changing, and naked structures are being clad. This is an improvement in many areas, such as furniture design, particularly from the point of view of touch.

This style derives from the impact that the new forms of bridges had on the aesthetic sense two hundred years ago. Fascination with these forms culminated in the monument to these forms, the Eiffel Tower, over 100 years ago.

Fig. 222: Eiffel Tower, Paris, France, 1889.

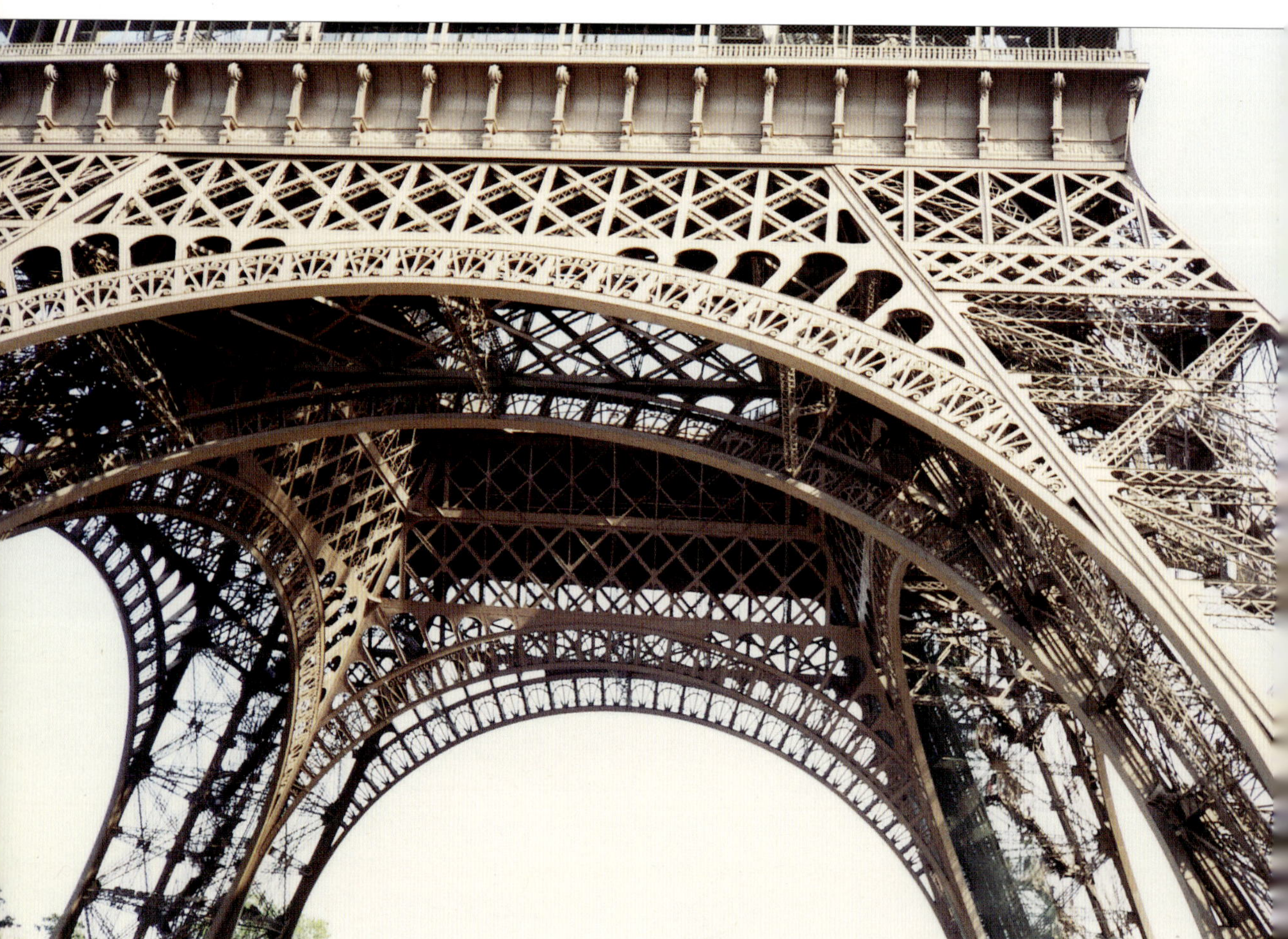

Geometric Forms & Patterns

The artistic demonstration of the geometry of solid shapes in rectangular arrangement appeared at the end of the nineteenth century. This style of geometry began in the design of architectural ornament and expensive furniture. It was later bestowed with social meaning by the *Neue Sachlichkeit* (New Objectivity) and became more generally accepted in all aspects of the modern movement. This basic geometry became the aesthetic ideal and the symbol of eternal values.

Rather early in the twentieth century, these so-called basic shapes were already being used in both high and low-brow art and had been endowed with moral principles in the rarified sphere of style. The Bauhaus, the Supremitists and other "ists" created geometric fantasies some of which are remarkably like our present-day cityscapes.

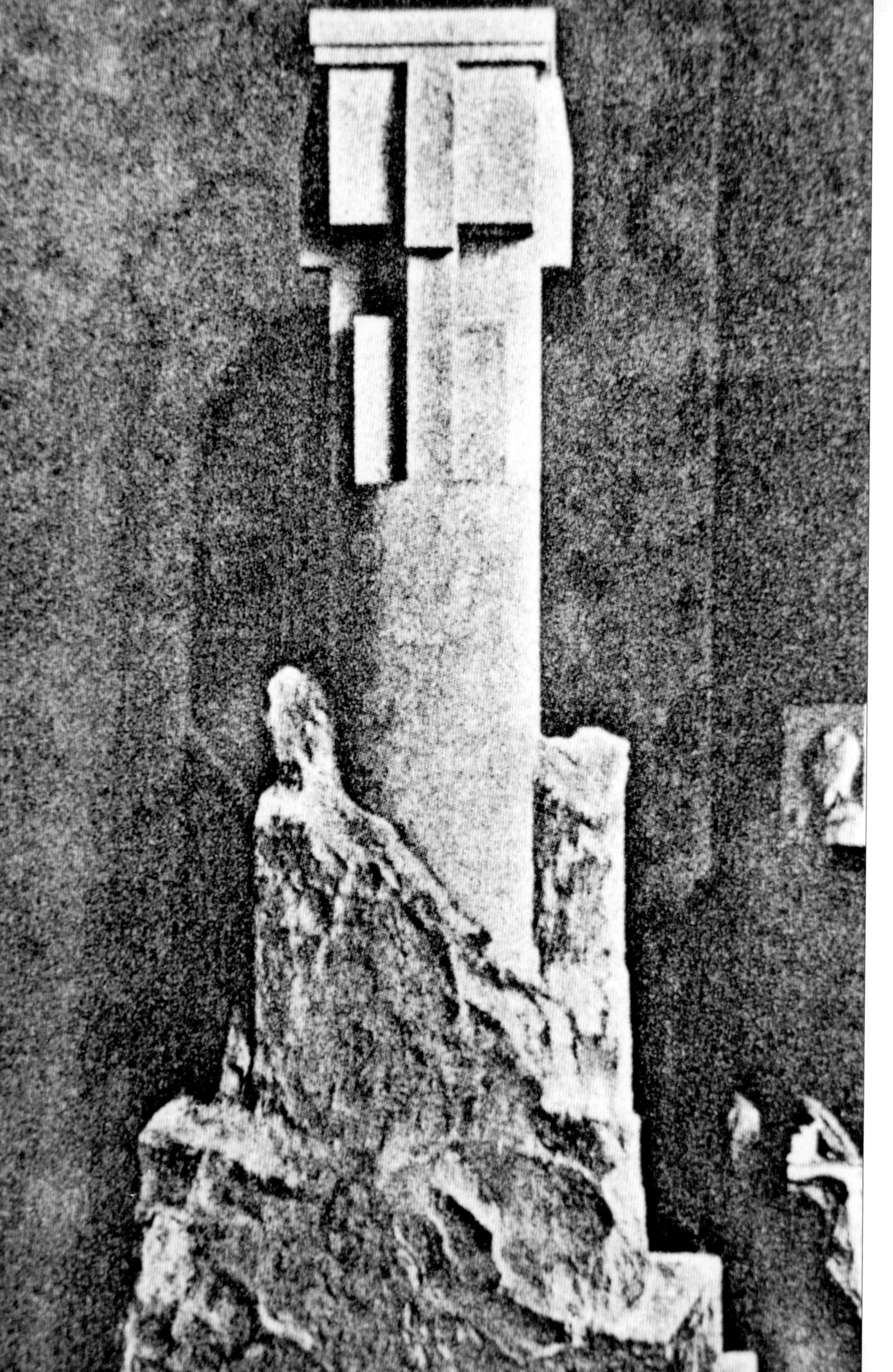

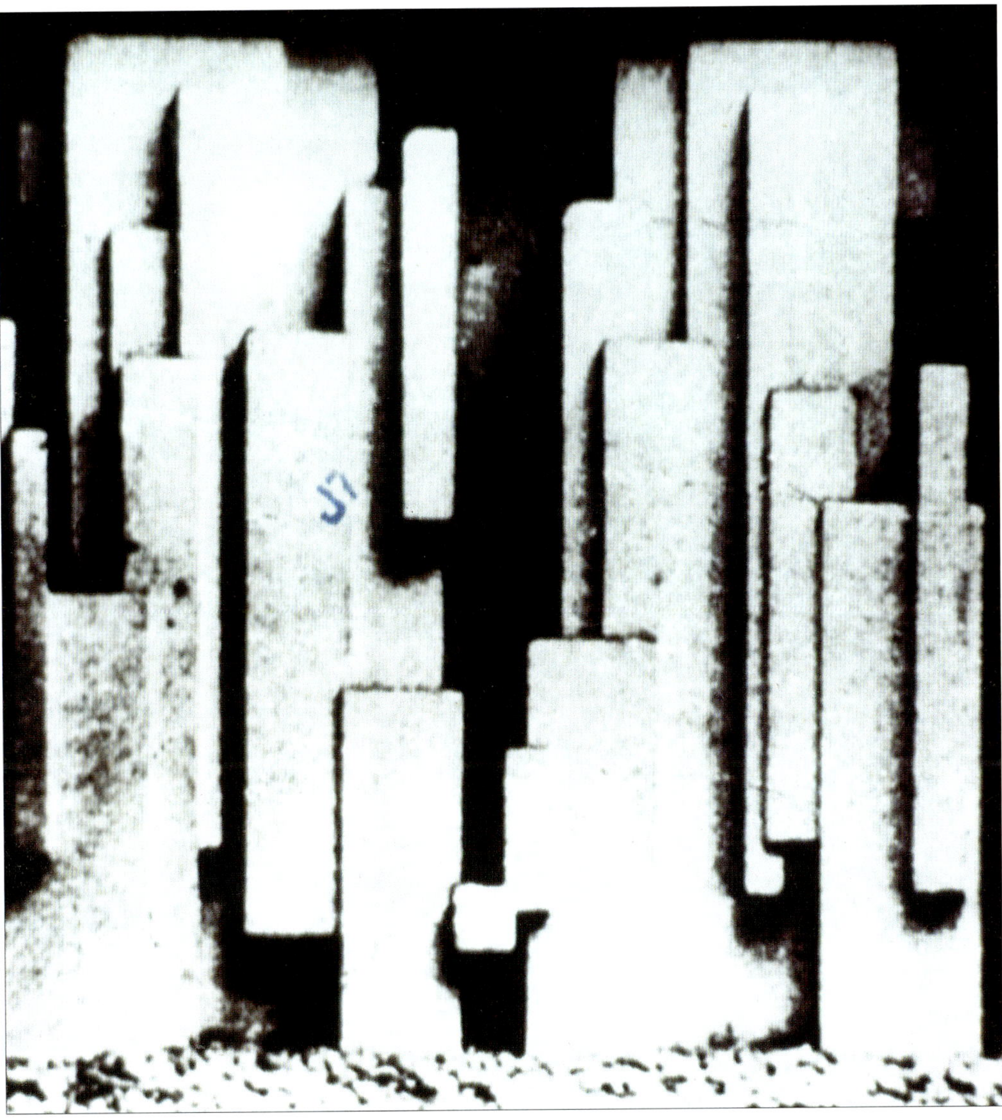

Fig. 224: Josef Hoffmann, 1902

Fig. 223: Secessionist visions, 1901.

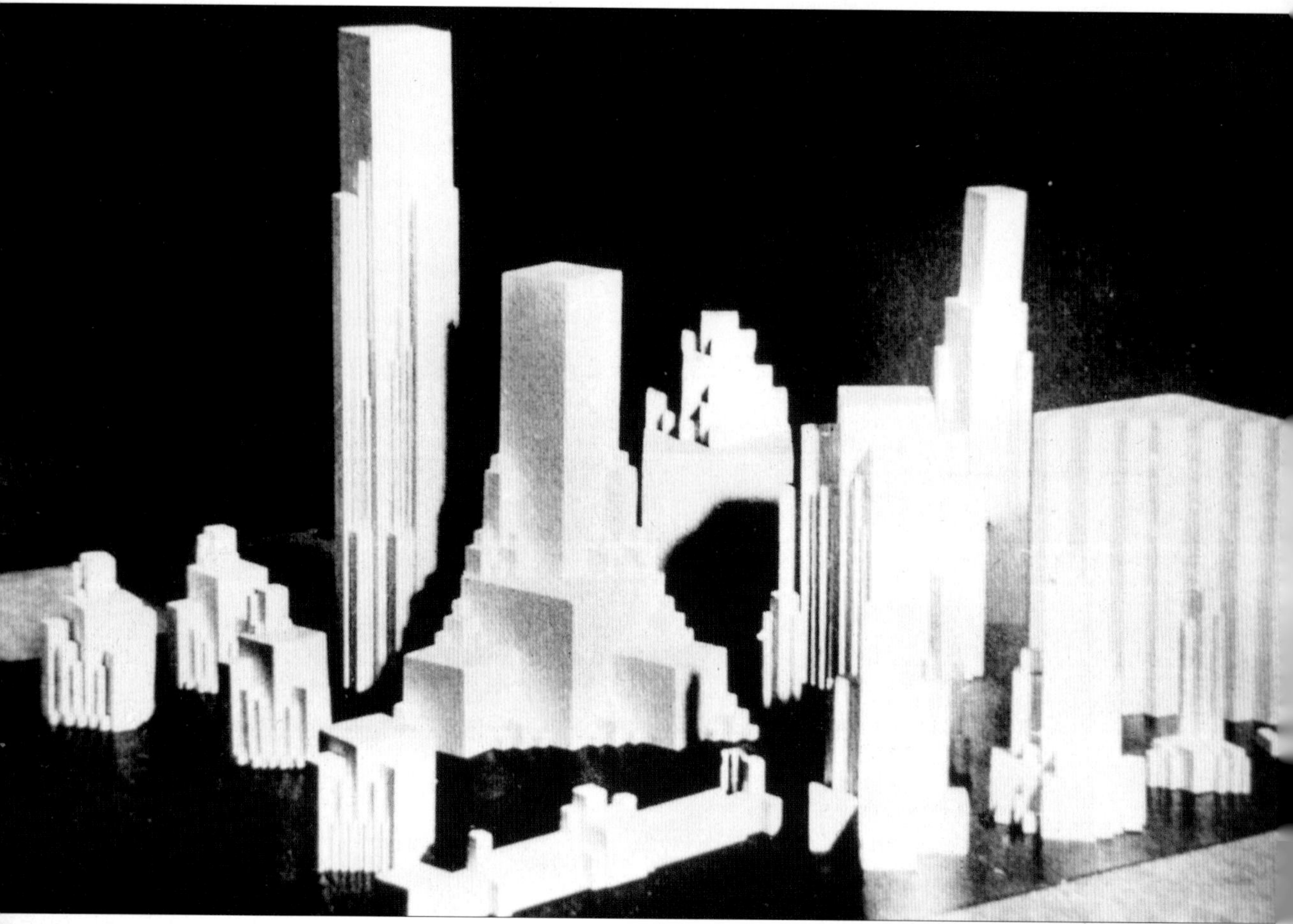

Fig. 225: Russian Suprematist model,
by K. Malevich and N. Suetin, ca. 1930.

Fig. 226: Aerial view of Manhattan island.

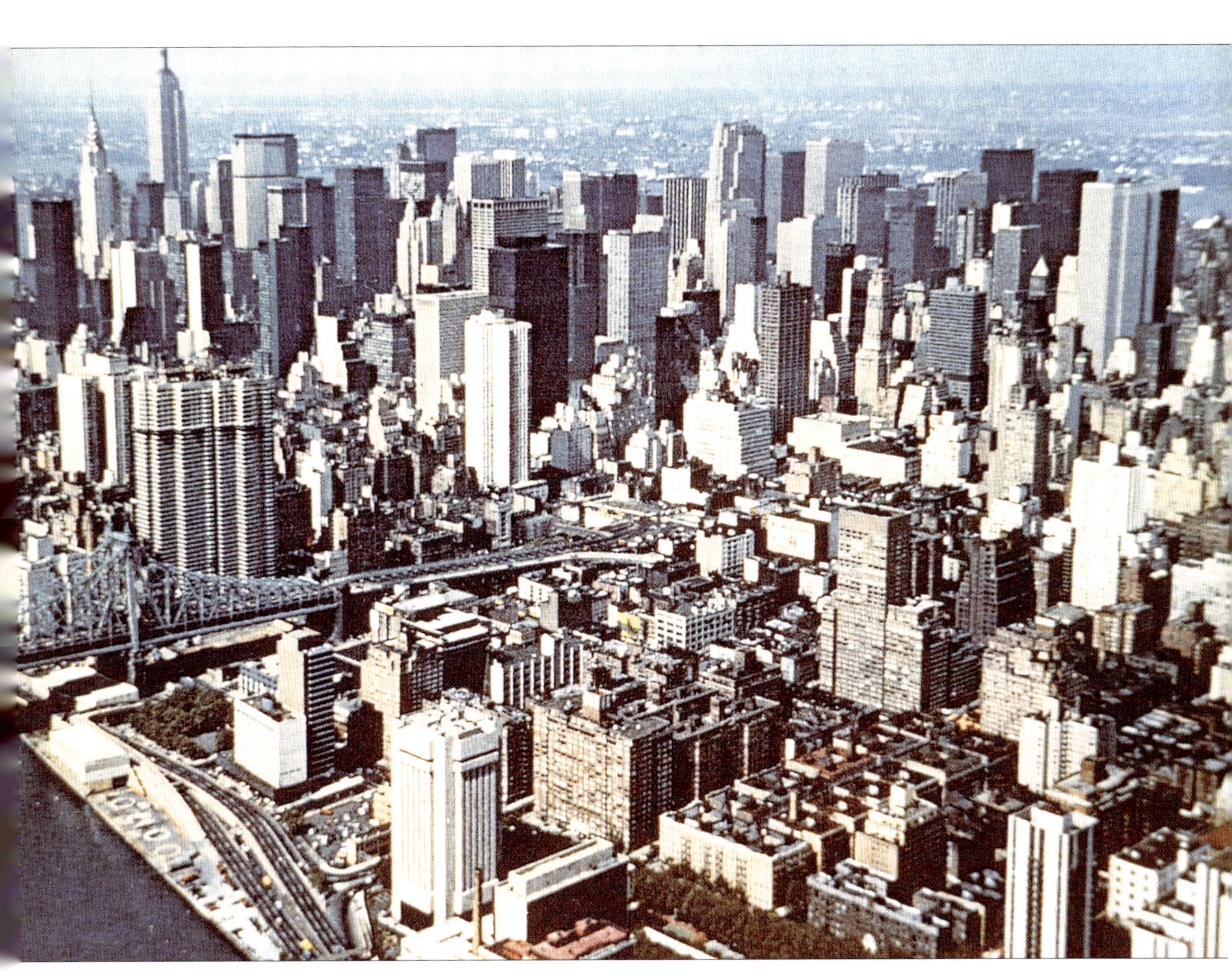

Moreover, the geometry of Dutch painter Piet Mondrian was soon being applied to the design of linoleum, doormats, and dishes. The geometric style so popular in the 1920s, 30s and 40s continues to this day.

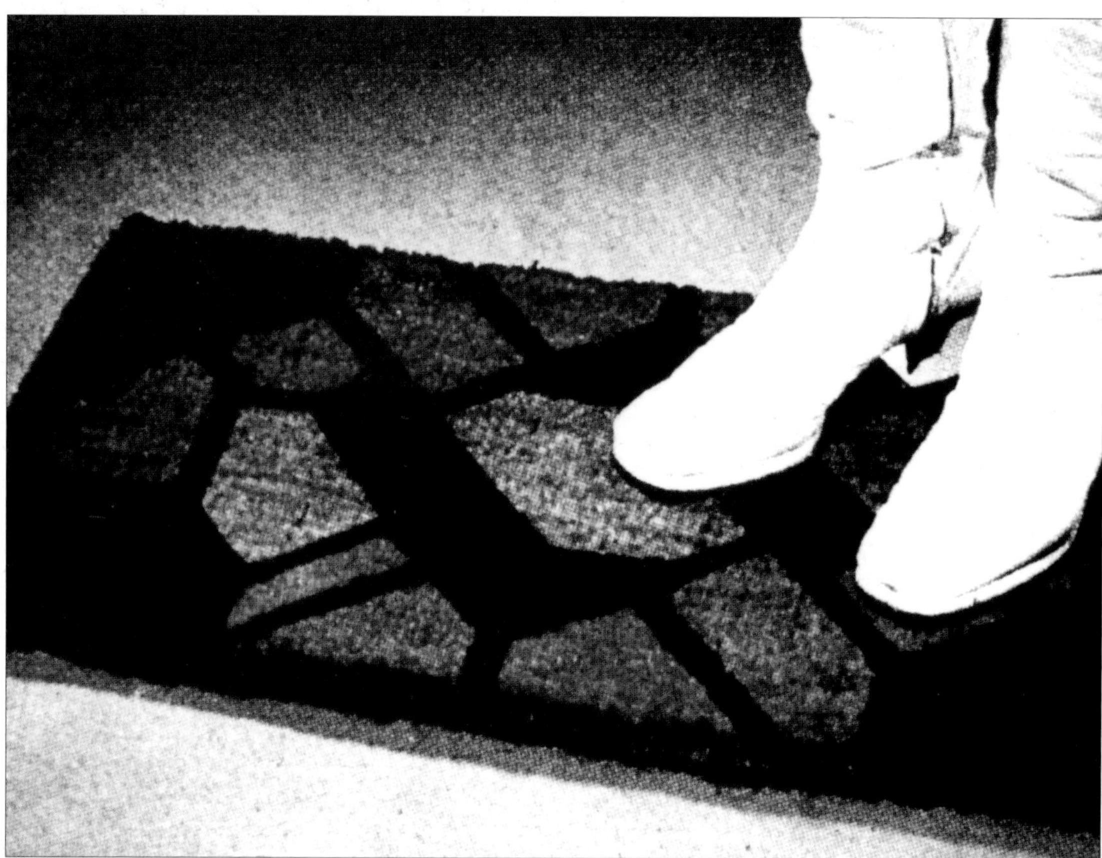

Fig. 227: Mondrian-style doormat, from 1950s catalog.

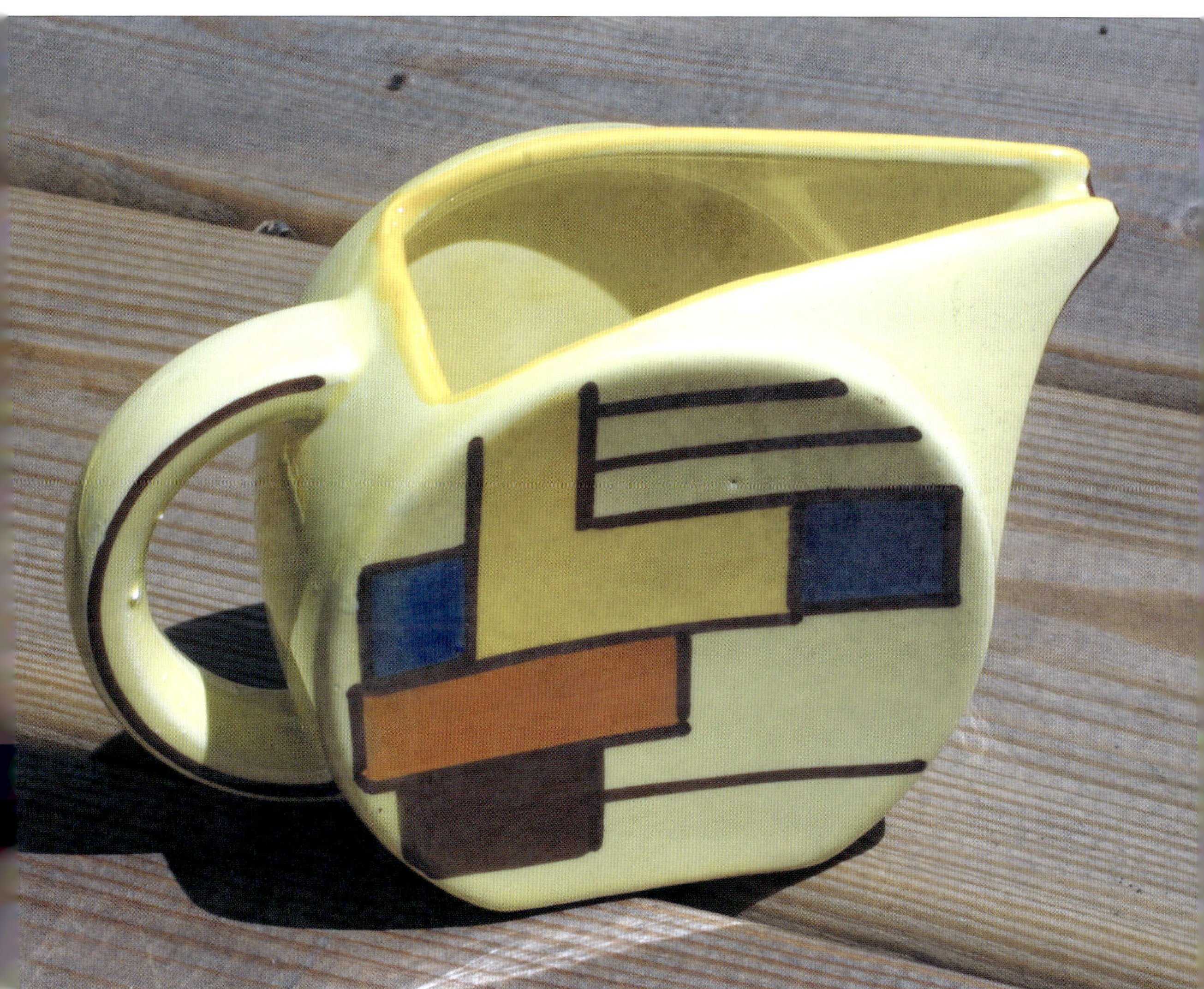

Fig. 228: Schramberg pitcher with Mondrian-style design, Eva Zeisel, 1929–30.

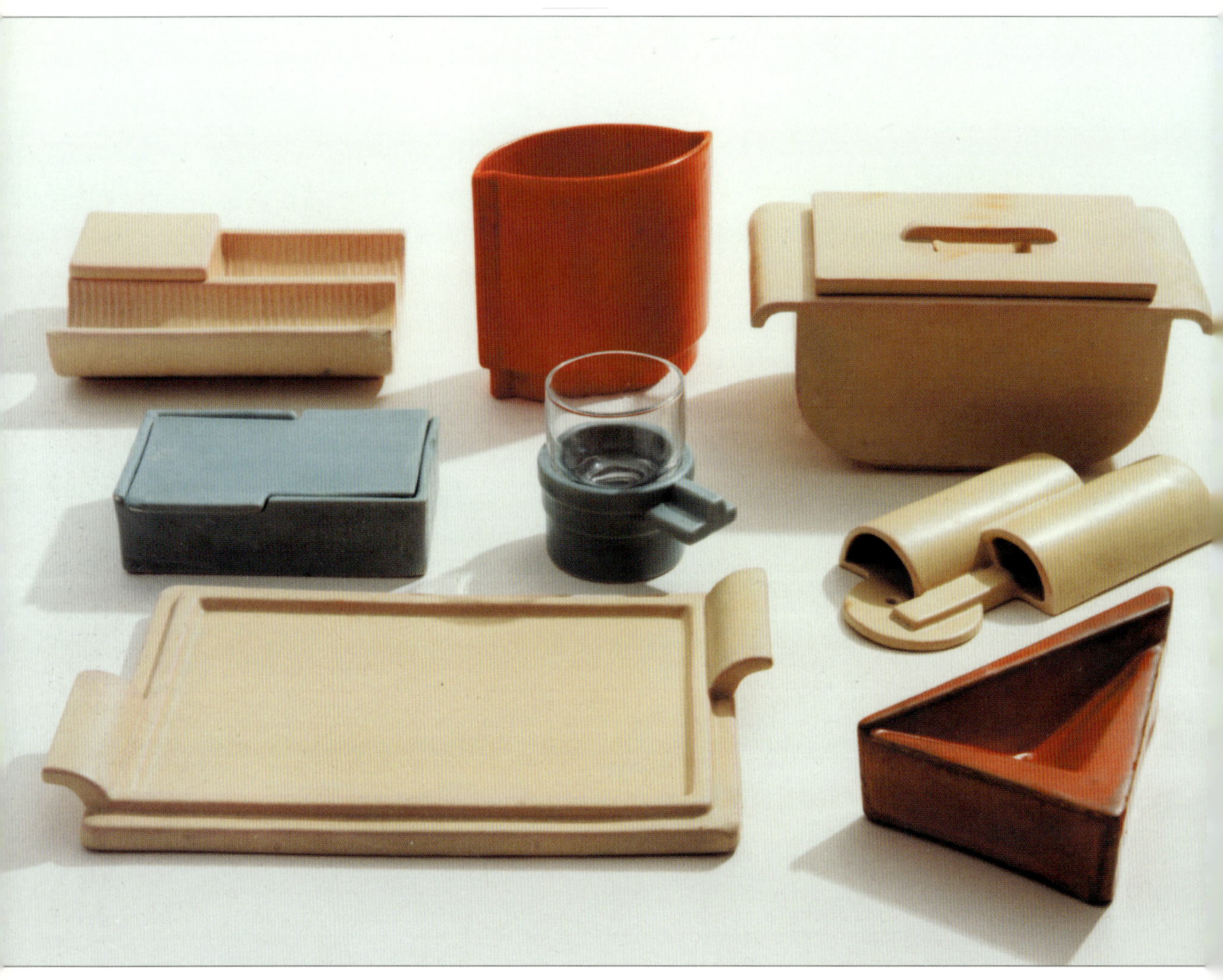

Fig. 229: Schramberg pieces, Eva Zeisel, 1929–30.

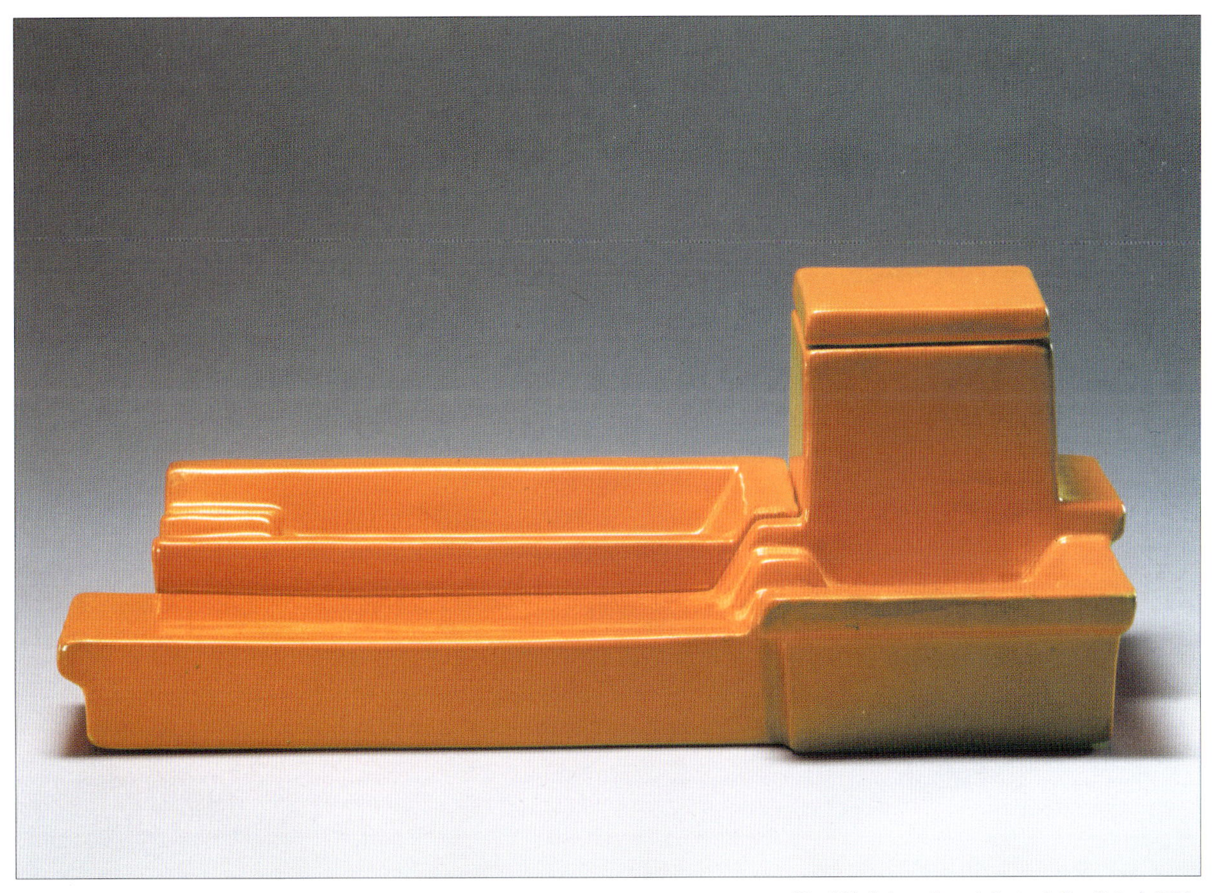

Fig. 230: Schramberg ink stand. Eva Zeisel, 1930.

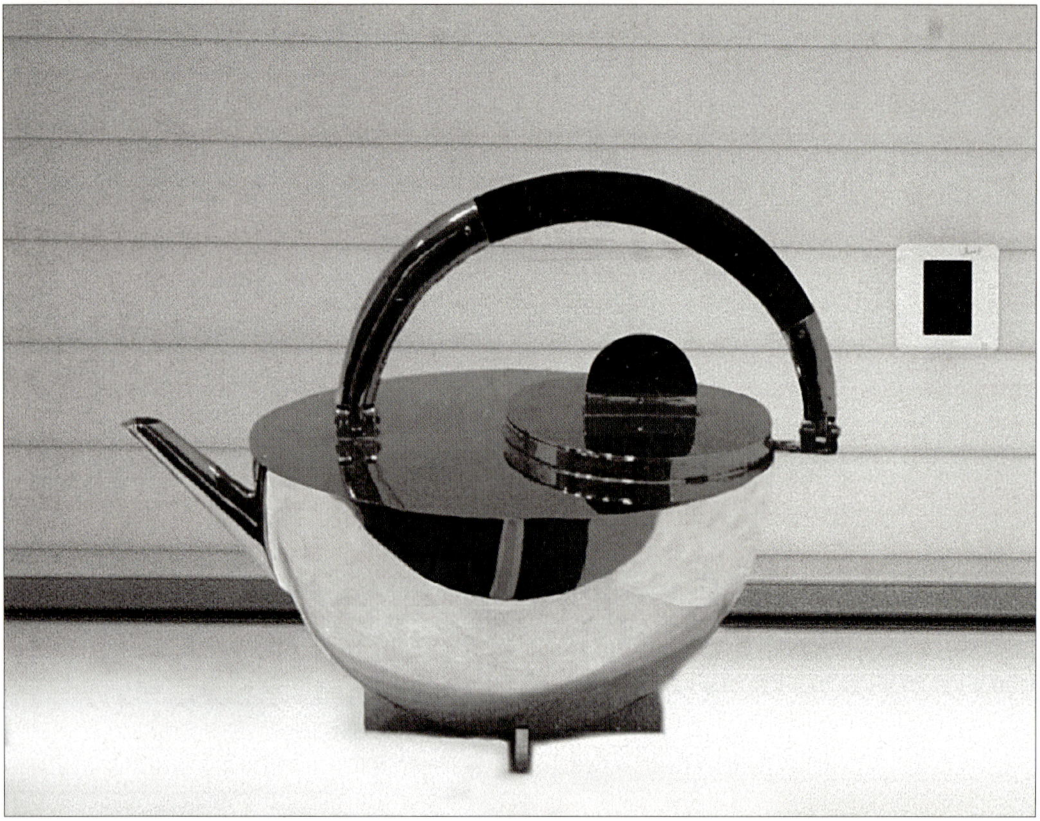

Fig. 231: Marianne Brandt teapot, 1924.

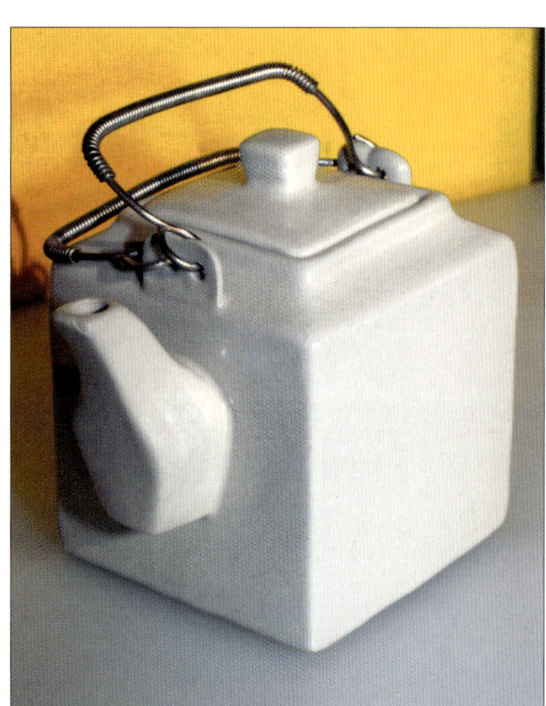

Fig. 232: Cubic teapot, 2003.

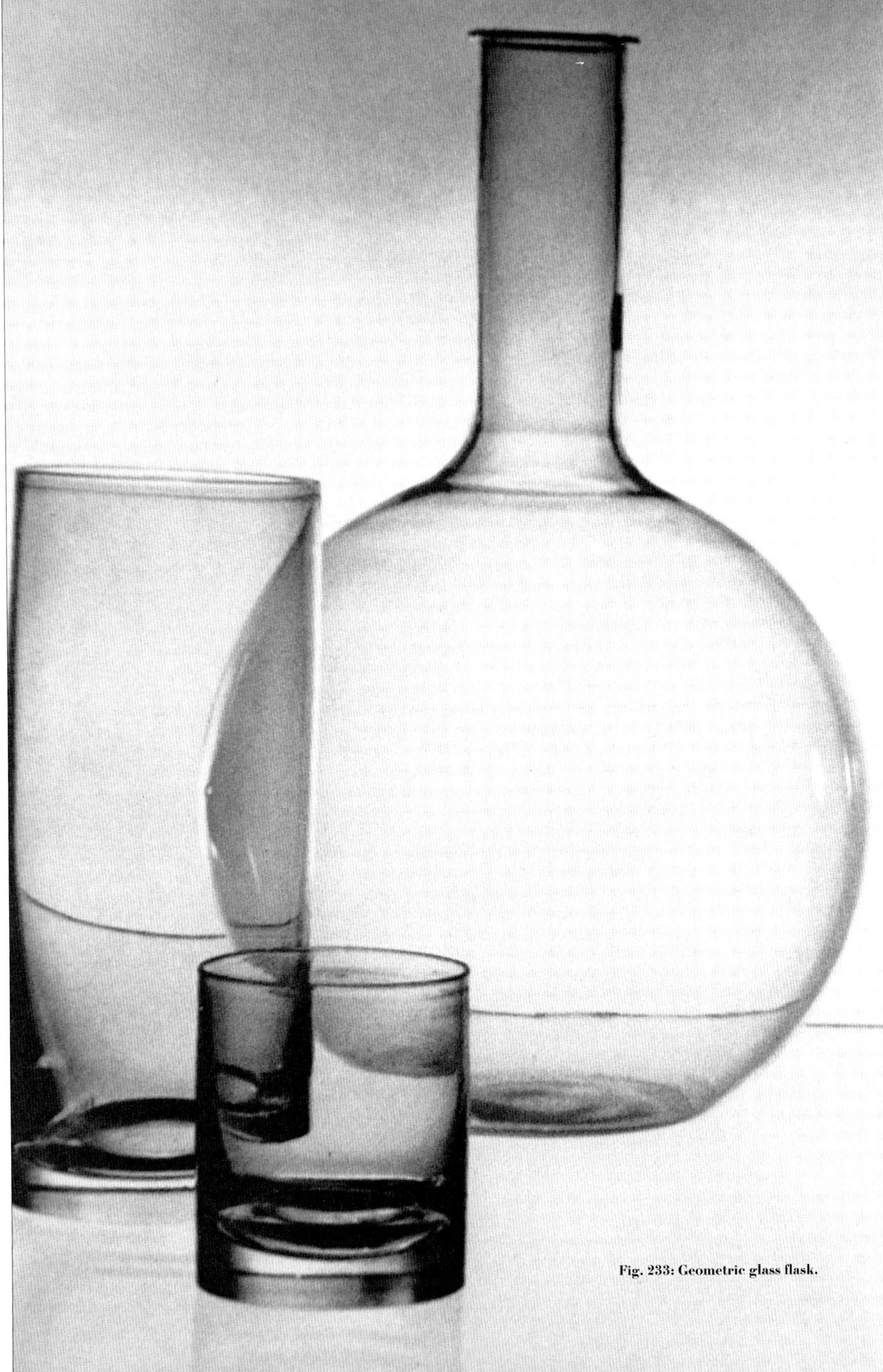

Fig. 233: Geometric glass flask.

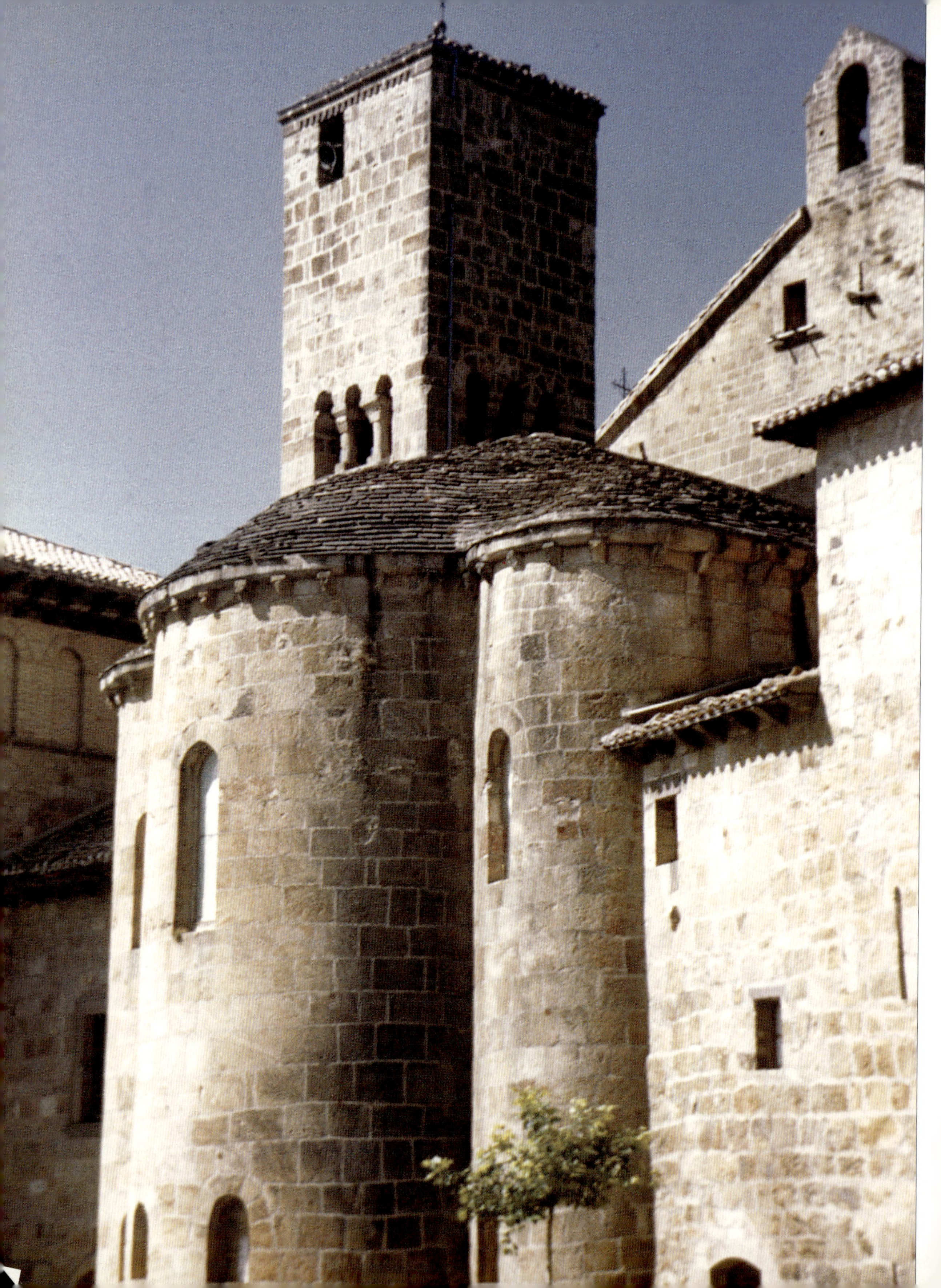

Geometry can be expressed in three-dimensions—spheres, cubes, cylinders—as well as in two-dimensions. Three-dimensional geometry is the backbone of much of design. I would say that such geometry should be implied rather than explicitly revealed. However, two-dimensional geometry can be used for decorative ornament.

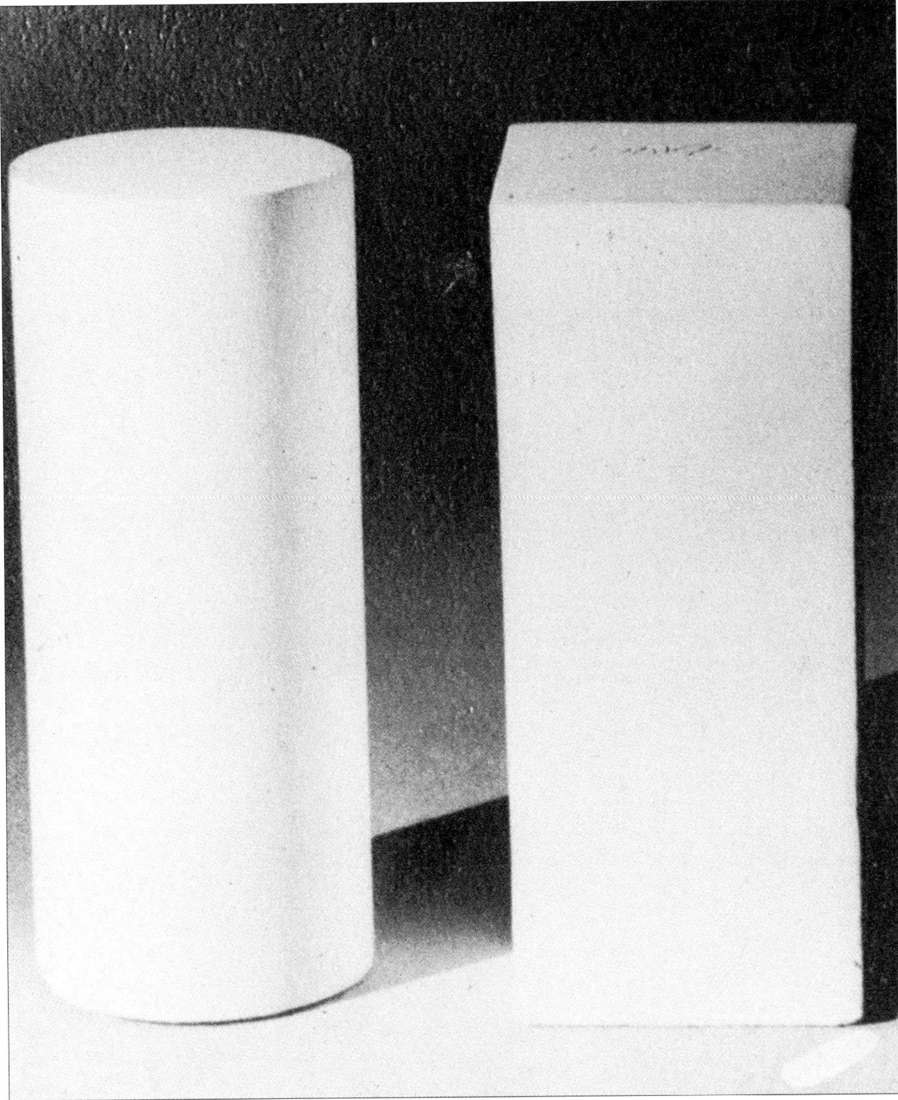

Fig. 235: Three-dimensional geometric forms.

Fig. 234: Romanesque church, France.

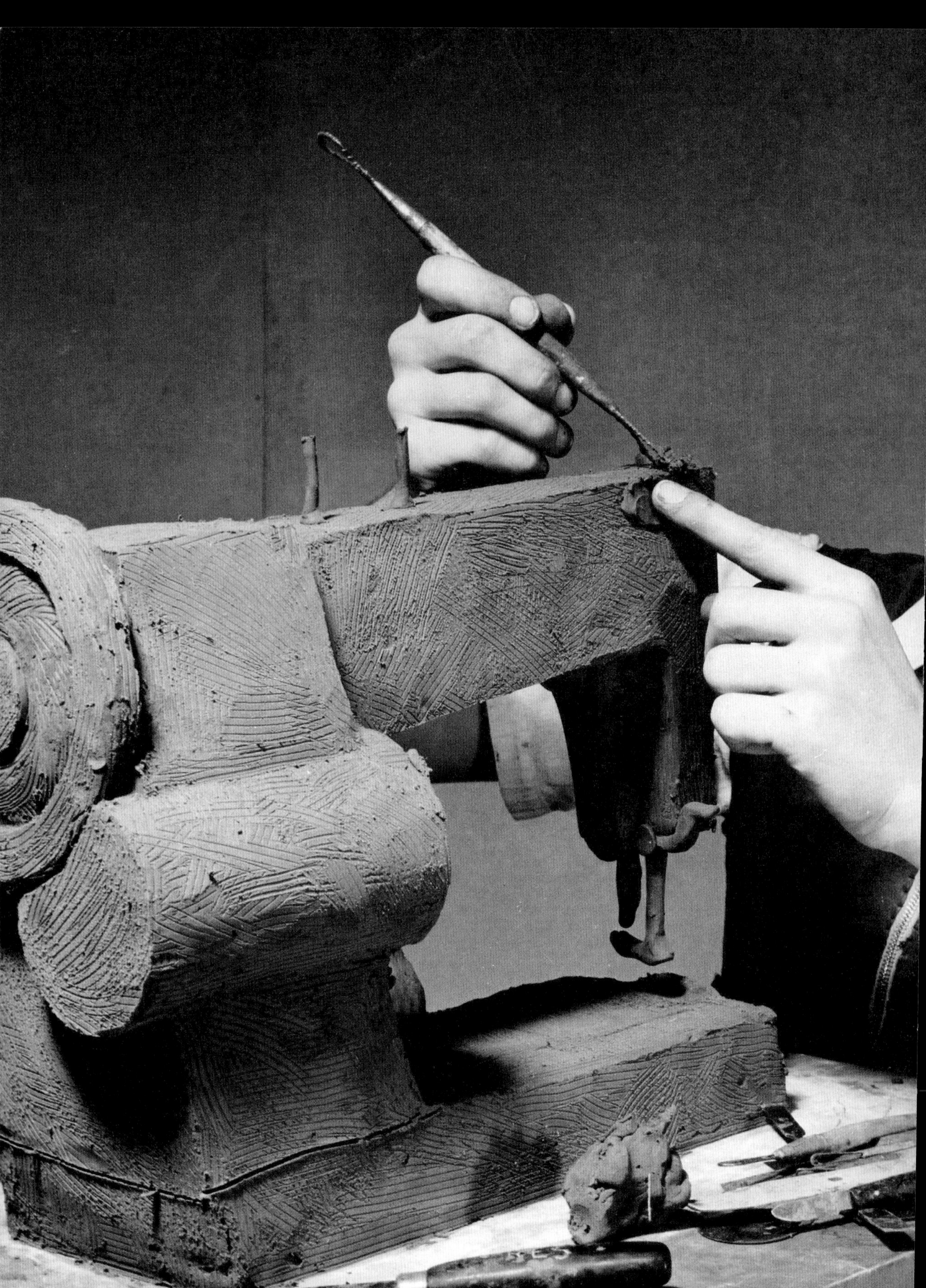

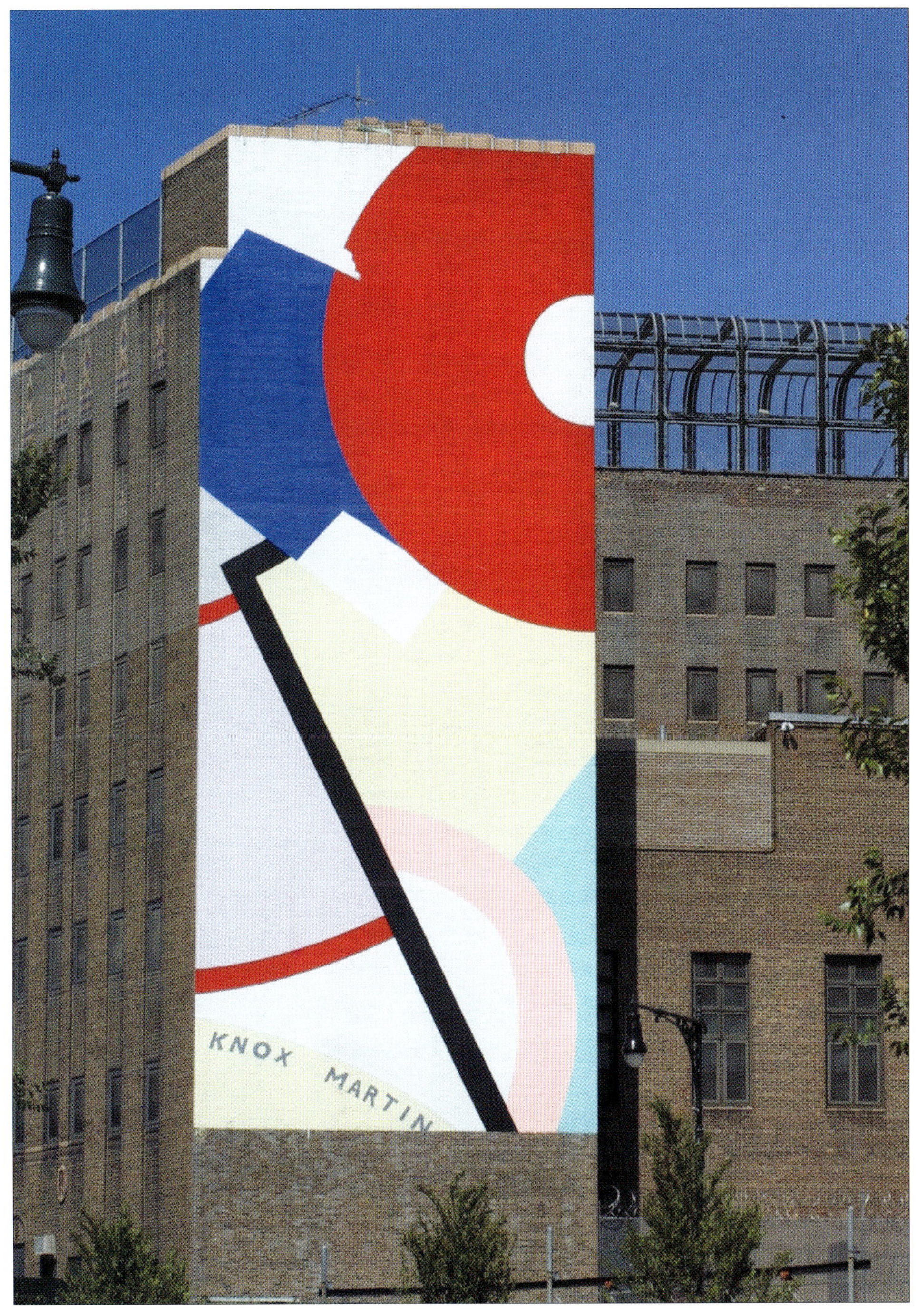

Fig. 237: Knox Martin mural, New York City.

Fig. 236: Clay model of sewing machine.

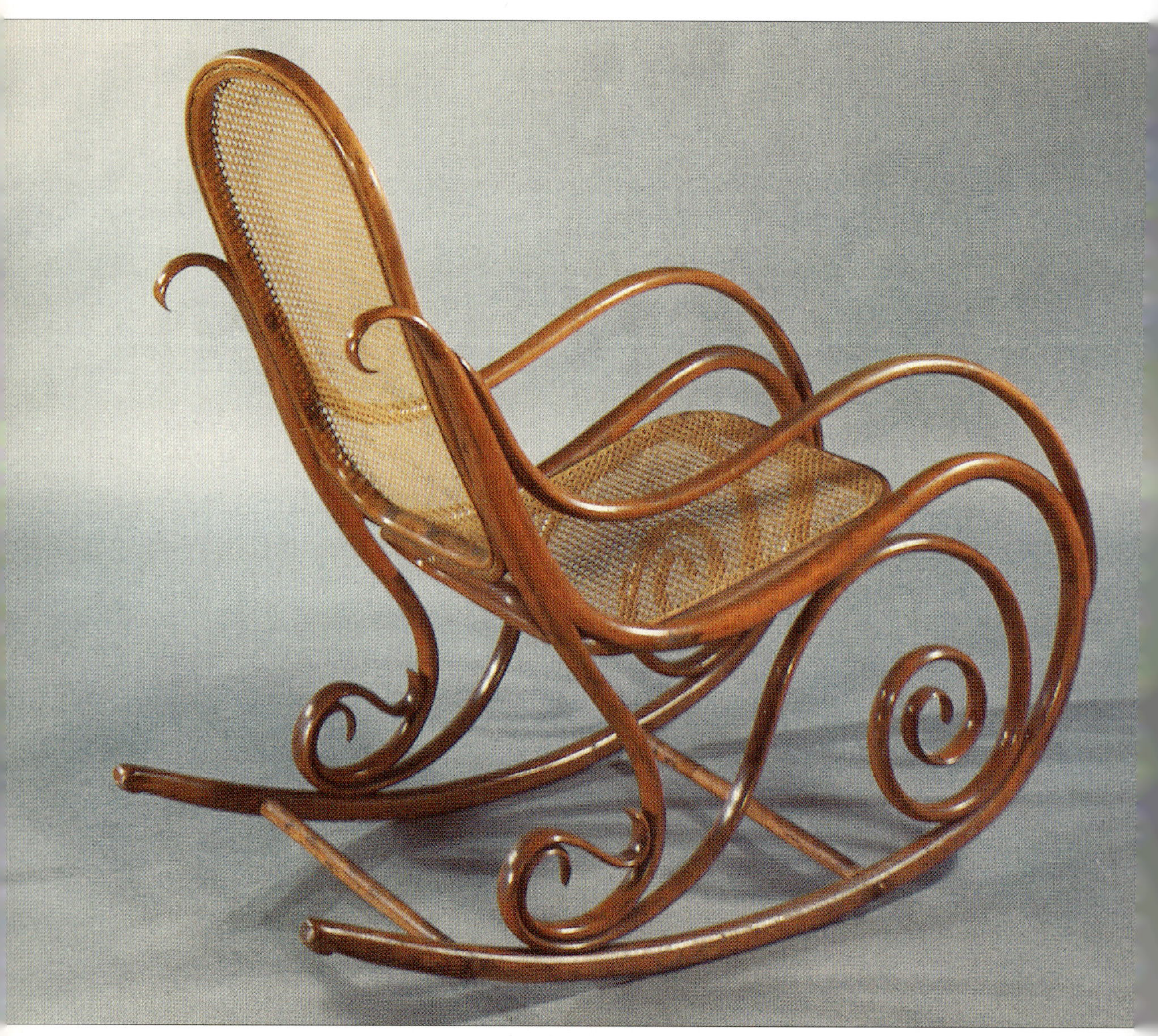

Curves: Stress & Compound

Fig. 238: Thonet chair.

The curve of the Thonet chair, which continues from a line of the circle into

one in the opposite direction is an example of the compound curve, also known as the "S" curve–was considered objectionable by Modernists, who called it gratuitous and extravagant.

The stress curve, the only curve accepted by modernists, bends the straight just a bit. It evokes the feeling of speed and elegance, in contrast to the soft, friendliness of the "S" curve. It might express tension or movement. It reminds us of the wing of a bird in flight, the forced bend of a bow. The word "stress" explains the feeling it evokes.

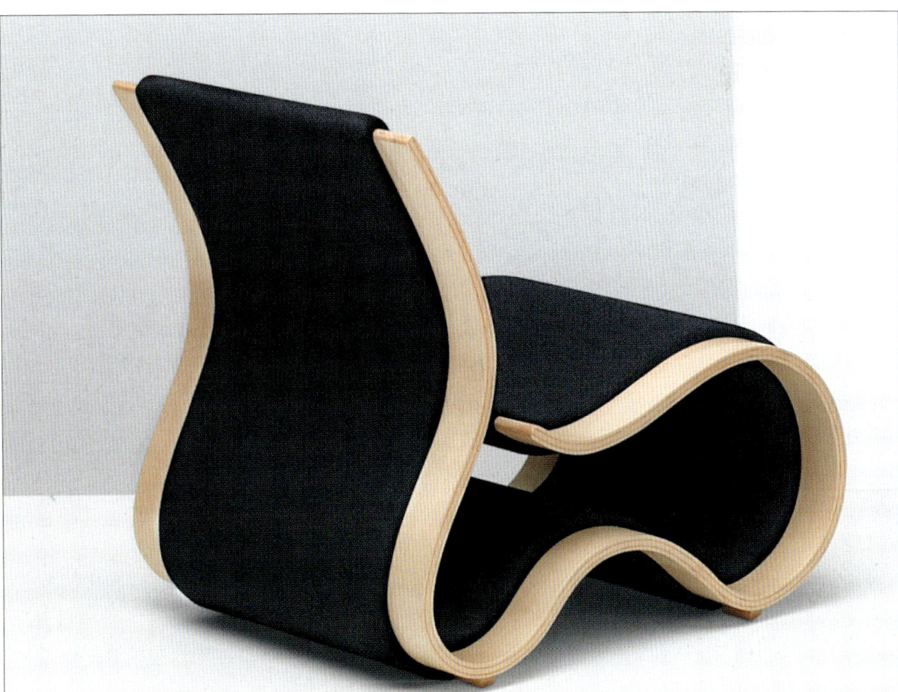

Fig. 239: Kurve Chair for Neinkamper, by Karim Rashid, 2002.

Eva Zeisel

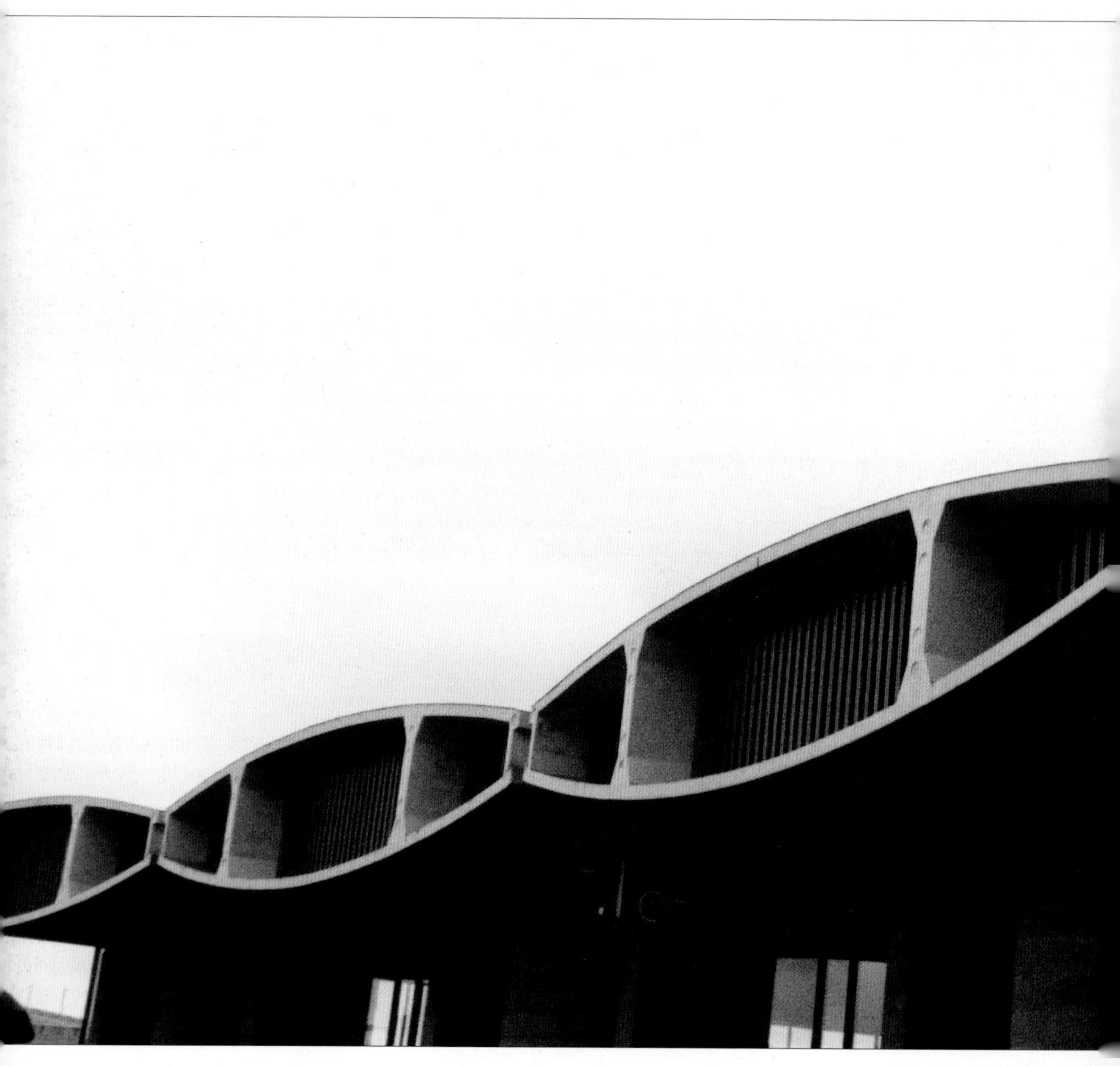

Fig. 240: Roissy/Charles de Gaulle Airport, Paris.

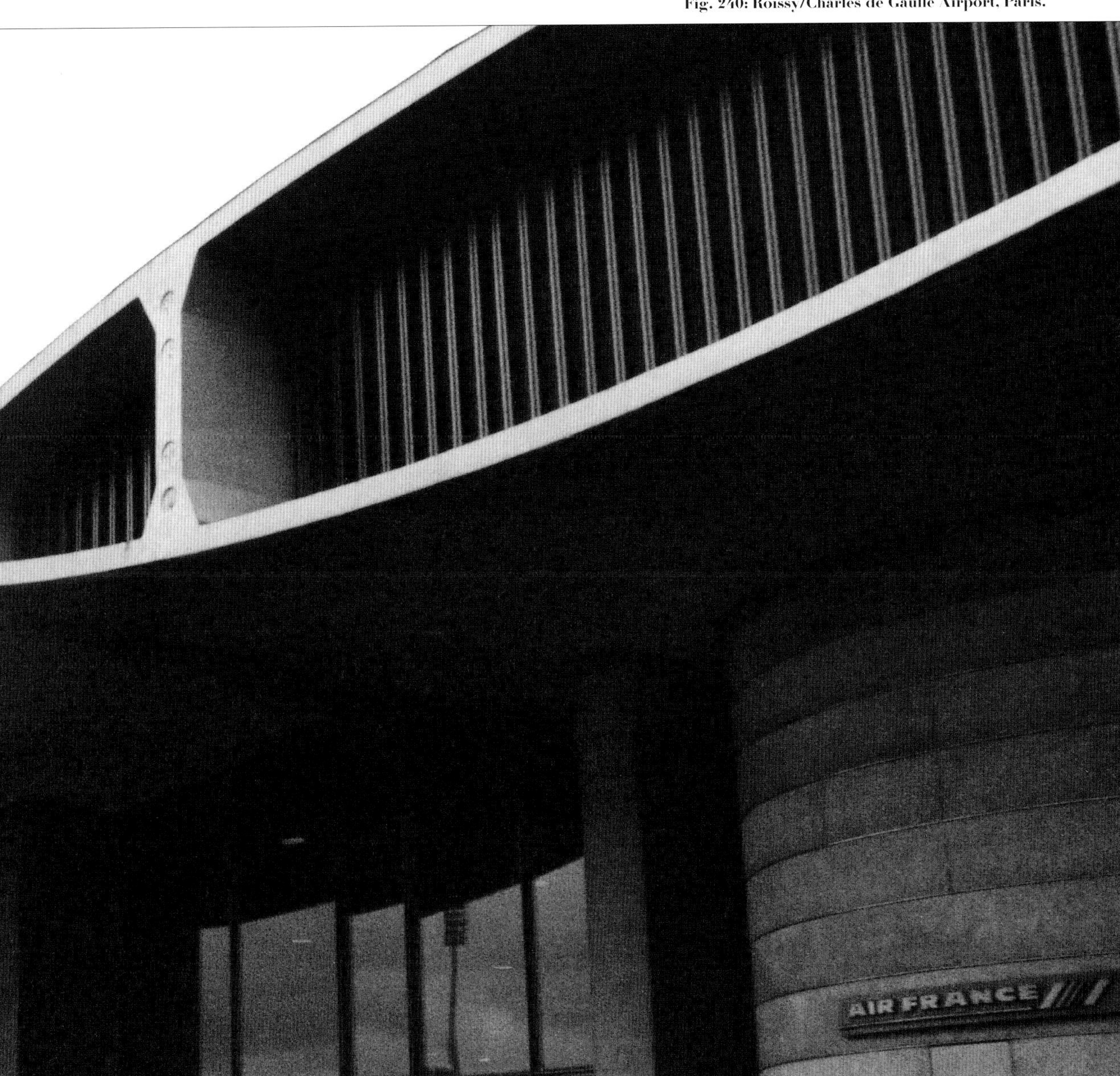

Fig. 241: Nesting bowls, designed by Gerald Gulotta.

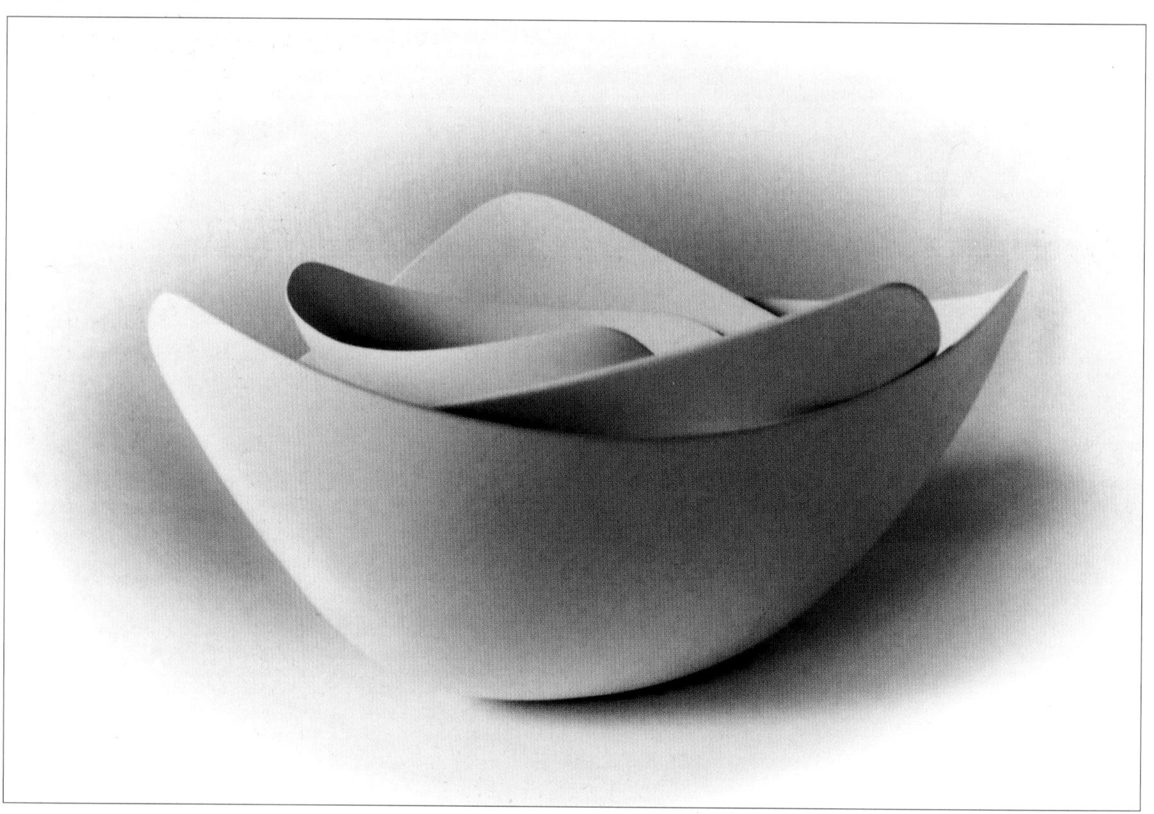

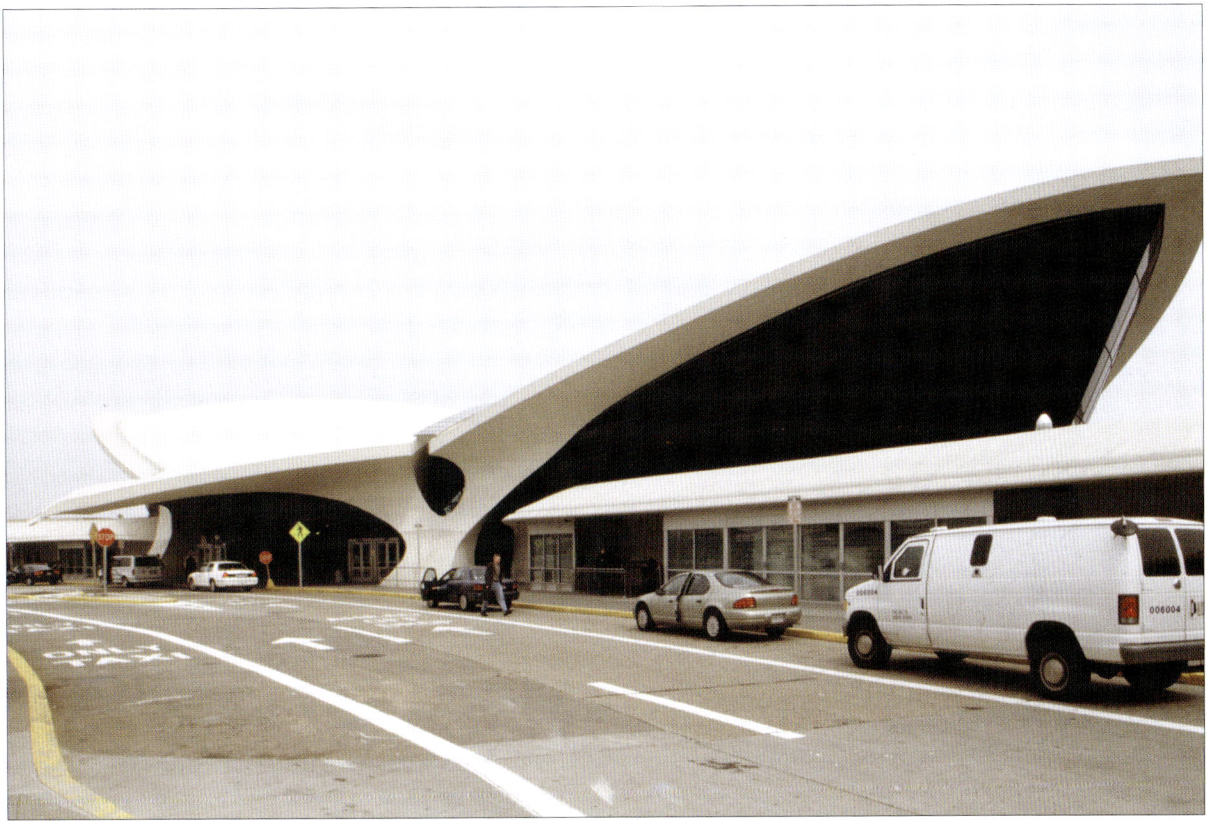

Fig. 242: TWA terminal, JFK airport, by Eero Saarinen.

Fig. 243 Barcelona Chair, Ludwig Mies van der Rohe, 1927.

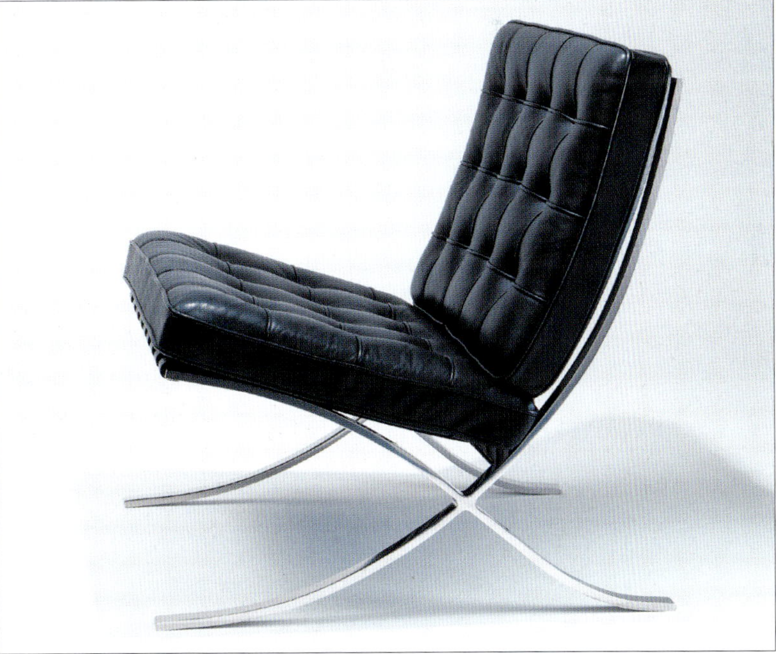

A compound curve can describe something slim, fat, extended or compressed. The friendly "S" curve is the line of nature. Things in nature are rarely straight or angular (with the exceptions of some crystals). Some hundred and fifty years ago, the painter William Hogarth wrote: "The 'S' curve is the line of beauty. Should any child practice forming this letter, he would be able to see beauty in nature that was invisible to the mere definer of straight lines."

The "S" curve is named after the letter S, rather than the harshly angular letter Z.

Earlier in this book I wrote of Peter Behrens's imaginary professor, who exclaimed "Hurrah, hurrah for the straight line!" We might now, with equal ardor, herald in the present millennium with the words: "Hurrah, hurrah for the friendly curve!"

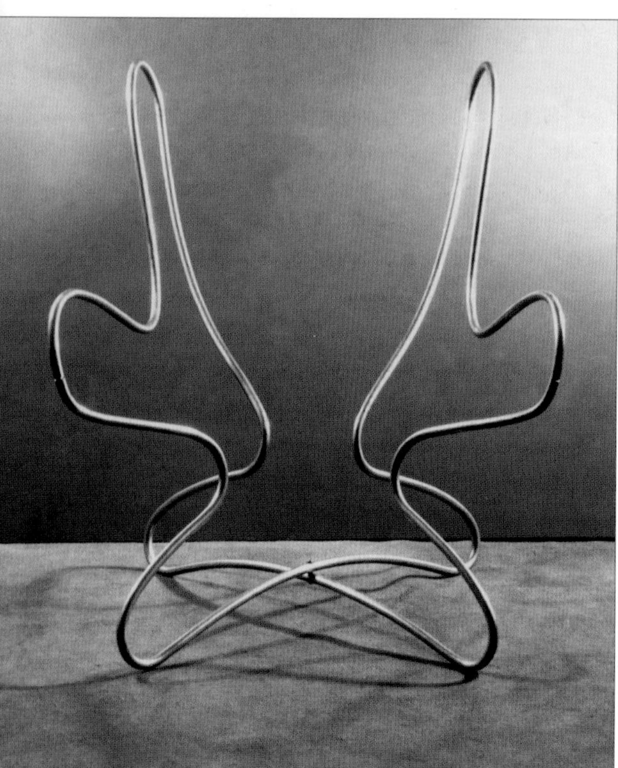

Fig. 244: Tubular metal chair, with and without cover, Eva Zeisel, 1954.

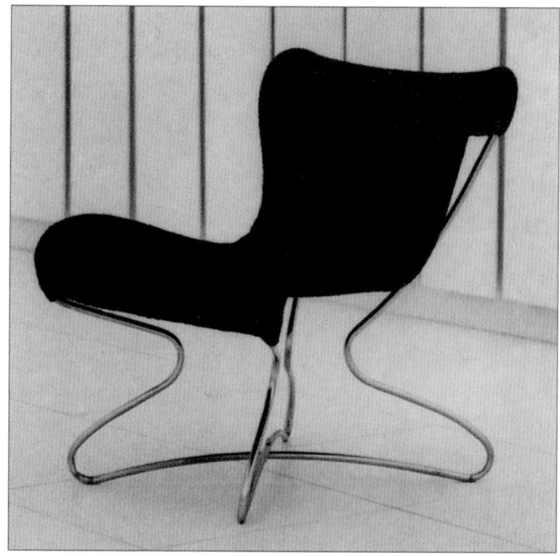

Beauty

The architect of the beginning of the twentieth century departed from the earlier definition of beauty—that only what is not useful can be beautiful—by declaring that only what is useful can be beautiful. During that century, the useful object become the *raison d'être* of design. Towards the end of the century, I wrote an article entitled "Beauty is Kitsch and Art is Shit." (The Guggenheim Museum was exhibiting canned excrement, the Brooklyn Museum displayed a Madonna in a painting smeared with elephant dung, and the Museum of Modern Art presented the process of human elimination in the image of a large pissoir adorning its lobby, an homage to the continuing influence of Dadaism.)

A young, industrial designer recently told me that it was a bit embarrassing to mention beauty, and it certainly could not be used as a selling point, although people do appreciated it once it's there. Another designer complained to me that he could not convince his students to try to make beautiful forms, as they felt that beauty was only a superficial attribute. Indeed, beauty is only skin deep, but it is only the skin that one sees. When one looks at a beautiful flower, or a mountain, or a field, it is only the surface that one sees. The surface is what informs us about the objects shape, texture, etc.

The goal of the designer should be to give pleasure to the audience through his designs. He may not succeed—because beauty is in the eye of the beholder and in the eye of the designer, and they may not agree. But the intention should be there. (The designer may also give pleasure through the sense of touch, but the touch may not be connected to visual beauty.)

We should not be embarrassed by beauty. In fact, beauty, harmony, loveliness, elegance, and usefulness—which were not the aims of twentieth century designers—should be what we designers strive for today in the twenty-first century.

Love

When you ask a designer or a maker of things which creation he or she is most proud of, the answer will probably be "I have no favorites among my children." The pleasure of making things useful or beautiful involves your feelings as well as your thinking. When your original sketch evolves into a tangible, three-dimensional object, your heart is anxiously following the process of your work. And the love involved in making it is conveyed to those for whom you made it.

To quote a fan letter from Seattle, Washington: "I just have two of your bowls and I absolutely love them. I just never felt such love for a piece of pottery before…"

Of course, love is a very personal matter.

Fig. 245: Excerpts from fan letters to Eva Zeisel (below).

Fan Letters Using The Word "Love"

"I just have two of your bowls and I absolutely *love* them. I just never felt such *love* for a piece of pottery before…I just fell completely in *love* with it."
—W.P., Seattle, WA

"I saw it, bought it and have *loved* it ever since." *—C. M. J., Chicago, IL*

"These dishes have served at many family celebrations and have always adorned our table in a magnificent fashion. I have always *loved* my dinnerware." *—E.F., New York*

"I have always *loved* these beautiful dishes…"
—L.T.

Conclusion

The tall museum doors have closed on the last century's decorative arts. The museum of the new century is now ready, its great halls eager to receive our new century's style, the style of elegance and beauty. Let us open the doors once again to the magic language of design.

Fig. 246: Eva Zeisel at Vienna exhibit.

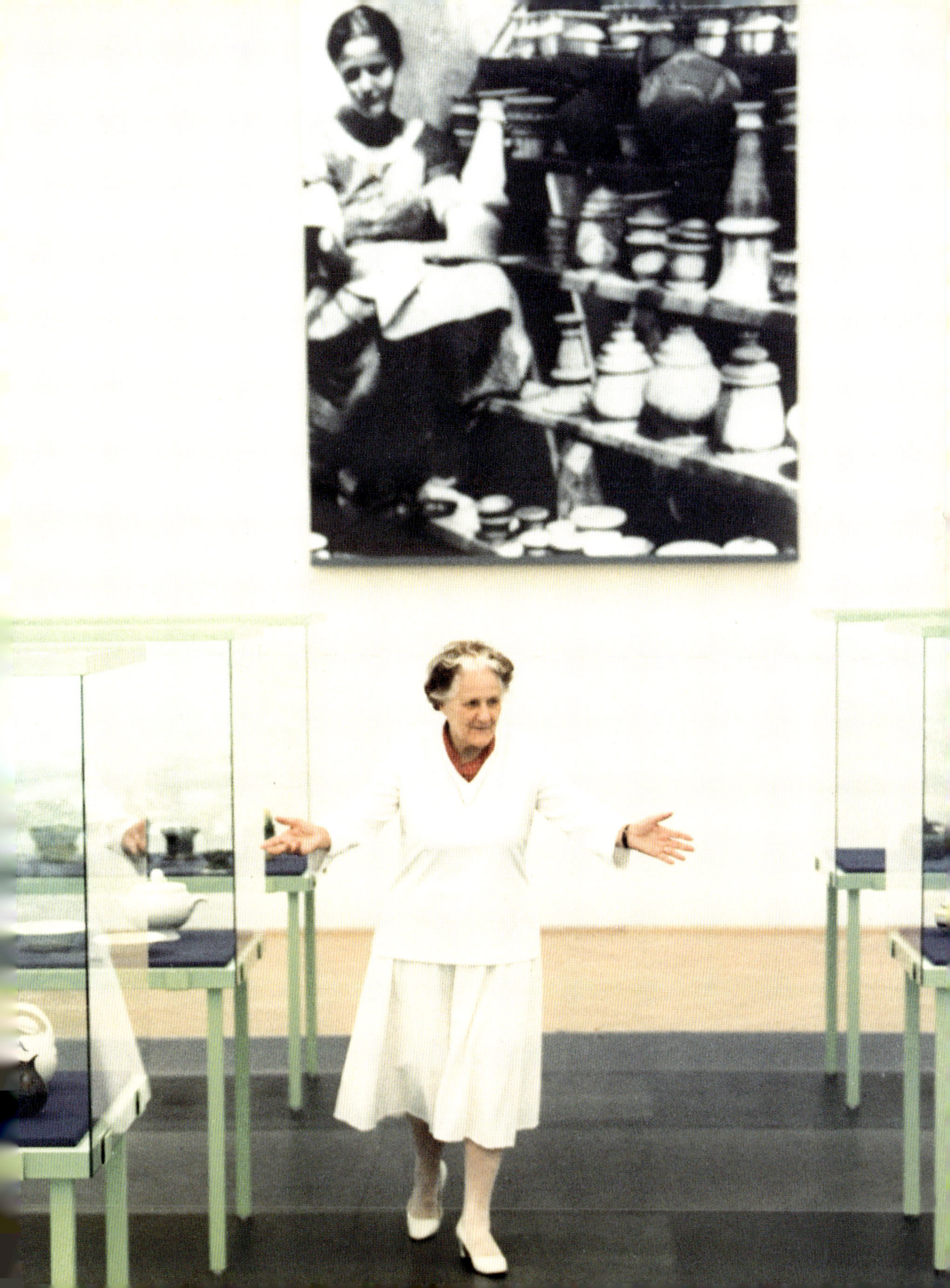

Bibliography

Caplan, Ralph, *Design In America; Selected Work by Members of the Industrial Designers Society of America*, New York: McGraw-Hill, 1969.

Constantine, Mildred and Arthur Drexler, eds., *The Object Transformed*, introduction by Mildred Constantine and Arthur Drexler, New York: Museum of Modern Art, 1966.

Crane, Walter, *Line & Form*, London: G. Bell & Sons, 1921.

Crane, Walter, *The Bases of Design*, London: Bell, 1904.

Drexler, Arthur and Greta Daniel, *Introduction to Twentieth Century Design, from the Collection of the Museum of Modern Art*, Garden City, NY: Doubleday, 1959.

Dyal, Donald H., *Norman Bel Geddes: Designer of the Future*, Monticello, IL: Vance Bibliographies, 1983.

Dyce, William, *Letter to Lord Meadowbank, and the Committee of the Honourable Board of Trustees for the Encouragement of Arts and Manufactures [microform]: On the Best Means of Ameliorating the Arts and Manufactures of Scotland in Point of Taste*, Edinburgh: T. Constable. 1837.

Flinchum, Russell, *Henry Dreyfuss, Industrial Designer: The Man in the Brown Suit*, New York: Cooper-Hewitt, National Design Museum, Smithsonian Institution & Rizzoli, 1997.

Fry, Roger, *Vision and Design*, London: Chatto & Windus, 1920.

Geddes, Norman Bel, *Miracle in the Evening: An Autobiography*, ed. William Kelley, Garden City, N.Y.: Doubleday, 1960.

Green, Christopher, ed., *Art Made Modern: Roger Fry's Vision of Art*, London: Merrell Holberton in assoc. with the Courtauld Gallery, Courtauld Institute of Art, 1999.

Gropius, Walter, *Architecture and Design in the Age of Science*, New York: The Spiral Press, 1952.

Gropius, Walter, *The New Architecture and the Bauhaus*, translated by P. Morton Shand, with a preface by Joseph Hudnut, New York: Museum of Modern Art, 1937.

Hannah, Gail Greet, *Elements of Design: Rowena Reed Kostellow and the Structure of Visual Relationships*, New York: Princeton Architectural Press, ca. 2002.

Hiesinger, Kathryn B., and George H. Marcus, eds., *Design Since 1945*, Philadelphia: Philadelphia Museum of Art, 1983.

Hoffmann, Josef Franz Maria, *Josef Hoffmann, Architect and Designer, 1870-1956*. Vienna, New York: Galerie Metropol, 1981.

Jeanneret, Charles Edouard (Le Corbusier), *Étude sur le mouvement d'art décoratif en Allemagne*, New York: Da Capo Press, 1986.

Jeanneret, Charles Edouard (Le Corbusier), *Le Corbusier Talks with Students from the Schools of Architecture*, Tr. by Pierre Chase, New York: Orion Press, 1961.

Jeanneret, Charles Edouard (Le Corbusier), *The Decorative Art Of Today*, tr. with an introduction by James I. Dunnett, Cambridge, MA: MIT Press, 1987.

Jeanneret, Charles Edouard (Le Corbusier), *Towards a New Architecture*, tr. with an introduction by Frederick Etchells, New York: Payson & Clarke, 1927.

Loos, Adolf, *On Architecture*, tr. by Michael Mitchell, Riverside, CA: Ariadne Press, c2002.

Loos, Adolf, *Ornament and Crime: Selected Essays*, tr. by Michael Mitchell, introduction by Adolf Opel, Riverside, CA: Ariadne Press, c1998.

Morris, William, *Hopes and Fears for Art*, New York: Longmans, Green, and Co., 1901.

Morris, William, *The Aims of Art*, London: Office of The Commonweal, 1887.

Morris, William, *William Morris on Art and Design*, ed. Christine Poulson, Sheffield: Sheffield Academic, 1996.

Morris, William, Oscar Wilde, and W. C. Owen, *The Soul of Man under Socialism: The Socialist Ideal—Art, and the Coming Solidarity*, New York: The Humboldt Publishing Co., 1892.

Muthesius, Hermann, *Style-Architecture and Building-Art: Transformations of Architecture in the Nineteenth Century and Its Present Condition*, translated and introduced by Stanford Anderson, Santa Monica, CA: Getty Center for the History of Art and the Humanities: 1994.

Muthesius, Hermann, *The English House*, ed. and introduction by Dennis Sharp, translated by Janet Seligman, New York: Rizzoli, 1979.

Noever, Peter, ed., *Josef Hoffmann Designs*, Munich: Prestel, c1992.

Schezen, Roberto, *Adolf Loos: Architecture 1903-1932*, introduction by Kenneth Frampton, New York: Monacelli Press, 1996.

Sekler, Eduard F, *Josef Hoffmann: The Architectural Work: Monograph and Catalogue of Works*, translated by John Maass, Princeton, NJ: Princeton University Press, c1985.

Smith, Cyril Stanley, *A History of Metallography: The Development of Ideas on the Structure of Metals before 1890*, Cambridge, MA: The MIT Press, 1988.

Teague, Walter Dorwin, *Design This Day: The Technique of Order in The Machine Age*, New York: Harcourt, 1949.

Wagner, Otto, *Die Baukunst unserer Zeit: dem Baukunstjünger ein Führer auf diesem Kunstgebiete*, Vienna: A. Schroll, 1914.

Wagner, Otto, *Modern Architecture: A Guidebook for His Students to This Field of Art*, (based on 1902 edition, with additions), translated and introduced by Harry Francis Mallgrave, Santa Monica, CA: Getty Center for the History of Art and the Humanities, 1988.

Wagner, Otto, *Otto Wagner, Vienna 1841-1918: Designs for Architecture*, Oxford: Museum of Modern Art, 1985.

Windsor, Alan, *Peter Behrens, Architect and Designer*, New York: Whitney Library of Design, c1981.

Photo/Illustration credits

Fig. 1: © Irene Hass

Fig. 2, 8, 12, 44, 48, 51, 79, 84, 94, 99, 101, 109, 110, 124-125 (reprinted from *The Designer's Eye* with permission from W.W. Norton, Inc.), 126, 137, 139, 140, 141, 155, 156, 161, 171, 173 (Courtesy of Jonathan Adler), 180, 197, 200, 201, 203, 205, 210, 214, 219 (Courtesy of Yuni Jie/Pratt Institute), 227, 229 (Courtesy of John Striker), 231, 232 (Courtesy of Moxa Coffee, New York City), 237, 238, 242 © Brent C. Brolin

Fig. 3, 4, 5, 6, 7, 9, 10, 11, 13, 14, 15, 16, 17, 18, 19, 20, 21, 22, 23, 24, 25, 26, 27, 28, 29, 30, 31, 32, 33, 34, 35, 36 (Courtesy of the Walker Art Center), 37, 41, 42, 43, 45, 46, 49, 50, 52, 53, 54, 55, 57, 59, 60, 62, 63, 64, 66, 67, 68, 69, 70, 71, 72, 74, 75, 77, 78, 82, 83, 85, 86, 87, 88, 89, 90, 91, 95 (Courtesy of the Chicago Art Institute), 96, 97 (Courtesy of *I.D. Magazine*), 98, 100, 102, 103, 104, 105, 106, 107, 108, 111, 112, 113, 115, 116, 117, 118, 119, 120, 121, 122, 127, 128, 129, 131, 132,133, 135, 138, 143, 144, 145, 146, 147, 148, 148, 150, 151, 152, 153, 157, 160, 162, 163, 164, 166, 168, 169, 170, 172, 176, 177, 178, 179, 181, 182, 183, 184, 185, 186, 189, 190, 191, 192, 193, 194, 195, 199, 202, 204, 206, 207, 208, 213, 217, 218, 221, 222, 223, 224, 225, 226, 229, 233, 234, 235, 236, 244, 245, 246: Eva Zeisel Archives

Fig 38, 56, 73, 76, 142, 158, 175: Courtesy of Editions Hannibal, 46 Kifissodotos St., 11825 Athens, Greece. Tel/Fax 30 (210) 3453941.

Fig 39: Courtesy of Stedelijk Museum, Amsterdam.

Fig. 40: Courtesy of Macklowe Gallery, New York.

Fig. 47: Courtesy of Keramikmuseum, Mettlach, Germany

Fig, 58, 61, 167: © Walter Civardi.

Fig. 65: Courtesy of Alessi.

Fig: 80, 81, 93 (Courtesy of *Tea A Magazine*), 216, 240: © Talisman K. Brolin.

Fig 92: Courtesy of Jason Jacques, Inc., New York.

Fig, 114: Courtesy of Jean Genest, SA Jos La Doare.

Fig. 123: The Orange Chicken.

Fig. 130, 230: © Ira Garber.

Fig. 159: © Milton Glaser.

Fig 134: Courtesy of KleinReid.

Fig. 154: Courtesy of Ross Miller.

Fig, 165: Courtesy of Scott Dooley.

Fig. 174: Courtesy of Elizabeth Kohlweiss, Vienna, Austria.

Fig. 187: Digital Image © Museum of Modern Art/Licensed by SCALA.

Fig. 188: Courtesy of Vitra.

Fig. 196: Courtesy of NASA.

Fig. 198: Courtesy of Nymphenburg Porcelain.

Fig. 209: © Dominic Habsburg.

Fig. 211: Courtesy of OutdoorDecor.com.

Fig. 212: © George Kopp.

Fig. 215: © Marie France Radvanyi.

Fig: 220: Courtesy of Gretchen Raber.

Fig. 239: Courtesy of Karim Rashid.

Fig. 241: Courtesy of Gerald Gulotta.

Fig. 243: Courtesy of Knoll International.